Comparative
LITERATURE
*for the*
NEW CENTURY

# Comparative LITERATURE for the NEW CENTURY

EDITED BY
*GIULIA DE GASPERI AND
JOSEPH PIVATO*

FOREWORD BY
*LINDA HUTCHEON*

MCGILL-QUEEN'S UNIVERSITY PRESS
MONTREAL & KINGSTON · LONDON · CHICAGO

© McGill-Queen's University Press 2018

ISBN 978-0-7735-5449-8 (cloth)
ISBN 978-0-7735-5536-5 (ePDF)
ISBN 978-0-7735-5537-2 (ePUB)

Legal deposit third quarter 2018
Bibliothèque nationale du Québec

Printed in Canada on acid-free paper that is 100% ancient forest free (100% post-consumer recycled), processed chlorine free

We acknowledge the support of the Canada Council for the Arts, which last year invested $153 million to bring the arts to Canadians throughout the country.

Nous remercions le Conseil des arts du Canada de son soutien. L'an dernier, le Conseil a investi 153 millions de dollars pour mettre de l'art dans la vie des Canadiennes et des Canadiens de tout le pays.

---

LIBRARY AND ARCHIVES CANADA CATALOGUING IN PUBLICATION

Comparative literature for the new century / edited by Giulia De Gasperi and Joseph Pivato ; foreword by Linda Hutcheon.

Includes bibliographical references and index.
Issued in print and electronic formats.
ISBN 978-0-7735-5449-8 (cloth). – ISBN 978-0-7735-5536-5 (ePDF). –
ISBN 978-0-7735-5537-2 (ePUB)

1. Comparative literature. I. Pivato, Joseph, editor II. De Gasperi, Giulia, editor

PN865.C62 2018                    809                    C2018-902085-7
                                                         C2018-902086-5

---

This book was typeset by Sandra Friesen in 10/13 Calluna.

# Contents

Foreword
*Linda Hutcheon*      vii

Acknowledgments      xi

Introduction: The State of the Art
*Giulia De Gasperi*      3

**SECTION ONE**
**Comparative Arguments**      19

Anonymous: Animating Ecologies of Belonging
*Sneja Gunew*      21

The Languages of Comparative Literature
*Joseph Pivato*      41

**SECTION TWO**
**Future Directions in Comparative Literature**      65

Dialogue between Francophone and Anglophone Literatures in Africa
*Ndeye Fatou Ba*      67

"What a Caring Act": Geographies of Care and the Posthuman in Canadian Dystopian Fiction
*Dominique Hétu*      87

Why Not an "African-Canadian" Epic? Lessons from Pratt and Walcott, Etc.
*George Elliott Clarke*      117

Reading Literature through Translation: The Case of Antonio
D'Alfonso into Italian
*Maria Cristina Seccia* 153

Exile, Media, Capital: *Calendar*'s System of Exchange
*Monique Tschofen* 174

SECTION THREE
## International Comparative Studies 197

A Many-Tongued Babel: Translingualism in Canadian
Multicultural Writing
*Deborah Saidero* 199

"Like a Dancing Gypsy": A Close Reading of *Cockroach*
*F. Elizabeth Dahab* 215

The Power to Narrate: Representing Italian Migrant Working-Class
Experiences in Two Steel Cities in Australia and Canada
*Gaetano Rando* 229

Gunn, Edwards, and di Michele: Nomadic Spaces
*Anna Pia De Luca* 246

Peasant Boots, Dancing Boots: Assimilation and Hyphenation in
Vera Lysenko's *Yellow Boots* and Hiromi Goto's *Chorus of Mushrooms*
*Jolene Armstrong* 267

SECTION FOUR
## Looking Back at Traditions 287

Comparative Literature in Canada: A Case Study
*E.D. Blodgett* 289

Haunting Tradition Properly: Studies in Ethnic Minority Writing
*Mark A. McCutcheon* 304

Contributors 321

Index 327

# Foreword

The "discipline" of Comparative Literature has often proved fruitfully un-disciplined over the many years of its existence and, if this lively volume is any indication, it promises to retain its healthily contrarian identity into the new century. Gathering together the work of several generations of "complitters," *Comparative Literature for the New Century* offers readers a cross-section of where the field has gone and is going, as it looks both backward and forward, exploring its history and speculating on its future.

This is a discipline that (at various moments of its existence) has been said to be in crisis or even dead. E.D. Blodgett, in his contribution to this collection, claims that the driving force of Comparative Literature is *hubris*, but I confess that I have always found it was more *angst* than *hubris* that propelled its students and teachers. Whatever the diagnosis, what we comparatists and our (un)discipline share is a penchant for self-conscious self-interrogation, as will be especially clear in the first section of this collection, entitled "Comparative Arguments." By self-interrogation, I do not mean simply the frequent institutionalized re-examinations of our working assumptions in light of the changes in the profession as a whole – as witnessed in the American Comparative Literature Association reports of 1965, 1975, 1993, 2004, 2014–15 – though I firmly believe that the regularity of this process has made our discipline uniquely sensitive to change in a way that national language and literature departments have not always been. I also mean by self-interrogation the kind of conscious questioning of disciplinary limits that individuals and departments/centres have undertaken around the world in the name of Comparative Literature.

Sometimes, as this volume illustrates so well, this interrogatory expansion of our discipline has been carried out under the interdisciplinary aegis of cosmopolitanism, migrant studies, transculturality, or even World Literature (as read in a global or diasporic context); at other times it has been done through serious engagement with either translation studies or various forms of cultural or critical theory. Even for comparatists, of course, some of these boundary-questioning moves have been a cause more for alarm (or at least angst) than for celebration. But without these challenges, I would want to argue, the discipline would not be in the happy position that it is today in the new century: that is, armed with the tools – linguistic, cultural, theoretical, ideological, digital – to make the vast literary, cultural, and historical relationships between east and west, south and north, our broadened focus. It is not simply the multicultural reality of a global population constantly in motion that demands this broadening; nor is it only the easy and inevitable connectivity provided by electronic media. It is, rather, the ethical imperative of living in and writing about our twenty-first-century world.

Our discipline is ready for this ethical challenge in part, as I have always felt, because our self-interrogations prepared the ground for the systematic and systemic thinking and rethinking of the guiding assumptions that constitute what came to be referred to under the general label of "theory." And as the chapters collected here show so well, "theory," in turn, has opened doors to new comparative perspectives on topics as specific as ethnic minority writing, as well as on topics as general as literature and its study as part of (not mere illustrations of) philosophical and ethical life. This is the "theory" that, in the late 1960s and early 1970s, found its North American home in French departments (because many of the theoretical writings came by way of Paris) and especially in Comparative Literature. When I graduated as the first PhD in the new program in Comparative Literature from the University of Toronto in 1975, I would never have guessed that this exciting new "theory" in which I had been immersed during my graduate years would have become, over the next forty years, as "naturalized," as bred-in-the-bone, as these chapters reveal it to be: if this volume is to be believed, it is almost our lingua franca. But whether the specific theory invoked be that of Mikhail Bakhtin, Jacques Derrida, Edward Said, Ngũgi wa Thiong'o, or Homi Bhabha, whether it involves feminist perspectives or those of material history and culture, whether it engages the post-colonial or the post-human, what is most striking to me in this volume is the rich *variety* of theories, rather than any stifling uniformity – as is also the case, in fact, in our discipline as a whole.

The comparative and theoretically sophisticated close readings of texts in this collection testify to the productivity of this kind of pushing outward of the boundaries of our discipline – or to use a different but equally apt image, of its methodological and ideological inclusivity. It is this richness, variety, and inclusivity, however, that have also contributed, for different reasons, to both the hubris and the angst experienced by the field and its practitioners. We do not "do" just one thing; we "do" many things. We study different languages and thus different national and regional cultures, but we also study different media. Over the years, as a comparatist, I have found myself lured into teaching and writing about everything from opera to film adaptations of fiction, from photography to architecture. But we do not simply "compare" literatures or even media: the social, political, and philosophical are inevitably dimensions of the linguistic and the literary (and now the digital) for us today. Issues of translation and translingual practices are clearly central to what we do, as a number of the chapters here explore – whether the focus be broadly international or more locally Canadian – for since its early days in the Sherbrooke School, Canadian Comparative Literature has shared all these concerns with the broader discipline around the world. The institutional and the intellectual come together in many of the Canadian-focused chapters, in part because the university departments and centres, not to mention the Learned Societies like the Canadian Comparative Literature Association and the Association for Canadian and Quebec Literatures, have been the enabling local homes to the diversity that is now our discipline.

It is no accident that many chapters in this collection address central themes of comparative ethnic minority and diasporic writing, specifically in Canada, and the reason is that they are all engaged responses to the important work in the field of one of this volume's editors, Joseph Pivato. A pioneer in the area of Italian-Canadian writing, Joe made it possible for a generation of scholars (many of us, like him, sharing the ethnicity of the writers we studied) to undertake another kind of self-examination, this time less of the discipline of Comparative Literature in general than of literary canon formation and the role of minority writing within it. Speaking for myself, I can say that the Bortolotti who is crypto-ethnically hidden beneath the marital Hutcheon took both heart and inspiration from Joe's example.

And I am not alone, as these chapters reveal. The writers take his fine example and run with it, so to speak. They use comparative methodological tools to bring together Ukrainian- and Japanese-Canadian writing, Italian-Australian and Italian-Canadian, Caribbean-Canadian and Caribbean, anglo- and francophone African or Canadian, American and Canadian, European and Arab-Canadian. En route, they engage central issues of translation as interpretation and cultural mediation; they explore the especially timely topic of the fluidity of "nomadic" cultural allegiances and identities; they tease out the constant and dynamic interplay of culture and language in translingual writing practices. In short, though the comparative focus of the volume is largely Canadian, the implications extend far beyond our national borders, for in our globalized world today, the volume's concerns with diversity and identity, exile and belonging, metropolis and colony, traditional and new worlds, language and translation, class and gender are the concerns of everyone everywhere. As Joe Pivato astutely begins his article, "Comparative Literature has many languages" – and they are, happily, all ours to study.

*Linda Hutcheon*

# Acknowledgments

We would like to thank the following for their indispensable assistance with the preparation of this manuscript.

Emma Pivato read many of the essays submitted for inclusion in this collection. Giulia De Gasperi would like to thank her husband, Dr Tiber Falzett, for his continued support throughout this project. The two anonymous readers who peer-reviewed the final draft made many valuable suggestions for improving individual essays.

The editors at McGill-Queen's University Press were most supportive of this project and we thank them: Mark Abley, Jonathan Crago, and Ryan Van Huijstee. We were very fortunate to have the skill and experience of our copy editor, Patricia Kennedy of Toronto.

Linda Hutcheon of the University of Toronto encouraged us from the beginning and articulated this positive energy in her foreword for this collection.

Licia Canton of Montreal has been a creative force for this project on multicultural literature and a great help to both editors.

We would like to recognize each of the contributors for their original essays, and for their support for the general promotion of Comparative Literature.

Joseph Pivato would like to thank his colleagues in the Language and Literature program at Athabasca University, who made it possible to teach courses in Comparative Literature at the graduate and undergraduate levels and carry on many years of research in comparative studies.

The Canadian Comparative Literature Association/Association Canadienne de Littérature Comparée (CCLA/ACLC) has promoted Comparative Literature across Canada for fifty years. Many of the contributors to this volume are active members of the CCLA, and some of the chapters included here were inspired by the annual conferences organized by the CCLA.

The American Comparative Literature Association published reports on the state of the discipline in 1965, 1975, 1993, 2004, and 2014–15. Sometimes these reports are later published in larger volumes accompanied by critical essays written by senior members of the ACLA. Several chapters in this volume, *Comparative Literature for the New Century*, are written in response to essays in the ACLA volumes.

E.D. Blodgett's "Comparative Literature in Canada: A Case Study" originally appeared in *Canadian Review of Comparative Literature/Revue Canadienne de Littérature Comparée* 40, no. 3 (September 2013): 308–20. We would like to thank the editors, J.L. Hart and I. Sywenky, for permission to reprint it here.

Comparative
LITERATURE
*for the*
NEW CENTURY

# Introduction: The State of the Art

*Giulia De Gasperi*

## OF (NON)-DEFINING COMPARATIVE LITERATURE

The aim of this volume is threefold: to present some of the most recent work carried out by academics and scholars actively engaged in the field of Comparative Literature in Canada and abroad; to promote the value of the field of Comparative Literature as an area of interdisciplinary study; and to assess the future directions it might take.

Comparative Literature has been characterized, since its beginning, as always being "en crise,"[1] "nomade,"[2] "dying,"[3] and "un-disciplined," as Hutcheon writes in the foreword to this volume. As an academic discipline, it has blurred, undefined boundaries, but its mobility and resilience provide reason for optimism[4] and hope for further change and growth in the future.

The chapters that make up this collection are, for the most part, examples of how the knowledge and tools offered by Comparative Literature can be applied to read, explore, and understand not only literary productions, but also the world at large. These chapters engage with – but not exclusively – theory, history, media studies, psychology, translation studies, post-colonial studies, gender studies, and close reading in two languages.

Since its first appearance on Canadian university campuses, Comparative Literature has shown the ability to reach out to other disciplines, to co-operate and collaborate, making interdisciplinarity, multidisciplinarity, and multilingualism three of its most important and distinctive characteristics. The hope is that this volume will testify to this and will also shed some light on the future course of the discipline. My brief overview of Comparative Literature programs in Canada is below.

Linda Hutcheon, in her 1995 review of *Comparative Literature in the Age of Multiculturalism*, writes that the volume is "a book for provoking thought"[5] and "a provocative challenge to broaden the scope of what we teach in CompLit departments."[6] The editors and contributors of *Comparative Literature for the New Century* offer this volume as a valuable addition to the work carried out up to now in the field of Comparative Literature in Canada and abroad, in the hope that it will broaden the scope of, spur debate on, and provide constructive criticism of this field.

This collection is organized into thematic sections, each of which defines aspects of Comparative Literature and begins with a brief introduction. In Section 1, comparative arguments examine questions of theory and methodology; Section 2 presents future directions for Comparative Literature; Section 3 considers the close relationship between international Comparative Literature and Comparative Canadian Literature; and finally, Section 4 reviews our relationship with traditions in both Europe and North America.

In this volume we include work by senior academics such as E.D. Blodgett, Sneja Gunew, and Gaetano Rando, but we also feature work by younger scholars such as Dominique Hétu, Mark McCutcheon, Maria Cristina Seccia, and Ndeye Fatou Ba.

## AMERICAN AGENDAS FOR COMPARATIVE LITERATURE

Perhaps because of its very nature, Comparative Literature has often been at the centre of debate:

> Debate has surrounded Comparative Literature for so long. The Levin report to the American Comparative Literature Association in 1965, the Greene Report in 1975, the Bernheimer Report in 1993 and the Saussy Report ... have all expressed the double movement of frustration and attraction, of definition and criticism that Hutcheon suggests.[7]

It is with this tendency to critique, discuss, and self-reflect every ten years or so the American Comparative Literature Association undergoes a thorough and in-depth review and, as a result, a report on its state is published. The two most recent documents, in a traditional print format, are *Comparative Literature in the Age of Multiculturalism*, edited by Charles Bernheimer (1994), and *Comparative Literature in an Age of Globalization*, edited by Haun Saussy (2006). We live in a fast-changing world, where innovations and advancements happen every day and touch every facet of our society. Even a decennial report is not immune to such changes, and for the first time the 2014-15 *State of the Discipline Report* has appeared online – demonstrating both a difference in format and in the variety of submissions. It is clearly a new way of approaching and engaging with the discipline and of sharing topics, thoughts, and ideas. The 2014-15 overview includes papers dealing with areas of interests, study, and research and shows how "Literature and Comparative Literature are changing: reading in an age of electronic media ... does change,"[8] supporting the thought that "the centre of gravity in Comparative Literature and other disciplines outside of science, in which facts make corrections, shifts according to curiosity, interest and the need for change"[9] was pushed forward by changes in societies. Indeed, more and more papers are dedicated to the impact the digital world is having on our lives and demonstrate how Comparative Literature can be used to analyze that impact, making it understandable and usable to the majority of us (see, for example, Scott Kushner's "Comparative Non-Literature and Everyday Digital Textuality," "Paradigm Shift in Comparative Humanities: Digital Humanities, Pedagogy with New Media Technology, and Publishing Scholarship Online" by Steven Tötösy de Zepetnek and Graciela Boruszko, and Dennis Tennen's "Digital Displacement"). In his essay, Kushner argues that digital textuality has given birth to textual culture in the forms of blogs, social-networking platforms, and short messaging services in as many genres as they come. These do not represent literary examples. Their beauty lies in the recognition of what they are, that is, non-literary texts, and the possibilities of engagement they represent for Comparative Literature. This way Kushner moves the attention away from the traditional discussion of canonical texts and asks what literary studies is and what it should include. Digital media deeply affected his generation – pushing it to finding answers to two new questions: What are we to do with everyday digital textuality and what is the function of the literary? Kushner encourages the discipline to welcome this new flood of textuality, because in studying it we can learn about the ethics and cultural practices of an era. If instead we choose to strictly apply the notion of the canon, "by forsaking other forms of writing, the field passes up opportunities to deploy its tools in sites of textual production and consumption that are much closer to both the lived experiences of contemporary digitally mediated society and the lives of the students who should populate its courses."[10]

Kushner's argument looks back at the 1993-94 Bernheimer Report, which had already declared that Comparative Literature "should include comparisons between media, from early manuscripts to television, hypertext, and virtual realities,"[11] and continues by listing two earlier examples of works of Comparative Literature dealing with non-literary material: Janice Radway's treatments of dime novels and popular literature, in which she compares the Harlequin novels of the 1970s and the selections of the Book-of-the-Month club; and Tom Conley's work, in which he studies maps and cartography to bring to the fore two important aspects of early modern literature: the emergence of the self and the rise of the nation. Kushner's final argument is that comparative literature should study this new body of texts, which allows us to better understand the societies in which they are currently produced through interpretation of what they mean and not what they are.

Other essays in this report present the history and development of departments which are now thriving but had to face a difficult start, such as, for example, "Arabic and the Paradigms of Comparison" by Waïl S. Hassan, while others deal with the further expansion of the blurred boundaries of Comparative Literature to include studies and comparisons drawn from the world at large ("Aesthetic Humanity and the Great World Community: Kant and Kang Youwei" by Ban Wang, and "World Literature as Figure and as Ground" by David Damrosch).

## A MULTICULTURAL PERSPECTIVE

The essays mentioned above are examples of the current trends of studies and of the research being conducted by comparatists working in the United States. They represent the breath, possibilities, and advancement of the discipline in American university programs, but also set the trends for literary studies in other countries, such as Canada. Even though comparatists are preoccupied with introspection about the nature and future of this discipline, there are few published self-examinations in Canada. The most significant self-critique of the state of Comparative Literature is a 1996 issue of the *Canadian Review of Comparative Literature* that includes articles in English and French and looks at programs beyond North America, including those in Eastern Europe and Brazil. This is where we find Linda Hutcheon's self-reflexive review, "Comparative Literature's 'Anxiogenic' State."

The present volume intends to examine the current state of the discipline in Canada and beyond. I begin here with a brief overview of the history and establishment of Comparative Literature programs in Canada, which were founded by several multilingual émigrés from Europe. At Carleton University in Ottawa, the Comparative Literature program was founded by Eva Kushner, who was born in Prague in the former

Czechoslovakia in 1929, lived in France from 1939 to 1945, and then emigrated to Canada, beginning to teach at Carleton in 1961. Her degrees are from McGill University, including a PhD in French literature (1956).

At the Université de Montréal, the program in Littérature Comparée was pioneered by Paul Zumthor, who was born and educated in Geneva. It included Wladimir Krysinski, Antonio Gomez Moriana, Walter Moser, Philip Stratford, and Silvestra Mariniello, who introduced film studies into the program in the 1990s. It is referred to as "l'école montréalaise."

The Department of Comparative Literature at the University of Alberta was founded by Milan Dimić, who was born in Belgrade, in the former Yugoslavia, and studied at the University of Belgrade, the University of Tübingen, and the University of Vienna. In 1966 he moved to Canada after being hired at the University of Alberta as a professor of German and Comparative Literature. In 1969 he helped to establish the program in Comparative Literature, and in 1974 was founding editor of the *Canadian Review of Comparative Literature*, which became an important international journal. Along with Eva Kushner, he was one of the founders of the Canadian Comparative Literature Association, a bilingual society.

At the University of Toronto, the founding of the Comparative Literature program is credited to Northrop Frye, the well-known Canadian scholar of literary theory. I will discuss this program below. Another Canadian, Ronald Sutherland, established the Comparative Literature program at the Université de Sherbrooke, in the 1960s, as the first bilingual graduate program in Comparative Canadian Literature/Littérature canadienne comparée, and it continues to develop its French content, with increasing attention to literary translation. Because of the unique nature of this program, Joseph Pivato has called it "the Sherbrooke School of Comparative Canadian Literature."

I must clarify that, in Canada, Comparative Canadian Literature is seen as part of the international area of study, Comparative Literature. In this volume, we argue that Comparative Canadian Literature, which studies not only English and French writing, but also work by ethnic minority and indigenous authors, can serve as a model for scholars in many other countries. I can mention other Canadian scholars who support similar views for future comparative studies: Antoine Sirois, Pat Smart, E.D. Blodgett, Sherry Simon, Winfried Siemerling, Marie Vautier, Louise Ladouceur, Marie Carrière, and Licia Canton.

The promising future for comparative literary study in Canada is indicated by emerging programs, such as the doctoral program in Comparative Literature that began at the University of Western Ontario in

2002 and the Graduate Diploma in Comparative Literature that was launched at York University (Toronto) in 2014. We can add to this list the Université de Moncton, with the bilingual study of Acadian literature, and the bilingual studies programs at Concordia University in Montreal, the University of Alberta, and the University of Victoria. The University of Ottawa has a School of Translation, which often conducts research on comparative literary topics.

I have focused on some pioneer founders of Comparative Literature in Canada, but I must also mention the many foreign students who were attracted to these multilingual programs. In the 1950s and 1960s, many bilingual students came with the mass migration of Europeans after the Second World War, and later formed part of the second generation of North American academics in Comparative Literature. By the 1970s and 1980s, students from all over the world had come to North America and brought their various languages with them. They often benefited from programs in Comparative Literature that supported the study of different languages and literatures, including those from their countries of origin. These students and academics expanded the languages of Comparative Literature beyond Europe. An example of this is Manijeh Mannani's book *Divine Deviants: The Dialectics of Devotion in the Poetry of Donne and Rumi*, which compares the Persian poems of the Sufi poet Rumi to the verse of John Donne.

It seems appropriate then that *Comparative Literature for the New Century* appears following the report discussed above and offers an overview of the kind of research that academics in the fields of Comparative Literature and Canadian Comparative Literature are conducting in Canada and beyond. Indeed, of great significance is the uniqueness of this anthology: a collection of chapters that begins with Canadian Comparative Literature and expands beyond North America to include Africa, Australia, the United Kingdom, and Italy. Until recently, works on Comparative Literature in this country were scattered among different publications, almost exclusively specialized journals and magazines: ARIEL, *Studies in Canadian Literature, Canadian Review of Comparative Literature, Mosaic, Canadian Literature*, Études littéraires, *Journal of Canadian Studies*, TOPIA, and the *International Journal of Canadian Studies*.

The multidisciplinary aspect that this discipline is built upon is mirrored in this volume by the provenance and the specialty of each contributor – from ethnic minority writing, translation studies, and post-colonial theory to filmography. The chapters that make up this collection rise from a habit this discipline seems to have, one that is so well described by Linda Hutcheon in the essay she wrote for *Comparative Literature in an Age of Globalization*: "It is this habit of self-interrogation that makes the discipline perhaps uniquely responsive to change: comparative literature has always been open to rethinking."[12] And rethink and evolve it certainly does. Things have changed considerably since the Sherbrooke School of the 1970s with its revolutionary approach to the study of Canadian literature through its production in both English and French texts. The influence of the Sherbrooke School was, and still is, great. Thanks to it, not only does Comparative Literature in Canada have status and recognition as a legitimate discipline, but its approach and its application to Canadian Literature can now be found in universities all across the country. From the introduction of studies of Canadian texts in English and French (see, for example, the literary journal *ellipse*, founded in 1969 and devoted to francophone and anglophone poems, published with their translation in the other language), to the founding of the Association for Canadian and Quebec Literatures (ACQL) in 1974, the Sherbrooke School has laid the foundations for this discipline to grow and expand, embracing not only the use of more than two languages but also exploring relationships with other disciplines, thus making it inter- and multidisciplinary.[13] Unfortunately, these achievements did not come easily. One need only read E.D. Blodgett's chapter, included in this volume, where he presents the history and development of the discipline through his own career at the University of Alberta, a career running from the end of the 1960s to 2010, to have a sense of its trials and tribulations.

More recently, who can forget the outpouring of support for the discipline that came in from academics and researchers all around the world following the 2010 announcement that the University of Toronto had plans to shut down its Centre for Comparative Literature in an attempt to save costs? The University of Toronto eventually pulled back from its plan, keeping the centre and the other departments that had risked being shut down at the beginning of 2010. Even though a colossal catastrophe was avoided, there remains a bittersweet aftertaste, a lingering sense that, if something needs to be sacrificed, the Centre for Comparative Literature, and the Centre for Ethics, the Centre for Diaspora and Transnational Studies, and the Centre for International Studies along with it, would be at the top of the list of possibilities. What does this say about the value given to this discipline by our educational establishment? Would the department of English literature ever be a candidate? What does such a choice mean when a critical entity such as the Centre for Comparative Literature, created more than forty years ago by one of the most brilliant minds Canada has ever produced, a centre that during its life has established itself and the University of Toronto as pivotal in literary and critical theory, is at risk of seeing its core structure reshaped and renamed?

## THE CONTRIBUTION OF THIS VOLUME

In his article "The Futures of Comparative Literature," Jonathan Hart briefly examines the state of the discipline in 2005 and suggests some possible general directions for future research. While he refers to a number of literary theorists, such as Gayatri Chakravorty Spivak, David Damrosch, and Richard Rorty, he gives few examples of literary texts. In contrast to Hart's theoretical-historical review, we present in this volume concrete examples of studies in Comparative Literature which engage creative works in a variety of languages and from different countries. While many texts are from Canadian literature, they nevertheless serve as models of comparative study for scholars in many countries.

Based on the quality of the chapters in this volume and on the success of the annual conferences of the Canadian Comparative Literature Association (CCLA) held during the Humanities and Social Sciences Congress (HSSC) each year we can argue that Comparative Literature in Canada is thriving and expanding its teaching and research scope to embrace its interdisciplinary, multidisciplinary, and multilingual approach.

Comparative Literature is a stubborn discipline, one whose temperament is often "contrarian" as Linda Hutcheon described it in her essay for *Comparative Literature in an Age of Globalization*. She was using that adjective hoping that the discipline in Canada would break free from a Eurocentric approach without forgetting Europe, choosing instead to embrace this ever-evolving geography and help it to understand and (re)define itself.[14] Some of the chapters in this collection are proof that Europe is still much part of the discipline's scope of study, but show the international links Comparative Literature fosters and the broader possibilities for collaboration and co-operation that exist in the Humanities at large.

In Canada, where many academics and students are bilingual and trilingual, work in Comparative Literature is often exemplary, as these chapters demonstrate.

What we hope will emerge from the pages of this volume is the importance of language use beyond English in Comparative Literature and the broadening of the academic curricula and research topics in order to reflect the indefinable realm of Comparative Literature that strives to mirror our ever-changing world. Because of, and thanks to, these open-minded approaches, this discipline does not only give voice to literary production but also embraces cultural expression in all its forms and provenances, bringing to the fore individuals and groups that would otherwise be left voiceless. Think, for example, of ethnic writing, immigrant writing, or diaspora writing, fields that McCutcheon in his chapter defines as "*uncanny* – in the psychoanalytically fraught, ambivalent sense of the original German term, *Unheimlich*: un-homelike" (306). There are several chapters in this volume that deal with ethnic minority writing, with the works of authors that feel the need to express how they mediate between two cultures, between an old "there" and a new "here," old/lost and new traditions, and old and new language(s). The discipline of Comparative Literature also gives voice to the quest for self and sense of belonging: The role of women and their place and space in society is the topic of much of the writing and research conducted through this discipline. Indeed, it is through the studies of women's writings and the literary and critical theories that sprang from them that Italian-Canadian writing in particular and ethnic writing in general have become more defined, established, recognized, and accepted in Canada and are increasingly subjects of studies in Comparative Literature.

Even though in Canada the primary languages chosen by authors belonging to ethnic minority groups are English or French, the need remains to understand the culture these writers come from, especially considering that, quite frequently, their pages are peppered with sounds derived from the language they left behind but that was never forgotten. There are numerous examples of books that are written in more than one language. The Anglo-Irish writer Samuel Beckett is a favourite example of an author who self-translates his own works from English to French. Russian-American writer Vladimir Nabokov (who also taught Comparative Literature) translated his Russian novels into English. In African literature, the best examples of self-translation are Ngũgi wa Thiong'o and André Brink. Karen Blixen (Isak Dinesen), who lived in Kenya for many years, wrote in Danish, French, and English. The current mistress of self-translation is Nancy Huston, who was born in Calgary, Alberta, and educated in Paris. She writes in both English and French, self-translating her own books from one language to the other. See her powerful introspective book *Losing North: Musings on Land, Tongue, and Self* (2002), in which she examines the expressions of life and language in circumstances of cultural exile.

In his chapter on the languages of Comparative Literature, Joseph Pivato argues that looking at the world from purely anglophone or American points of view is limiting. He maintains that the Canadian models of embracing different languages and various cultural perspectives form part of the future directions for Comparative Literature.

The strong emphasis on the importance of languages expands to include Translation Studies, especially when combined with Literary Criticism, as shown in the chapter by Maria Cristina Seccia, "Reading Literature through Translation: The Case of Antonio D'Alfonso into Italian." Being able to read both the original work and its translation into another language allows the student or researcher to analyze not only the quality of the translation itself but most importantly the level of understanding and sensitivity toward both cultures – the one translated from and the one translated into – that the translator conveyed through his/her work.

The importance and validity of the contributions presented in this volume are made evident in a chapter that responds to the challenge posed by Scott Kushner around opening the field of Comparative Literature to less-traditional themes, topics, and disciplines, referred to as "Comparative Non-Literature." The chapter by Monique Tschofen, "Exile, Media, Capital: *Calendar*'s Systems of Exchange" explores the Canadian film, *Calendar* (1993) by director Atom Egoyan, about a couple that travels back to Armenia. This offers possibilities for comparison, thanks to its dramatization of cross-cultural fertilizations and misunderstandings. Its value to literary studies emerges from its continued acceptance of the significance of media in the construction of cultural encounters, and their role in complex global structures of production, circulation, and exchange. We could argue that Comparative Literature is not only open to "rethinking itself,"[15] but can also "reimagine what the discipline of literary studies takes as its object of study and its *raison d'être*,"[16] hoping that such a statement will open the gate to more interactions and engagements with visual arts, digital media, photography, and filmography. As Scott Kushner writes: "Every living discipline thrives by interrogating its practices and objects of study with regularity. If the way we read now is more screen than page, more tweet than blank verse, then let's deploy the power of literary studies to understand how those textual forms work, how they communicate meaning, what textual practices thrive and falter, and how all of these traits might compare with other and earlier textual cultures."[17]

Some of the chapters in this volume will raise controversy. Elizabeth Dahab questions the canonical status of Rawi Hage's novel *Cockroach*. Ndeye Fatou Ba contrasts language policies among the British and French colonies in Africa. The original work of Dominique Hétu explores theories of care ethics as applied to dystopian novels. We welcome these and other literary controversies.

## PERSONAL EXPERIENCES WITH COMPARATIVE LITERATURE

Before concluding, I would like to share my own personal experience with Comparative Literature, since I was not academically and officially trained in it. I was a student of Canadian literature in Italy during the late 1990s and the beginning of the 2000s. I am now a literary translator, and I focus my work on the literary production of Canada, hoping to increase the numbers of works by Canadian authors being translated and published in Italy. My interest and passion for this country comes from a year I spent on Prince Edward Island as an exchange student. That experience changed my life, and it shouldn't come as a surprise that Canada is now my new home. My year abroad was my first exposure to a different culture and language. Experiencing on a daily basis a constant need to compare where I was and where I came from was my first encounter with comparative studies. I learned by living. And when I returned to Italy and time came to choose a faculty, I had no doubts: Foreign Languages and Literatures. My chosen languages were, of course, English and French, and my main research interest was Canadian Literature. Year by year, this course was alternatively hosted by the English department and the Anglo-American one, to which I belonged. To me it seemed that this utterly fascinating reality, Canadian Literature, this realm of endless reading and research possibilities, was treated by the faculty like a hot potato that no one really wanted to deal with. I realize there was probably not enough funding or enough interest to give it a permanent, more stable, home. But I had got *un'infarinatura*, as we would say in Italian, a bit of a taste of English Canadian Literature, and I continued my career hoping I would have the chance, perhaps not as an undergraduate but as a PhD student, to explore territory that was new and uncharted, at least to me. But alas, I was to be disappointed.

Discouraged, I applied for a Government of Canada scholarship and upon receiving it I made a very, let's say, bold choice. I chose to delve into Celtic Studies and explore the language and culture of the Scottish Gaelic-speaking immigrants that settled in Canada. It was Hugh MacLennan who inspired me to embark on such a research path. In some of his essays I found mention of other realities present in Canada, realities that went beyond the two solitudes he wrote about in one of his better-known novels. It might be a surprise to many, but here is another example of marginalized ethnic/immigrant/minority writing. My choice clearly put an end to my academic career, and still to this day I get questioned as to why I have chosen such an "esoteric" topic. Here "esoteric" refers both to Canadian literature in general and the literature of the Scottish Gaelic diaspora in particular. (This reminds me that Joseph Pivato, upon trying to place his first essay on Italian-Canadian writing, saw it being rejected because it was too esoteric.) You may think that such a judgment was uttered by an Italian, someone with very little knowledge or understanding of the Canadian literary and cultural landscape. Would you be surprised to know that "esoteric" was actually uttered by a fairly educated Canadian? What does it say about this particular individual's perception of Canadian literature? I do not regret my choices. The research I have conducted, the knowledge I have gained, and the mentors I have found along the way are irreplaceable. I still remember how proud I felt when, during my oral exam on Italian literature, I compared the personality of Carlo Altoviti, the main character of the novel I was discussing – *Confessioni di un ottuagenario* by Ippolito Nievo – to the novel *Waverley* by Walter Scott, which we were studying in my course on Scottish literature. Although we weren't encouraged to draw connections and make comparisons – as if courses were separate entities on their own (there were courses on Comparative Literature at the university I attended, but they did not explore what I was truly interested in) – the process of reading different books in different languages at the same time made it quite natural to draw associations.

Nowadays my personal and professional contribution to this country and to the discipline of Comparative Literature is to export as much Canadian literature in translation as possible, moving away from the big names – those are already taken care of – and focusing instead on lesser-known but equally talented writers and authors. I would like to make ethnic and minority writing a recognizable component of Canadian literature. It should be its strength, what makes it stand out from the literary production of other English-speaking countries.

In the past, I translated excerpts of literary works for an online literary journal that focuses mainly on Canadian minority writings. Of the utmost importance when doing translations is, at least to me, to be extremely sensitive toward the author's writing, keeping in mind where s/he comes from and the message the writing is meant to convey. Not every translator has the chance to directly discuss doubts with authors or travel to the place where a piece of writing is set. Comparative Literature and Canadian Studies are thus two extremely important disciplines that can prepare a translator-to-be to face and solve problems that arise during the translation process. I have frequently come across examples where the translator did not have a clear understanding of the work s/he was translating.

Let me offer you two examples: as I live on the island of Lucy Maud Montgomery, a few years ago I reread *Anne of Green Gables*. Mine was an exercise that brought together Comparative Literature and translation studies. I read side by side the original work, in English, and one of the many Italian editions available. What an excruciating experience. I was appalled. Not only were there mistakes in the translation itself, showing that the translator did not have a thorough-enough knowledge of the English language, but there were also many misinterpretations, proving that the translator did not understand the culture, the history, and the geography of this island, and had no knowledge of the type of person and writer Lucy Maud Montgomery was. More recently, I had to write a review of *John Barleycorn* by Jack London for an Italian literary magazine. I was given an Italian translation of the many available, and I had to resort to the English original, because the translation I was reading was extremely poorly done. I think the translator did not understand the time the novel was set in and mistranslated quite a few words, leaving out explanations and passages he did not know how to present to the Italian readership. These two examples demonstrate that studies such as the one by Seccia are extremely important, and that Comparative Literature should prepare students to be able to read and interpret correctly a piece of writing in another language before comparing it with or attempting a translation.

## CONCLUSION

The chapters in this volume are proof that the discipline of Comparative Literature in Canada is constantly growing and that its research and study topics are expanding in order to analyze and understand our ever-evolving world. *Comparative Literature for the New Century* argues that the discipline of Comparative Literature in Canada offers the right tools to better interpret this world – a world of different languages and different literary traditions – and to face and resolve the many problems arising from miscommunication. Comparative Literature in Canada is flexible, stubborn, and contrarian. It constantly self-reflects, rethinks, re-invents, and re-imagines itself. It creates connections and forges alliances with other disciplines, thus strengthening its inter- and multidisciplinary aspects. It encourages the study of more than two languages and is excited about innovations and advancements. It is eager to explore the future and to let it enter its university campuses and classrooms.

## NOTES

This collection is not a Festschrift for Joseph Pivato, though over his long career he has been a mentor to many writers and academics with his research work and publications in ethnic minority writing, Canadian literature, and Comparative Literature. Some of the contributors to this volume make references to his publications. Early in his career, Joseph Pivato pursued diverse interests that matched his languages: English, Italian, and French. Below I list some of his early publications as an indication of his work in Comparative Literature:

"Nouveau Roman Canadien." *Canadian Literature* 58 (1973), 51–60.
"Wyatt, Tudor Translator of Petrarca: Italian Plain Style." *Canadian Review of Comparative Literature* 8, no. 2 (1981): 239–55.
"Eight Approaches to Canadian Literary Criticism." *The Journal of Commonwealth Literature* 13, no. 3 (1979): 43–53.
Edited. *Contrasts: Comparative Essays on Italian-Canadian Writing.* Montreal: Guernica Editions, 1985. (This became a model for future research and publications on ethnic minority writing.)
Edited. *Literary Theory and Ethnic Minority Writing*, special issue of *Canadian Ethnic Studies* 28, no. 3 (1996).

1. Gnisci, "La Littérature comparée comme discipline," 67.
2. Moser, "La Littérature comparée et la crise," 43.
3. Spivak, *Death of a Discipline*, 2003.
4. Hart, "The Future of Comparative Literature," 6.
5. Hutcheon, "Productive Comparative Angst," 299.
6. Ibid., 302.
7. Hart, "The Future," 9.
8. Ibid., 8.
9. Ibid., 16.
10. Kushner, "Comparative Non-Literature."
11. Bernheimer, *Comparative Literature in the Age of Multiculturalism*, 45.
12. Hutcheon, "Congenially Contrarian," 225.
13. Pivato, "The Sherbrooke School."
14. Hutcheon, "Congenially Contrarian," 228.
15. Ibid., 225.
16. Kushner, "Comparative Non-Literature."
17. Ibid.

## BIBLIOGRAPHY

ACLA *Report on the State of the Discipline, 2014–2015*, edited by Ursula Heise et al. http://stateofthediscipline.acla.org/about.

Bernheimer, Charles. *Comparative Literature in the Age of Multiculturalism*. Baltimore: Johns Hopkins University Press, 1995.

Damrosch, David. "World Literature as Figure and as Ground." In ACLA *Report on the State of the Discipline, 2014–2015*. http://stateofthediscipline.acla.org/entry/world-literature-figure-and-ground-0.

Gnisci, Armando. "La Littérature comparée comme discipline de décolonisation." *Canadian Review of Comparative Literature/Revue Canadienne de Littérature Comparée* [CRCL/RCLC] 23 (1996): 67.

Hart, Jonathan. "The Futures of Comparative Literature: North America and Beyond." *Revue de littérature comparée* 317, no. 1 (2006): 5–21.

Hassan, Wail S. "Arabic and the Paradigms of Comparison." ACLA *Report on the State of the Discipline, 2014–2015*. http://stateofthediscipline.acla.org/entry/arabic-and-paradigms-comparison-1#sthash.l7wOhSkS.dpuf.

Huston, Nancy. *Losing North: Musings on Land, Tongue, and Self*. Toronto: McArthur, 2002.

Hutcheon, Linda. "Productive Comparative Angst: Comparative Literature in the Age of Multiculturalism." *World Literature Today* 69, no. 2 (Spring 1996): 299–303.

– "Comparative Literature's 'Axiogenic' State." *Canadian Review of Comparative Literature* 23, no. 1 (March 1996): 35–41.

– "Congenially Contrarian." In *Comparative Literature in an Age of Globalization*, edited by Haun Saussy, 224–9. Baltimore: Johns Hopkins University Press, 2006.

Kushner, Scott. "Comparative Non-Literature and Everyday Digital Texuality." In ACLA *Report on the State of the Discipline, 2014–2015*. http://stateofthediscipline.acla.org/entry/comparative-non-literature-and-everyday-digital-textuality-0.

Moser, Walter. "La Littérature Comparée et la crise des études littéraires." *Revue Canadienne de Littérature Comparée* [CRCL/RCLC] 23 (1996): 43.

Pivato, Joseph. "The Sherbrooke School of Comparative Canadian Literature." *Inquire*. http://inquire.streetmag.org/articles/25.

Spivak, Gayatri Chakravorty. *Death of a Discipline*. New York: Columbia University Press, 2003.

Tenen, Dennis. "Digital Displacement." ACLA *Report on the State of the Discipline, 2014–2015*. http://stateofthediscipline.acla.org/entry/digital-displacement#sthash.w9Es9YDN.dpuf.

Tötösy de Zepetnek, Steven, and Graciela Boruszko. "Paradigm Shift in Comparative Humanities: Digital Humanities, Pedagogy with New Media Technology, and Publishing Scholarship Online. *ACLA Report on the State of the Discipline, 2014–2015*. http://stateofthediscipline.acla.org/entry/paradigm-shift-comparative-humanities-digital-humanities-pedagogy-new-media-technology-and.

Wang, Ban. "Aesthetic Humanity and the Great World Community: Kant and Kang Youwei." *ACLA Report on the State of the Discipline, 2014–2015*. http://stateofthediscipline.acla.org/entry/aesthetic-humanity-and-great-world-community-kant-and-kang-youwei.

SECTION ONE

# COMPARATIVE ARGUMENTS

Comparative Literature has always had an identity problem, as scholar René Wellek pointed out in his 1958 essay "Crisis of Comparative Literature." The reports of the American Comparative Literature Association over the years have tried to deal with the various questions in this "undisciplined" discipline, be they in theory, methodology, or pedagogy. Some of our colleagues and students have turned to cultural studies or post-colonial theory for possible directions. There, too, they confront questions of legitimacy and appropriation of voice and subject matter. There are many debates about these and other questions in literary studies. One example of such discussion is in the essay "Godzilla vs Post-Colonial," by Indigenous writer Thomas King. King challenges the view that all Indigenous literature is a reaction to colonialism, rather than an extension of a longer native tradition. In King's opinion, the term post-colonial serves to reinforce the legacy of colonialism.[1] Our response to this rejection of post-colonial theory is to consider the possibilities of Comparative Literature.

The historical development of Comparative Literature has the problem of being Eurocentric, but the practice of dealing with different languages and cultures means that the study of literary texts does not depend on power relations, such as those found in post-colonial studies. In practice, the comparison of two or more texts usually means that they meet on a level playing field. We are suggesting, therefore, that more comparative work needs to be done with the literary works of Indigenous authors in North America, which may also involve work with Indigenous languages. A good place to start is with the volume *Introduction to Indigenous Literary Criticism in Canada*, which includes essays by a number of Indigenous writers, such as Tomson Highway, Emma LaRocque, Lee Maracle, Jeannette Armstrong, Kateri Akiwenzie-Damm, and Daniel David Moses.[2]

Many Indigenous writers make us aware of concerns about the stewardship of our land and problems raised in ecocriticism. Bilingual comparatist Sheena Wilson is promoting critical work relating literary culture to oil and energy, which she sees as offering promising new research directions for Comparative Literature beyond post-colonial theory.[3]

The two contributions in this section raise many other questions about the future directions for Comparative Literature.

## NOTES

1 King, "Godzilla vs Post-Colonial," 10–16.
2 Macfarlane and Ruffo, *Introduction*.
3 Wilson, "Shake Up, Not Shake-Down," 226–30.

## BIBLIOGRAPHY

King, Thomas. "Godzilla vs Post-Colonial." *World Literature Written in English* 30, no. 2 (Autumn 1990): 10–16.

Macfarlane, Heather, and Armand Garnet Ruffo, eds. *Introduction to Indigenous Literary Criticism in Canada*. Peterbrough: Broadview Press, 2015.

Wellek, René. "The Crisis of Comparative Literature." In *Comparative Literature: Proceedings of the Second Congress of the ICLA*, edited by W.P. Friederich. 2 vols. 2:149–59. Chapel Hill: University of Carolina, 1958.

Wilson, Sheena. "Shake Up, Not Shake-Down: Comparative Literature as a Twenty-First Century Discipline." *Canadian Review of Comparative Literature* 41, no. 2 (2014): 226–30.

# Anonymous: Animating Ecologies of Belonging

*Sneja Gunew*

Consider the two dynamics: those who are caught up within the supposed hyper-individualism of the First World, who apparently yearn for group identity; in contrast, those individuals who are primarily perceived in terms of a group identity (often designated subaltern or abjected) and desirous of being situated (at least provisionally and fleetingly) as individuals. E.D. Blodgett's essay on the history and development of Comparative Literature in Canada alludes to the ways in which the dynamics of belonging operate within a certain period and place in literary studies. That they are always implicated in a more general politics is also vibrantly illustrated by the nationalist and Cold War politics that permeated the era in which Comparative Literature developed. We academics are now in a new phase of suspicion and surveillance, as Marina Warner's recent analysis of the modern university makes starkly clear (2015). Let me therefore situate this discussion within the framework of a cosmopolitanism that sets itself against globalization.

What has been termed the new cosmopolitanism explores possible frameworks for rethinking cultural difference in relation to reading multicultural, post-colonial, diasporic texts. In other words, we are dealing with ecologies of belonging within the framework of neo-cosmopolitanism. To sketch this in quickly: unlike the old elitist cosmopolitanism that dealt with a type of privileged mobility, the new cosmopolitanism deals with the perspectives of those left out of triumphalist globalization. The new cosmopolitanism is often characterized by qualifying terms such as vernacular, abject, moral, ecological, and armoured cosmopolitanism, etc. There are many disputes around whether the terms generate new perspectives or whether they camouflage the same neo-liberal structures. The political scientist Ulrich Beck's "Cosmopolitan Manifesto" (1998) was intended to mobilize a concept of "world citizens." Beck is often seen as one of the architects of these new debates in the context of risk management, summarized by Claire Colebrook as "threats to this cosmopolitanism – resource depletion, rising sea levels, global heating, desertification, species extinction, viral apocalypse, violent fundamentalism, bio-weapons" (166). Clearly, the institutions associated with nation-states are not able to manage all these threats, so how might we imagine new global institutions, which are predicated on new alliances that can comprehensively involve the greatest number of participants, can deal with these problems? Because of Beck's focus on Europe (albeit a redefined Europe) and his debt to Immanuel Kant (and Habermas), many critics see his position as being inherently Eurocentric, referring to universalist principles that covertly enshrine the old Euro-US hegemonies through this humanitarian appeal to maintaining world peace – in spite of the fact that Beck alludes to such dangers in the Manifesto.

A more familiar North American manifestation of the new cosmopolitan debates may well be Kwame Anthony Appiah's *Cosmopolitanism: Ethics in a World of Strangers*. One notes a contradiction that is at the heart of these debates, such as the two versions of anonymous: the fact that cosmopolitanism is structured in relation to the tension between individuals and groups. In Jean-Luc Nancy's terms: "From one singular to another, there is contiguity but not continuity" (5). How one receives the stranger, for example, depends very much on how the group situates itself temporally and spatially. For example, critics of the West often create a version of the West that is defined by a rampant individualism that is seen to be responsible for the ills associated with globalization, the irresponsible expenditure and waste of resources – human and other. Others suggest that, indeed, the heart of cosmopolitanism is that individuals are the central component – all individuals. Here, for example, is Thomas Pogge:

> First, *individualism*: the ultimate units of concern are human beings, or persons – rather than, say, family lines, tribes, ethnic, cultural or religious communities, nations or states. The latter may be units of concern only indirectly, in virtue of their individual members or citizens. Second, *universality*: the status of ultimate unit of concern attaches to every living human being equally – not merely to some

sub-set, such as men, aristocrats, Aryans, whites or Muslims. Third, *generality*: this special status has global force. Persons are ultimate units of concern for everyone – not only for their compatriots, fellow religionists, or such like. (142)

This rings false to our increasingly post-humanist conception of "human beings," and does not work so easily when we consider our intertwining with other species, as well as the notion of fractal individuals, who are linked with one another as well as with non-human elements. We want to believe, after Judith Butler's influential work, that all lives are grieveable. We also want to avoid the kind of model uncovered by Lili Chouliaraki, who analyzes "cosmopolitan solidarity" in connection with responses to suffering (92) to suggest that recent campaigns to do with eliciting charitable donations from First World subjects are linked to celebrity figures within a symbolic economy of promoting self-awareness – that is, if you engage in this giving, you will grow into a better person, become more yourself. This ecology is very different from the work of grassroots activists such as Cambodian-US artist Anida Ali, who campaigns on behalf of deported Cambodian-US citizens, and whose video work endows the statistics of human tragedy with individual faces.[1]

So what does cosmopolitanism have to offer English Studies, for instance? Here we need to pause to assess the nature of the "English" in that term – how is it situated in relation to time and space and what kind of analytical subject-in-process does it call into being? For example, to what extent do English Studies continue to be defined by their link to the history of the United Kingdom, to a European periodization of major artistic movements such as Modernism? To what extent do English Studies engage with English as a global language? How situated are these engagements? Taking stock after several years of immersing myself in this material, I found that one repetitive element is the question of whether cosmopolitanism is most easily defined as being in opposition to nationalism or is primarily animated by post-nationalism? I should pause here to explain that the way in which I use "post" in my work is in the Lyotardian sense. The logic proposed by Lyotard was that the condition of Postmodernism consists in part of going back to elements not taken up by Modernism, so that the "post" of Postmodernism becomes not simply a future orientation so much as the future anterior (the future in the past or back to the future) structured by anamnesis, a recollection or going back that discovers other possibilities for alternatives to the period and movement we have come to call Modernism:

> Tu comprends qu'ainsi compris, le "post-" de "postmoderne" ne signifie pas un mouvement de *come back*, de *flash back*, de *feed back*, c'est-à-dire de répétition, mais un procès en "*ana-*," un procès d'analyse, d'anamnèse, d'anagogie, et d'anamorphose, qui élabore un "oubli initial."
>
> [You understand that when understood like that, the "post" of the postmodern does not mean a movement as in come-back, flash-back, feed-back, that is to say a repetition, but a process of "ana," a process of analysis, anamnesis, anagogy, anamorphosis, which elaborates on an "initial forgetting." (Lyotard 126; author's translation)]

In other words, in this precondition to Modernism we would not find the grand narratives of nationalism or internationalism, or even of West and non-West, but the *petits récits* of those differences within: ethnicity, indigeneity, and gender, all of which had of course always been lurking there. In this context, we might consider a paradigm that is post–English Studies, suggesting that we need to expose the cosmopolitan dimensions that connect us to a world that should not remain fully mediated by the nation-state or by capitalist globalization.

Long-term critics of cosmopolitan, such as Tim Brennan (75–8), maintain that the death of the nation has been too hastily invoked – that the nation remains a much-needed bulwark against the more rapacious and predatory incursions of global capitalism. In this version of the tensions between local and global, the nation counts as a version of the local. In the same continuum, Pheng Cheah (2012) reminds us that the nation signifies differently when it is one that is post-independence and in the process of decolonization. Cheah also argues that, in addressing global inequities, cosmopolitan solidarity must connect with institutions situated within nation states.

One of the ways of thinking about "institutions" more broadly is in the sense of Althusser's Ideological State Apparatuses (ISAs), within which literary cultures have their ideological role to play. What on earth is at stake now in this ISA we call English Literature? What are the expectations now? In general terms, you get a kind of cultural history and a management plan that is organized around periodization and genres. But what about the fact that the core medium, English, has now become a global language that is to some degree untethered from this history, spinning out of its initial imperial orbit? What are the implications of studying "Eng Lit" now, of studying writings in English (are they the same)? English as a global language can never inherently provide a neutral mediation. For example, Aijaz Ahmad expresses a somewhat bitter evaluation of the role English has played in Indian literature:

> Meanwhile, it is in English more than any other language that the largest archive of translation has been assembled ... The difficulty is that it is the language least suitable for this role ... because it is, among all the Indian languages, the most removed, in its structure and ambience, from all the other Indian languages ... This disability is proportionately greater the closer the original text is to the oral, the performative, the domestic, the customary, the assumed, the unsaid. (250)

To give a sense of another, or parallax view,[2] consider the following statement by Ashis Nandy (which appears to merge English and the West):

> The West's centrality in any cultural dialogue in our times has been ensured by its dominance over the language in which dialogue among the non-Western cultures takes place ... All such dialogues today are mediated by the West as an unrecognized third participant. For each culture in Asia today, while trying to talk to another Asia culture, uses as its reference point not merely the West outside, but also its own version of an ahistorical, internalized West. (144)

The inter-Asia cultural studies project under the direction of Kuan-Hsing Chen and Chua Beng Huat represents an attempt to decolonize the internalized process Ashis Nandy describes.

The texts I have assembled in over forty years of teaching in English Studies have generally been considered non-canonical, although some over that vast period have attained a foothold in the canon. They've been dubbed multicultural, post-colonial, diasporic, or Third World. In respect to the last, Aijaz Ahmad (1992) has produced a thorough critique of Fredric Jameson's enormously influential essay on postmodernism that labels all Third World texts as national allegories, but perhaps there is some purchase in considering world literatures as parables or allegories of cosmopolitanism. Central to the quest to flesh out a cosmopolitan framework for literary studies is to ask whether it is the text, the writer, or the reader that determines a cosmopolitan approach? For example, do we agree with Tim Brennan's somewhat scathing dismissal of neo-cosmopolitan debates as largely synonymous with a globalized Americanization, including the fetishization of elite cosmo-celebratory figures such as

Salman Rushdie or Amitav Ghosh, who have become the iconic representatives of so-called Third World cultures? Robert Spencer is "interested less in cosmopolitan texts than in cosmopolitan readings" (7). Berthold Schoene locates a cosmopolitan sensibility within writers that allows them "to open up and yield to the structuring of the world as she or he finds it, however bewildering, turbulent or self-contradictory" (16), and situates this within the context of "literature as a specialized set of ethical tools for cultural critique and creative world-formation" (32). In other words, the cosmopolitan author helps to activate a cosmopolitan reader. But how does this come about? Neil Lazarus describes cosmopolitan writers as not just setting the scene but allowing us to comprehend the "symbolic economy – or 'structure of feeling'... to ground his readers in the novel's *mise en scène* thereby making it possible for them to appreciate the full human implications of his story" (123–4).

To try and push this further, here is a series of questions that will structure the rest of this chapter. In relation to these writings: Who am I/are we? When am I/are we? Where am I/are we? What forms of interpellation or hailing into being of fractured subjects are exercised here?

### SUBJECT-IN-PROCESS: WHO AM I/ARE WE?

In post-colonial studies there has been a lot of work that looks at the rise of "englishes," a kind of creolization of English that now has a robust existence, for example, dialect and dub writings.[3] In *The Idea of English Ethnicity*, Robert Young asserts that "[i]t is, finally, English itself ... which holds the Anglo-Saxon world together fraternally in its impatient, perpetual circulations" (6). But what does this mean for those who are not part of the Anglo-Saxon diaspora, but who are nonetheless "in" English, an English perpetually haunted by other languages?

Robert Young contends that all Englishness is performative (3), and that it comes into being through the Anglo-Saxon diaspora. However, if Englishness is performative, then logic dictates that it is not only available to Anglo-Saxon diasporas but, arguably, to anyone. Young's thesis resonates with Gauri Viswanathan's (1989) important contribution to post-colonial studies, the view that English Literature came into being via colonialism – to form a covert ideological system (unlike missionary proselytizing) that would produce those mimic subjects that allowed colonialism to flourish. It resonates as well with Homi Bhabha's notion (1994) of colonial mimicry, a mimicry of the colonizer that undoes his authority. In other words, taking on the "masquerade" of Englishness needs to be aspirationally available to anyone. However, within global English (clearly a key component within Englishness), the meanings attached to linguistically enunciative positions differ (I speak; I am spoken), as do the geopolitical positions from which one speaks English. Such making of meaning began early with England's first colony – Ireland:

> Someone once remarked that Synge wrote in Irish and English simultaneously. The English of this novel is inhabited from the inside by the tones and rhythms of Irish, so that from the viewpoint of Standard English its idiom is as persistently off-key as its realism ... the spectral presence within them of a language other than English ... Being stranded between two tongues in this way was one reason Ireland proved so hospitable to modernism ... typically the work of literal or internal émigrés, men and women caught on the hop between different cultures and languages. (Eagleton 23–4)

Eagleton's comment reinforces Deleuze's and Guattari's notion of "minoritarianism" and language, in this instance in relation to a major language – English.[4] Such "minor" explorers of a major language are consistently characterized as having a heightened sensitivity to the linguistic components that would lend themselves so well to the evolution of Derridean deconstruction – those fertile internal contradictions.

After Derrida, we have assimilated the fact that we are all strangers within language, any language. Whether this understanding is absorbed through the modernist writers characterized by Eagleton, or through the teachings of Wittgenstein, Saussure, Benveniste, or Derrida, we understand that the ability to assume a speaking position cannot be taken for granted and always involves a splitting (I speak; I am spoken). It certainly does not provide a stable foundation for identity, "[n]o, an identity is never given, received, or attained; only the interminable and indefinitely phantasmatic process of identification endures" (Derrida 28). So then, what does it mean to be asked to reside precariously in another language, a language that always comes with historical (including ideological) baggage? Some of the answers depend on the prevailing "monolingualism" of the culture in question:

> The monolingualism imposed by the other operates by relying upon that foundation, here, through a sovereignty whose presence is always colonial, which tends, repressively and irrepressibly, to reduce language to the One, that is, to the hegemony of the homogeneous. This can be verified everywhere, everywhere this

homo-hegemony remains at work in the culture, effacing the folds and flattening the text. (39–40)

In attaining the status of a global language, English is phantasmically attached to the assumption that it is the only language required, Umberto Eco's (1995) "perfect language," with its allusion to Paradise before the Fall and Babel. Communication (as in the womb) was once characterized by plenitude and required no effort. Thus, it is *more* difficult to assert the legitimacy of other languages within post-colonial cultures that strenuously reiterate their monolingualism, such as Australia, than within officially bilingual cultures such as Canada.[5]

Post-colonial studies are filled with contemplations of those approximations of the colonial tongue – patois, creole, pidgin – the terms proliferate, and all indicate an inferior relationship to the "homo-hegemony" of the master tongue. There is also the sense that they carry the subversive elements of secret codes that allowed the enslaved or oppressed to communicate with each other within earshot of the "masters." But what happens when these groups, these diasporic communities, finally assert their rights to change or challenge authoritative versions of the master language? This is, for example, the basis for Evelyn Nien-Ming Ch'ien's lively study *Weird English* (or the assumption behind Dohra Ahmad's anthology *Rotten English*). What happens when these new speakers and writers of English subtend it with other resonances (the acoustic element predominates)? Indeed, the authority or legitimation resides in the claim that these are embodied and oral, representing the everyday use of the language that clamours to be recorded:[6]

> weird-English writers denormalize English out of resistance to it, and form their own language by combining English with their original language. In immigrant communities where weird English is exclusively an oral phenomenon, pidgins and misspellings may have meant a lack of education or fluency. But for weird-English writers, the composition of weird English is an active way of *takin' the community back*. (Ch'ien 6)

It is here that Joseph Pivato's work on Italian-Canadian writing has been so important to revising our sense of Canadian literature. In a recent essay, he analyzes the ways in which such writers contend with the concept of Italiese, "a dialect spoken by Italian immigrants that is the result of mixing Italian and English, and in Quebec, Italian and French" (198).

But while English is momentarily the leading global language, there are other aspirants. Pascale Casanova's *World Republic of Letters* organizes world literature around the primacy of French. André Aciman's new novel *Harvard Square* (2013) moves between English, French, and Arabic.[7] The linguistic shifts harness other allegiances. The unnamed narrator, an Egyptian-Jewish graduate student, befriends a Tunisian taxi-driver who is desperately attempting to obtain his green card:

> And yet what finally cemented our friendship from the very start was our love of France, and of the French language, or, better yet, of the idea of France – because real France we no longer had much use for, nor it for us ... it hovered over our lives like a fraught and tired heirloom that dated back to our respective childhoods in colonial North Africa. (56)

The narrator's sense of a networked identity is manufactured from French and Arabic, by movies, by an Egyptian childhood, by a sense of masculinity and homo-sociality that arises from this fecund blend. This networked, fractal self also interpellates a certain kind of reader. At a superficial level, the taxi-driver, Kalaj (short for Kalashnikov), sinks back into subaltern anonymity at the end of the book:

> No matter how long you knew him, and how he disrupted the world of those around him, eventually he'd be out of your life and things would go back to being what they'd been before him. Despite his dogged efforts to recast the world in his own image, he made no impact, changed nothing, left no mark. In fact, he'd already walked out of history and the family of man before he or any of us knew it. (214)

In one sense, this could represent an evocation of an abjected subject – a Spivakian subaltern who can, of course, speak but cannot be accommodated, cannot be meaningfully heard. Because of the kind of reader contract set up traditionally by a first-person narrator, the reader is at one level meant to collude with this devastating indictment. However, this superficial reading is undermined by the fact that Kalaj is the dynamic centre of the novel – the essence of its affective economy. The statement may mark a point of separation between the values of the narrator and an implied reader: Kalaj is named, whereas the narrator never acquires a name. *Harvard Square*, I would suggest, explores various forms of cosmopolitanism in which a sense of ethics is attached to an abjected figure rather than to the normatively situated narrator.

## TIME: WHEN AM I/ARE WE?

> How strange it is to exist with a purpose, with something to do, something to be engaged in, but to have no sense of time in which to place it. (Kincaid, *Among Flowers* 157)

Time is most easily apprehended in the past, but whose history is our primary reference point? If modernity functions to bestow full humanity, whose modernity is being evoked? For example, Nigel Lazarus's work involves the analysis of "co-eval modernities" (121-3). In her essay "Imperative to Re-imagine the Planet," Gayatri Spivak refers to the Second World War in relation to India as "a remote instrument for the end of specifically territorial imperialism" (336). Once again, we are presented with a parallax view also associated, for example, with Dipesh Chakrabarty's injunction in the title of his book, *Provincialize Europe* (2000). In that context, consider Amitav Ghosh's masterpiece, *In an Antique Land*, which is summarized in the following manner on his website:

> History in the guise of a traveller's tale ... moves back and forth between Ghosh's experience living in small villages and towns in the Nile Delta and his reconstruction of a Jewish trader and his slave's lives in the eleventh century from documents from the Cairo Geniza. In the 1980s, Amitav Ghosh moved into a converted chicken coop. It was on the roof of a house in Lataifa, a tiny village in Egypt. During the day he poured over medieval letters sent to India from Cairo by Arab merchants. In the evenings he ... wrote stories based on what he had seen in the village ... [A]nd, of course, the story of Amitav Ghosh himself, known in the village as the Indian doctor, the uncircumcised, cow-worshipping kaffir who would not convert to Islam. This book is the story of Amitav Ghosh's decade of intimacy with the village community. Mixing conversation and research, imagination and scholarship, it is also a charged, eccentric history of the special relationship between two countries, Egypt and India, through nearly ten centuries of parochialism and sympathy, bigotry and affection.[8]

Ghosh's recent trilogy, *Sea of Poppies*, *River of Smoke*, and *Flood of Fire*, continues this trajectory of a history that does not take European history as the primary temporal coordinate. Ghosh considers the Chinese opium wars and the imbrication of British imperial interests from a parallax historical perspective that concentrates on non-European participants across the social spectrum.

Walter Mignolo (2002), whose critical cosmopolitanism is largely focused on Latin America, identifies four moments of what he calls "global design":

> The first of these designs corresponds to the sixteenth and seventeenth centuries, to Spanish and Portuguese colonialism, and to the Christian mission. The second corresponds to the eighteenth and nineteenth centuries, to French and English colonialism, and to the civilizing mission. The third corresponds to the second half of the twentieth century, to U.S. and transnational (global) colonialism, and to the modernizing mission. Today we witness a transition to a fourth moment, in which the ideologies of development and modernization anchored in leading national projects are being displaced by the transnational ideology of the market – that is, by neoliberalism as an emergent civilizational project. (161)

One could say that colonial histories are being rewritten or simply that the colonial underpinnings of histories we are used to encountering are made obvious. What we consider to be our historical knowledge is revealed to be saturated with continuing imperial interests.

## SPACE: WHERE AM I/ARE WE?

So, finally, to the spatial: The tensions between mobility and residentialism. Nineteenth-century travellers' tales are filled with examples of the old cosmopolitanism, of effortless mobility that could only be sustained by the resources that comprised colonialism. But now we have something else, a parallax view. Apart from someone like Amitav Ghosh, Jamaica Kincaid is a formidable writer of what it feels like to be assimilated into a colonial English education. Her first novel, *Annie John*, famously describes the internal colonization involved, and her extended meditation on Caribbean tourism and the neo-colonialism it implies is succinctly explored in *A Small Place*. Her scathing essay "On Seeing England for the First Time" remains a staple of post-colonial critique. The narrator of Jamaica Kincaid's 2005 travel memoir, *Among Flowers: A Walk in the Himalaya*, is part of a group of privileged First-World seed-gatherers, who trek through Nepal, sponsored by the *National Geographic*. Kincaid's narrator walks a fine line between acknowledging a First-World privilege situated in a US lifestyle, at the same time that the narratorial persona also articulates an awareness of her historical baggage of colonization and slavery: "I saw the people and I took them in, but I made no notes on them, no description of their physical being since I could see that they could not do the same to me" (77). Fearful of the Maoist insurgents who are active in the area, the group treads warily. Kincaid's narrator expresses her ambivalence toward a spatial entitlement in numerous ways.[9] For example:

> No sooner had we set up camp than the Maoists appeared ... Perhaps that moment is one of many that holds in it a metaphor of the very idea of the garden itself: we had in our possession seeds that, if properly germinated, would produce some of the most beautiful and desirable flowering plants to appear in a garden situated in the temperate zone; at the very same time we were in danger of being killed and our dream of the garden in the temperate zone, the place in which we lived, would die with us also. (168–9)

Another way in which the spatial has been re-imagined is through the city. Theorists such as Saskia Sassens (1991) have given us the concept of global cities – the city as microcosm of the world. The city becomes the place for intersecting histories and models for the subject-in-process. Kiran Desai's *The Inheritance of Loss* is partially set in New York, whereas Zadie Smith's *NW* is set in London. Less well-known (for the moment) are those other global cities, Orhan Pamuk's Istanbul or Aatish Taseer's Delhi. In Taseer's novel *The Temple-goers*, a complex text that juxtaposes differing models of cosmopolitanism, a layered cartography prevails:

> It was a city with a fragmented geography: a baggy centre of bungalows and tree-lined avenues, the British city; a walled and decaying slum to the north, the last Muslim city ... a post-independence city of gated colonies, with low houses and little gardens, stretching out in all directions; and beyond, new unseen cities, sometimes past city lines. But the sprawl was being slowly sewn together by new roads, buses and metros. (73)

Anita Rau Badami's evocation of Vancouver in her novel *Can You Hear the Nightbird Call?* maps the long history of the Sikh community there and extends from the events of the *Komagata Maru* to the 1985 Air India bombing, linking these to the 1984 invasion of the Golden Temple in Amritsar, the subsequent assassination of Indira Gandhi, and the anti-Sikh killings across India. Here is a description of the Delhi Junction café on Main Street circa 1967:

> Every morning when Bibi-ji came into the restaurant, the first thing she did was to sprinkle water on the plastic roses. On one wall she hung lithographic prints of the ten Sikh gurus, a highly coloured painting of the Golden Temple with a garland of flashing bulbs around it, maps of India and Canada, pictures of Nehru, Gandhi, Bhagat Singh, Marilyn Monroe, Meena Kumari, Clark Gable and Dev Anand. On another wall were clocks displaying the time in India, Pakistan (East and West), Vancouver, England, New York, Melbourne and Singapore. The clocks were Pa-ji's favourite item of decoration ... It pleased him to be reminded that Sikhs were scattered all over the world, like seeds that had exploded from a seed pod. (60)

In a somewhat different vein, Dionne Brand's *What We All Long For* depicts Toronto as another global city:

> Lives in the city are doubled, tripled, conjugated – women and men all trying to handle their own chain of events, trying to keep the story straight in their own heads. At times they catch themselves in sensational lies, embellishing or avoiding a nasty secret here and there, juggling the lines of causality, and before you know it, it's impossible to tell one thread from another. In this city, like everywhere, people work, they eat, they drink, they have sex, but it's hard not to wake up here without the certainty of misapprehension. (5)

In her novel there are tragic consequences to these misapprehensions. So, in a number of different forms, we have depictions of the tensions between the individual and the group. As Stuart Hall reminds us, both are needed:

> We witness the situation of communities that are not simply isolated, atomistic individuals, nor are they well-bounded, singular, separated communities. We are in that open space that requires a kind of vernacular cosmopolitanism, that is to say a cosmopolitanism that is aware of the limitations of any one culture or any one

identity and that is radically aware of its insufficiency in governing a wider society, but which nevertheless is not prepared to rescind its claims to the traces of difference, which makes its life important. (30)

Cosmopolitanism deals with the world, worlding, the planetary, and with Jean-Luc Nancy's notion of *mondialisation*, explained by Berthold Schoene as "the creation of the world ... it originates and stays rooted in the specific, unassimilable singularities of the local ... *mondialisation* promotes cosmopolitan agency as non-directive 'struggle'" (24). We are catapulted back to the oscillation between presence and absence at the heart of Derridean deconstruction. Ironically, the proliferation of writing (the substitution for presence) helped to confirm the death of the sovereign subject – a limited form, as it turned out, of presence. The presence we contend with now is the posthumanist one of fractal selves, the continuum of the new materialism, of the concept of animacies (Chen). In anthropologist Marisol de la Cadena's work, the political life of "earth-beings" such as mountains have their political agency in Andean indigenous coalitions. So, the elements that comprise the spatial (cities, villages, homes) also have their connections to the formation of the subject-in-process.

## WORLD LITERATURE

And so we come to the question of world literature. In my attempts to construct a cosmopolitan methodology I have taken from Paul Gilroy's (2006) work the notion of a cosmopolitan pedagogy as involving a process of denaturalization, in which one works to distance oneself from the familiar (Gilroy uses George Orwell as emblematic of this process). Berthold Schoene puts it thus: "to call oneself a cosmopolitan involves not so much excising one's local affiliations, or rounding off one's personal repertory of identities with a final outer finish, as opening oneself up to a radical unlearning of all definitive modes of identification" (21).

In my own work I have reconceptualized so-called multicultural writers as mediators between national literatures and a world literature. While the nation state and its anxious reiterations continue, there are competing terrains, such as the diasporic, and the latter often comes together in the metropolitan city – the microcosm as macrocosm or possible model for a differing conception of the literature of the world. In this vision, world literatures are not stratified into nations, and their supposedly evolutionary histories into a progress towards modernity, but consist of the coeval existence of many histories, languages, and forms of the human and posthuman coexisting and sometimes interacting across borders – zones of the city, of the global that includes the detention camps, or the spaces of provisional asylum. For example, Paul Gilroy's evocation of a Black European presence demonstrates that it has always been there; Leela Gandhi's (2006) study of affective relations and friendships across colonial interests includes our sense of the journeys of those servants who accompanied their masters from the outposts of empire back to the imperial centres.

What does it feel like to be part of a group for which you don't necessarily have the right connections in terms of the old identity politics (recall Derrida's point that identity is always phantasmatic)? And it's not as though you have the correct ethical DNA just because you do have those connections. The examples I have given in relation to space and time and the fractured subjectivities these invoke constitute ways of engaging with literary studies. At present, for us here, these circle around the qualifier "English," but in order to extend the potential contained in the term English studies or English literature, it is important to subtend it with literatures in English, including weird English and rotten English, so that global legibility includes a robust understanding of literatures of the world. "Despite its apparent diversity and worldliness English literature still fundamentally serves a 'mosaic' of nations ... renders English literature international, but not necessarily cosmopolitan" (Schoene 16).

My final example is Taiye Selasi's first novel, *Ghana Must Go*. The enigmatic title refers to those ubiquitous striped plastic bags that appear globally as cheap hold-alls. Here is a description taken from a website, http://www.alamodewearhouse.com/2013/03/ghana-must-go.html:

> It is the go to bag for market women to travel within their countries and to carry their goods. The term "Ghana Must Go" was coined in the late 1900s by Nigerians when an influx of Ghanaian refugees fled to Nigeria during political unrest. The bags were Nigerians' way of telling Ghanaians its time to pack and go back home. Typically anyone you see carrying the bag is on a voyage of some sort. You have to be Ghanaian or Nigerian to understand the mockery/humor behind the phrase ... Lately, designers like Louis Vuitton and Celine have used the rather "iconic" duffle bag print in their collection.

So the title and novel allude cleverly to both versions of cosmopolitanism – the old consumerist cosmopolitanism and the new sense of subaltern solidarity. Taiye Selasi (2005) some years ago coined the term Afropolitan, which she defined in the following ways:

Perhaps what most typifies the Afropolitan consciousness is the refusal to oversimplify; the effort to understand what is ailing in Africa alongside the desire to honor what is wonderful, unique. Rather than essentialising the geographical entity, we seek to comprehend the cultural complexity; to honor the intellectual and spiritual legacy; and to sustain our parents' cultures ... Most of us grew up aware of "being from" a blighted place, of having last names from countries which are linked to lack, corruption. Few of us escaped those nasty "booty-scratcher" epithets, and fewer still that sense of shame when visiting paternal villages. Whether we were ashamed of ourselves for not knowing more about our parents' culture, or ashamed of that culture for not being more "advanced" can be unclear. What is manifest is the extent to which the modern adolescent African is tasked to forge a sense of self from wildly disparate sources.

Her novel can certainly be seen as an allegory of cosmopolitanism in which a family is dispersed among Ghana, Massachusetts, and London and come together after the death of the father in Accra, a father who had abandoned his first family. Olu, the eldest son, voices some of what Selasi indicates in her essay: "You live your whole life in this world, in these worlds, and you know what they think of you, you know what they see. You say that you're African and you want to excuse it, explain *but I'm smart*. There's no value implied. You feel it ... No one gives a shit. You want them to see you as something of value, not dusty, not irrelevant, not backward" (305).

While his father was a surgeon, as he is, Olu's return to the village from which his father, Kweku, came also shows how real that ascent had been and from what deprivations. In 2014, Caryl Phillips gave a talk in Vancouver that dealt with his parents' generation of what he termed "colonial migrants," who moved to London in the postwar period. He spoke of figures like Sam Selvon, who re-emigrated to Toronto, because he could not bear the rejection of what had become for this generation (and others before them) a sense of England as their motherland. This had come via the colonial education that Kincaid describes so well. Olu's father had also believed he could succeed in that other empire, the USA, but had been capriciously and undeservedly ejected – hence the shame which led him to flee the country and his family there. As Caryl Phillips stated in his talk, it is the tenacity of those colonial migrants that we should recognize – that they are visible on their own terms (even at the cost of their lives). It is an experience beautifully delineated in Phillips's own fiction, including his novel *A Distant Shore* (2003).

This chapter has tried to set out a different vision of what English Studies/literatures in English might mean today. I have also attempted to indicate the consequences of a cosmopolitan analysis that involves taking the time to learn the histories and understand the spaces that undergird the singularities of anonymity within the plurality globalization.

## NOTES

1  Consider her video *My Asian Americana*, http://www.youtube.com/watch?feature=player_embedded&v=YQxtfCz4B10.
2  The apparent displacement, or difference of position, of an object, as seen from two different stations, or points of view.
3  I have written about English as a technology that structures certain kinds of subjectivity in a chapter of my book *Haunted Nations*.
4  Deleuze and Guattari linked their study to Kafka's use of German.
5  It is interesting here to consider the role of the oral/acoustic. Derrida spends a lot of time registering the "accent" as a sign of "impurity" within one's mother tongue. I have written more about "acoustic accent" in writing in Gunew, *Post-multicultural Writers as Neo-cosmopolitan Mediators* (London: Anthem Press, 2017).
6  There is also the question of melancholic relations to the old language. Ch'ien refers to melancholia, but one thinks as well of Anlin Cheng's extended study (*The Melancholy of Race*) around the mechanisms of psychoanalytical melancholia and racialized grief. In relation to this paper, one might imagine the first language as encrypted in the body and providing resistance to assimilation.
7  See, for example, 54, 56, 214.
8  See http://www.amitavghosh.com.
9  See also Kincaid, 83–4.

## BIBLIOGRAPHY

Aciman, André. *Harvard Square: A Novel*. New York: Norton, 2013.
Ahmad, Aijaz. *In Theory: Classes, Nations, Literatures*. London: Verso, 1992.
Ahmad, Dohra, ed. *Rotten English*. New York: Norton, 2007.
Ali, Anida. *My Asian Americana*. Video. http://www.youtube.com/watch?feature=player_embedded&v=YQxtfCz4B10.
Appiah, Kwame Anthony. "Case for Contamination." *New York Times*, 1 Jan. 2006.
– *Cosmopolitanism: Ethics in a World of Strangers*. New York: Norton, 2006.

Badami, Anita Rau. *Can You Hear the Nightbird Call?* Toronto: Knopf, 2006.
Beck, Ulrich. "The Cosmopolitan Manifesto." *New Statesman* 127, no. 4377 (1998): 28–30.
Bhabha, Homi. *The Location of Culture.* London: Routledge, 1994.
Blodgett, E.D. "Comparative Literature in Canada: A Case Study." *Review of Comparative Literature* 40, no. 3 (September 2013): 1–13.
Brand, Dionne. *What We All Long For.* Toronto: Knopf, 2005.
Brennan, Timothy. "Cosmopolitanism and Internationalism." *New Left Review* 7 (Jan./Feb. 2001): 75–84.
Cadena, Marisol de la. "Indigenous Cosmopolitics in the Andes: Conceptual Reflections beyond 'Politics.'" *Cultural Anthropology* 25, no. 2 (2010): 334–70.
Casanova, Pascale. *The World Republic of Letters.* Trans. M.B. DeBevoise. Cambridge, MA: Harvard University Press, 2004.
Chakrabarty, Dipesh. *Provincializing Europe: Postcolonial Thought and Historical Difference.* New Jersey: Princeton University Press, 2000.
Cheah, Pheng. "What Is a World? On World Literature as World-making Activity." In *The Routledge Handbook of Cosmopolitan Studies*, edited by Gerard Delanty, 138–49. London & New York: Routledge, 2012.
Chen, Kuan-Hsing, and Chua Beng Huat, eds. *The Inter-Asia Cultural Studies Reader.* London: Routledge, 2007.
Chen, Mel Y. *Animacies: Biopolitics, Racial Mattering, and Queer Affect.* Durham, NC, and London: Duke University, 2012.
Cheng, Anne Anlin. *The Melancholy of Race.* New York: Oxford University Press, 2001.
Ch'ien, Evelyn Nien-Ming. *Weird English.* Cambridge, MA.: Harvard University Press, 2004.
Chouliaraki, Lili. "Cosmopolitanism as Irony: A Critique of Post-humanitarianism." In *After Cosmopolitanism*, edited by Rosi Braidotti, Patrick Hanafin, and Bolette Blaagard, 77–110. London: Routledge (GlassHouse Book), 2013.
Colebrook, Claire. "Destroying Cosmopolitanism for the Sake of the Cosmos." In *After Cosmopolitanism*, edited by Rosi Braidotti, Patrick Hanafin, and Bolette Blaagard, 166–82. London: Routledge (GlassHouse Book), 2013.
Deleuze, Gilles, and Félix Guattari. *Kafka: Toward a Minor Literature.* Trans. Dana Pollan. Minneapolis: University of Minnesota Press, 1986.
Derrida, Jacques. *Monolingualism of the Other; or, The Prosthesis of Origins.* Trans. Patrick Mensah. Stanford, CA: Stanford University Press, 1998.
Desai, Kiran. *The Inheritance of Loss.* Toronto: Penguin, 2006.
Eagleton, Terry. "An Octopus at the Window." *London Review of Books* (19 May 2011): 23–4.

Eco, Umberto. *The Search for the Perfect Language*. Trans. James Fentress. Oxford: Blackwell, 1995.
Gandhi, Leela. *Affective Communities: Anticolonial Thought, Fin-de-siècle Radicalism, and the Politics of Friendship*. Durham, NC: Duke University, 2006.
Ghosh, Amitav. *In an Antique Land*. London: Granta Books, 1992. http://www.amitavghosh.com/antique.html.
– *Flood of Fire*. New York: Viking, 2015.
– *River of Smoke*. New York: Viking, 2012.
– *Sea of Poppies*. New York: Viking, 2008.
Gilroy, Paul. *After Empire: Melancholia or Convivial Culture?* New York: Routledge, 2006.
Gunew, Sneja. *Haunted Nations: The Colonial Dimensions of Multiculturalisms*. London: Routledge, 2004.
Hall, Stuart. "Political Belonging in a World of Multiple Identities." In *Conceiving Cosmopolitanism: Theory, Context, and Practice*, edited by S. Vertovec and R. Cohen, 25–31. Oxford: Oxford University Press, 2002.
Jameson, Frederic. "Postmodernism, or the Cultural Logic of Late Capitalism." *New Left Review* 1, no. 146 (July–August 1984): 53–94.
Kincaid, Jamaica. *Among Flowers: A Walk in the Himalaya*. Washington, DC: National Geographic, 2005.
– *Annie John*. London: Picador, 1985.
– "On Seeing England for the First Time." *Transition* 51 (1991): 32–40.
– *Small Place*. New York: Farrar, Straus, Giroux, 1988.
Lazarus, Neil. "Cosmopolitanism and the Specificity of the Local in World Literature." *Journal of Commonwealth Literature* 46, no. 1 (2011): 119–37.
Lyotard, François. *Le Postmoderne éxpliqué aux enfants: Correspondance, 1982–1985*. Paris: Galilée, 1986.
Mignolo, Walter. "The Many Faces of Cosmo-polis: Border Thinking and Critical Cosmopolitanism." In *Cosmopolitanism*, edited by C. Breckenridge, S. Pollock, H.K. Bhabha, and D. Chakrabarty, 157–87. Durham, NC: Duke University Press, 2002.
Nancy, Jean-Luc. *Being Singular Plural*. Trans. Robert D. Richardson and Anne E. O'Byrne. Stanford: Stanford University Press, 2000.
Nandy, Ashis. "A New Cosmopolitanism: Toward a Dialogue of Asian Civilizations." In *Trajectories: Inter-Asia Cultural Studies*, edited by Kuan-Hsing Chen, 142–9. London and New York: Routledge, 1998.
Phillips, Caryl. *Color Me English: Reflections on Migration and Belonging before and after 9/11*. New York: The New Press, 2011.
– *A Distant Shore*. London: Vintage. 2005.

Pivato, Joseph. "1978: Language Escapes: Italian-Canadian Authors Write in an Official Language and Not in Italiese." In *Translation Effects: The Shaping of Modern Canadian Culture*, edited by Kathy Mezei, Sherry Simon, and Luise von Flotow, 197–207. Montreal: McGill-Queen's University Press, 2014.

Pogge, Thomas. "Cosmopolitanism and Sovereignty." In *Cosmopolitanism: Critical Concepts in the Social Sciences*. 2 vols. Edited by Gerard Delanty and David Inglis, 2:142–68. London: Routledge, 2011.

Sassen, Saskia. *Global City: New York, London, Tokyo*. Princeton, NJ: Princeton University Press, 1992.

Schoene, Berthold. *The Cosmopolitan Novel*. Edinburgh: Edinburgh University Press, 2009.

Selasi, Taiye. "Bye-Bye Barbar." *The Lip Magazine*, 3 March 2005. http://thelip.robertsharp.co.uk.

– *Ghana Must Go*. New York: Penguin, 2013.

Smith, Zadie. *NW*. New York: Penguin, 2012.

Spencer, Robert. *Cosmopolitan Criticism and Postcolonial Literature*. London: Palgrave Macmillan, 2011.

Spivak, Gayatri. "Imperative to Re-imagine the Planet." In *An Aesthetic Education in the Era of Globalization*, 335–50. Cambridge, MA: Harvard University Press, 2012.

Taseer, Aatish. *The Temple-goers*. London: Viking, 2010.

Vardoulakis, Dimitris. "The 'Poor Thing': The Cosmopolitan in Alasdair Gray's *Poor Things*." *SubStance* #117, 37, no. 3 (2008): 137–51.

Viswanathan, Gauri. *Masks of Conquest: Literary Study and British Rule in India*. London: Faber, 1989.

Warner, Marina. "Learning My Lesson." *An Octopus at the Window, London Review of Books* 37, no. 6 (19 March 2015): 8–14.

Young, Robert. *The Idea of English Ethnicity*. Oxford: Blackwell, 2008.

# The Languages of Comparative Literature

*Joseph Pivato*

> Dal lavôr si cognos il mestri.[1]
> Old Friulan proverb

## INTRODUCTION

Comparative Literature has many languages. This is what distinguishes it from the study of traditional national literatures such as English, French, or Spanish. These are also the three languages of major colonial powers which spread across the globe. In direct contrast to a monolingual focus, core studies in Comparative Literature begin with the examination of two literatures in different languages and cultures and then expand to include questions of theory, history, psychology, and other media. The positive future of Comparative Literature is built on the study of different languages.

In the continuing tradition of self-interrogation, we will examine some of the different languages of Comparative Literature, in order to help us understand the state of the art in this new century and its possible future directions. We will consider not only English, French, and other European languages, but also those from developing countries. We will briefly look at the languages of theory and the literary tools in the new technology.

The term Comparative Literature in English is a short form for the Comparative Study of Literature, the main practice of this discipline. This is clear in the German version, *die Vergleichende Literaturwissenschaft*. In Italian the term *Letteratura comparata* was first used by Benedetto Croce in 1903. In Spain, *Literatura comparada* began to develop only in the 1980s and 1990s.

Because this is an argumentative essay, I must declare my biases: Both my MA and my PhD are in Comparative Literature, and I work in English,

French, and Italian. My research and publications have included work in Canadian literature, ethnic minority writing, women's literature, African-Canadian literature, Italian-Canadian writing, translation, theory, and Renaissance literature.

## BEGINNING WITH LANGUAGES

Many introductions to Comparative Literature begin with a brief review of its history. There is often a reference to Johann von Goethe's call for the study of world literature (*Weltliteratur*) from his conversations with Eckermann in 1827. At the time Goethe had been reading Chinese novels in translation, as well as Persian and Serbian poetry. From 1786 to 1788, he travelled in Italy and so became personally aware of the overlap of different languages and cultures. For example, Goethe was particularly struck by the Greek architecture in Agrigento, Sicily. This led him to re-evaluate Roman influences in Europe. Just before Goethe, there was Madame de Staël's *De la littérature dans ses rapports avec les institutions sociales* from 1799, which raises questions about globalization from an early European perspective. Goethe was interested in literature outside of Europe; however, in the twentieth century, Comparative Literature became quite Eurocentric.

There is a much earlier example of a writer who compared different languages and literatures. The Italian poet Dante, in his long essay *De Vulgari Eloquentia* (1305), advocated writing in the languages of the people, rather than in Latin, the lingua franca of what became Europe. Dante argued for giving writing in vernacular languages the same dignity and legitimacy as Latin. His comparative examples were not just from Italian but from the Occitan language of southern France for songs and poetry, and he also made references to the *Razos de trobar* (1210) by Catalan troubadour Raimon Vidal de Bezandum. Dante's essay should be considered a founding document for Comparative Literature.

In addition to his essay on languages and literature, Dante's work in the *Convivio* and the *Divina Commedia* demonstrate his knowledge of Greek and Arabic writing and philosophy. In the *Convivio* he refers to the Persian Sufi writer Al-Ghazali (1058–1111). His use of allegory reveals certain similarities with Sufism, that is, Islamic mysticism. In Dante's time, translations of the *Qur'an* existed, as well as the "Night Journey, The Isra and Miraj," in Latin, Spanish, and Old French. And there were also commentaries by other writers and philosophers. The *Commedia* achieves a summa-like quality with its encyclopaedic references to different cultures, writers, and philosophers, and so it is a good example of comparative work by an accomplished writer (Ziolkowski).

Many national languages in Europe are the by-products of the ancient Roman occupation. The Roman Empire spread across the territory of Europe and beyond, and made Latin the standard form of communication. Greek continued to be an important language in the Eastern Mediterranean. After its decline, Latin remained the common language and was supported by the spread of Christianity, but regional languages began to emerge. In the Italian peninsula, for example, the Veneziano language developed around Venice and the surrounding mainland. Veneziano was the language of the Venetian Republic for about one thousand years. In the border region of Friuli, the Friulan language became the oral form of communication. There exist written texts from the 1100s in this distinct rural language. In Tuscany, a common language grew around the cities of Florence and Siena. This is the language of Dante and many other writers from Central Italy and was adopted as the national language of Italy in the 1800s.

From the Vulgar Latin roots, many more regional languages developed in Italy, France, Spain, Portugal, and Romania. But before these became national languages, there were also a number of regional minority languages, such as Aragonese, Catalan, Galician, Valencian, Neapolitan, Sicilian, Sardinian, and other languages that are still used today. The Germanic languages of Europe, such as English, German, Dutch, and Swedish, have a different history.

When writers move between a minority language and the national language, they often deal with translation and adaptation from one language code to the other. These practices lead to comparative study of texts, styles, and genres. In the works referred to above, both Dante and Raimon Vidal de Bezandum explained and defended their use of language and genres. These comparative practices are based on a knowledge of different languages and literary texts and are still the basis of Comparative Literature today.

## COMPARATIVE LITERATURE IN THE MODERN ERA

The term *littérature comparée* first appeared in French in 1816, and by 1848 Matthew Arnold was using the English term in the plural: comparative literatures. As an area of study in universities, Comparative Literature began to emerge in the late 1800s and was promoted by Irish–New Zealand scholar Hutcheson Macaulay Posnett with his 1886 book, *Comparative Literature*. While teaching at the small University of Auckland, Posnett found that he had the freedom to draw on many different literary sources. In Hungary, Hugo Meltzl de Lomnitz founded the journal *Acta*

*Comparationis Litterarum Universarum* in 1887 to promote Goethe's idea of *Weltliteratur*. French, Russian, and German scholars slowly began to write about comparative study. By 1907, Frederio Lolice had written *A Short History of Comparative Literature from the Earliest Times to the Present Day*.

The Great War of 1914–18 can be viewed as primarily a European war, in which many lives were lost fighting over mere acres of territory. But the Second World War was truly an international conflict, involving many countries around the world. After its devastation, there was a general consensus among national leaders and many intellectuals that better understanding across international borders should be promoted. Many countries banded together to establish the United Nations in order to work towards international cooperation and peace.

In universities and colleges, many people promoted the study of foreign languages and cultures as a way of fostering international understanding, cooperation, and possibly trade. In North America, universities began to develop programs in Comparative Literature with the arrival of European émigrés before, during, and after the Second World War. These were scholars who had a solid knowledge of two or three languages and literatures from their early education and training in various European universities. I will briefly profile a number of these early pioneers of Comparative Literature in North America to illustrate their various language skills.

One of the founders of Comparative Literature in the US was René Wellek, who was born and raised in Vienna and spoke Czech and German. He studied literature at Charles University in Prague. He taught at the London School of Slavonic and East European Studies (1935–39), and then emigrated to the US to teach at the University of Iowa (1939–46) before moving to Yale University to establish the Comparative Literature program in 1948. In 1949 he co-wrote, with Austen Warren, *Theory of Literature*, a systematic review of theory and an important text for comparative study. One of the Europeans also at Yale was Erich Auerbach, who was born in Berlin, had a doctorate from the University of Greifswald, taught at the University of Marburg, and in 1935 left Nazi Germany for exile in Istanbul, Turkey. He emigrated to the US in 1947 and taught at Penn State University until he moved to Yale in 1950. His book *Mimesis: The Representation of Reality in Western Literature* (1946) is considered a seminal work in Comparative Literature, and from his work on Dante it is evident that he read Italian, as well as other languages. At Indiana University the Comparative Literature department was founded by Henry H.H. Remak, who was born in Berlin, studied in France (1934–36), and emigrated to the US in 1936. He earned his PhD at the University of

Chicago (1947), and then taught Comparative Literature at Indiana until he was eighty-eight years old. He helped to establish the American Comparative Literature Association as an academic society to foster the study of different languages and literatures.

In her introduction, Giulia De Gasperi reviews how the first Comparative Literature programs in Canada were also founded by academics from Europe: Eva Kushner at Carleton University in Ottawa, Paul Zumthor at the Université de Montreal, and Milan Dimić at the University of Alberta. She points to the promising future for comparative literary study in the emerging bilingual programs across Canada. Nevertheless, we should be aware of the problems that we face as academics and scholars of languages and literatures.

## THE AMERICAN CASE

There are many people in Canada who speak different languages every day. We often find these bilingual or trilingual people on university campuses. Canada also attracts thousands of students from all over the world. Given these human resources, you would expect that Canada would be an international leader in developing and promoting programs in Comparative Literature. In the 1970s and 1980s it looked as if Canada was moving in this direction, but then in the 1990s literature and language programs began to shrink, and some eventually disappeared from university campuses. One of the main reasons for this was reduced funding for the humanities.

It is a sad irony that, in a bilingual country like Canada, we often take for granted the common use of different languages and do not value the study of our national literatures in two languages: English and French. Only when these language programs disappear do we become conscious of the loss, but by then it is often too late.

While Canadian universities and bilingual academics have failed to take a leadership role in Comparative Literature, academics in the United States have assumed that role and set the agenda for the future. We should be concerned about this for two reasons: the negative effects of the culture wars on some American university campuses and the frequent lack of appreciation for working in the original languages rather than in translation. To illustrate the last point, I have a striking example from an MLA congress.

In January 2015, I participated in the huge MLA congress held in Vancouver, BC. The four-day convention consisted of 783 sessions, running simultaneously, thirty-eight at a time. There were many sessions, but few languages used. I heard only English. The MLA is the Modern Languages

Association of America and reflects the predominantly monolingual professoriate in the US. (The only exception to this is the growing use of Spanish in some American states.)

Comparative Literature in the English-speaking world has been defined and redefined more and more from this monolingual American perspective. The American Comparative Literature Association, in its reports on the state of this discipline, reflects this ongoing crisis in identity: Comparative Literature in English only. I must point out that most of the bilingual pioneers of Comparative Literature that I listed above have passed away.

I will look briefly at two reports of the ACLA published as books: Charles Bernheimer's 1995 volume, *Comparative Literature in the Age of Multiculturalism*, and Haun Saussy's 2006 volume, *Comparative Literature in an Age of Globalization*. I will consider what implications, if any, these American reports have for the future of Comparative Literature. For some literary scholars, the 1990s marked a decade of decline for comparative study in North America. Are there clues to this decline in the Bernheimer report?

The seventeen essays in the Bernheimer volume consider several different questions in Comparative Literature. Collectively they examine its relationship to literary criticism, literary history, elite culture, feminist theory, university politics, the cultural wars, cultural studies, media, and the other arts. Several writers give lip service to the need for students to learn different languages, but this is not the focus of the volume. Many of the contributors hold positions in English programs, so it is doubtful that they read or teach foreign-language texts, except possibly in English translation.

Only three of the seventeen contributors explicitly declare the need to focus on learning, reading, and speaking foreign languages. The first is Mary Louise Pratt, an expatriate Canadian who teaches Spanish at New York University. The others are Rey Chow, who teaches Comparative Literature at Duke University and writes on Chinese women and Chinese cinema; and K. Anthony Appiah, who teaches the work of African-American and African writers at Harvard.

In her essay, "Comparative Literature and Global Citizenship," Mary Louise Pratt argues:

> Comparative literature should remain the home for the polyglots; multiculturalism and polyglossia should remain its calling card. But it might help to update our rhetoric on this issue. Instead of producing students who "know foreign languages," maybe we should start

talking about producing *bilingual, bicultural* people (or multilingual, multicultural people). Maybe we should link our endeavours to the need for deeply informed, culturally competent individuals in a globalized world. This seems a good moment to reverse the United States' blind commitment to monolingualism and the tendency to cede the terrain of "globalization" to English. To the monolingual Anglophone it may look like everyone in the world is learning English, but the more accurate statement, visible from where we stand, is that the world is becoming increasingly multilingual ... Anglophones place themselves at a great disadvantage if they rely solely on this medium [English] to conduct their relations with the rest of the planet. (Bernheimer 62)

In the Bernheimer volume, Mary Louise Pratt is a voice calling for the study of languages in order to balance the unilingual focus on theory. Bernheimer himself explains some of the problems faced by literary studies in America:

In those years (1980s), the study of comparative literature at some of the best graduate schools gave priority to theory over literature, to method over matter. The trend that Harry Levin had deplored in 1968 was intensifying: we weren't comparing the literature so much as we were comparing theories about comparison. Anxiety was fashionable. Indeed, it was de rigueur, rigor being the fetish of theory.

But as the Reagan-Bush years gradually eroded the liberal social agenda, it became more and more painful for professors in literature departments to continue in an attitude of skeptical detachment and sophisticated alienation. The inevitable aporia of deconstructive undecidability began to seem too much like the indecipherable double-talk of the politicians we detested. Even those, myself included, who had been deeply influenced by deconstruction were feeling tired of systemic, suspicious vigilance, tired and demoralized by the work of displacing the ground from under our own feet, tired of being morally rigorous, tired of comparisons that always collapsed into indifference. (5)

It seems as if the American academy has abandoned literary texts and the study of languages for theory, European theory in English translation. They embraced theory about the death of the author, and theory about the deconstruction of the texts. We have the image of a French theorist writing some clever word-play, a novel metaphorical expression, to impress his colleagues and students in Paris. This is later translated into English like a biblical passage, and the metaphor becomes the literal gospel truth in Madison, Wisconsin, Ann Arbor, Michigan, and Yale.

In Canada, professors and students of literature also embraced European theory, but many of us remained skeptical of its long-term directions. Maybe this was because, in Canada, we have more bilingual students in universities than they do in the United States and a thriving multicultural population, with approximately one-third of Canadians now having cultural backgrounds that are neither English nor French. We understand the limits of translation. We can read the original French texts and see what Derrida's "différance" could possibly mean, if in fact intelligible meaning is possible.

In a 2013 essay, E.D. Blodgett pointed out the problems with translations of French theory, problems that departments of English tend to ignore. He explained the question of unreliability, "the issue of theory in translation ... a number of my colleagues pointed out that the French language as used by Derrida, Barthes and Foucault, for example, was not quite as clear as the translations suggested" (311).

The French used by the philosophers listed above can be quite complex and difficult to understand, even for French readers. English translations tend to simplify the language for the sake of making it easier to understand, but may be distorting the intended meaning.

An example of Derrida's misdirection is from his essay "Le dangereux supplément," in which he uses the phrase, "il n' y a pas de hors-texte" (204), which literally means "there is no outer-text," but is often translated as "there is nothing outside of the text." If Derrida is trying to explain that the text must be read in context, it is not clear here, since the French phrase seems to suggest the opposite idea. We should maintain a healthy skepticism with regard to French theory in English translation. Living with different languages in a multicultural society helps us to develop an understanding of the limitations of translation.

The bilingual writer Nancy Huston, a former student of Barthes and his part-time translator, explains: "The problem, of course, is that languages are not just languages. They're also world views – and therefore, to some extent, untranslatable" (38).

In my experience, multiculturalism in Canada contributed to the growing diversity of Comparative Literature programs. Bernheimer's volume *Comparative Literature in the Age of Multiculturalism* seems to suggest that multiculturalism and cultural studies are threats to literary studies.

In some of the essays in his volume, multiculturalism is a difficult problem that challenges the academy. To me it soon becomes evident that some of these American academics, entrusted with the task of investigating multiculturalism, do not understand it. In his critical introduction, Bernheimer tactfully tries to explain the problems identified by the various contributors to the volume. From reading the individual essays, it is evident that there is much disagreement among the seventeen American academics about the problems confronting Comparative Literature and how to deal with them. We can list the problems in this way: (1) the need to compare works in the original languages and not in translation; (2) the role of European theory in the future of Comparative Literature; (3) the Eurocentrism of much teaching and research in Comparative Literature; (4) the perceived conflict between literary studies and cultural studies; (5) the response to changing cultural and linguistic diversity in North America and Europe.

Various contributors raise questions about the multicultural model as not being representative and possibly essentializing a culture. Michael Riffaterre favours working with cultural studies, while Emily Apter suggests moving into post-colonial studies. How would some of these contributors approach non-European masterpieces such as: García Márquez's *Cien anõs de soledad* (1967), Gabrielle Roy's *Bonheur d'occasion* (1945), Ngũgi wa Thiomg'o's *Caitaani mutharaba-Ini* (Gikuyu novel, 1980), and Chimamanda Ngozi Adichie's *Half of a Yellow Sun* (Nigeria, 2006)? I could list others, but I have chosen these novels because I have taught them in my Comparative Literature courses over the years. In all cases, I was not troubled by questions about being representative, being authentic, or essentializing minority cultures. Instead, these questions were openly discussed with students as part of our readings. The methodology of Comparative Literature can provide nuanced approaches to the study of cultural differences.

The open development of multiculturalism in literary study in America is impeded by disputes over identity politics. Americans must deal with their long history of racism, racial segregation, and nativism. These are all controversial areas, with which American comparatists have been unable or unwilling to deal. With some evident hostility toward different cultures and different languages in many parts of American society, we may ask: what kind of Comparative Literature is being promoted in American universities? The wide support for President Donald Trump's administration and the repeated protests against it give us some indication of the divisions in American society.

In my experience, some of these negative attitudes have entered the Canadian academy and have led to funding cuts for programs in the humanities. In July 2010, the University of Toronto planned to shut down the Centre for Comparative Literature. It was saved by hundreds of petitions and letters. But at the University of British Columbia, the program closed. The Comparative Literature program at the University of Alberta is gradually being starved to death. In her 2011 online article "State of the Discipline," Linda Hutcheon identifies some of the dangers faced by Comparative Literature in recent decades.

Let us now look briefly at the 2006 ACLA report. The volume edited by Haun Saussy, *Comparative Literature in an Age of Globalization* (2006), is a much more hopeful volume on the current state of the discipline. To me, the significant difference is that eight of the nineteen contributors teach foreign languages as well as Comparative Literature. The essays present diverse points of view, and multilingual perspectives. Many explicitly support the study of languages and the reading of literature in the original languages. For example, Françoise Lionnet, quoting Spivak, says, "While I agree completely with the need both to include a diversity of languages and to stress the importance of the 'literary,' or the slow 'reading and teaching of the textual' (Spivak), I am uneasy about any kind of prescription" (101). She proposes not just binary comparisons but a "transversal comparative approach" that studies many intersecting lines and points of contact. Roland Greene argues that the focus of comparative study should be not just texts but networks.

The essay by Steven Unger, "Writing in Tongues: Thoughts on the Work of Translation," argues for the useful contributions of translation studies for Comparative Literature:

> The centrality of translation within literary studies is at odds with the fact that it often remains under-analyzed and under-theorized. Rather than simply bemoan this condition, I want ... to consider how issues surrounding practices of an emergent field of translation studies over the past twenty-five years has contributed to the evolving discipline, discourse, and institution of comparative literature. (Saussy 127)

Like George Steiner before him, Unger advocates for a model of Comparative Literature centred on the process and limitations of translation. They both see the different traditions, theories, styles, and forms of translation as pivotal to comparative study. They argue that the failures and incompletions of even the best translations help us to understand the genius of a given language. The difficulties of translating words from one language to another are concrete expressions of cultural differences.

Rather than dismissing the process of translation of a literary work as a second-order representation, Unger argues that translation is a re-reading and re-writing engaged with the production of meaning. This activity depends on knowing other languages reasonably well.

In Canada, students of Comparative Literature are generally familiar with the problems of translation. We also have a tradition of translation studies that has often been involved in Comparative Literature programs. In her book *Gender in Translation*, Sherry Simon argues that translation is a feminist practice, a mode of re-engagement with the literary text, and is often contesting the received values related to language communication. Simon proposes an altered understanding of translation as an activity "which destabilizes cultural identities and becomes a basis for new models of cultural creation" (135). Simon uses the example of Third World literature in English translation. Close comparative study reveals imbalances inherent in a wilful monolingualism, and a "flat international translatese" wholly inadequate to the transmission of literary and cultural specificity (Simon, 142). What she describes is the experience of reading English translations of texts from very different parts of the globe and finding that they tend to sound alike. This negative homogenizing effect on distinct cultures is one of the dangers of globalization.

In Canadian Literature, we read many Quebec works in English translation, and sometimes find that they have been turned into English Canadian works. This is a common experience with the novels of Gabrielle Roy. To illustrate this problem, E.D. Blodgett wrote an essay entitled "How Do You Say Gabrielle Roy?" (1983). In Comparative Canadian Literature, we read the original French texts and sometimes follow the bilingual model of the Sherbrooke School of Comparative Canadian Literature, in which an English and a French text are studied in parallel (Pivato, "The Sherbrooke School").

The Haun Saussy volume *Comparative Literature in an Age of Globalization* has some promising directions for the future of Comparative Literature in North America. One of these directions is to focus on the study of different literatures in their original languages.

In my reading, some of the contributors to the Bernheimer volume (1995) have abandoned the goals of studying different languages and literatures, the goals envisioned by the founders of Comparative Literature in North America. By contrast, the writers in the Saussy volume (2006) re-affirm their commitment to the study of languages and literatures.

## TEXT VERSUS THEORY

The relationship between a literary work and theory is a problematic one. When we assign our students a new literary work to read, we often ask them to simply read it on their own, without reference to literary theories, critical commentaries, or other aides. The concern is that the other secondary material will influence individual students in how they read the new text before they have a chance to develop their own interpretation based on their own emotional and intellectual response to the work. We believe that students need to develop these critical skills as readers by dealing directly with the text. Only later, in discussions about their responses to the text, can we begin to introduce the critical commentaries and theories that other academics and writers have applied to the literary work. We can then analyze the critical commentaries and compare them to the observations of various students. In Comparative Literature, this process can be complicated when reading texts in languages other than English. Both Bernheimer and Blodgett, above, complain about the preoccupation with theory among the comparatists in the 1990s.

Now, as readers we all encounter powerful theories which may preempt our own reading and understanding of a given text. When we write literary criticism we often use theory that we have absorbed in our reading or education, either consciously when we deliberately focus on a particular theory or unconsciously when we use ideas or approaches. The conjunction of theory and criticism implies a relationship between the two activities, but also denotes the separation between them.

Theory, or theoretical criticism, can be distinguished from practical criticism or interpretive criticism. Theory makes general statements on literary forms, genres, structures, techniques, styles, periods, and literary movements. Theory develops the hypotheses about the nature and function of literature and about the general principles that underlie the achievements of art and literature.

Interpretive, or practical, criticism, usually refers to the study of actual works. In the examination of a work, such as a novel, this type of criticism may involve one or more of the following: observation; classification; analysis; close reading; the determination of historical, social, or formal qualities; and intertextuality. There is also the emphasis on evaluation, that is, determining the quality of the literary work. Is one play better than another, and why? Practical criticism, then, is the application of general literary theory to individual texts.

Writers sometimes combine theory and criticism under the term "poetics." For example, in his work *Poetics,* Aristotle discussed the structure of literary genres such as tragedy, and also gave us guidelines for evaluating the qualities of individual works. The history of poetics includes works by Horace, Dante, Sir Philip Sidney, Pope, Wordsworth, T.S. Eliot, and Northrop Frye.

The writing of literary theory and criticism is distinct from the production of literary works, such as novels, lyric poems, or comedies. This separation is a convention firmly established in the Western literary tradition. In the literatures of Europe, teachers often call the works of creative writers "primary texts," whereas they call the commentary by literary critics "secondary texts." The implication is clear: in the study of literature, the most important texts are those by the creative authors; the less-important ones are by the critics. To me, this distinction reflects the biases found in the New Criticism, the broad movement that has dominated the study of literature in the universities of North America and the UK from the 1940s to the 1980s. The academics who follow this approach hold that the focus of literary study should be the text, rather than secondary material, and that the preferred method of study is a close reading of the text. This approach often leads to the belief in a single or correct interpretation of a work of literature, setting aside all other information about the author, his or her expressed intentions in composing the work, divergent interpretations about the work, the social or historical context in which the work was produced, and other direct influences. We can see that limiting the study of texts to close reading in this way may not always be compatible with comparative study, which often considers all the external elements of the text.

In French literature programs, this type of close reading is called *explication de texte*, and we find similar practices of exegesis in Italian and Spanish. In German literature, we have the tradition of hermeneutics, which follows the methodology of close reading.

The view that theory and criticism are secondary to literary texts is not supported by many literary theorists. They read the essays on theory as though they were primary literary texts. We apply this approach to a feminist essay or an essay in Comparative Literature. These essays can be the objects of close reading as much as any poem or short story. Another reason we support close reading of critical texts is our belief that students should be encouraged to do criticism and not just read about it.

This general approach is supported by two considerations: the long European tradition of *belles-lettres* that regards literary criticism as literature, and the practice of contemporary writers who see all literature and criticism as participating in a discourse. In this approach, there is a dissolving of the barriers between not only creative writing and criticism, but also among the many different genres of written communication. If we adopt this broad view of human discourse, we begin to see the interrelations among the various types of writing in literature, history, philosophy, psychology, science, politics, and art. And beyond the different forms of writing there are also the other forms of verbal and visual communication, such as theatre, film, TV, and music.

In the 1980s and 1990s, academics at North American universities began to embrace theory to the point that it has become a dominant activity in literature programs. But at the same time, many academics in Comparative Literature have been questioning the role and value of various theories now being promulgated, because some of these theories neglect the distinctions of different languages and the problems of translation. We will now briefly examine some of the problems with theory.

In her book *Art: Sublimation or Symptom* (2003), Parveen Adams has collected essays that examine the relationship between psychoanalytic theory and works of art and literature. She observes that theory is often privileged over art: "The apparent modesty of this formula conceals a certain theoretical arrogance – the transaction between the two has increased the power of psychoanalysis but not that of art" (13). The psychological premise in these essays is to examine artistic works as the sublimation of the sex drive or a symptom of some mental problem. Do we understand these works better as a result of these theories?

As the example above shows, the power of theory is one of the problems. There is the perception that powerful theories will overwhelm the young writer. These forces can disallow the natural development of culturally specific works. The writer is looking for an authentic voice, a true representation of the community, a meaningful expression of his or her experiences and ideas. For some critics the question is: will immersion into theory help the writer (Gunew 17)?

Some authors also fear the influence of theory on the reading and reception of their books. If a work does not subscribe to a popular theory, will it be valued less; will it be seen as lacking in complexity, depth, or the elusive quality of literariness? Writers who work in the realist tradition find themselves at a disadvantage with postmodern theories that question all interpretations. In my publications I have raised similar questions about theory (Pivato, "Shirt of the Happy Man" 30–1).

When French theorist Roland Barthes declared "The Death of the Author," it did not seem to be very helpful to ethnic minority writers who were just beginning to get some recognition for their work, their voices, and their stories. Barthes declared that "The removal of the author ... is not merely an historical fact or an act of writing; it utterly transforms the modern text (or – which is the same thing – the text is henceforth made and read in such a way that at all its levels the author is absent)" (255).

The markers of ethnic identity are the author's name, family ties, links to a different history, culture, and language. He or she gives voice to a whole community. The removal of the author diminishes this ethnic identity and history. The removal of the author silences a whole community. Far beyond appropriation of voice, theory can obliterate a whole human existence. This approach is not compatible with comparative studies designed to consider all the elements dismissed by Barthes.

In her article "Theory: Beauty or Beast? Resistance to Theory in the Feminine" (1990), Smaro Kamboureli explores the debate over the role of theory among women writers in Canada, suggesting that part of writers' reluctance to embrace theory is that it is difficult to define and to control the different ways in which it manipulates the meanings of a given text. For some, this slippage in meaning is a positive quality, which allows us to re-evaluate many texts both canonical and marginal. Kamboureli argues that

> one of the primary goals of women writers interested in theory is their desire to position themselves as subjects of discourse, hence the readiness with which they question the very theories they practise. Indeed, the fact that they find suspect any appropriating tendencies that might be inherent in the ideology of a given theory is one of the main characteristics of their attitude towards theory, whether feminist or not. (9)

In the past, critical theory was able to accommodate the intention and authority of the writer, but this has changed. Current literary theories proclaim the death of the author (Barthes). Reader-response theory privileges the interaction of the reader with the text. Umberto Eco claims that the author is only a strategy of the text, and that the real text is a product of the reader's consciousness (65–6). We can see the gap here between the sophisticated urban cultures of Europe with their self-reflexive theories, meant to honestly do away with the cult of personality, and the basic activities of the minority writer, who is trying to articulate an experience, develop an identity, and find a space in society. These ethnic minority writers were not included in the literary institution, the literary canons of various national literatures. And now that they are about to get some small recognition and raise their collective voice, we are told by high theory that the author is dead.

My training in Comparative Literature has taught me the importance of intertextuality. But my work with ethnic minority texts in different languages has caused me to question all the assumptions of intertextuality and such axioms as "Works of literature are the products of other works of literature, and not necessarily a reflection of the life experience of the author." The works of Italian-Canadian authors are based on their life experiences. Mary di Michele, in her novel *Tenor of Love* (2004), could explore the life of Caruso, his migration to America and return to Italy, because she herself had similar immigration experiences and a conflicted relationship to Italy. The primordial text here is actual experience and memory and not other publications.

Intertextuality is a problematic term, since it has at least two meanings. The first is a purely literary one; the second is socio-historical. The first type of intertextuality comes from French literary theory and focuses on the relations between two texts or among several texts. Often this takes the form of studies on the influence of one text or author on other texts or authors. Examples of this are studies on the influence of Dante on English literature. This study of *"les rapports de fait"* was the foundation of *la littérature comparée*, or the French School of Comparative Literature.

There is another type of intertextuality, the socio-historical theory of Mikhail Bakhtin, which sees each utterance as the interaction of several systems of signs (263). Julia Kristeva applied this theory of intertextuality to literary texts (69). Each text is seen as a network of sign systems, situating the literary structure in a social environment. This reading of the text as an interaction of different codes, discourses, or voices, not only permits the inclusion of the ethnic minority work, but may in fact privilege it. Bakhtin's term for this phenomenon was "heteroglossia," a way of describing the different discursive strata within any given utterance. These strata are derived from what Bakhtin called "the socio-ideological languages" in a culture, and depend on the contesting voices of a historical context (288–91). To me Bakhtin's theory fits well with comparative studies of texts that involve more than one language.

Along with questions of authenticity and identity, the question of language use leads us to the problem of realism. Here we mean classical realism and the expressive theory of literature. We recall Auerbach's *Mimesis* (1946). Realism is an appealing mode of writing for both creator and reader, because it offers itself as transparent. Unlike much postmodern writing, which explicitly draws attention to itself as a constructed text, the realistic work tends to efface its own textuality and its existence as discourse. Realism is most effective when it leads to the recognition of the already familiar. In ethnic-minority writing, realism is even more appealing, because this experience is emphasized through the shock of recognition for the ethnic reader. The pleasure of the text comes not so much from the verisimilitude of the detailed depiction of events, as from the recognition of familiar experiences encountered for the first time in literature.

The form of the classical realist text in conjunction with the expressive theory of writing and ideology privileges the interpolation of the reader as subject. The ethnic-minority reader is given a reality, an existence, in society that he or she never had before. The authority of the author with the ethnic signature reinforces this.

This model of intersubjective communication, of shared understanding of a text which represents a familiar world, is the guarantee not only of the truth of the text – that is, realism – but of the reader's existence as an autonomous and knowing subject in a world of intelligent subjects. This realist reading of the ethnic-minority text by the minority reader constitutes an ideological practice. The meaning is constructed by the reader, but it is a meaning he or she can recognize in the text.

## THE POST-COLONIAL QUESTION

As critics, scholars, and academics in Comparative Literature, we are often conscious of the fact that we are also helping to bring into existence these new ethnic-minority literatures. Two recent examples are Elizabeth Dahab, who is advancing the cause of Arab-Canadian writers with her book *Voices of Exile in Contemporary Canadian Francophone Literature*, and George Elliott Clarke, who is promoting African-Canadian writers with *Odysseys Home: Mapping African-Canadian Literature*. As academics, we are often in the privileged position of freely using terms like post-colonial theory without much thought to what the consequences may mean for the ethnic-minority author.

This questioning of theory by some ethnic-minority writers, this reluctance to abandon the conventions of classical realism, is as much a political position as a literary tendency. Many of us of minority backgrounds are well aware that our subject positions are discursively constructed, and we want to determine the discourse, since it is the location of resistance. Our position is similar to that of many women writers and Indigneous writers; in the end all we have are our stories.

One topic that has been mentioned several times in the books discussed above is the relationship between post-colonial theory and Comparative Literature. The Canadian scholar Winfried Siemerling has the best explanation for the possible future collaboration between the two areas of study:

> Much recent work on intralingual relations and emergence generally has been produced under the heading of postcolonial studies rather than comparative literature. Postcolonial studies works comparatively across lines of unequal power or juxtaposes situations of "common sociohistorical conditions" and is often considered a specific form of comparative literature. Theoretically it also holds, like comparative literature in general, great promise for approaching contexts of emergence and cultural transformation in North America. (10)

In our work with post-colonial theory, we must also be sensitive to the concerns of Indigenous writers such as Kateri Akiwenzie-Damm and Thomas King, who are referenced in the introduction to this section on comparative arguments. King argues that "the idea of post-colonial writing effectively cuts us off from our traditions, traditions that were in place before colonialism ever became a question, traditions which have come down to us through our cultures in spite of colonialism, and it supposes that contemporary Native writing is largely a construct of oppression" (12).

This different experience of Indigenous history in North America is also forcefully argued by Kateri Akiwenzie-Damm in her 1998 essay "We Belong to This Land: A View of 'Cultural Difference.'" It is clear to me that one of the future directions for Comparative Literature is to study the work of Indigenous writers in North America, such as Scott Momaday, Louise Erdrich, Leslie Marmon Silko, Basil Johnston, Tomson Highway, Eden Robinson, Daniel David Moses, Ruby Slipperjack, and Jeannette Armstrong. In my Comparative Literature courses of the 1980s and 1990s, I often had my students read works by these authors. In general practice, now we find works by Indigenous writers separated into courses on Indigenous Literature. While it is a positive development to have courses on

Indigenous literature, the separation may sometimes duplicate the segregation of the remote reserve. In Quebec, we have Indigenous authors working in French, which directs us away from English-only post-colonial theory and can open possibilities to study Indigenous languages and oral literature. It will be up to comparatists to include works by Indigenous authors while being sensitive to concerns about appropriation of voice and post-colonial theory. In my article "Representation of Ethnicity as Problem: Essence or Construction," I discuss appropriation of voice with regard to both ethnic minority communities and Indigenous communities.

Indigenous writers make us aware of concerns about the stewardship of our land and the ethical issues raised in ecocriticism. Sheena Wilson, the bilingual director of the Petrocultures Research Group, has written about the work of comparatists who address new research problems related to oil, energy, and culture and bring valuable perspectives to serious twenty-first-century problems. She argues that these are some of the new research directions for Comparative Literature beyond post-colonial theory.

## COMPARATIVE LITERATURE AND DIGITAL MEDIA

There are two developments in digital technology that are transforming literary studies: the Open Access (OA) movement and the emergence of online journals, E-journals. Many academics are celebrating the advent of Open Access as a boon to research and scholarly publishing, especially with online journals. However, when many of these writers explain the value of Open Access, they are referring only to the English-speaking world. We know that there is a vast amount of scholarship beyond the English language and that comparatists who know other languages can have direct access to these sites. They also have access to other points of view, and often different information. For example, the German Wikipedia has many pages that are different from the English version, and even the criteria for including and editing articles are different. Comparatists can research the different Wikipedias in France, Spain, Italy, Sweden, Brazil, and other countries. We can directly explore *la Biblioteca Virtual Miguel de Cervantes*, which includes writers in the Iberian peninsula, as well as in Latin American countries. Other examples are the *Grand Larousse encyclopédique* in France and the *Istituto dell'Enciclopedia Italiana Treccani* in Italy. In these international developments, Open Access speaks the different languages of Comparative Literature.

Online journals include both traditional print journals which have online versions available and new e-journals which exist only in digital formats. Two examples of the latter are *Inquire: Journal of Comparative Literature*, which was established at the University of Alberta in 2011, and CLCweb: *Comparative Literature and Culture* at Purdue University, which was created in 1999 by international comparatist Steven Tötösy de Zepetnek.

Online journals can take advantage of the benefits of digital technology, especially as they apply to time, space, and costs. The new technology allows journals to publish and edit on an ongoing basis, rather than being limited to issues three of four times a year. Evaluations can be done in a timely fashion with email. E-journals can encourage interaction among contributors and readers, with commentaries and critiques which can lead to possible international collaboration on other projects. E-journals have the option of adding links to other sites, such as external references, as well as video, sound, visual arts, and translations. They cost less to produce and disseminate than print journals and can be easily accessed across the globe. By promoting the literary arts more widely and in different languages, E-journals are more inclusive across diverse global locations and economic conditions. There are also blogs, wikis, and portals in different languages, which promote read-write systems of direct international communications. Future developments in Comparative Literature will benefit from this new technology, which speaks many different languages and reaches many different cultures.

In 2010-11, Geoffrey Rockwell (Alberta) and Stefan Sinclair (McGill) developed Voyant Tools, a Web-based text-analysis environment that is used to study single texts in comparison to other single texts, as well as massive amounts of literary data. This free, open-access tool has been translated into nine languages, including Japanese, Arabic, Hebrew, and Italian, and is now in use in 156 countries. From the list of projects on the Voyant site, it is clear that it is being used by researchers in Comparative Literature. Rockwell and Sinclair released Voyant 2.0 in April 2016, as well as their book *Hermeneutica.ca: Computer-Assisted Interpretation in the Humanities* (MIT Press, 2016).

I began my exploration of literary studies and digital technology in 2000 with my course on Literature and Hypertext, built around a text by George Landow, *Hypertext 2.0: The Convergence of Contemporary Critical Theory and Technology*. Landow, who taught Victorian literature at Brown University, began exploring the potential for computers to help with literary research and became an expert in what is now called Digital Humanities. He begins *Hypertext* with an observation that is still true today:

Others who write on hypertext and literary theory argue that we must abandon conceptual systems founded on ideas of centre, margin, hierarchy, and linearity and replace them by ones of multilinearity, nodes, links, and networks. Almost all parties to this paradigm shift, which marks a revolution in human thought, see electronic writing as a direct response to the strengths and weaknesses of the book ... This response has profound implications for literature, education and politics. (1)

It is my hope that in the future students and scholars in Comparative Literature will become more fully involved in this paradigm shift and use their different languages.

In 1958, René Wellek published "The Crisis of Comparative Literature," to decry the homelessness of this discipline among humanities programs built around national literature departments. In 2004, Spivak published *Death of a Discipline* to refocus comparative study on close reading and local knowledge. In her 2006 response to these ongoing problems in Comparative Literature, Linda Hutcheon gives a more hopeful explanation: "It is this habit of self-interrogation that makes the discipline perhaps uniquely responsive to change: comparative literature has always been open to rethinking; it is always aware of the state of the intellectual economy, if you will" (225).

### NOTE

1 *"Dal lavôr si cognos il mestri"*: this old Friulan proverb is translated into Italian as *"Dall'opera si conosce il maestro"* and into English as "From the work we recognize the master." This is often only possible if we read the literary work in its original language.

### BIBLIOGRAPHY

Adams, Parveen, ed. *Art: Sublimation or Symptom.* New York: Other Press, 2003.
Akiwenzie-Damm, Kateri. "We Belong to This Land: A View of 'Cultural Difference.'" In *Literary Pluralities*, edited by Christl Verduyn, 84–91. Peterborough, ON: Broadview Press, 1998.
Auerbach, Erich. *Mimesis: The Representation of Reality in Western Literature.* Princeton, NJ: Princeton University Press, 1953.
Bakhtin, M.M. *The Dialogic Imagination.* Austin: University of Texas, 1981.
Barthes, Roland. "The Death of the Author." In *Falling into Theory*, edited by David H. Richter, 253–7. New York: St Martin's Press, 2000.

Blodgett, E.D. "Comparative Literature in Canada: A Case Study." *Canadian Review of Comparative Literature* 40, no. 3 (Sept. 2013): 311.

– "How Do You Say Gabrielle Roy?" In *Translation in Canadian Literature Symposium*, edited by Camille La Bossière, 13–34. Reappraisals: Canadian Writers 9. Ottawa: University of Ottawa, 1983.

Bernheimer, Charles, ed. *Comparative Literature in the Age of Multiculturalism*. Baltimore: Johns Hopkins, 1995.

Clarke, George Elliott. *Odysseys Home: Mapping African-Canadian Literature*. Toronto: University of Toronto Press, 2002.

Dahab, F. Elizabeth. *Voices of Exile in Contemporary Canadian Francophone Literature*. Lanham, MD: Lexington Books, 2009.

Del Fabro, Adriano. *Provèrbis dal Friûl*. Verona: La Libreria di Demetra, 1998.

Derrida, Jacques. "Ce dangereux supplément." In *De la grammatologie*, 203–34. Paris: Les éditions de minuit, 1967.

di Michele, Mary. *Tenor of Love*. Toronto: Penguin, 2004.

Eco, Umberto. *Interpretation and Overinterpretation*. Edited by Stefan Collini. Cambridge, UK: Cambridge University Press, 1992.

Gunew, Sneja, and A. Yeatman. *Feminism and the Politics of Difference*. Halifax, NS: Fernwood, 1993.

Huston, Nancy. *Losing North: Musings on Land, Tongue, and Self*. Toronto: McArthur & Company, 2002.

Hutcheon, Linda. "Comparative Literature: Congenitally Contrarian." In Saussy, 224–9.

– "State of the Discipline." *Inquire: Journal of Comparative Literature* 1, no. 2 (June 2011), inquire.streetmag.org/articles/36.

Kamboureli, Smaro. "Theory: Beauty or Beast? Resistance to Theory in the Feminine." *Open Letter* 7, no. 8 (1990).

King, Thomas. "Godzilla vs Post-Colonial." *World Literature Written in English* 30, no. 2 (1990): 10–16.

Kristeva, Julia. *Desire in Language*. New York: Columbia. 1980.

Landow, George. *Hypertext 2.0: The Convergence of Contemporary Critical Theory and Technology*. Baltimore: Johns Hopkins, 1997.

Pivato, Joseph. "Representation of Ethnicity as Problem: Essence of Construction." In *Literary Pluralities*, edited by Christl Verduyn, 152–61. Peterborough, ON: Broadview Press, 1998.

– "The Sherbooke School of Comparative Canadian Literature." *Inquire: Journal of Comparative Literature* 1, no. 1 (2011), inquire.streetmag.org/articles/25.

– "Shirt of the Happy Man: Theory and Politics of Ethnic Minority Writing." *Canadian Ethnic Studies* 28, no. 3 (1996).

Pratt, Mary Louise. "Comparative Literature and Global Citizenship." In Bernheimer, 58–65.
Rockwell, Geoffery, and Stefan Sinclair. *Hermeneuti.ca: Computer-Assisted Interpretation in the Humanities*. Cambridge, MA: MIT Press, 2016.
Saussy, Haun, ed. *Comparative Literature in an Age of Globalization*. Baltimore: Johns Hopkins, 2006.
Siemerling, Winfried. *The New North American Studies: Culture, Writing and the Politics of Re/cognition*. New York: Routledge, 2005.
Simon, Sherry. *Gender in Translation: Cultural Identity and the Politics of Translation*. New York: Routledge, 1996.
Spivak, Gayatri Chakravorty. *Death of a Discipline*. New York: Columbia University Press, 2003.
Stone, Gregory B. *Dante's Pluralism and the Islamic Philosophy of Religion*. New York: Palgrave Macmillan, 2006.
Tötösy de Zepetnek, Steven, and Joshua Jia. "Electronic Journals, Prestige, and the Economics of Academic Journal Publishing." CLCWeb: *Comparative Literature and Culture* 16, no. 1 (2014). http://dx.doiorg/10.7771/1481-4374.24.26.
Wellek, René. "The Crisis of Comparative Literature." In *Concepts of Criticism*, edited by Stephen G. Nicholas, 282–95. New Haven: Yale University Press, 1963.
Wellek, René, and Austen Warren. *Theory of Literature*. 3rd ed. New York: Harcourt, Brace & World, 1956.
Wilson, Sheena. "Shake Up, Not Shake-Down: Comparative Literature as a Twenty-First Century Discipline." *Canadian Review of Comparative Literature* 41, no. 2 (2014): 226–30.
Ziolkowski, Jan M., ed. *Dante and Islam*. New York: Fordham University Press, 2015.

SECTION TWO

# FUTURE DIRECTIONS IN COMPARATIVE LITERATURE

This section presents a selection of contributions that illustrate possible directions for Comparative Literature studies in the future. We will highlight three of them. Ndeye Fatou Ba's "Dialogue between Francophone and Anglophone Literatures in Africa" is an original comparative study of two literary traditions in Africa and a model that can be followed for other studies in the future which can also include African languages. For many years, some scholars have wanted to combine academic writing with creative writing. In his chapter, "Why Not an 'African-Canadian' Epic?" George Elliott Clarke explores the possibilities of this interdisciplinary approach, while Monique Tschofen, in "Exile, Media, Capital: *Calendar*'s System of Exchange," uses comparative methodology to critically analyze a film on an ethnic minority topic.

Below is a list of book titles that we consider good models of Comparative Literature studies, which investigate cultural differences, diasporic writers, and Indigenous authors:

Aziz, Nurjehan, ed. *Floating the Borders: New Contexts in Canadian Criticism*. Toronto: TSAR, 1999.
Boldini, Lucia, Marina Grishakova, and Matthew Reynolds, eds. CLCWeb: *New Work in Comparative Literature in Europe*. Special Issue. CLCweb: *Comparative Literature and Culture* 15, no. 7 (2013). http://docs.lib.purdue.edu/clcweb/vol15/iss7.
Carrière, Marie, and Catherine Khordoc, eds. *Comparing Migrations: The Literature of Canada and Quebec*. Bern: Peter Lang, 2008.
Chao, Lien. *Beyond Silence: Chinese Canadian Literature in English*. Toronto: TSAR, 1997.
Dahab, F. Elizabeth. *Voices of Exile in Contemporary Francophone Literature*. Boulder, CO: Lexington Books, 2009.
Dvorak, Marta, and Jane Koustas, eds. *Visions/Division: l'oeuvre de Nancy Huston*. Ottawa: Presses de l'Université d'Ottawa, 2004.
Gunew, Sneja. *Post-multicultural Writers as Neo-cosmopolitan Mediators*. London: Anthem Press, 2017.

Heise, Ursula K., ed. *Futures of Comparative Literature: ACLA State of the Discipline Report*. New York: Routledge, 2017.

Isaacs, Camille A., ed. *Austin Clarke: Essays on His Works*. Toronto: Guernica, 2013.

Kamboureli, Smaro. *Scandalous Bodies: Diasporic Literature in English Canada*. Waterloo: Wilfrid Laurier University Press, 2009.

Lindberg, Tracey, and David Brundage, eds. *Daniel David Moses: Spoken and Written Explorations of His Work*. Toronto: Guernica, 2015.

Macfarlane, Heather, and Armand Garnet Ruffo, eds. *Introduction to Indigenous Literary Criticism in Canada*. Peterborough: Broadview Press, 2015.

Mannani, Manijeh, and Veronica Thompson, eds. *Selves and Subjectivities: Reflections on Canadian Arts and Culture*. Edmonton: AU Press, 2012.

Mezei, Kathy, Sherry Simon, and Luise von Flotow, eds. *Translation Effects: The Shaping of Modern Canadian Culture*. Montreal: McGill-Queen's University Press, 2014.

Moyes, Lianne, Licia Canton, and Domenic A. Beneventi, eds. *Adjacencies: Minority Writing in Canada*. Toronto: Guernica, 2004.

Nischik, Reingard M., ed. *The Palgrave Handbook of Comparative North American Literature*. New York: Palgrave Macmillan, 2014.

Sayed, Asma, ed. *M.G. Vassanji: Essays on His Works*. Toronto: Guernica, 2014.

Sharma, Ram. *New Directions in Diasporic Literature*. Jaipur: Aadi Publications, 2016.

Siemerling, Winfried. *The Black Atlantic Reconsidered: Black Canadian Writing, Cultural History and the Presence of the Past*. Montreal: McGill-Queen's University Press, 2015.

– *New North American Studies: Culture, Writing, and the Politics of Re/cognition*. New York: Routledge, 2005.

Ty, Eleanor, and Christl Verduyn, eds. *Asian Canadian Writing: Beyond Autoethnography*. Waterloo: Wilfrid Laurier University Press, 2008.

Verduyn, Christl, ed. *Literary Pluralities*. Peterborough: Broadview Press, 1998.

Wilson, Janet, Cristina Sandru, and Sarah Lawson Welsh, eds. *Re-Routing the Postcolonial: New Directions for the New Millennium*. New York: Routledge, 2010.

# Dialogue between Francophone and Anglophone Literatures in Africa

*Ndeye Fatou Ba*

In this chapter, I draw comparisons between African authors writing in French and those writing in English in the hope that this will promote dialogue between the two post-colonial language groups. I see this comparative study as an example of future directions in Comparative Literature, which can include studies between African literatures and those of the Caribbean, India, New Zealand, Australia, and Canada. This chapter is also a demonstration of the value the methodology of Comparative Literature can bring to post-colonial studies, which are often focused on the single language of English.

While both the British and the French empires colonized territories in Africa at about the same time, their approaches to the dissemination of their own languages and cultures were different, as were their attitudes toward the indigenous languages of Africa. In this chapter, I briefly compare the separate developments of Francophone and Anglophone literatures in selected African countries.

### ON FRANCOPHONE LITERATURE

From its origins in colonization to its present-day understanding as a linguistic community, what it means to be Francophone has for the longest time, especially in France, carried some hegemonic undertones. In literature, African Francophone authors have, traditionally, written with a sense of commitment in their works. With René Maran's *Batouala* (1921)[1] – considered the first Francophone novel – and later the Négritude movement, the first generation of African authors trained in the

French school essentially wrote to showcase a certain cultural richness and to correct exotic Eurocentric views often channelled through colonial narratives. Later, with the first wave of local governments that took over responsibilities from the former colonizers, Francophone literature moved from a critique of colonization to denouncing national dictatorial regimes. More recently, with women writers joining in the literary scene, gender considerations have been brought forth to challenge the way black subjectivity has primarily been articulated as a male concern. Francophone literature then, as can be inferred from this general overview, is, and has been since "birth," a literature of protest. This is particularly true of women writers who have asserted their subjectivity with their novels: Mariama Ba, *Une si longue lettre* (1979), Aminata Sow Fall, *La Grève des Bàttu* (1979), Calixthe Beyala, *Tu t'appelleras Tanga* (1988), and Monique Ilboudo, *Le mal de peau* (1992).

### DEFINITION OF FRANCOPHONE LITERATURE

The adjective "Francophone" comes from the word *Francophonie*, a term first coined in 1880 by Onésime Reclus to refer to places, around the world, where French was used as a vehicular language. Beside natives of France, a few European countries, and a part of Canada, the majority of people deemed Francophone do not claim French as their first language. However, rarely – if at all – are French people from the Hexagon (France) referred to as Francophone; more often than not, the term applies to French-speaking people other than the natives of France. As a consequence, what it means to be Francophone involves complex interfacings between various languages. The term, by definition, refers to someone who speaks, usually, another language besides French. The qualifier Francophone then is a terminology used on the basis of linguistic diversity and geographical home; "it designates both a socio-linguistic and geographical phenomenon: to describe French-speaking population and to describe a French-speaking bloc" (Jack 17).

The adjective "Francophone" to refer to the body of literature written in French – and distinct from metropolitan French literature itself – is a denomination that has greatly evolved over time. Simply referred to, in its early stages, as "literature written in French," "literature of French expression," or "Negro-African literature," the denomination Francophone literature passed into popular usage only in the late 1970s. This lack of consistent denomination to refer to the body of writings originating from the ex-colonies mirrors a more insidious lack of early recognition of Francophone literature as an independent and worthy literary field with a legitimacy of its own. Indeed, France, which has for the longest time been considered the cultural capital of all writings in French, showed a deep-seated mistrust[2] of this new protest literature that was, in many regards, critical of the French empire (or what was left from it), a literature that called for a "contemporary assessment of the culture and history of empire from the moment of conquest" (Forsdick and Murphy 5). This mistrust however was not limited to social settings only. In academia as well, mainstream French literature shunned this new discipline born out of France's ex-colonies. In his article entitled "L'université a-t-elle peur de la littérature négro-africaine d'expression française," Bernard Mouralis wrote, back in 1982, over two decades after the Négritude pioneers, "[L]a littérature négro-africaine d'expression française demeure dans l'ensemble du tissu universitaire français, une discipline fragile et pas encore vraiment reconnue" (In the fabric of the French university, Black African literature in French remains in a precarious position, still falling short of true recognition) (2; translation mine).

In fact, when the adjective "Francophone" is applied to literature, specifically to the African novel, cultural, historical, political, and even ideological paradigms come into play. Francophone literature refers to the body of writings, outside of the French metropolis, that usually originate from countries previously colonized by France, and where authors have retained the French language as their vehicular means. This latter issue of language choice constitutes one of the major points of controversy in the discussion of the Francophone African novel. Even if the debate over the authorial language of Africans is less heated in Francophone studies than it is with the Anglophone novel, critics have still, nonetheless, debated the pertinence of the choice of the French language to write a literature often aimed at denouncing the very ideologies that are embedded in that language. More often than not, the Francophone views on the French language fall squarely within the teachings of the French direct colonial project.

In 1880, the same year the word Francophone was coined, the French language was promulgated by the French minister of education, Jules Ferry, as the mandatory and sole medium of instruction throughout the French Empire. By this decree, the French outlawed all local languages – at least in schools – and placed the French language at the forefront of their colonizing mission in Africa, which they came to equate with their "mission éducatrice et civilisatrice" (educational and civilizing mission) (Ferry, qtd. in Parker 92). In Senegal, for example, the specific decree outlawing local languages in school was signed in May 1924. It clearly stated that "Le Français est seul en usage dans les écoles. Il est interdit aux maitres de se servir avec leurs élèves des idiomes du pays" (French only is to be used in schools. It is forbidden for teachers to speak to pupils in the local languages) (Moumouni 55). For Canadian readers, this assimilation policy is similar to that used in residential schools, which controlled Indigenous education for decades in Canada.

For the French, more so than the British, colonization was not just about territorial expansion: "both territories and minds were objects of conquest, and language was identified as a key tool [in the] conquest" (Parker 92). The "indigenes" in French-ruled colonies had to be assimilated and taught "the values of the French Republic, both for their own humanity and for the survival of the empire itself" (92). This assimilation policy, carried through a most direct colonial rule, accounts (at least partially, and for what it is worth) for the Francophone writer's accepting attitude toward the French language. The French minister of education Jean Jaures's famous 1884 declaration about the status of the French language is very eloquent, and is, to this date, still very much quoted in most discussions of France's assimilation policy. Jaures said:

> Our colonies will only be French in their understanding and their heart when they understand French ... For France above all, language is the necessary instrument of colonization ... More new French schools, to which we shall invite the natives, must come to help the French settlers, in their difficult task of moral conquest and assimilation ... when we take possession of a country, we should take with us the glory of France, and be sure that we will be well received, for she is pure as well as great, imbued with justice and goodness. (qtd. in Ager, *Identity, Insecurity, and Image* 238)

Indeed, from the poets of the Négritude movement to women writers such as Mariama Ba through Cheikh Hamidou Kane or even such harder-liners as Ahmadou Kourouma or Sony Labou Tansi, all these authors are known to have taken the indigenization of the French language to a superior level. In literary criticism today, people commonly talk about Kourouma's "Malinkismes" and Labou Tansi's "Tropicalités" – the debate over the authorial medium of African writers has not been pushed to the extremes of calling for an abandonment of the French language in favour of the vernaculars, despite some loud critics who call for the rejection of French.

We should note that the founders of Négritude ideology, Léopold Sédar Senghor, Aimé Césaire, and Léon Damas, were all educated in the

French colonial system. Their adherence to French language and culture is demonstrated by the fact that Négritude was initially invented in Paris. In 1973, Senghor wrote, "Quand je dis 'nous,' il s'agit de la poignée d'étudiants noirs, dans les années 1930, au Quartier Latin, à Paris, qui lancèrent ... le movement de la Négritude" (When I say "us" I am referring to a handful of black students in the 1930s in the Latin Quarter of Paris who launched ... the Négritude movement) (Senghor, vii; translation mine). In contrast to this, Ngũgĩ's rejection of English language and culture was consolidated in a jail cell in Kenya.

By definition, when discussing the African Francophone novel, the question no longer is which language to develop as the writers' authorial means; rather, it becomes how they – authors – take charge of these new languages inherited from colonization to forcefully convey their purpose and subject matters. The literary tradition in Africa being in the majority oral, and in keeping with the direct policy and the French's belief in the "superiority" of their language, local languages in French-ruled colonies were rarely – if they were at all – codified; as a consequence, they could not be used for literary purposes. Furthermore, given the large plurality of languages in use in Africa[3] and the lack of intelligibility among different ethnic groups, the colonizers' languages imposed themselves as lingua franca across the continent. Not to mention that, for merely practical reasons related to publications and readership, it was indicated and expected that the language of writing be French or English. However, these "foreign" languages would have to be crafted to become new languages, able to capture new subject matters and serve a greater goal of self-affirmation.

In Francophone literature, one general tendency was to try to deconstruct skewed French colonial narratives from within by using the very language which was once used for civilizing purposes. Senghor's strong statement in defence of his use of French as his authorial means is memorable. He contends:

> Parce que nous sommes des métis culturels, parce que, si nous sentons en nègres, nous nous exprimons en français, parce que le français est une langue à vocation universelle, que notre métissage s'adresse aussi aux français de France et aux autres hommes, parce que le français est une langue de "gentillesse et d'honnêteté."
> (*Éthiopiques*, afterword)
> [Because we are of mixed cultures, because if we feel ourselves Black, we express ourselves in French, because French is a language with a universal vocation, that our mixed race can address both the French

of France and other people, because French is a language of graciousness and honesty. (translation mine)]

As Jean-Paul Sartre famously argued in *Orphée Noir*: "Puisque l'oppresseur est présent jusque dans la langue qu'ils parlent, ils parleront cette langue pour la 'détruire'" (Since the oppressor is present even in the language that they speak, they will speak this language in order to destroy it) (247; translation mine), a statement that most writers and critics seemed to agree with, as they proudly claim the French language as their own, even if the latter, they contend, would at times have to be "défrancisé" and crafted to suit their narratives. This philosophy and attitude toward the French tongue was to inform, for generations to come, the somewhat non-dramatic acceptance of the language for literary purposes.

This total hegemony of the French tongue, however, along with the diglossic situations it brought about, would not fail, as one can easily imagine, to create some tensions within the colonial subject. From Léopold Sédar Senghor's *Négritude et Humanisme* and Frantz Fanon's *Peau noire, masques blancs* (*Black Skin, White Masks*) to Micheal Syrotinski's *Deconstruction and the Postcolonial: At the Limits of Theory*, through Patrick Chamoiseau's *Écrire en pays dominé*, the interface between European languages – French particularly – and the psyche of the indigene has often been studied. While Fanon is famous for his description, in *Black Skin, White Masks*, of the "almost pathological response of educated West Indians vis-à-vis the French language" with "anything less than pure Parisian [relegating] the speaker to a less human category" (qtd. in Michelman 219), Paulin Hountondji addresses the same relationship with the French language as Fanon, but this time, vis-à-vis the African subject specifically. In *Présence Africaine*, Hountondji claims that "The linguistic behaviour of the African, when expressing himself in French, has all the characteristics of a neurosis" (16). Hountondji's description is echoed by Oludare Idowu, who provides a detailed account of a perfectly "Westernized" indigenous person. In "Assimilation in 19th Century Senegal," the assimilated native is described as follows:

> He was like a typical French citizen, governed not by native law and custom but by the French codes. He was not a polygamist. Literate in French, he was expected to have imbibed as much of the French way of life as possible, and to have contributed in his own way to the success of the *mission civilisatrice* in the colony. Thinking French, living French, more at home in French society than elsewhere, he

was expected to be in everything except in the colour of his skin, a Frenchman. (205)

As can be inferred from this quote, a good knowledge of the French language was often associated with a more insidious abandonment of traditional ways of life in favour of an adoption of "French codes." Indeed, the connections Idowu drew back in 1969 between "litera[cy] in French," "thinking French," and ultimately "living French" very much resonate with Fanon's observations. And even today, with newer research on the intrinsic relationships between language and culture demonstrated by Ngũgĩ wa Thiong'o, J.R. Gladstone, and Claire Kramsch, among others, the use of language for purposes other than mere communication has been established. Indeed, Gladstone argues in "Language and Culture" that "language is at once an outcome or a result of the culture as a whole and also a vehicle by which the other facets of the culture are shaped and communicated" (212). Applying these critiques to the context of African Francophone natives who choose to write in French instead of their native languages highlights the loss of their original culture and world view in favour of a Western one carried through the French language.

This being said, however, one cannot help noticing that, from the Nigerian Idowu to the Kenyan Ngũgĩ, mistrust toward the use of foreign languages in African literature emanates mostly from critics originating from the English-speaking world. Francophones, as argued earlier, because of the role of the French language in the "mission civilisatrice" and the subsequent particular "close" relationships natives had with the colonizers' language, more readily accepted the French language as their authorial means. Unlike in the Anglophone world, the use of French in African literature has been subjected to fewer heated and controversial debates. However, past the differences in the relationships with the colonizers' languages, Francophone and Anglophone literatures share similar thematic concerns, and can both be qualified as literature of protest. And for this reason, a reassessment of normative readings of the Francophone novel that does not always display obvious signs of linguistic difference is long overdue. The heterogeneity of the Francophone novel, I contend, cannot simply be measured by the level of indigenization of the French language only. Both in its content and its form, the Francophone novel is and has been a literature of protest.

Traditionally, in sub-Saharan Africa, Francophone literature, like its English counterpart, seeks to re-inscribe indigenous natives as worthy subjects of study, with rich and complex cultures of their own. It provides alternative narratives from that of colonial literatures, as it aims to deconstruct Orientalist representations of Africa and Africans. In that regard, Francophone and Anglophone literatures share similar objectives, which are to challenge representations where Africans hardly ever spoke for themselves. At the heart of both literatures is the will to expose an African perspective on history. In applying the teaching of Amadou Hampathé Ba, who famously declared that "Quand une chèvre est présente, on ne doit pas bêler à sa place" (When a goat is present, do not bleat on its behalf) (qtd. in Merand 9; translation mine), Francophone and Anglophone literatures then provide variances to stories where the African is spoken, as they challenge "an accepted grid for filtering through the Orient into Western consciousness" (Said 6). Up until the birth of the African novel, English- and French-ruled sub-Saharan Africa were knowable on the international scene mostly through "a sovereign Western consciousness out of whose unchallenged centrality an Oriental [African] world emerged" (Said 8).

The evocation of Edward Said's seminal work *Orientalism* to address the problematic of both Francophone and Anglophone literatures implies a close relationship between the two disciplines and post-colonial criticism. Just as I did for the qualifier Francophone, I should give a brief overview of the history of Anglophone literature.

## GENESIS OF AFRICAN ANGLOPHONE LITERATURE

In its most literal sense, "Anglophone literature" simply refers to literatures written in English; however, in literary studies, the term has many inflections, because of historical, political, and ideological considerations that inform the genesis of the discipline. As a consequence, a working definition of the qualifier Anglophone seems appropriate.

In social settings, the adjective Anglophone refers to someone who speaks English in countries where other languages – next to English – are spoken. In academia, Anglophone literature refers to productions written in English – outside Great Britain and the United States of America – from formerly colonized countries, such as Canada and Australia. At the heart of the discipline is the project to reclaim and disseminate an African voice, an African side of history, long stifled by colonial narratives. Anglophone literature and the ensuing area of literary criticism it generated – namely post-colonialism – were ambitious to unveil and deal with titles and authors not normally included in the regular English curriculum. Unlike the qualifier Francophone, however, which often designates things related to French but not of proper French origins, there is no over-determined will to separate an Anglophone from a native of British origins.

Though it shares similar ontological goals with Francophone literature, the advent of Anglophone literature can be traced further back than its French counterpart. Indeed, as early as the birth of Commonwealth Literature,[4] around the 1950s, before most African countries became independent, pieces were already being written by Africans in the English language. If we include narratives written in English by former slaves who originated from the continent, then we could trace the birth of African Anglophone literature much further back. Indeed, Olaudah Equiano's *The Interesting Narrative* (1789) and Phillis Wheatley's *Poems on Various Subjects* (1773) were works of two former slaves, respectively from Britain and the United States of America, who both published their works in English. However, it was not until Amos Tutuola, in 1952, with *The Palm-Wine Drinkard and His Dead Palm-Wine Tapster in the Deads' Town*, that the first major English novel by an African was published. Tutuola's novel, written in a predominantly awkward English, is often considered to be the starting point of Anglophone African literature.

The form of Tutuola's novel, specifically the integration of local vernaculars and unconventional English grammatical rules, would later set the "paradigms" by which the "authenticity" of the Anglophone African novel was commonly to be measured. In fact, unlike their Francophone counterparts, African writers who chose English as their authorial means showed far less "deference" toward their language; in Anglophone literature from Africa, the English language is often experimented with, and local vernaculars as well as literary traditions typical of an African oral art readily stand out. This early presence of different languages and literary traditions in Anglophone narratives finds its roots in the indirect British colonial language policies in the continent.

Where the French took pride in their assimilation policy and their "mission civilisatrice," the British showed less protectiveness toward their language and kept at a distance in their interactions with the indigenes. In "Linguistic Apartheid: English Language Policy in Africa" (2004), Augustin Simo Bobda, discussing the language situation in his native Cameroon, denounces the more general segregationist attitude of the British in regard to the implantation of their language in Africa. In 1922, Lord Frederick Lugard, a former British Governor General in Nigeria, wrote extensively about what was later to be more commonly referred to as the "dual mandate," a policy that outlined British quasi-racist attitudes toward colonized people.

Lugard developed the ideological basis, as well as the practical application, of the "indirect rule" policy, which was to govern the expansion of the British Empire in its (African) colonies. Convinced that the Black Africans were inherently different from their White European counterparts, Lugard theorized a segregationist policy, whereby a "dual mandate" of reciprocal benefits for both parties – indigenes and colonizers – would be put into place. In *The Dual Mandate in British Tropical Africa*, Lugard argues for a state-sponsored colonization, in which, contrary to the assimilationist French policy, local populations would take an active role in the management of their localities. In fact, out of a concern to avoid potential rebellion and claims for more independence from the natives, Lugard argues for an intermediary class of an educated elite directly selected from among the natives. In focusing on educating only a small percentage of the local population for practical supervisory purposes, the British made their language available only to a selected few. Contrary to the promulgation of the French language as mandatory and sole language of education throughout the French Empire, early education in the British colonies was carried out in the local vernaculars, and wherever the English language was used as a medium of education, it existed alongside various other languages and in varied registers.[5] To better understand the high degree of malleability of the English language, a quick analysis of its role in the expansion of the British Empire is necessary.

Indeed, the English language was introduced in Black Africa around the mid-nineteenth century by Christian missionaries whose aim was to convert African "pagans" and spread the word of the Bible. To that end, they established schools throughout the country, but unlike the French, the British promoted local vernaculars and an English-based pidgin to ensure that they effectively succeeded in communicating with the masses. Schools in British-ruled colonies then did not assume the classical mission of education they are known to have today; rather, they were synonymous with Christian evangelism and were essentially considered as incidental to converting indigenes. Language – in this case the English language – was a mere accessory to the greater goal of the British civilizing mission in Africa. To that effect, and to gain access to as wide an audience as possible, the language of education was usually the mother tongue of the natives, in which the British also made the Bible available. To make the translation of the Bible effective in local vernaculars, the British went to great lengths and developed systems of writing for the languages in question, which prior to colonization did not have a written form, as the majority of them belonged to essentially oral cultures.

This interest in local vernaculars and the civility of Africans hides a deeper concern about the relationship between the indigenes and the colonizers. Indeed, in British-ruled colonies, the majority of indigenes did not have access to the English language, as education – religious mainly – was also carried out in local languages. And at times when the autochthons were actually introduced to English, they were usually taught a lower register, different from the high standard that the colonizers themselves spoke. As a result of this discrepancy, a pidgin-based English developed throughout most Black African countries. This reticence to widely disseminate a higher register of English was justified by deeper concerns of cultural domination. In fact, the wish of the British to keep their "space" different from that of the colonized in social settings transpired even into the realm of language. In *Second Language Learning: Myth and Reality*, Paul Christophersen hints at some of the reasons that account for the colonizers' lack of real effort to promote a high standard of English among the natives. Christophersen claims that some British people felt threatened and "violated" by a non-native speaker who had a good command of their language, hence their protectiveness towards it. He writes, "it is as if an uninvited guest started making free of the host's possession" (83). This thought is echoed by Braj Kachru, who, in *The Alchemy of English*, contends that "English language deficiencies made the colonized an object of ridicule [while] the acquisition of native-like proficiency made them suspect" (75). The British, then, were at ease and even promoted different mechanisms of relexification of the English language, an attitude at the antipodes to that of the French, who had faith in the beauty and humanizing quality of their language to the point that people like René Étiemble considered the language sacred. In *Parlez-vous franglais*, addressing the growing influence of English in the French language, Étiemble contends, "[t]he French language is a treasure. To violate it is a crime. Persons were shot during the war for reason of treason. They should be punished for degrading the language" (87).

As this brief overview shows, the British colonial language policy in Africa made room not only for local vernaculars, but for other "deviant" forms of English as well, as it encouraged the flourishing of English-based pidgins throughout its empire. On balance, however, regardless of the British racist attitude toward their language, most newly independent colonies still retained English as their sole official language after the departure of the British. Throughout former British colonized countries, writers also adopted the English language as their authorial medium. In fact, because of the multitude of languages spoken in Africa, where a language is often equated with the tribe who speaks it, the English language "naturally" imposes itself as a federating and more effective medium of communication across diverse linguistic communities. In "Language Policy in Africa," Bernd Heine reflects on the quasi-general tendency in the populations of sub-Saharan Africa to adopt the languages of their former colonizers as their official ones. He writes:

> Most African states have adopted the general framework of language policy inherited from the respective colonial power ... The motivation for such a policy was obvious: In a situation where dozens or even hundreds of ethnic groups coexisted within the confines of a given nation competing for economic and political power, the European language constituted a convenient tool for bridging sociolinguistic, cultural, and political antagonisms which endangered the national unity of the young nation states. Furthermore, the political leadership of the first generation after independence were trained in Europe or North America and usually those leaders took for granted that a modern state should be run in a European language. (173)

While Heine was right in his observation of how naturally foreign-trained African leaders used their ex-colonizers' languages for political matters, what he overlooked was criticism of the use of these Western languages for the purpose of writing African literature. Indeed, regardless of the existence of codified local vernaculars at the time of independence, authors in former British colonies, just like their French counterparts, retained the English language as their authorial medium. And this very choice of language would create one of the largest topics of controversy in any discussion of the African novel – particularly the Anglophone one. Contrary to the African Francophone, for whom French seemed like the natural language to use for writing literature, Anglophone African writers struggled more forcefully and debated more loudly their choice of English for authorial means. Indeed, critics like Ngũgi wa Thiong'o, Chinweizu, and Obiajunwa Wali, among others, have called for an abandonment of the English language in African literature in favour of local vernaculars and more typical African ways of communication.

The Kenyan author Ngũgi wrote his first three novels in English, but after *A Grain of Wheat* in 1967, he renounced the use of English as colonial-minded, and so began to write in Gikuyu and Swahili. After he was arrested by the Kenyan regime in 1977, he wrote a novel in Gikuyu from prison. He translated *Caitaani mûtharaba-Inî* (1980) into English as *Devil on the Cross* (1982). In his collection of critical essays, *Something Torn and New* (2009), Ngũgi continues to make the argument that African languages are critical for the recovery of African memory and the identity of various cultural groups.

## THE LANGUAGE DEBATE IN AFRICAN ANGLOPHONE LITERATURE

In his book *Decolonizing the Mind: The Politics of Language in African Literature* (1986) Ngũgi wa Thiong'o argues that not only are foreign languages unable to carry a true African experience, but they also participate in perpetrating Western political hegemony on the African continent. For Ngũgi and other critics such as Wali and Chinweizu, language and culture are interchangeable; the loss of the former will result in the loss of the latter. In *Decolonizing the Mind*, Ngũgi affirms: "Language as culture is the collective memory bank of a people's experience in history. Culture is almost indistinguishable from the language that makes its genesis, growth, banking, articulation and indeed its transmission from one generation to the next" (15). From Ngũgi's description, one understands that language carries the weight of experience people accumulate throughout their history to the point that language and the culture it defines become a blend: one cannot go without the other.

More forcefully in this debate regarding African writers and their language of expression, Obi Wali from Nigeria asserts in "The Dead End of African Literature" that "until African writers accepted that any true African literature must be written in African languages, they would be pursuing a dead end" (282). Wali's pessimism is great. To him and his like-minded critics, "indigenized" French or English are no less Western languages, and they still carry all the weight of cultural hegemony brought about by colonization. This position is echoed by Chinweizu Ibekwe, who, in addition to his fight for the promotion of local languages, also argues for a replacement, in the university curricula, of British subject matters by African ones. Chinweizu is not alone in arguing for a change in African curricula. The now-famous Makerere conference on African writers of English expression touched on the issue as well. We remember that Ngũgi, for example, vigorously called for a suppression of English departments in Africa. As early as 1983, in *Toward the Decolonization of African Literature* (1983), Chinweizu and fellow critics called for a cleansing of imperialism in all spheres of African life. Here is how they articulated their project:

> The cultural task in hand is to end all foreign domination of African culture, to systematically destroy all encrustations of colonial and

slave mentality, to clear the bushes and stake out new foundations for a liberated African modernity. This is a process that must take place in all spheres of African life – in government, industry, family and social life, education, city planning, architecture, art, entertainment, etc. This book is intended as a contribution to this process in the realm of African letters. (1)

Indeed, according to Chinweizu and his allies, English was more than simply a language for communication purposes, it was also a subject that was taught to the indigenes and through which cultural dependence on a colonial reference was maintained. In Francophone and Anglophone Africa then, it was not just the language policy which was marked by continuity after independence. The colonizers' cultural and imperial domination over the colonized was sustained as well. The colonizers' history, literature, and culture – that is, their world view – was still being presented to the indigenes as the models to emulate. Reclaiming the African languages in literature then, according to Ngũgi and his like-minded critics, constitutes the necessary first step toward reclaiming a more global African sense of worth and validity.

For these critics of English, there is an urgent need to supplant Western literature by African literature. And for a piece of writing to be appropriately labelled African, the latter would have to be written in local languages and in a style that reconnects to the continent's traditions and past. For Ngũgi, any failure to return to local vernaculars would merely produce "Afro-European literature" by "intellectuals from the petty bourgeoisie" that "is likely to last for as long as Africa is under this rule of European capital in a neo colonial set-up" (*Decolonization* 27). The connection Ngũgi makes between language and identity is echoed by Fanon, who declares, "to speak is to exist absolutely for the other … The negro of the Antilles will be proportionately whiter – that is, he will come closer to being a real human being – in direct ratio to his mastery of the French language" (*Black Skin, White Masks* 17). For Fanon as well, as can be inferred from this quote, the use of former colonizers' language could – and to a degree does – participate in an attempt by the colonized to imitate Western cultural code. While Fanon's study was by no means specific to Africans – he specifically mentioned "the negro of the Antilles" – his conclusions can effortlessly be applied to all former colonized people who make the choice to express themselves in the languages of their former colonizers. A psychiatrist and philosopher, Fanon is very much in tune with Ngũgi in denouncing a black subject's rampant loss of personal identity in favour of a split self at best and a cultural "bastardization" at worst.

Fanon's understanding of the colonized mind did not necessarily translate into an awareness of the black female subject. In his book *Peau noire, masques blancs* (1952), he attacks colonialism and racism, but ignores the problem of sexist oppression. His damning critique of Mayotte Capecia's *Je suis martiniquaise* (1948), a woman's autobiography, suggests that black women are to be subservient to men, rather than to be viewed as subjects with agency in their own right. In more general terms, despite the sexism that they have encountered in their patriarchal societies, African women writers have asserted their independence in such novels as Tsitsi Dangarembga's *Nervous Conditions* (1988), Ken Bugul's *Le Baobab Fou* (1982), Chimamanda Ngozi Adichie's *Half of a Yellow Sun* (2006), and Fatou Diome's *Le Ventre de l'Atlantique* (2004).

This socio-cultural and political project to debunk hegemonic Western models and faulty representations of Africa as a locus of primitivism and alienation led to the creation of Commonwealth literature first and later Anglophone or post-colonial studies. The central place Chinweizu, Wali, and Ngũgĩ attempted to give to local languages, Anglophone post-colonial literatures sought to accomplish at the level of education. These newer "disciplines" were intended to end the domination of British literature in African university curricula. Faculties of Arts, more specifically English departments in most African countries, historically tended to exclusively teach authors of British origin, along with the world view that came with their narratives. The most radical critics found this an aberration, and they called for changes that would actually allow authors from the African continent to take a central place in their own home countries. This is precisely what Francophone, Anglophone, and post-colonial studies seek to do: namely, position African authors and their works as central and worthy subjects of study. Both Francophone and Anglophone literatures are concerned with "the interplay between the colonial past and the post-colonial present" as they "reflect on unfinished processes of representation and remembrance" (Forsdick and Murphy 3). In fact, because of ongoing political links, a shared history, and a common use of the French and English languages, both France and the UK are engaged in a post-colonial relationship with their former sub-Saharan colonies, even though the colonial ties that used to unite them are severed.

If the parallels between post-colonialism and Anglophone literature are more obvious and more documented than in Francophone writing, there exists, nonetheless, an intrinsic relationship between the objectives of post-colonial criticism and the ideological paratext of Francophone studies; and this despite some critics' reluctance to view the two disciplines as connected in any way. The relationships between post-colonialism and Francophone studies have more recently been the object of controversy and debate. While it is common knowledge that post-colonialism largely grew from Anglophone expatriates from ex-colonies established in Western universities, who felt their history and culture were not acknowledged enough in literary criticism, the intrinsic link between Francophone literatures and the newer paradigm of literary criticism (post-colonialism) has aroused a lot of skepticism, mostly from French scholars. For further information on how post-colonialism is diversely appreciated within Francophone studies, see Alec G. Hargreaves and Jean-Marc Moura's article entitled "Editorial Introduction: Extending the Boundaries of Francophone Post-colonial Studies."

Indeed, the same irony that excludes French hexagonal literature from the definition of Francophone literature also informs this "literary protectiveness" from a theory that has mainly been developed in Anglophone studies.[6] Furthermore, the productions within *la Francophonie*, the present-day network that gathers countries which use the French language (whether exclusively or partially), still continue to reflect on questions of representation that arose from the imperial meeting between France and its former colonies. Along with the work of Hargreaves and Moura, I hope that this comparative study will stimulate further work in different African literatures.

## CURRENT TRENDS IN FRANCOPHONE AND ANGLOPHONE LITERATURE

The recent trends, in both post-colonial and Francophone studies, consist of a move away from the question of empire and imperialism into the newer paradigm of globalization, which is now the critics' primary topic of concern in this area. With new growth areas such as migrations, transnationalism, and diaspora (among others), the immutable centre of the Western colonial empire is actually starting to shift. The discourse that has for too long opposed a hegemonic West to a subdued East is now giving way to a more ambivalent narrative, as spaces, cultures, and identities are in a constant process of becoming.

In "Towards a World Literature in French," signatories simply proclaim the death of Francophone literature because of this very disappearance of the centre which makes this discourse "from the margins" an oxymoron. But when we, as critics, ask who exactly the signatories in question are, from which position they are speaking, and for what ultimate motives, we realize that questions of power cannot so easily be done away with, and that globalization often hides a darker imperialist side than some critics are willing to acknowledge.

In the Anglophone world, theorists such as Homi Bhabha and Stuart Hall increasingly argue, and this long before their French counterparts, against the large place given to the referential colonial past. Indeed, with the concept of hybridity, Bhabha and Hall propose a much-less-historical reading of post-colonialism as they shift the focal point from a colonial experience to the more current situation of permanent contact, wherein a most relevant encounter – according to them – takes place.

It is hoped that this article will contribute toward bridging the linguistic barrier between French and English by reinforcing the validity of Francophone literary criticism within the larger realm of post-colonial studies in which English constitutes the dominant language. In other words, this chapter will help alleviate what is commonly referred to as the Anglophone "bias" of post-colonial studies by creating a dialogue between the two linguistic areas, an enterprise that will not only shine more light on Francophone literature but will also contribute in dispelling Harish Trivedi's fear that "the post-colonial has ears only for the English" (qtd. in Forsdick and Murphy 7). By using methods from Comparative Literature in this post-colonial study of African literatures in French and English, I support the argument that, in order to understand the writing and cultures of former colonies, we need to acknowledge and value the presence (obvious or not) of languages beyond English and French. I see the future of Comparative Literature pushing post-colonial research into comparative studies among the African literatures and also those of the Caribbean, India, and other former colonies.

## NOTES

1 This book, winner of the Goncourt Prize in 1921, is often considered the pioneer novel of Francophone literature. René Maran, it should be emphasized, was not from Africa. He was originally from Martinique, but he wrote and published *Batouala* while working for the colonial service in French Equatorial Africa.
2 Case in point, Michel Le Bris, reacting to *Orientalism*, one of the foundational works of post-colonial studies, qualifies the concept as "l'hystérisation de toute pensée, le refus de toute complexité, de toute nuance" (the hystericization of all thoughts, the refusal of any complexity or nuance) (qtd. in Forsdick and Murphy 8).

3 According to *The Ethnologue*, an average of 36 languages, next to the official French, are spoken in Senegal alone; 505 languages in Nigeria; and some 19 languages in Zimbabwe.
4 For more information on Commonwealth Literature, see Ken Goodwin's article entitled "Studying Commonwealth Literature," published in 1992.
5 For more information on what registers of English were taught to whom and on what basis (in Nigeria specifically), see Ayorinde Dada's "The New Language Policy in Nigeria: Its Problems and Its Chances of Success."
6 For more information, see Richard Serrano's *Against the Postcolonial: Francophone Writers at the End of the French Empire*, or the interview with Jean-Marc Moura entitled "Postcolonial Criticism: A Study of Specificities."

## BIBLIOGRAPHY

Adichie, Chimanda Ngozi. *Half of a Yellow Sun*. New York: Knopf, 2006.
Ager, Denis. *"Francophonie" in the 1900s: Problems and Opportunities*. Clevedon: Multilingual Matters, 1996.
– *Identity, Insecurity, and Image: France and Language*. Philadelphia: Multilingual Matters, 1999.
Ba, Mariama. *Une si longue lettre*. Dakar: Les Nouvelles Editions Africaines, 2006.
Beyala, Calixthe. *Tu t'appelleras Tanga*. Paris: Éditions J'ai lu, 2001.
Bobda, Augustin Simo. "Linguistic Apartheid: English Language Policy in Africa." *English Today* 20, no. 1 (January 2004): 19–26. (Accessed 12 Jan. 2009).
Bugul, Ken. *Le Baobab Fou*. Dakar: Nouvelles Éditions Africaines, 1982.
Chamoiseau, Patrick. *Écrire en pays dominé*. Paris: Gallimard, 1997.
Chinweizu, Onwuchekwa Jemie, and Ihechukwu Madubuike. *Toward the Decolonization of African Literature*. Washington, DC: Howard University Press, 1983.
Christophersen, Paul. *Second Language Learning: Myth and Reality*. Harmondsworth, UK: Penguin Education, 1973.
Dada, Ayorinde. "The New Language Policy in Nigeria: Its Problems and Its Chances of Success." In *Language of Inequality*, edited by Nessa Wolfson and Joan Manes, 285–96. New York: Mouton, 1985. Googlebooks. (Accessed 26 Feb. 2009).
Dangarembga, Tistsi. *Nervous Conditions*. London: The Women's Press Ltd, 1988.
Diome, Fatou. *Le Ventre de l'Atlantique*. Paris: Éditions Anne Carrière, 2004.
Etiemble, René. *Parlez-vous franglais*. Paris: Gallimard, 1973.

Fanon, Frantz. *Black Skin, White Masks*. Paris: Éditions du Seuil, 1952.
Forsdick, Charles, and David Murphy, eds. *Francophone Postcolonial Studies: A Critical Introduction*. London: Arnold, 2003.
Gladstone, J.R. "Language and Culture." *ELT Journal* 23, no. 2 (1969): 114–17. www.eltjoxfordjournals.com (accessed 21 Nov. 2009).
Goodwin, Kevin. "Studying Commonwealth Literature." *College Literature* 19/20, no. 3/1, Teaching Postcolonial and Commonwealth Literatures (Oct. 1992–Feb. 1993): 142–51. Jstor. (Accessed 15 Sept. 2012).
Hargreaves, Alec G., and Jean-Marc Moura. "Editorial Introduction: Extending the Boundaries of Francophone Postcolonial Studies." *International Journal of Francophone Studies* 10, no. 3 (2007): 307–1.
Heine, Bernd. "Language Policy in Africa." In *Language Policy and Political Development*, edited by Brian Weinstein, 167–84. Norwood, NJ: Ablex Publishing Corporation, 1990.
Hountondji, Paulin. *Africa and the Problem of Its Identity*. New York: P. Lang, 1985.
Ilboudo, Monique. *Le mal de peau*. Paris: Le Serpent à plumes, 2001.
Idowu, Oludare. "Assimilation in 19th-Century Senegal." *Cahiers d'Études Africaines* 9, no. 34 (1969): 194–218. Jstor. (Accessed 23 Mar. 2009).
Jack, Belinda. *Francophone Literatures: An Introductory Survey*. Oxford: Oxford University Press, 1996.
Kachru, Braj. *The Alchemy of English: The Spread, Functions, and Models of Non-native Englishes*. Toronto: Pergamon Institute of English, 1986.
Le Bris, Michel, Jean Rouaud, et al. *Pour une littérature-monde*. Paris: Gallimard, 2007.
Lewis, M. Paul, ed. *Ethnologue: Languages of the World*. Sixteenth edition. Dallas, TX: SIL International, 2009. Online version: http://www.ethnologue.com
Lugard, Frederick. *The Dual Mandate in British Tropical Africa*. Edinburgh: William Blackwood and Sons, 1922.
Maran, René. *Batouala*. London: Heinemann, 1973.
Merand, Patrick. *La vie quotidienne en Afrique noire: A travers la littérature*. Paris: L'harmattan, 1977.
Michelman, Frederic. "French and British Colonial Language Policies: A Comparative View of Their Impact on African Literature." *Research in African Literatures* 26, no. 4 (Winter 1995): 216–25. Jstor. (Accessed 16 Jan. 2010).
Moumouni, Abdou. *L'Éducation en Afrique*. Paris: Maspero, 1964.
Moura, Jean-Marc. "La critique postcoloniale: étude des spécificités – Interview." www.afribd.com (accessed 21 Nov. 2010).

Mouralis, Bernard. "L'université a-t-elle peur de la littérature négro-africaine d'expression française." *Recherche, Pedagogie, Culture* 57 (April/May/June 1982): 19–31.

Parker, Gabrielle. "'Francophonie' et 'universalité': Evolution of Two Notions Conjoined." In *Francophone Postcolonial Studies: A Critical Introduction*, edited by Charles Forsdick and David Murphy, 91–101. London: Arnold, 2003.

Said, Edward W. *Orientalism*. New York: Pantheon Books, 1978.

Sartre, Jean Paul. *Orphée noir*. Paris: Présence Africaine, 1963.

Serrano, Richard. *Against the Postcolonial: "Francophone" Writers at the End of the French Empire*. Lanham, MD: Lexington Books, 2005.

Senghor, Léopold S. *Éthiopiques: poèmes*. Dakar: Nouvelles Editions Africaines, 1974.

– *Négritude et Humanisme*. Paris: Editions du Seuil, 1964.

Senghor, L.S. " Les Leçons de Leo Frobenius. " In *Leo Frobenius 1873/1973: Une Anthologie*, edited by Eike Haberland, vii. Wiesbaden: Franz Steiner Verlang, 1973.

Tutuola, Amos. *The Palm-Wine Drinkard and His Dead Palm-Wine Tapster in the Deads' Town*. London: Faber and Faber, 1952.

Wali, Obiajunwa. "The Dead End of African Literature." *Transition* 75, no. 76 (1997): 330–5. Jstor. (Accessed 16 Jan. 2010).

Wa Thiong'o, Ngũgi. *Devil on the Cross*. Trans. from the Gĩkũyũ by the author. London: Heinemann, 1982.

– *Decolonizing the Mind: The Politics of Language in African Literature*. London: Heinemann, 1986.

# "What a Caring Act": Geographies of Care and the Posthuman in Canadian Dystopian Fiction

*Dominique Hétu*

Margaret Atwood's novel *The Year of the Flood* and Karoline Georges's novel *Sous béton* dramatize post-apocalyptic worlds in which ordinary and extraordinary encounters, as well as shared living spaces with non-human others, disrupt human life. Informed by the ethics of care and critical posthumanism, a comparative analysis of both texts sheds light on their depictions of alternative configurations for intersubjective relationships. On the one hand, everyday, subtle caring gestures participate in the characters' survival strategies as they try to find meaning in unexpected relationships and solidarity. On the other, extraordinary actions and experiences impact their capacity for caregiving and self-care, disrupting anthropocentric configurations of subjectivity. The following analysis addresses how critical discourses on care and the posthuman can contribute to literary analysis, and how literature also informs, if not complicates, these two paradigms by imagining and anticipating responses to crises that extend caring capacities to nonhuman beings.

The fictional work of Margaret Atwood has shown concern with several ethical and environmental issues, as well as with the patriarchal treatment of women. Amelia DeFalco suggests, for instance, that a central problem often addressed in Atwood's writing is how "ethical commitment can prove to be a high-wire act, a struggle to balance distance and presence, evaluation and interaction, abstraction and action, the needs of others and the self" ("Moral Obligation" 236). Drawing on DeFalco, I want to suggest that Atwood's second novel of her latest trilogy,[1] *The Year of the Flood*, dramatizes such tensions and conflicts. More precisely, the book engages with an ethic of posthuman care. It addresses the burden of individual responsibility with the demands of distant others in extreme social and environmental conditions. It also plays with the malleability of memory to fight isolation and despair, and, more importantly, it imagines some of the struggles that come with caring and with needing care when the frontiers between human, nonhuman, and posthuman become messy. For instance, the text dramatizes the tensions involved in caring interactions between humans and other living creatures. It uses two female protagonists, Toby and Ren, who, by recalling past events to better cope with the present, make use of strategies of resistance that foster solidarity, healing, and an easier adaptation to technoscientific excesses.

Multidisciplinary artist Karoline Georges's short novel *Sous béton*[2] is also set in a post-apocalyptic, dystopian world. Caged in a mile-wide and mile-high bunker called "l'Édifice" (the Tower) (*UTS* 9) and mostly made of a material called "Béton Total" (Total Concrete) (*UTS* 13) a nameless child comes of age in dehumanizing conditions. Living in an oppressive environment that reduces human beings to an emotionless, mechanical working force, the young protagonist develops strategies to escape physical and psychological abuse and to cope with isolation. Written in a desensitized language that participates in the dehumanization of life in the text, Georges's depiction of the child's meaningless life touches upon the dark side of technoscientific progress. The text also maintains some degree of hope by suggesting a new disembodied form and force of life for the child. To better understand this negotiation, care ethics is a useful tool for interpreting the confrontation between careless and caring interrelations. In a language of care ethics, Georges's text complicates the modern idea of the unity of the self, of its supposed self-sufficient independence. It does so by dramatizing the protagonist's physical mutability, not as an expression of self-destructive behaviour, but rather as a form of responsibility for a human subject and a world that demands reinvention.

While the settings, contexts, and styles vary, both novels seem to suggest, through their representations of interdependent characters, that, in the words of care ethicists Patricia Paperman and Pascale Molinier, "la relation est l'unité appropriée" (the relationship is the proper unit) (16; translation mine). Paperman and Molinier, like most care ethicists and theorists, argue that this relationship of interdependence, marked by vulnerability and reciprocity, is fundamental to the development of a sense of being-in-the-world, especially in situations of struggle, where the underprivileged are often invisible and treated with indifference. The following comparative analysis relies on this language, and on the central arguments of care ethicists like Paperman and Molinier, to better understand the problematic relational processes at play in the two novels, in which the characters are often neglected, dehumanized, and silenced. Both texts use narrative and textual strategies that, despite their differences and despite a dystopian context that does not leave much space for hope, illustrate how "the relationship between us is no less important than universal rules" (Held 99). As both novels also show, this kind of relationship, based on attention to detail, to what is often left unseen, allows expressions of solidarity, healing, and survival in unexpected places and from unexpected others. Also, the two novels use haunting, non-living objects, and living spaces in the protagonists' negotiation with, and at times reconciliation processes with, family and community. These negotiations and socio-spatial interactions show how care operates, not only in human relationships but also in interactions with the non-human.

## BRIDGING CARE AND POSTHUMAN ETHICS

Most of the work in care ethics has focused on human relationality and has developed in accordance with Joan Tronto's definition of care as "a species activity that includes everything that we do to maintain, continue and repair our 'world' so that we can live in it as well as possible" (103). But second-wave care ethicists, such as Sandra Laugier, Catherine Larrère, and Sherilyn MacGregor, have argued that care ethics also concerns environmental, animal, and bioethical issues. Their work shares points of tension with posthuman discourse, as they each work to "destabilize the dominant biopolitical order" (103) by bringing to attention new ways of inhabiting the world "away from species-based anthropocentrism" (Ciobanu 160). Both care ethics and critical posthumanism address the need for "a de-centring of 'Man,' the former measure of all things," or, in the words of care ethicist Nel Noddings, they question why "the male model still establishes the dominant norm" (Braidotti, *Posthuman* 2; Noddings 266). In addition to an unsettling of traditional anthropocentric world views, what characterizes the posthuman paradigm is an appeal to technology and scientific progress as sources of enhancement and compensation: robots, monsters, hybrid human constructs, and virtualities are used to challenge the limits of the human body. Critical theorists of the posthuman usually credit Donna Haraway and Katherine Hayles as being the first to "critically embrac[e] the ambiguous potential that 'becoming posthuman' might bring, both liberating and regressive" (Herbrechter). Other theorists such as Cary Wolfe, Karen Barad, and Sheryl Vint are also critical of the posthuman, and question the risks of repeating oppressive patterns that favour mind over body through technological and scientific enhancement. Hence the term "critical posthumanism" serves to challenge different approaches to the posthuman and raises question about the many facets of this projected state of humanity.

These two research fields are well established critically and theoretically in the Western humanities, and recent Canadian and Québécois critical work shows there is a continuing interest in both domains.[3] Also, a growing number of literary scholars are exploring issues at the intersection of the ethics of care and literature,[4] and they provide additional interdisciplinary knowledge for comparative literature. Relying on DeFalco's remarks about the potential of literature for theorizing care, I suggest that both domains, because of their shared "resistance to abstraction" and emphasis on relationality, benefit from "narrative fiction as an ideal form for the study of care and the posthuman ... in their representation of particular scenarios of dependence, responsibility, compassion and care" ("Caretakers" 1).

Indeed, the connections between care, posthumanism, and literature go beyond what moral philosophers such as Martha Nussbaum have suggested: literature is not merely a source of examples to be used by moral philosophy to validate theory (DeFalco, "Moral Obligation" 243). Despite rejecting care ethics for a liberal moral approach (Held 94), Nussbaum remarks that literature contributes to moral philosophy and moral life "by inviting the reader to perform ethically significant acts of perception and attention, acts that are themselves part of a well-lived ethical life" (10). She adds that "the text in this way does not simply represent ethical deliberation, it incites it; and the reader's acts are valuable sorts of moral activity" (Nussbaum 10, 16). Drawing on Nussbaum's argument that literature contributes to the understanding of ethical matters, and departing from the belief that fiction only serves to provide examples for moral theory, I agree with DeFalco that literature deepens and complicates critical theory. It dramatizes and renders visible the intricacies of ethical responsibility, creating an opportunity to raise the readers' awareness of the "desirable and debilitating" aspects of care ("Moral Obligation" 243). Therefore, I am not suggesting that *The Year of the Flood* and *Sous béton* exemplify or mirror care ethics and posthuman discourse. Rather, they raise awareness of other living possibilities, of imaginary lives that thrive because of caring gestures and attitudes in contexts that demand "the possibility of reconstituting humanity apart from the dominant male order" (Ciobanu 157). Also, in both novels, the characters' accountability and requirements for hospitality are affected by living spaces and interdependent relationships that make a place for new ways of inhabiting the world. The fictional texts provide access to a posthuman ethic of responsibility and spatial politics centred on care-related processes. The goal is therefore not to argue for an all-encompassing model of posthuman care ethics in literary analysis. Instead, reading the fictional intersubjectivities and interrelationships' "turbulent processes" brings to attention alternative, more caring, and careful states of being (Murdoch 3, 16).

Besides, in the novels, geographies of care symbolize a preoccupation with the self and others articulated through living spaces. The protagonists engage, carefully, with the world, and their unique experiences of that world lead to alternative spatial practices and better self-care. The characters' attempt to resist traditional and often oppressive domestic roles, and their geographies of care expose how the search for a sense of belonging is found outside the traditional home space and with unexpected figures. Land- and caring-scapes work together in the texts and unveil another facet of relationality that operates in a fluid, shifting intersubjective system of caring encounters. This interplay works between the characters' need to escape their home space, their longing for a feeling of belonging, and their caring gestures toward building an alternative "home" in unfamiliar settings. Reading geographies of care thus highlights a rethinking of the shared space of domesticity and proximity in the two texts. In other words, understanding spatial imagery with an ethics of care "offers a more flexible and less deterministic view of caring and space" (Phillips 118). Using care ethics and critical posthumanism together sheds light on how fictional environments and relationships "challenge the hegemonic notion of individuals as isolated, atomistic entities" and ideas of intersubjectivity and interdependency as a solely interspecies process (Massey 5). And reading "geographies of care" in these literary texts allows initiation of a conversation about "posthuman care." More precisely, the two books make clear the "difficulty of responding to another's needs" (7) and challenge, rather than maintain, the dichotomies of human/non-human and life/death.

The notion of "posthuman care" might seem euphemistic, because care ethics is inscribed in social, cultural, and theoretical approaches that seek to disrupt humanist, male-oriented Western thought based on individualism, anthropocentrism, and patriarchy. However, the term "posthuman care" proposed here serves to differentiate a conceptualization of care from that of other researchers who focus on work-related and material forms of care, such as care work and "para-ordinary" care (DeFalco). This comparative analysis thus centres on care ethics' fundamental disruption of "human exceptionalism" (LaGrandeur), which connects to the umbrella term of the posthuman. In other words, "care" is used in its widest definition, as an abstract and polysemous notion, to read the different moral and spatial trajectories of posthuman relationality. I also use critical posthumanism to engage creatively with the representations of caring and distrustful relationships between human and non-human figures.

I borrow and adapt the figuration of "geographies of care" from emotional geography, a branch of human and social geography interested in the interconnections between emotions and space that conceptualizes both the spatial experience and the methods of geographical analysis as situated ensembles of socio-ethical and emotional, even therapeutic, practices. Geographies of care procure, maintain, and reinforce healing possibilities in the texts. Reading geographies of care uncovers "hidden emotional [and ethical] experiences" (Davidson, Bondi, and Smith 8) and illustrates how "environment might ameliorate or exacerbate troubling emotions" (9). With this methodology, I wish to shed light on the impact of care practices on different and overlapping systems of oppression and domination. The selected texts share similarities in their treatment of domesticity, scientific and medical progress, and patriarchy, and in their dramatization of "the self as being immersed in a network of relationship with others" (Benhabib 403), others that are human, non-human, and at times non-living things. To better understand the geo-emotional processes that characterize these networks of relationships, I use second and third waves of care ethics and subtopics of emotional geography. The latter has developed a language of care ethics with field-specific concerns about relationality, and echoes other related fields in geography that use care-related notions, such as emotions and healing, namely medical and health geography. I configure the novels' interdependent interactions as "geographies of care" to stress the relational aspect of the characters' lived experiences in chaotic and dangerous spaces and to bring to attention the caring gestures and attitudes that inform these experiences.

Also, the field of human geography, through the subtopics of emotional and feminist geography, has exposed how space is made of contextualized positionalities, and that it is "a situational marker" (Friedman 23). Emotional geography, for instance,

> is composed of ways of considering how emotions, along with linked modalities such as feeling, mood or affect, are constitutive elements within the ongoing composition of space-time, and exploring how learning to respond to and intervene in such

modalities could or perhaps should disrupt human geography's methodological and theoretical practices. (Gregory et al. 188–9)

It is also important to note that

> emotional geography responds, on the one hand, to the claim that emotions are an intractable aspect of life and thus potentially a constitutive part of all geographies (Anderson and Smith, 2001) and, on the other, to the recognition that emotions have long been manipulated and modulated as a constitutive part of various forms of power. (Gregory et al. 188)

Those "forms of power" are marked by different positionalities, such as "class, race, gender, ethnicity, religion, national origin," and they "function relationally as sites of privilege and exclusion" (Friedman 23). Bridging emotional and feminist geography, Kay Anderson and Susan Smith write that

> [e]motions are an intensely political issue, and a highly gendered one too. The gendered basis of knowledge production is probably a key reason why the emotions have been banished from social science and most other critical commentary for so long. This marginalization of emotion has been part of a gender politics of research in which detachment, objectivity and rationality have been valued, and implicitly masculinized, while engagement, subjectivity, passion and desire have been devalued, and frequently feminized. (2–3)

Accordingly, emotional geography shares common ground with care ethics. They are both concerned with gender issues, values, and feelings. They also share a commitment to "the relationality of emotions" and "an assumption that emotions are not contained by, or properties of an individual mind" (Gregory et al. 189).

Drawing on Gregory et al.'s definition of emotional geography in *The Dictionary of Human Geography*, I suggest that both this sub-discipline and care ethics

> perform a sensibility that attends to the ebb and flow of everyday life. First, and most prominently, there is the careful attention in feminist geographies to the silencing or repressing of differential, often gendered, emotional experience and the subsequent attempts

to reclaim and give voice to emotional experiences. Second, attention is paid [...] to the emergence [...] of emotions from within more or less unwilled assemblages that gather together human and non-human bodies. (189)

There is a language of care in this definition, as the text refers to "careful attention" and mentions that "attention is paid" to differentiated experiences and power forces that limit the expression of emotional experience.

The presence of a language of care further stresses the interconnections between the two disciplines, from which I borrow theoretical material to better read the geographies of care in the novels. It is also important to note that emotional geographers Anderson and Smith acknowledge the role of the arts in emotional configurations. They remark that the traditional rationalist paradigm has tended to evacuate emotions from the public and social spheres, whereas access to emotions "is gained through settings where the emotional is routinely heightened, for example in musical performance, film and theatre, spaces of mourning and so on" (3). Therefore, emotional geography helps to bridge a gap between care ethics and literature, as the stories make use of spatial imagery to dramatize relational proximity. The two texts address different forms of struggle that blur boundaries between public and private, as well as between human and non-human life, using textual and narrative strategies that bind the characters to one another and that emphasize a co-constitutive intersubjectivity and relationality.

The geo-emotional processes that the texts dramatize also shed light on the survival strategies developed by the characters to recover from abusive, harmful caregiving. Drawing on Astrida Neimanis's critical discussion of the term "concept" in *Bodies of Water: Posthuman Feminist Phenomenology*, I suggest that geographies of care are a figuration, an "embodied concept" rooted in a posthuman feminist genealogy. Following Donna Haraway, Neimanis theorizes "figurations as 'living maps' that acknowledge 'concretely situated historical positions'" (8). She adds that

> [f]igurations are keys or imagining and living otherwise, but unlike a concept unfettered by the world we actually live in or as, figurations are importantly grounded in our material reality (I have never been entirely convinced by theory that frames anything as wholly "immaterial" ... ) I like the idea that our best concepts are already here, semi-formed and literally at our fingertips, awaiting activation. (8)

Then, quoting Braidotti, she adds that "figurations can also be a mode of feminist protest: a 'literal expression' of those parts of us that the 'phallogocentric regime' has 'declared off-limits' and 'does not want us to become'" (8). Geographies of care, along with posthuman care, resonate with this "feminist impetus" (8) and, like Neimanis's bodies of water, they are "not arbitrary, but arise in response to a particular contemporary question or problem" (8). My inquiry is rooted in the resurgence of the theme of vulnerability (Ferrarese 132) and an ethical and political "rethinking [of] bodily matters beyond a humanist imagination" (Neimanis 9). Such a configuration of geographies of care is useful for reading Atwood's and Georges's depictions of vulnerable lives, because they raise questions about "the political ramifications of gendered [and human] obligations to care" (DeFalco, *Imagining Care* 15). Subsequently, this figuration of posthuman care sheds light on the potential of thinking beyond interhuman relationality. Neither "conceptual fantasy nor metaphor," geographies of care and posthuman care question differently the ethical, political, and intersubjective vulnerabilities that characterize the human experience of being in the world. Both terms inform, in the two novels, the "geography of the relations through which the identity ... is established and reproduced" (Massey 6). They also provide material with which to critically approach how the novels imagine a "corporeal relational ethics *that begins to extend beyond the individual human*" (Neimanis 11; emphasis in the original).

## GEO-EMOTIONAL VULNERABILITIES IN *THE YEAR OF THE FLOOD*

*The Year of the Flood* alternates between Ren's first-person narrative and Toby's story, told by a third-person omniscient narrator. The two voices recall a pre-pandemic world in rich and disturbing detail. They both hold on to the words of Adam One, leader of their environmentalist, biosphere-friendly group called God's Gardeners, as well as to their need for creating a more liveable and hospitable world: "For all the works of Man will be as words written on water" (Atwood 312). Suffering and solitude characterize Toby and Ren's daily lives, and it is their encounters with one another and with the Gardeners that make place for solidarity and attachments. Their interactions also draw attention to the paradoxical, ambivalent space of caring for self and others, between "the selfishness and sacrifice that can arise within the praxis of care" (DeFalco, "Moral Obligation" 236).

Ren and Toby's interdependent stories are told separately through seventy-seven short chapters, some that are flashbacks and some that are narrated in the present, stressing their distance and their proximity following a Waterless Flood that caused the death of most living creatures, both human and non-human. This Waterless Flood forces the remaining inhabitants, organized in hierarchical groups, such as the Gardeners, to cope with their past and with an uncertain future. They do so by negotiating a new socio-spatial relationship between human and non-human, forcing interactions with hybrid animals and eventually with the Crakers, an "improved" version of the human created by Crake, who is also the person responsible for the Flood.

Atwood complicates the moral lesson that humans must treat other living creatures equally and respectfully, as well as protect the environment. In a post-apocalyptic context that introduces new forms of life and disrupted social boundaries and conventions, Atwood's novel places into dialogue and confronts multiple intersubjectivities of the oppressed that are organized socially, in classes, as well as spatially, in partially safe and dangerous areas. The text also uses different forms of care, such as medicine and alternative health care, gendered tasks, and moral gestures, such as solidarity, hospitality, and healing. On the one hand, the text illustrates the social pervasiveness of gendered and class-related roles and caretaking jobs. On the other, the text exposes spaces of solidarity that emerge in the particularity and context of each relationship, and in the wake of new parameters for life development and sustenance. The geographies of posthuman care that characterize Toby and Ren's experiences in this dystopian world expose the modalities at play between constraining and rigid dominant structures of oppression and the transformative potential of a renewed attention to non-human forms of life.

I also want to stress that they expose how the alternative living spaces are inscribed in a perspective of care. Mostly told in flashbacks of Toby's and Ren's life, the novel is built on the singularity, rather than on the individuality, of both characters. This singularity stresses the characters' interdependent relationships as they experience tragedy and healing while adjusting to the new world order. What stands out, as Toby and Ren try to cope with different forms of violence, is how a language of care illuminates a relational proximity that fosters solidarity and care between the protagonists. This language also exposes the difficulty of generating new responses to vulnerability and to oppressive social institutions and structures that use science and technology to further control human and non-human beings. Drawing on Susan Dodds's theory of the "relationship between situational vulnerability and dependency" (190), I read Toby and Ren's own caring gestures and attitudes of care as responses to their shared vulnerable status as dispossessed women. They are also forms of response to the need for alternative spaces of hospitality and healing.

But I also consider how their respective dysfunctional social environments, which they at times share, exacerbate their sense of isolation and their vulnerability. This context decreases their capacity to provide care and to cope with oppression. Indeed, the novel represents two active women who occupy significant places in their community and who manage to find and participate in "supportive networks [that] alleviate the isolation and dependency" (187). It also carefully recognizes, in the narrative structure, the severe structural and systemic interactions that prevent the protagonists from fully taking charge of their lives. These structures limit the subjects' capacity to provide care for others and themselves. For instance, before being a Gardener, Toby worked in a SecretBurger, where she was abused and exploited by a character named Blanco. Rescued by the Gardeners, given a place in which to heal, Toby is initially both grateful and suspicious of the group, questioning their motives and keeping a distance: "She was accepting Gardeners' hospitality, and under false pretenses at that – she wasn't really a convert" (Atwood 45).

Paradoxically, Toby eventually becomes the Gardeners' healer, but keeps struggling to show her emotions and to take expressions of care. She is refusing to show vulnerability and to accept her need for others – her dependency – two values that, to borrow the words of Genevieve Lloyd, have been traditionally and historically qualified as weaknesses and obstacles to autonomy under rationalistic moral imperatives (3). One of those instances involves Blanco, whose extreme patriarchal violence and misogyny typify Atwood's concern with the historical disposability of women and with male entitlement, attacking Toby. The narrator expresses Toby's reluctance to receive help from others, even in situations of extreme pain and danger: "Toby feels bludgeoned – that was brutal, it was horrifying – but she can't show her feelings to Ren" (Atwood 380). Spaces of solidarity are not easy to build between female characters who struggle to come together and to liberate themselves from patriarchal expectations that place women as caregivers without considering their need for care. Refusing to commit fully to a relationship, afraid of vulnerability, Toby accumulates emotional distress and the need for care while she takes on greater responsibility as the Gardeners' healer. The asymmetrical relationship between Toby and her community leads to different conflicts that care practices and gestures partially solve, exposing how care is a response to a vulnerability that might lead to new responses to individual and social crises (Dodds 187). The dystopian novel thus makes clear the moral difficulties that come with providing care when one is "exposed to increased situational vulnerability" (193).

*The Year of the Flood* presents how caring relationships are not and should not be limited to exchanges between humans. The protagonists' vulnerability operates in the geographies of care. It is illustrated by their need for survival strategies, including the healing relationships with bees and plants, emotional trajectories between Toby's parents' house and the bunker, her becoming a teacher and a healer as a Gardener, and thus her participation in building and preserving caregiving and care-receiving spaces. These geo-emotional processes create more hospitable living spaces that maintain hope and alternative forms of solidarity.

After the Waterless Flood, isolated from the Gardeners and unsure if there are other survivors, Toby lives on her own for several years in the Spa where she worked. She eventually becomes paranoid, hallucinates voices, and develops a very close relationship with objects and animals surrounding the area. Toby ends up shooting at Ren – who is already in bad shape – and at her friends when they get to the Spa to see if she is still there. Realizing it is her long-lost friend, Toby brings her inside the spa and demands that she does not move: "'Stay here,' Toby says unnecessarily: Ren isn't going anywhere" (Atwood 355). This order to Ren is a symbolic demand for care that opens wider their shared space for mutual healing. Albeit straightforward and short, this imperative verb followed by the narrator's comment nevertheless acknowledges the inevitability of, if not the need for, interdependency. Reading with an ethics of care directs our attention to these small gestures that, given visibility in the text, expose the key role of caregiving to maintain good and to foster safety despite the risks.

Also, Toby is a character strongly affected by her interconnections to the non-human. Her father's shotgun, the bees on the roof of the Gardeners' bunker, and the healing materials that the previous healer passed on to her "serve not only to introduce alternatives to normative forms of existence, but also function as fictional engagements with trauma, with experiences of precarity interwoven with the broader framework of male domination and with a dystopian, post-apocalyptic, biopolitical system of power forces" (Hétu, "Of Wonder and Encounter" 160). Also, new types of animals and hybrid creatures also complicate the sovereignty of the human being by representing unique relational processes that do not posit the human as the hero and that stress the importance of caring interspecies encounters. The unusual relationships between Gardeners, hybrid animals, Crakers, and plants transform the characters' sense of belonging and alter their understanding of what it means to be living in the world. Having to provide care in atypical contexts and to negotiate the moral and political tensions between self-care and care for others that are not only human disrupts their living environments as well as their sense of responsibility.

How the novel imagines relationships between living creatures and the ability of human subjects to alter their bodies endorses Rosi Braidotti's claim that standing firm against political, patriarchal, and technoscientific systems of domination requires "dislocations and re-assemblages of intersecting subject positions ... that express strong and affirmative recomposed subjectivities of those who were previously labeled as other" (Braidotti, *Transpositions* 132–3). In a similar manner, but not in posthuman terms, Stephen David Ross's ethic of inclusion

> pursues an ethical rethinking of natural kinds in memory of the repeated movements in Western thought that sort and order nature's and humanity's kinds into superiors and inferiors, dominants and subordinates, pure and impure, setting some to rule over others, excluding some from the good: men over women, humans over animals. (1)

Drawing on his theorization, I suggest that speculative fiction exacerbates these tensions between harm and care, between "cherishment and sacrifice," by showing distrust toward the dominant ideology of what constitutes the living world. It reminds the reader, through anticipation, that to undertake the good in situations of struggle and chaos "is to face unceasing sacrifice and loss" (1). Toby and Ren, in their reaching out to different others and in their singular, yet intersubjective, experiences, symbolize both the limits of care and its potential for support and healing, despite ongoing practices and regulations of exclusion. The novel does not idealize or romanticize caring practices and attitudes: it depicts forms of care that enable growth, healing, solidarity, and that also deprive, as illustrated, for example, by the characters of Blanco and the CorpSeCorps, the protagonists of self-care, of emotional and material comfort. There is certainly an "inescapability of injustice" (Ross 2) and a dark side of care in *The Year of the Flood*. However, that the text uses caring practices and dramatizes responses to suffering as well as to demands of care also shows how the novel rests on an ethic of care. Combined with a posthuman stance, it serves not only to interpret different forms of crisis from a relational understanding of persons but also to decentre a limited anthropocentric, interspecies perspective to a more-than-human collectivity.

The novel fictionalizes forms of posthuman care, as Toby spends a lot of time on the bunker's rooftop, where she cares for bees and plants, reciprocally caring for herself as the insects give her a sense of purpose. Her ritual with the bees is an expression of posthuman care, for her caring for bees, for non-human beings, provides them with healthy living conditions, and this ritual provides her with stability, responsibility, and healing. Toby's body is another important site of struggle. She must heal it several times, as well as modify it with technological suits that provide her with animal features, symbolically blurring further the boundaries between humans and other living creatures. Because those physical changes occur in contexts where Toby and Ren are working in a men's club or attempt to escape dangerous men, Ciobanu argues that Atwood's dystopia exposes the risks of converging animal and women as disposable life if the posthuman perspective is about "replicating the human of its past" (156). In her analysis of the dichotomized representations of male and female characters in Atwood's trilogy, Ciobanu suggests that *The Year of the Flood* "is an affirmation that if the post-Anthropocene (post) human is to resist replicating the hu*man* of its past, it will have to think carefully – and differently – about how to structure the community of the living of which it forms a part" (156). The female human body is, in several instances, represented as a disposable product. Toby modifies her body so that Blanco won't recognize her when she is forced to leave the Gardeners' bunker. Violent and voluntarily cruel, Blanco symbolizes the ongoing oppression of neoliberal and patriarchal dynamics by exploiting both financially and sexually the disposable bodies of women workers.

Imagining a character such as Blanco, along with the technoscientific progress that seems to cause as much damage as it brings improvement, and the human-made pandemic echoes, it appears, what Vint names "the writing of reverse discourse" (170) in *Bodies of Tomorrow*. This reverse discourse is a tool that helps uncover "social and subjective change" (170). While Vint centres her argument on science-fiction texts, I borrow her notion of "reverse discourse" to argue that Atwood's novel uses narrative strategies to comment on culture and science's participation in the production of identity. It is important to note that Vint does not refer to care ethics in her theory. However, when she writes that "rewriting the self through reverse discourse is only successful in the context of community belief," I am tempted to connect this "belief" to a sense of togetherness and solidarity that echoes values related to the paradigm of care ethics. Vint bridges further the gap between the posthuman and the underlying presence of care ethics in her argument when she concludes that "an effective model of posthumanism must be one of an engaged, social subject, not an isolated individual" (170). Her statement supports the idea that care and posthuman perspectives share similar objectives for the formation of new relational subjectivities. Vint also writes that "the kinds of posthumanism that appear in SF [science fiction] texts function as both potential models for and current critiques of the ways in which technology and culture are producing a new model of human identity" (170). I would suggest that, like science fiction texts, Atwood's dystopia and *Sous béton* do not offer "potential models," but certainly imagine the undesirable effects of technoscientific progress. They also dramatize inhospitable environments, commenting on the present and future possibilities for human life by complicating conventional and traditional ideas of subject positions.

Atwood not only fictionalizes social structures that reproduce patriarchal and neo-liberal hierarchies. She also depicts the male figure mainly as a heroic character who should save animals from an unfair world. It is important to note that the mad scientist, Glenn, who caused the pandemic, is a male character with a God complex. Also known as Crake, he is the co-creator of the Crakers, whose male subjects have bright-blue erections that seem impossible to control, not only celebrating the male organ as the key to world repopulation and salvation but also maintaining the male figure in a posture of domination. The text seems to question the difficulty of deconstructing male privilege and the deeply rooted naturalization of man as the norm, challenging how "technology, like patriarchy, fails to provide workable substitutes" for women (Meyers 47). Toby's extremely violent episode of financial and sexual exploitation with Blanco at SecretBurger is another event from the text that warns against deeply rooted historical patterns of patriarchal oppression, possibly problematizing utopian world views of the future and undoubtedly underlining the need for social alternatives.

Issues of environmentalism and feminism are woven together in the story. The novel reproduces sex-gendered oppression through the hierarchical social categories of Adams and Eves, Blanco's sexual and financial exploitation of women, and the Crakers' uncontrollable erections, to name just a few. These elements operate in tension with the biosphere-friendly behaviours of the Gardeners and alternative living choices. While the Gardeners push for an eco-friendly, vegetarian lifestyle, the human dynamics struggle to reflect that "loving care for all creatures." As Virgina Held suggests, "the ethics of care envision caring not as a practice under male domination, but as it should be practiced in post-patriarchal society, of which we do not have yet have traditions or wide experience" (19). Both novels, albeit very differently, confront those issues, "evoking ethical quandaries in which characters feel compelled to choose between the self and the other" (DeFalco, "Moral Obligation" 243).

## RETHINKING SPACES OF RESPONSIVENESS IN *SOUS BÉTON*

*Sous béton* also uses textual strategies that emphasize the continuum between the child's immobility and mobility, first describing his existence in the immense building as passive and stagnant, with variants of the word "immobilité" being used repeatedly. Other characters are also described as motionless. For instance, the child says that "Avant, j'avais été longtemps immobilisé sur mon siège, mais toujours occupé à ne pas bouger" (Before, I'd often been immobilized on my seat, always busying myself with not moving) (133; *UTS* 107), and that he is caught between his two parents, "entre le père et la mère, en silence, sans trop bouger, que la mâchoire quelques secondes" (Between the father and the mother, in silence, without moving, only my jaw a few seconds at a time to swallow nutrients) (87; *UTS* 67). He adds: "Le père et la mère étaient bel et bien des adultes. Mais le père s'abrutissait de plus en plus. Et la mère pourrissait au même rythme" (The father and the mother were adults. But the father was numbing himself more and more. And the mother rotted at the same rhythm) (97; *UTS* 76). The text makes clear the characters' paralysis. The child explains his daily routine, which consists of learning and faking sleep: "Je patientais toute la journée assis sur mon drap gris, tête enserrée dans le cubicule d'apprentissage, immobilisé entre les murs de béton sans fenêtre aucune et le sifflement du filtre à oxygène. Le reste du temps, je cumulais exactement deux autres occupations: dormir, ou feindre le sommeil" (I waited all day, sitting on my grey sheet, my head tucked snugly into the learning box, immobile between the concrete walls without windows and the whistling of the oxygen filter. The rest of the time, I did exactly two other things: I slept, or pretended to sleep) (25; *UTS* 19), and of accepting, passively and quietly, the father's violence: "Il fallait accepter, passif, les humeurs ou les silences. Il ne fallait pas manifester souffrance après punition ... Alors j'ai ravalé larmes, arguments et gémissements, malgré l'état de tension qui grandissait en moi. Nul autre choix que l'immobilité. Réaction béton" (You had to passively accept his moods or silences. You could never show suffering after punishment, no matter the depth of the wound. I swallowed my tears, arguments, and moaning, despite the tension that grew in me. There was no choice but immobility. React like concrete) (110; *UTS* 87). This "état de tension" marks the transformation of the child. When he realizes that the building seems to contain other singularities that acknowledge his presence, he finds the strength to leave and to resist the alienated life he is expected to live: "Mais plutôt que de me protéger, j'ai alors affirmé avec une certitude qu'on ne me connaissait pas: Je ne peux pas faire comme vous. Ça n'a aucun sens. Vous êtes déjà le pire. Vous êtes déjà la mort" (But instead of protecting myself, I declaimed with newfound certainty: I don't want to do as you do. It makes no sense. You are the worst possibility. You are already dead) (119; *UTS* 97).

His desire to act differently, to defy death, is manifested in this imaginary breach in the wall of "Béton Total," in his capacity to question his existence and to search for new forms of life. His parents try to make him understand that the only thing to do is to accept their situation and listen to instructions, but he wonders what death means in this lifeless existence and rejects his parents' submissive attitude. Thinking back on their advice, he says:

> J'aurais pu capituler, comme toujours, comme on me l'avait enseigné, et me concentrer sur le va-et-vient au seuil de l'Édifice, sur la venue du prochain fou ... Un noeud en moi, qui s'était densifié par la répétition aliénante du même ... J'étais beaucoup trop grand malgré ma petitesse, beaucoup trop présent. Je ne voulais plus être là, du tout. Mais il n'y avait nulle part où aller, je savais bien. (119–20)
>
> [I could have given up, as I always had, as I'd been taught, and instead concentrated on the comings and goings at the bottom of the Tower, on the next insane person wandering through the screen ... A knot in me that had become denser through the alienating repetition of sameness ... I was already too big despite my smallness, too present. I no longer wanted to be *there*, at all. But there was nowhere to go, I knew that well.] (*UTS* 97–8)

This knot that he feels inside him sparks a sense of wonder at the new possibility before him, through this breach that will eventually allow him to disincarnate and to merge with the concrete building.

In an interview about *Sous béton* in *Le Devoir*, Georges comments on her protagonist's disembodying process. She describes it as a way to surmount pain and as a strategy to imagine life beyond the human: "J'ai toujours été fascinée par la transcendance, par cette idée que l'être humain est transition, que le corps est embryonnaire. L'idée ... c'est d'atteindre un niveau plus avancé. C'est dégager un corps subtil d'un corps grossier; se libérer pour atteindre une qualité, une finesse" (I've always been fascinated by transcendence, by this idea of the human being as transitional, that the body is embryonic. The idea ... is to reach a higher level. It is about pulling out a subtle body from a rough body; to be free as to obtain quality, finesse) (Lalonde n.p.; translation mine). Georges then shares a possible source of inspiration for this posthuman disembodiment: "j'ai des cicatrices, j'ai vécu des accidents assez graves dans ma vie ... Je sais ce que c'est que la souffrance physique, profondément, et je crois qu'on poursuit dans notre vie des thèmes, un peu comme une forme de résilience" (I have scars, I've had serious accidents in my life ... I know what physical pain is, deeply, and I think we pursue themes in our life, as a form of resilience) (Lalonde n.p.; translation mine). The building might thus be read as a symbol of this body in pain, struggling to adapt to the side-effects of pain and trauma symbolized by a post-apocalyptic environment and enforcing a regime of terror on what Georges names "la conscience," in her efforts to reimagine and rewrite relational proximity and processes of intersubjectivity. That the child cannot find recognition from human others but from the voices of the disembodied others within the building structure suggests a demand for ethical and spatial alternatives illustrated by the transgressive practices of the protagonist who refuses to give in to the "répétition aliénante du même" (the alienating repetition of sameness) (Georges 120; *UTS* 97). The language of care used in the text sheds new light on the post-apocalyptic future. It brings necessary attention to the difficult harmonization between the needs of the self and the needs of others when life is threatened, when all is left seems to be the imagination of new forms of relational beings.

The work of care in the novel demands new configurations for improving the quality of life: caregiving fails more often than it succeeds for the child. However, his caring attitude toward the voices that he hears through the breach, along with his willingness to resist dehumanization like his parents and death like his siblings, lead to his "singularité" (singularity) (*UTS* 49). This intersubjective awakening thrives on a constellation of affects and on his interactions with the non-human others, in a different dimension of relational proximity: "mon oeil s'est ouvert ailleurs" (And my eye opened elsewhere) (151; *UTS* 122). It is thus an expression of care as underlying vulnerability, as an intrinsic quality of being. The text does not only subordinate physical, embodied pain to the emotional struggle of the mind: it reimagines life "along alternative arcs, according to different ethical structures" (Mintz 147). Hence, rather than a confirmation of traditional configurations of dualism that represent subjectivity as separated from the body, the figure of the child can be interpreted as a symbol of a revitalized subjectivity. He finds, in an alternative relationality with non-human matter, a shared and empowered sense of embodied self. The child's desire for a sense of belonging and his careful attention toward the breach lead to a new form of relationality and to a new way of living that assert posthuman care.

Posthuman care might thus be a pivotal point toward theorizing intersubjective bonds with others that are not human. *Sous béton* seems to suggest that, even in the darkest dystopian environment, there is place for possibilities, for promises of a better life, independent of the form it takes. The child refuses to capitulate, to become like his parents, and to abdicate to a lifeless existence. Through the breach come "promises of possible reembodiments" (Braidotti, *Nomadic* 68) that allow the protagonist to reinvent himself and to find an alternative space, despite the confinement and the close controlling of bodies.

The novel illustrates the potential of care to either harm or heal. Under the ethics of care, these problematic gestures are brought to attention by questioning whether the practices of care serve to reproduce naturalized roles or whether they benefit both caregiving and care-receiver. A care ethics framework provides a structure for "keeping a critical eye trained on the marginalizing, denigrating structures of care within a culture that idealizes autonomy and self-reliance" (DeFalco, "Caretakers" 243). For instance, the child and his mother, in *Sous béton*, fail to protect the other siblings from the father's killing hands. The nameless mother, portrayed as weak and depressive, does express a certain guilt for failing to help her child fit into the system. She also fails to protect him from the father's violence. The child is "coincé entre deux êtres programmés" (I was stuck between two beings programmed) (Georges 77; *UTS* 62). The figure of the father dominates at home and pushes the child to seek a sense of safety and belonging elsewhere, outside of his body: "Aucune place pour moi au 804 étage 5969. Aucune place dans mon propre corps" (But there was no room for me at number 804, floor 5969. There was no place in my own body) (120; *UTS* 98). These care-related attitudes and activities are mechanical. Caring gestures respond to basic needs of nutrition and sleep, as well as serve to control the inhabitants of the building. How the authorities provide food, shelter, work, and entertainment are forms of care that endanger human life rather than protect it. These caregiving strategies also affect the emotional caregiving in the family, and participate in their dehumanization process.

The protagonist's process of disembodiment through the breach in the building of "Béton Total" resonates with Katherine Hayles's critical posthumanist perspective, namely what she identifies as one of the blind spots of the scientific discourse on the evolution of the concept of flesh. Suspicious of several posthuman trends that, in her opinion, repeat the liberal paradigm of abstraction rather than celebrate how "human life is embedded in a material world of great complexity," Hayles suggests thinking beyond a "deeply pessimistic" posthuman paradigm (283). She argues that such a model might encourage a fear of breached human boundaries (290) and the continuation of "an imperialist project of subduing nature" (288). Her image of the breach sheds important light on the representation of the breach that appears in the wall of the apartment where the child lives. How the child reacts to this breach, in wonder and with attention, is symbolic of a different "kind of account" that Hayles's posthuman theory of embodiment brings to attention. It "evokes the exhilarating prospect of getting out of some of the old boxes and opening up new ways of thinking about what being human means" (285). Indeed, the child notices, after his "emmuration" (immured presence) (Georges 133; *UTS* 107), a significant change but not a total transformation: "Je n'avais pas vraiment disparu. Au contraire, je sentais battre en moi quelque chose de nouveau. Une puissance qui grandissait" (I hadn't truly disappeared. On the contrary, I felt something new beat in me. A growing power) (134; *UTS* 108).

Also, the novel dramatizes a post-apocalyptic environment in which humans compare to zombies. Authorities secretly feed the inhabitants of the building with the processed dead bodies of the sick and those they do not want to keep inside. This undisclosed anthropophagy contrasts with the child's empowering experience of wonder when finding the breach and becoming aware of his "singularité," suggesting that thinking in posthuman terms might shed light on narrative details that engage hope, survival strategies, and possibly healing processes, despite extreme living conditions:

> To conceptualize the human in these [posthuman] terms is not to imperil human survival but is precisely to enhance it, for the more we understand the flexible, adaptive structures that coordinate our environments and the metaphors that we ourselves are, the better we can fashion images of ourselves that accurately reflect the

complex interplays that ultimately make the entire world one system. (Hayles 290)

While Hayles's discussion addresses literary texts and cybernetics, her critical analysis of the posthuman paradigm is useful for reading *Sous béton* and for decoding the complexity of the child's shared embodiment with "l'Édifice." How she stresses the importance of "adaptive structures" and "metaphors" in the shaping of one's environment echoes my configuration of geographies of care and their posthuman implications.

Indeed, the geographies of care in Georges's text are characterized by problematic caregiving and caretaking practices, violence, and isolation in an apartment described by the narrator with words such as "cellule étroite," "cellule minuscule," and "dortoir." These words evoke coldness, confinement, prison, and the invasion of the workplace in the home. The parents move to their "cellule" to do their task, and the child's brain is plugged in a learning machine that reminds us of propaganda tactics: "Chaque matin, le père s'enfermait dans sa cellule de travail ... La mère disparaissait au même moment dans sa cellule minuscule, également adjacente au salon ... Et je m'isolais alors dans mon dortoir, cerveau enserré dans le distributeur du Savoir" (Each morning, the father locked himself in his small work cell ... The mother disappeared at the same time into a tiny cell, also adjacent to the living room ... Meanwhile, I isolated myself in my dormitory, brain tight in the Knowledge box) (Georges 37; *UTS* 30). It is the child's uncanny relationship with the non-human – as he sees the breach in the wall, manages to escape from this apartment, and develops a caring attentiveness towards this mysteriously welcoming structure – that creates a place for thriving. The child, in the last pages, comments on his merging experience: "J'émerge. Par-delà l'océan du vivant fusionné. Un nouvel étage de l'Édifice déborde de l'astre" (I emerge. Beyond the ocean of life in fusion. A new floor of the Tower flows out of the sun) (183; *UTS* 147). In addition to this significant relationship with the non-living, using the verb "to emerge" suggests a coming into existence, a coming into view that is made possible because of the child's interconnection with the building. It becomes apparent that the child cannot escape on his own, that he is dependent on his environment to find a way out.

The narrative also articulates geographies of violence and dehumanization in the representations of those spatialized relationships exempt of care. But the child's awakening and refusal to become like his parents create a space for a form of posthuman relationality that, within the building, disrupts social conventions and expectations and allows the child's construction of identity within more hospitable configurations. I would add that the geographies of care circumscribe well those complex interplays dramatized in the texts. The language of care as well the constellation of affects that trigger caring gestures participate in the identification of more inclusive structures and strategies. The latter are put in place by subjects whose social positions and situated knowledge tend to be devalued and discarded, but who nevertheless manage to reinvent themselves.

Moreover, reading these imaginary lifeworlds with a perspective of care allows "new kinds of cultural configurations" that expose what Hayles names "the scarce commodity of human attention" (286). I suggest that complicating her theorization of the posthuman with a language of care helps to avoid "reinscribing and thus repeating some of the mistakes of the past" (289). Attention is a central feature of care ethics that serves to highlight gestures and attitudes that would otherwise be invisible because of an often taken-for-grantedness of caregiving and caretaking roles in social interactions. That Hayles uses this word in her discussion supports my hypothesis that the concept of the posthuman provides solid ground for thinking and for reading configurations of human life in terms of care and in terms of justice. It is an attention to the ordinary and to particularities that affirms the importance of embodiment by focusing on the multiplicity of "ways of living as bodies in space" (Grosz 93). It stresses the contextuality of experience rather than it "identif[ies] the experience of a specific group of subjects as the paradigmatic case of the human as such" (Benhabib 406).

In *Sous béton*, the flesh and cement structures seem to merge to make a place for what would otherwise be invisible without this shared mutual attention. The body of the child is the site of multiple affective, caring, careless, and violent gestures that lead to his uncanny emancipation from the apartment into the walls of "l'Édifice." His corporeal transformation expresses a necessity for new models of subjectivity that this text takes to an extreme, while also stressing how "embodiment replaces a body seen as a support system for the mind" (Hayles 289). The child's physicality is not denied: it is revitalized and transgressed into a different embodied experience. Hayles suggests that narrative – especially the literary text – fosters an awareness of the significance of embodiment:

> the literary texts do more than explore the cultural implications of scientific theories and technological artifacts. Embedding ideas and artifacts in the situated specificities of narrative, the literary texts

give these ideas and artifacts a local habitation and a name through discursive formulations whose effects are specific to that textual body. (22)

Hayles argues that the literary text can be "a resistance to disembodiment and abstraction," a textual illustration that "the abstract pattern [of the liberal humanist tradition] can never fully capture the embodied actuality" (22). She also claims that certain posthuman perspectives replicate "traditional ideas and assumptions" (6) by proposing a "disembodied immortality": "Although in many ways the posthuman deconstructs the liberal humanist subject, it thus shares with its predecessors an emphasis on cognition rather than embodiment" (5).

*Sous béton* complicates Hayles's theorization. The novel challenges the understanding of the reader by never clearly establishing in which state the child is when the "singularité" appears. This process of identity trans/formation may be a sign that he is dying, hallucinating voices he wished to hear, meeting welcoming, hospitable others that would make him feel wanted and accepted. Or, it may act as a posthuman shift in the configuration of life and death, stressing the disposability of human beings and their vulnerability in the face of techno-scientific progress and patriarchal domination. The novel confronts the reader with moral, ethical, spatial, and social consequences of problematic uses of technology. It dramatizes, through the figure of the unwanted and vulnerable child, a possible transformation of the world order through his posthuman emancipation. The latter is possible because of strategies of resistance to "l'Édifice" that allow the child to develop an apparently fluid self: "J'ai alors compris que je pouvais maintenant circuler. Autrement" (I understood I could move now. Differently) (139; *UTS* 111). It is when the child can move more freely in and out of the apartment to discover the system of "l'Édifice" and to dwell on his newly found singularity that he finds purpose and comfort.

Georges fictionalizes a disembodied state of being with this character, whose consciousness reaches beyond the traditional configurations of life and death and whose transformative experience, despite careless human relations and emotional deprivation, sheds light on the potentiality of the posthuman framework for new, "non-dualistic understanding of nature-culture interaction" (Braidotti, *Posthuman* 6). For instance, the child realizes that the building both preserves and destroys life. He quickly comprehends that the building, as it encages and enslaves its inhabitants and expulses the sick, the old, and the rebellious, serves, ironically, to protect human life:

Il fallait comprendre que la construction d'un édifice indestructible avait occupé toute l'existence de l'ancêtre initial et celle de sa descendance entière. Qu'on avait tout mis en œuvre pour protéger la chair fragile ... toutes les menaces du vivant, pour créer un environnement protégé de tout pour toujours. (Georges 79)

[It must be understood that this ancestor spent his life and his childrens' lives and his entire descendants' lives in search of some indestructible building, an edifice, a tower. Everything had been done to protect fragile flesh. To counter the vagaries of time, the threats accrued by being alive, to create an environment protected from everything, forever.] (*UTS* 63)

The building is characterized by a desire to protect human life, but does so with violent, alienating, dehumanizing methods. Life must be protected, whereas human life, immobilized and micromanaged, becomes instrumental for the enterprise. In this complex, harsh, and threatening environment, the child's encounters with nonhuman others (the breach in the wall, the rumble coming from within the walls) make extraordinary use of caring gestures. The latter encourage the development of a sense of belonging and safety that consequently allows an alternative living space for the child.

### READING POSTHUMAN CARE

A comparative analysis of the two novels exposes what Marie-Anne Casselot, following environmental political theorist Sherilyn MacGregor, identifies as "the inevitability of care": "[i]mportantly, seeing care as necessary work also acknowledges our inherently interdependent nature. It is impossible not to do care work for ourselves and others, and we reciprocally need care from others" (3). The combination of discourses on care and the posthuman as an approach to comparative literature is a strategy that illuminates the variations in the figure of geographies of care in the two novels. And such a dialogue between care ethics, critical posthumanism, and comparative literature attests to conceptual and textual issues.

Reading strategies that focus on the fictionalization of care practices help to decode how the texts expose the moral contradictions and polarized situations that come with post-apocalyptic worlds. For instance, in *The Year of the Flood*, the Gardeners' vegetarianism and respect for the names of the animals clash with the popular fast-food restaurant SecretBurger, a name that clearly suggests how labelling the origins of the meat contained in the hamburgers has no importance. It plays on the mystery, on the concealment that characterizes the notion of secret to catch attention. More importantly, SecretBurger symbolizes the triviality of killing living creatures, celebrating the disposability of animal and human bodies. These two systems of beliefs collide in the text. They show how alternatives are needed under these messy ethical and political boundaries surrounding respect for the living and the dead, highlighting a need for new "patterns of association that compromise the distinction between the 'human' and the 'nonhuman'" (Whatmore 159). Careful and careless attitudes towards the living, combined with fictionalized futuristic events that help readers imagine possible consequences to the "global commodification of living organisms" (Braidotti, *Posthuman* 8), shape geographies of care as a non-linear, webbed ensemble of socio-spatial successes and failures. They characterize the fictionalized subjects as "nodes of attachments": "une conception – essentielle au *care* – de la personne comme noeud d'attachements qui font d'un être plus, et autre chose, que la somme de ses propriétés non-relationnelles" (a conception – fundamental to care – of the person as node of attachments that make that person more, and something else, than the sum of her non-relational properties) (Laugier 107–8; translation mine). Speculative fiction and dystopia allow the authors to imagine such intersubjective configurations and alternatives for understanding survival and thinking beyond the known, to some degree symbolically commenting on what is at risk if there are no changes made to our world system.

In *Sous béton*, the child first opts for immobility. However, he soon realizes that this corporeal and emotional paralysis replicates his parents' behaviour, pushing him to seek refuge in the small breach he finds in the wall of the building: "Alors je m'enroulais sur moi-même pour éviter toute provocation et, malgré les consignes de la mère, je tentais d'imaginer ma liberté ... Chaque fois, j'ouvrais les yeux sur l'étroitesse du logis. Et la sensation d'étouffement amplifiait" (I would fold into myself to avoid all provocation and, despite the mother's instructions, I tried to imagine my freedom ... Each time, I would open my eyes again on the narrowness of the dwelling. And the feeling of suffocation would grow) (Georges 75; *UTS* 60). The child chooses a new form of life, a new state of being that will welcome his singularity. In reaction to the violence and the carelessness of his parents, and in reaction to this moment of wonder that triggers a desire to survive, to remain alive despite the uselessness of the body, he imagines and finds refuge in a relational force coming from the building. It is the building that, strangely, offers him protection and escape, providing him with a sense of familiarity: "Que le Béton Total qui protégeait l'accès [...] Or, peu importe le point de vue, la sensation d'intense familiarité augmentait. Le réseau de fissures formait un visage. Semblables à tous les visages des pères, mères et enfants de l'Édifice" (Only Total Concrete that protected the way in ... But no matter my point of view, the sensation of intense familiarity increased) (155–6; *UTS* 125–6). "L'Enfant" finally disincarnates in ambiguous, fragmented scenes, where the reader questions whether this process symbolizes death or whether the character becomes one of the disembodied voices: "Il ne subsiste presque plus rien de moi" (Your limitations are fading) (85; *UTS* 136).

Also, the zombie-like parents of the child, the sick, the rebellious people ejected from the building, as well as the cadavers used to feed the inhabitants participate in the dark and gloomy world dramatized by Georges. And, perhaps more importantly, they are textual elements that raise ethical and political questions about matters of life and death in contexts where death seems "internal to the very possibility of an entity's being itself" (Kirby 120). Less radical in terms of human transformation, Atwood's imaginary alternatives to human/animal hierarchies suggest a need for horizontal politics, rather than for a vertical chain of beings. Indeed, while Atwood's chapters seem to centre on either Toby or Ren, as their names are placed at the opening of each section, it quickly becomes clear that Atwood displaces the focus of her narrative on the relationships and interactions between the characters, both human and non-human. The structure of the text stresses the need for something other than "self-centered individualism" (Braidotti, *Posthuman* 2).

In these novels, chaos, death, life, and hopes of a better future "interweave with caring and careless environments to produce complicated and sometimes confusing emotional geographies, negotiated by sufferers, carers, and others" (Davidson, Bondi, and Smith 4). Figures of posthuman care provide fertile ground for imagining alternative, more caring, forms of relationships. If reading fiction with care ethics and with a critical posthumanist approach does not necessarily resolve the historical and anticipated inhospitality toward minoritized groups in contexts of injustice and domination, at least it encourages mitigating dominant cultural and ethical scripts. Geographies of care and posthuman relationality expose the difficulties of caring, and remind us, subsequently, how the importance of care cannot be denied or dismissed.

## NOTES

Chapter title in Atwood, 89.

1 The first novel of the trilogy, *Oryx and Crake*, was published in 2003. It is told from the point of view of Jimmy, who remembers his young adult life with Crake and his struggle following the pandemic. *The Year of the Flood* chronicles the same set of events, but is told from the point of view of Ren and Toby, two female characters. It provides certain answers to *Oryx and Crake* and centres on God's Gardeners. The third and final book is *Maddaddam*, published in 2013. It continues the story and focuses on Toby and Zeb, who again revisit the past to come to terms with the new civilization to be built.

2 I use Jacob Homel's 2016 English translation of Georges's novel *Under the Stone*. From now onwards, the English version will be referred to as UTS.

3 For recent work on the ethics of care, see Bourgault and Perreault, Deschênes, and Collins. For key publications on critical posthumanist theory, see Wolfe, Asberg and Neimanis, Vint, and Wallace. For an insightful analysis of a posthuman perspective in Canadian literature, see García Zarranz.

4 See Carrière, DeFalco, Snauwaert, and Hétu.

## BIBLIOGRAPHY

Anderson, Kay, and Susan Smith. "Editorial: Emotional Geographies." *Transactions of the Institute of British Geographers* 26, no. 1 (2001): 7–10.

Asberg, Cecilia, and Astrida Neimanis. "Bodies of the Now: Feminist Values in Posthuman Times." *Visions of the NOW Conference*. Stockholm Festival for Art and Technology, Stockholm, Sweden. 24–26 May 2013. www.academia.edu/Bodies_of_the_Now_feminist_Values_in_Posthuman_Times (accessed 5 June 2016).

Atwood, Margaret. *The Year of the Flood*. New York, Toronto: Nan. A. Talese/Doubleday, 2009.

Benhabib, Seyla. "The Generalized and the Concrete Other: The Kohlberg-Gilligan Controversy and Feminist Theory." *PRAXIS International* 4 (1985): 402–24.

Bourgault, Sophie, and Julie Perreault, eds. *Le Care: Éthique féministe actuelle*. Montréal: Éditions du remue-ménage, 2015.

Braidotti, Rosi. *The Posthuman*. Cambridge: Polity, 2013.

– *Transpositions: On Nomadic Ethics*. Cambridge: Polity, 2006.

Carrière, Marie. "Mémoire du care: féminisme en mémoire." In *Women in French Studies: Selected Essays from Women in French International*

Conference "Femmes et Mémoire," 2015, edited by Dawn Cornelio, Margot Irvine, and Karine Schwerdtner, 1–13. 2016. (Accessed 4 Jan. 2017).

Casselot, Marie-Anne. "The Inevitability of Care in a Posthuman World." GNOSIS: Journal of Philosophy 14, no. 2 (2015): 1–7. (Accessed 12 Mar. 2016).

Ciobanu, Calina. "Rewriting the Human at the End of the Anthropocene in Margaret Atwood's *Maddaddam* Trilogy." *Minnesota Review* 83 (2014): 153–62.

Davidson, Joyce, Liz Bondi, and Mick Smith, eds. *Emotional Geographies*. 2005. Farnham, UK: Ashgate, 2007.

DeFalco, Amelia. "Caretakers/Caregivers: Economies of Affection in Alice Munro." *Twentieth-Century Literature* 58, no. 3 (2012): 377–98.

– *Imagining Care: Responsibility, Dependency, and Canadian Literature*. Toronto: University of Toronto Press, 2016.

– "Moral Obligation, Disordered Care: The Ethics of Caregiving in Margaret Atwood's *Moral Disorder*." *Contemporary Literature* 52, no. 2 (2011): 237–64.

Deschênes, Marjolaine. "Diagnostiquer le discours sur le care comme symptôme d'une culture désenchantée." *Les ateliers de l'éthique / The Ethics Forum* 10, no. 3 (2015): 66–100.

– "Identité narrative et temporalité chez Christian Bobin: L'écriture du care comme réplique poétique au désenchantement." PhD diss., Université de Montréal, 2012.

Dodds, Susan. "Dependence, Care, and Vulnerability." In *Vulnerability: New Essays in Ethics and Feminist Philosophy*, edited by Catriona Mackenzie, Wendy Rogers, and Susan Dodds, 181–203. Oxford, Oxford University Press, 2014.

Ferrarese, Estelle. "Vivre à la merci: Le *care* et les trois figures de la vulnérabilité dans les théories politiques contemporaines." *Multitudes* 2, nos. 37–8 (2009): 132–41.

Friedman, Susan Stanford. *Mappings: Feminism and the Cultural Geography of Encounter*. Princeton, NJ: Princeton University Press, 1998.

García Zarranz, Libe. "Queer TransCanadian Women's Writing in the 21st Century: Assembling a New Cross-Border Ethic." PhD diss., University of Alberta, 2013.

Georges, Karoline. *Sous béton*. Québec: Alto, 2011.

– *Under the Stone*. Translated by Jacob Homel. Vancouver: Anvil Press, 2016.

Gregory, Derek, et al. *The Dictionary of Human Geography*. 5th edition. Malden, MA, and Oxford: Blackwell, 2009.

Grosz, Elizabeth. *Space, Time, Perversion: Essays on the Politics of Bodies*. New York and London: Routledge, 1995.

Hayles, Katherine. *How We Became Posthuman: Virtual Bodies in Cybernetics, Literature and Informatics.* Chicago, London: University of Chicago Press, 1999.

Held, Virginia. *The Ethics of Care: Personal, Political and Global.* Oxford: Oxford University Press, 2006.

Herbrechter, Stephen. Interview with Jerome Garbah. *Critical Posthumanism*, November 2013. http://criticalposthumanism.net/the-posthuman-review/stefan-herbrechter-interview (accessed 23 Aug. 2015).

Hétu, Dominique. "'All I Ever Was to Keep Them Safe': Geographies of Care in Comparative Canadian Fiction." *Canadian Literature* 226 (Fall 2015): 36–53.

– "Of Wonder and Encounter: Textures of Human and Nonhuman Relationality in Two Novels." *Mosaic* 48, no. 3 (Sept. 2015): 159–74.

– "'The Wanderers Will Find a Way Home': Les géographies du *care* dans deux romans américains." *TransVerse* 14b (2014/2015): 80–95.

Kirby, Vicky. *Telling Flesh: The Substance of the Corporeal.* New York: Routledge, 1997.

Lagrandeur, Kevin. "What Is the Difference between Posthumanism and Transhumanism?" *Institute for Ethics and Technology*, 26 Dec. 2014. (Accessed 4 May 2015).

Laugier, Sandra. *Tous vulnérables? Le care, les animaux et l'environnement.* Paris: Payot et Rivages, 2012.

Lloyd, Genevieve. *The Man of Reason: 'Male' and 'Female' in Western Philosophy.* Minneapolis: University of Minnesota Press, 1984.

Massey, Doreen. "Geographies of Responsibility." *Geografiska Annaler. Series B, Human Geography* 86, no. 1 (2004): 5–18.

Meyers, Kristi Jane. "We Come Apart: Mother-Child Relationships in Margaret Atwood's Dystopias." Master's thesis, Iowa State University, 2011. http://lib.dr.iastate.edu/etd/12006 (accessed 9 Sept. 2016).

Mintz, Susannah B. *Hurt and Pain: Literature and the Suffering Body.* London, New Delhi, New York, Sydney: Bloomsbury, 2013.

Murdoch, Jon. *Post-Structuralist Geography: A Guide to Relational Space.* Thousand Oaks, CA: Sage, 2006.

Neimanis, Astrida. *Bodies of Water: A Posthuman Feminist Phenomenology.* Oxford, London, New York: Bloomsbury, 2017.

Noddings, Nel. *Starting at Home: Caring and Social Policy.* Berkeley, Los Angeles: University of California Press, 2002.

Nussbaum, Martha. "Literature and Ethical Theory: Allies or Adversaries?" *Frame* 17, no. 1 (2003): 6–30.

Paperman, Patricia, and Pascale Molinier. "Introduction. Désenclaver le care?" In *Carol Gilligan, Arlie Hochschild, Joan Tronto: Contre l'indifférence* des privilégiés: À quoi sert le care, edited by Patricia Paperman and Pascale Molinier, 7–34. Paris: Payot, 2013.

Phillips, Judith. *Care: Key Concepts*. Malden, MA; Cambridge, UK: Polity Press, 2007.

Ross, Stephen David. *Plenishment in the Earth: An Ethic of Inclusion*. Albany, NY: SUNY Press, 1995.

Snauwaert, Maïté. "Dépression et affection dans *Le juste milieu* d'Annabel Lyon: une poétique du care." Journal section Affecting Feminist Literary and Cultural Production / Affects féministes dans les productions littéraires et culturelles. *Atlantis: Critical Studies in Gender, Culture, and Social Justice* 39, no. 1 (Dec. 2016) [in press].

Tronto, Joan. *Moral Boundaries: A Political Argument for an Ethic of Care*. New York: Routledge, 1993.

Wallace, Jeff. "Literature and Posthumanism." *Literature Compass* 7, no. 8 (August 2010): 692–701.

Whatmore, Sarah. *Hybrid Geographies: Natures, Cultures, Spaces*. London: Sage, 2002.

Vint, Sheryl. *Bodies of Tomorrow: Technology, Subjectivity, Science Fiction*. Toronto, Buffalo, London: University of Toronto Press, 2007.

# Why Not an "African-Canadian" Epic?
# Lessons from Pratt and Walcott, Etc.

*George Elliott Clarke*

## I  POUND AND FRYE

In 1909, responding to maternal musing on the idea of an "Epic of the West" (Moody 121), the European-American poet Ezra Pound propounds four prerequisites for an American epic:

1  a beautiful tradition.
2  a unity in the outline of that tradition vid. The Odyssey.
3  a Hero – mythical or historical.
4  a dam [sic] long time for the story to loose [sic] its gharish [sic] detail & get encrusted with a bunch of beautiful lies. (qtd. in Moody 121)

Pound also opines that Henry Wadsworth Longfellow "tried to hist [sic] up an amerikan [sic] epik" [sic] (qtd. in Moody 121), referring, presumably, to his *Evangeline: A Tale of Acadie* (1847), which tells the story of two lovers separated nearly unto death by the British Expulsion of the Acadians from Nova Scotia in 1755, or to his *The Song of Hiawatha* (1855), retelling Ojibway legends. But, for Pound, Longfellow could not succeed in his efforts because America itself "has no mysterious & shadowy past to make her interesting" (qtd. in Moody 122), while the present is even worse. Pound also explains that the would-be epic poet "needs figures to move on the epic stage & they have to be men who are more than men, with sight more than mansight" (the latter neologism suggests they should possess supernatural or divine insight), and "[t]hey have to be picturesque" (qtd. in Moody 122). For those who might propose Walt Whitman and his *Leaves of*

*Grass* (1855) as an American epic, Pound shoots back that that poetry collection is merely "interesting as ethnology" (qtd. in Moody 122). Clearly, for him, the effective epic poem cannot be set among minorities – Acadian or Ojibway – or even utilize the miscellaneous speech of the variegated citizens of the United States of America. Heteroglossia, he suggests, cannot provide the model for the epic.[1] In his response to his mother's notion of the American epic, Pound moves, impishly, that only "a religion of 'Chivalry in affairs of money'" (with, presumably, lingo about stocks and mortgages) could provide the matter for an American poem of high purpose (qtd. in Moody 122). Ideally, Pound imagines, the American epic poet must be one who "will walk very much alone, with his eyes on the beauty of the past of the old world, or on the glory of a spiritual kingdom, or on some earthly new Jerusalem – which might as well be upon Mr Shackletons antarctic [sic] ice fields as in Omaha ... Canada, Australia, New Zealand, South Africa, set your hypothetical [epic] where you like" (qtd. in Moody 122).

The trouble is, Yanks lack the ethnic and national unity of the Portuguese poet Luis Vaz de Camões,[2] who Pound feels "is the only man who ever did a nearly contemporary subject with any degree of success & [who] had the line of [explorer] Vasco de Gamas voyage for unity ... & the mythical history of Portugal for back ground [sic]" (qtd. in Moody 122). Bereft of such homogeneity, the American poet must either parrot a polyglot babble, Pound suspects, or "parley Euphues" – that is to say, the seductive, false tongue of commerce (qtd. in Moody 123). Ultimately, Pound proposes, "[a]n epic in the real sense is the speech of a nation thru the mouth of one man" (qtd. in Moody 122). Note his emphasis on unities – of "race" ("nation"), rhetoric ("the speech of a nation"), and the "individual talent" ("one man"). Almost a decade later, in 1917–18, Pound maintains that heteroglossia, or the hubbub of many, cannot produce the epic voice, which must be national and even imperial: For him, "the province is always a series of impotent and diminishing ecchoes [sic]" (qtd. in Moody 330). "Province" is, here, a synonym for the ethnic, the minority, the ex-central (eccentric), and the marginal.

And Pound is not wrong. Generally, the epic seeks to answer the question, "Who are we?" Naturally, that answer arrives most easily if the poet is dealing with a singular, cultural entity, and one exuding mythic or imaginative force. The great Canadian critic Northrop Frye says as much when he posits that the epic poet – that is, one who "communicates as a professional man with a social function" (*Anatomy* 55) – may attempt "a single encyclopaedic form," descended from "a total body of vision," if he is "sufficiently learned or inspired" (55). The epic may also be generated

– as a set of communal, oracular verses – "by a poetic school or tradition, if the culture is sufficiently homogeneous" (55). Yet, the epic poet, being "a spokesman of his society," and explicitly *not* of "a second society" (54), finds articulated in himself "a poetic knowledge and expressive power which is latent or needed in his society" (54). Nevertheless, civilizations themselves may generate "traditional tales and myths and histories [that] have a strong tendency to stick together and form encyclopaedic aggregates" (55–6), such as, Frye believes, is true for the Homeric epics and the Finnish *Kalevala*, too, even though "everything that is unified or continuous about the poem is a nineteenth-century reconstruction" (56). Frye seems to accord with Pound, then, that epic is the voice of a civilization (or a culture), the vocalization of a unity of cultural experience, and he also holds that the form itself "makes some attempt to preserve the convention of recitation and a listening audience" (248). Frye also follows Pound in disparaging the "provincial": "The province or region ... is usually a vestigial curiosity to be written up by some nostalgic tourist" ("Canada" 89). One should not conceive such a limited or narrow space capable of supporting the epic imagination. Frye insists, then, that "culture seems to flourish best in national units ... the empire is too big and the province too small for major literature" (89).

Given these existential limitations for Canadian poetry, its provincial and colonial inheritance, and its immediately bifurcated national voice (French and English), it should be difficult for Canada to produce epic poets. But Frye elects one: E.J. Pratt; and one Pratt poem, namely, *Brébeuf and His Brethren* (1940). For Frye, "Canadian poetry is at its best a poetry of incubus and *cauchemar*," featuring "[n]ature ... consistently sinister and menacing," and so the martyrdom of the French Jesuit priest Brébeuf yields "the greatest single Canadian poem" (96–7). Herein, "the man with the vision beyond nature is tied to the stake and destroyed by savages who are in the state of nature, and who represent its mindless barbarity" (97). While Frye's description of the poem admits a reflex racialism, where European Christian civilization is crucified by North American heathens, unenlightened and irrational, Frye also notes shrewdly, "the black-coated figure at the stake is also a terrifying devil to the savages, *Echon*, the evil one" (97). Despite this almost noble moral relativism, Frye imposes the standard reading of Canadian colonial history that the poem indubitably affirms: Aboriginal Canadians are doomed savages, fated to endure as much justified annihilation as had been the avatars of Nazism (97).

Interestingly, both Pound and Frye read the possibility for twentieth-century epic through an ethnocentric and nationalist lens that advances the epic poet as the vatic articulator of the dominant – or administrating – ethnicity of a nation or imperial homeland. Playfully, Pound pretends that the true, unifying language of the United States is that of Wall Street and Madison Avenue, commerce and slogans. Yet his own epic, *The Cantos* (1917–87),[3] makes terrific – and terrifying – use of the bombast of both, while also exploiting ugly – if polyphonous – ethnic caricature (particularly of Jews). For his part, Frye elects Pratt English Canada's great epic poet, for a poem that represents the implantation of European Christianity upon Canadian soil and its displacement of Aboriginal civilization, which is pictured as regressive barbarism.[4]

## II DUDEK'S EUROPE

These provisos of Pound and Frye are echoed in Anglo-Polish-Canadian poet and scholar Louis Dudek's own attempt at an epic – or, simply, long – poem, *Europe* (1955), which he describes as an "ecstasy" exploring "three great subjects" or "thematic vehicles" (Preface 14), namely, "the Sea, the Cathedrals, and the Acropolis of Athens" (14–15), which also double as "themes of some redeeming good, either in the past, or in eternity, or yet again in the ever-living present" (15). (These principal principles might also correspond to Dudek's triad of devotions: "Democracy, yes, humanity and justice" [9].) The sea becomes for Dudek a tissue that connects the Euro/Franco–North American settlements of the St Lawrence River (Montreal and Quebec City) and the Euro/Franco–North Atlantic islands of Newfoundland and Saint-Pierre et Miquelon with the Northern European Christian heritage of cathedrals and the Mediterranean-anchored tradition of Plato and Aristotle. Dudek admits as much: "For the sea-waves were there in the first place, as Pound says of the birds which were there in the trees, before the 'Canzone degli uccelli' (Song of the Birds) in his 75th Canto had been written. And as the Sea at Paumanok was there before Whitman ever began to hear it" (Preface 17). European civilization is, for Dudek, borne from and by the sea – as is Venus herself in Botticelli's famous painting. Read thus, Dudek's *Europe* is an attempt to unify settler-civilization with the Old World. Moreover, Dudek undertakes this effort as an Anglophone-Polish-Canadian Catholic, one familiar with French-Canadian culture and Catholicism, but also with High Modernism as pioneered by a Europe-besotted American, namely, Pound. In this regard, for all its gestures toward European cultural and intellectual unity, *Europe* is as necessarily fractured – or encyclopedic – a project as

Pound's own *Cantos*, his already gargantuan and, in 1955, still ongoing poem of poems (begun in 1917). Still, Dudek is haunted by the possibility of achievable oneness, of unity, and decides that it is apprehended in the form of the poem itself:

> More particularly, what I discovered in writing *Europe* was the great wave of emotion, the cumulative energy of a sea-like rhythm, that gathers in a long poem. I discovered that a long poem, in this case a series of poems, achieves an intensity and a self-propelling force that can never be equalled by short poems or a mere collection of short poems written at different times. I discovered that poetry has actual momentum, that it is like a tide, or like the sea. (Preface 17)

To reinforce the unitary legitimacy of his poem, Dudek likens it to maritime organic structure. One should hear echoes of the primary, seafaring European epics here, including *The Odyssey, Beowulf*, Norse sagas, but also Hebrew scripture – Jonah and Genesis, and also Walt Whitman's ocean-imitating prosody and Pound's own Canto I. Dudek is explicit about the work of his poem as elaborating a European Atlantic-Mediterranean ethos, deciding that gestures toward Utopia refer really to "Atlantis, the never-realized ideal world, to which all reality must somehow be referred" (18). This statement should be read in tandem with Dudek's pronouncement, too, that poetry is "the epic that all men would live if they were free" (13). Hence, we should understand *Europe* as the epic effort of a Central European–immigrant culture spokesperson to explicate Euro–North American civilization through an examination of three great shaping forces: Nordic Catholic and Protestant Christianity and Mediterranean philosophy. However, Dudek's study is not a celebration. We must remember that Atlantis is lost, and the poet himself opines that *Europe* reflects a mind "involved in the tragedy of modern history" (13). (Frye's terms, "incubus and *cauchemar*," are freshly resonant here.)

In his poem, Dudek, as governing pilot or consciousness, takes us down the St Lawrence River and across the Atlantic in Part I; stops in England (Part II); crosses to France/Continental Europe (Part III); reconnoitres The Warm South (Part IV); enumerates What Greece Has Given (Part V); and concludes with Finis (Part VI), which is also a kind of envoy. His intellectual cartography echoes that of Pound and Frye, applying Euro–North American scrutiny to the Old World heritage. Thus, the Anglo-Canadian poet, Dudek, like his forerunners, Pratt and the American Pound, is empowered to speak with an illusion of oneness, as if Montreal, Southampton, Chartres, Athens, and, I will add, Pound's Rapallo are all, in any simple sense, *one* – even if the same sea water touches all of them.

But Dudek's history-informed, Euro-ethnic-related, North Atlantic and Mediterranean vision is striking for what it omits. In Part 1, Sea and Land, as his vessel steams down the St Lawrence, Dudek's persona meditates on Quebec and its cities "The river made" (26). (Here again one finds that, for him, European civilization and civilizing impulses are organic in ship-bearing water itself.) He also writes,

> Montreal
> raids on the world for population,
> Hungarians, Poles, Mongolians, Greeks and Jews,
> as well as the two conventional races [French and English]
> who stiffen against each other in their pride. (26)

In this case, the river brings Quebec – or Montreal –

> other people's broken wrongs; brought its
> accumulation of dead habits,
> the racial tics of other nations ...
> Raw matter for a raw country. (27)

Fascinatingly, for Dudek, the English and French are "conventional races," the rest of the "world ... population" are either European castoffs or "Mongolians" or "racial tics," all constituting "Raw matter for a raw country" (26–7). Indigenous people are absent here, of course, and other non-Caucasian and non-European people are encased and rendered spectacular by the pseudo-scientific and racialist term, "Mongoloid," and perhaps also by the belittling phrase, "racial tics." Out upon the Atlantic Ocean, Dudek's speaker remembers the famed, European drowned:

> Shelley, Edward King ...
> those athletes on the Titanic,
> all the Olympians [sailors], of Salamis, of Trafalgàr–
> familiar. And to the victor
> a crown of white foam (34)

but also "poets [who] sink with their laurels" (41). Given the racial or ethnic history that Dudek values, it is logical that he, looking at Montreal, sees neither Negroes nor Natives, and then, gazing upon the Atlantic, has no memory of The Middle Passage and the millions of Africans who were transported thereon as "Raw matter" to help build the so-called New World, and who also drowned in the millions therein. These omissions may be explained because Dudek seeks a unifying European (Caucasian) vision and voice that must cast non-European and non-Caucasian others as invisible, inaudible, and marginal – if not non-entities. As his persona sets foot on English soil, he remarks, "[w]e have left our world, we have left America, / and we are here" (48). Ironically, though "our world ... America" (48) assembles a "world ... population" (26), that variegated composition of people is reduced to only one of consequence: European and Caucasian (and implicitly Judeo-Christian, with an emphasis on Christian and/or Catholic). Disturbingly, too, Dudek's effort at North American–European unity shows instant cracks. Aboard ship, the musical program is African American–influenced "bebop / exclusively and German *Sehnsucht*"[5] (43) and these "jazz rhythms," plus the omission of "Mozart" or "the *Messiah*" (by Handel), render the vessel a "Ship of Fools" (43). Although we have been told to think of the sea as carrying, innately, European civilization, what it is bearing back to Europe is supposedly degenerate, pleasure-besotted, and Negroid. Dudek's persona confesses, "Having boarded the ship as an innocent / I had not realized that an ocean crossing / is one of our fucking institutions" (44). In this context, the epithet should be read literally: the jazz-serenaded Atlantic voyage is an occasion for singles (and couples) to couple, and, for Dudek's speaker, such lovemaking nixes classical ideals. But, read with the racial subtext highlighted, one might retort that jazz itself, born in the interracial brothels of New Orleans, is also rooted distantly in the ship-borne rape of African women by European sailors.

This comment occasions the reflection that Dudek, as an English-speaking Polish-Canadian poet and intellectual, may have modelled himself, not only on Pound, but on Joseph Conrad,[6] also Polish by birth, but famed as an English writer who also speculated on European history and European imperialism (especially in Africa), and who conceived of the world in explicitly racialist terms. Indeed, the Dudek speaker who sums up Montreal as an unsettled (and unsettling) mix of diverse settlers may be juxtaposed with Conrad's Marlow, who in *Heart of Darkness* (1899, 1902) spies, in coastal Africa, Europeans driven suicidally mad by their exploitive contact with "dark-souled" Africans.[7] In *Europe*, then, despite his quest for Occidental unity, Dudek joins Conrad in critiquing Europe as "fallen," though by its own hand, not by its enslavement and oppression of non-Europeans. His persona announces,

> [i]f now only the proud cathedrals remain,
>     it is because art
> outlives inhumanity.
>
> History is really the study of failures. (66)

In the great cathedral at Chartres, his epiphany is "Entertainment, amusement, have eaten up the arts!" (77). Shortly, he complains of "the monstrous sugar teeth / of 'money' and 'amusement'" and then of "sensuality / for the boudoir, decorativeness" (78). If jazz spells New World decadence aboard ship, so does popular desire for distraction and decoration represent European cultural decline. The word *sensuality* is important here, for it hints at a sensibility that views the "Oriental" as a source of decadence.[8] Thus, for Dudek, artistic and cultural disintegration occurs when jazz displaces classical music and when fucking displaces philosophy ... *Europe* is, in other words, a version of Oswald Spengler's *Decline of the West* or *Der Untergang des Abendlandes* (1918, 1922), a racialist manifesto. (Dudek tells us that *Europe* was indeed shaped partly by his teaching of a literature course stressing "A kind of down-going of the West," i.e., "a study of the disintegration of belief and of social coherence in western society" [Preface 10].) The alternative to Europe – Christian and classical – is always atavism and primitivism.

Yet, the New World – or, rather, "America (the continent, Canada / being a good part of it)" (127) – does have its virtues. Present-day Europe "is little more now / than an accumulation of bad habits," its heritage "wasted" (138). Now, America provides

>                   power
> ... like the clear sight of new races ...
>     unlike the Europeans,
> who are tired of it all, or helpless, or exhausted. (138)

On the return voyage to North America, Dudek's persona observes: "On this ship there are several Italians and a few Greeks / ... the raw matter / of democracy; Europe sends us its people" (144). Far from seeming degraded now, North America offers the renewed *promise* of Europe: "We have work to do. / Europe is behind us. / America before us" (145). Dudek's speaker even praises, now, "multi-national America" (129). However, *multi-national* isn't, likely, a synonym for multiracial.

### III PRATT'S *BRÉBEUF*

One finds identical reasoning in Pratt. The epic can never be as unifying as it seeks to be, because it is always beset by the Other's race-based irrationality. Though Pratt's "epics of national life, *Brébeuf and His Brethren* [1940] and *Towards the Last Spike* [1952] ... showed [younger poets] that the Canadian historical past could be transformed into a 'useable myth' for the present" (Djwa and Moyles, "Introduction" xviii), they do not escape, as I will justify via my reading of *Brébeuf*, imbrication in the basic racial hostilities indicated above.

Deemed to have become "and long remained Canada's national poet" (xvii), Pratt (1882–1964) was of the same generation as Pound (1885–1972) and T.S. Eliot (1888–1965), but his modernism never escaped a traditional – Victorian or perhaps Newfoundland – interest in what his editors and anthologists Sandra Djwa and Roger Moyles term "Determinist philosophy and [Thomas] Hardy's pessimism" (xxi). Rightly then, they judge Pratt an "uneasy ... early modern" (xxiii), for, unlike his internationalist contemporaries, who "portray man as an anti-hero, Pratt, the Newfoundlander, insists on his capacity for heroism" (xxxvi). This romantic and heroic stance, supported by Pratt's Christianity (though partially contradicted by his Darwinism), encouraged his desire to develop "the larger human currents, the democratic visions, the creative impulses at work on myths and national origins," to become, in this specific sense, "the 'Whitman,' or founding national poet"[9] (xlv). For Djwa and Moyles, then, Pratt's long poems – *Brébeuf and His Brethren* and *Towards the Last Spike* – fulfill this task: to render Canadian history with the force of myth, or literature, to give the common Canadian English reader and intellectual a *common* text through which to appreciate, interrogate, and comprehend the nation. My epithet *common* registers the anxiety here, though, between intent and accomplishment. Pratt sought to become English Canada's all-Canadian poet, to be our Whitman, but we must admit that he is not that. Rather, he is a very fine, mid-twentieth-century poet, perhaps the finest Canadian poet in English fifty years ago, but hardly is he unarguably a national sage or conscience or even, in Percy Bysshe Shelley's phrase, an "unacknowledged legislator,"[10] though Djwa and Moyles argue that Pratt projected "moral leadership" (xxxix). However, *moral leadership* is not a synonym for *incomparable poetry*.

But what does Pratt achieve in *Brébeuf and His Brethren*? First, I think he wants to answer Longfellow's *Evangeline* (1847), a successful, "national" poem – or epic – for French-Canadians, especially les Acadiens, even though it was imagined by an Anglophone and written by an American. So, Pratt follows Longfellow in borrowing a tale from French settlement in North America and employing it to create a "national" myth. Here are Longfellow's opening lines:

> This is the forest primeval. The murmuring pines and the hemlocks,
> Bearded with moss, and in garments green, indistinct in the twilight,
> Stand like Druids of eld, with voices sad and prophetic,
> Stand like harpers hoar, with beards that rest on their bosoms.
> Loud from its rocky caverns, the deep-voiced neighboring ocean
> Speaks, and in accents disconsolate answers the wail of the forest. (61)

Compare them to those of Pratt:

> The winds of God were blowing over France,
> Kindling the hearths and altars, changing vows
> Of rote into an alphabet of flame.
> The air was charged with song beyond the range
> Of larks, with wings beyond the stretch of eagles.
> Skylines unknown to maps broke from the mists
> And there was laughter on the seas. With sound
> Of bugles from the Roman catacombs,
> The saints came back in their incarnate forms. (ll. 1-9)

Although Longfellow can be cited for mystical anthropomorphism, giving us an Acadia of bearded trees and a barkative ocean, there is, nevertheless, an accent on nature and, eventually, on the Acadian peasantry as being rooted within it. In contrast, Pratt gives us a distinctly non-Canadian and otherworldly opening: In his vision, God's spirit stirs France to the point that, to the accompaniment of angelic bugles out of Rome, classical Christian-Catholic saints are reincarnated as specifically Gallic men and women. One might even say that Longfellow looks an abject pagan juxtaposed with Pratt's blatant Christian trumpeting (or "bugling"). That contrast gains further interest if one registers that, normally, it is the United States that sees itself as God's gift to humanity, while Canadians poke fun at that conceit. But, here, in *Brébeuf*, Pratt claims, audaciously, evangelical Christian France as the cradle of colonial Canada. His audacity intensifies when we consider that Martiniquan poet Aimé Fernand David Césaire (1913-2008), whose masterpiece - arguably, an epyllion, *Cahier d'un retour au pays natal* [*Notebook of a Return to My Native Land*], appeared in 1939, the year before *Brébeuf*, showcases a Martinique ruined and perverted by *French* racism and imperialism, let alone its native versions of Christianity.[11] Too, Pratt's Zombified "marble saints [who] leave / Their pedestals for chartless seas and coasts / And the vast blunders of the forest glooms" (ll. 51-3) arrive in North America with almost utter disregard for the commercial interests that pay their way. We are to believe that French settlement in northern North America is all about converting heathens to Christianity, and hardly about the enrichment of France: Not only by finding the mythical "western gateway to Cathay" through which "French craft / Freighted with jewels, spices, tapestries,[12] / Would sail to swell the coffers of the Bourbons" (ll. 1644-9), but through profits from fish, fur, and forestry.

Thus, as we have seen with Dudek, the poem soon pursues a racial binary that is as insidious as it is inevitable. To convert the Huron who, unlike the Iroquois, are pliable, Brébeuf and his brethren utilize "simple Huron rhymes" (l. 558) and infantilized images and deeds "which readily the Indian mind / Could grasp" (ll. 562-3). On the plus side, the "savages" – to use the standard epithet – show "[a] fighting courage equal to the French," "[e]ndurance," and "impassivity" (ll. 705-8). Nevertheless, they still represent "[a] race so unlike men that we [the French] must live / Daily expecting murder at their hands" (ll 802-3). "The Indian mind" cannot warm to "cold / Abstractions"; "fears and prejudices" haunt "the shadows of their racial past" (ll. 884-90). Pratt tells us that parts of New France are "*Infested* by the Iroquois" (ll. 1542 and 1698-9, my emphasis), who demonstrate a "keen ... lust for slaughter" (ll. 1711). So backward and unregenerate are the Aboriginal peoples that, when their crops fail or the rains don't come, they demonize Brébeuf and his brethren. One brave

> at the palisade with axe
> Uplifted says, "I have had enough ...
> Of the dark flesh of my enemies. I mean
> To kill and eat the white flesh of the priests." (ll. 1141-4)

Cannibalism is countenanced by this "forest primeval" Antichrist, but at least the "white meat" of the priests will be more pleasant to gnaw than that of unenlightened barbarians. Later, we read of "the Huron curse inspired by sorcerers / Who saw black magic in the Jesuit robes / And linked disaster with their ritual" (ll. 1766-8).

But the racial schema of the poem constructs bastardizing ironies. Natives enslave occasionally white French priests and colonists, and this captivity is rendered as martyrdom and horror. Yet Pratt ignores the truth that actual seventeenth-century New France harboured thousands of slaves, both Aboriginal and African.[13] In addition, the French missionary Jogues, hounded by non-Christian Iroquois, is, upon his return to Christian Europe, "robbed by a pirate gang" (ll. 1431), one of, presumably, nominally Christian but definite Euro-Caucasian provenance.

Even so, Pratt's heroic romanticism does produce a majestic Brébeuf, whose martyrdom is rendered in Part XII of the poem, in a metre distinctly different from the basic blank verse of the first eleven parts of the work. Here, in Part XII, the conclusion of *Brébeuf and His Brethren*, I believe that Pratt reaches for a longer, freer line, reminiscent of Longfellow's dactylic hexameter, which, as the wag Anonymous has it, features

> soft-flowing trochees and dactyls,
> Blended with fragments spondaic, and here and there an iambus,
> Syllables often sixteen, or more or less, as it happens,
> Difficult always to scan, and depending greatly on accent,
> Being a close imitation, in English, of Latin hexameters.

Certainly, Pratt approximates this use of trochees, dactyls, spondees, and iambs, in lines, generally of anapestic pentameter with frequent iambic substitutions, that range between twelve and fourteen syllables in length:

> Where was the source
> Of his strength, the home of his courage that topped the best
> Of their braves and even out-fabled the lore of their legends?
> ... Was it the blood?
> They would draw it fresh from its fountain. Was it the heart?
> They dug for it, fought for the scraps in the way of the wolves.
> (ll. 2052–61)

Soon, we learn that the "source" of Brébeuf's courage and strength is "the sound of invisible trumpets blowing / Around two slabs of board, right-angled, hammered / By Roman nails and hung on a Jewish hill" (ll. 2068–70). Pratt's concluding lines offer again a rich echo of Longfellow's *Evangeline*:

> Three hundred years have passed, and the winds of God
> Which blew over France are blowing once more through the pines
> That bulwark the shores of the Great Fresh Water Sea ...

Near to the ground where the cross broke under the hatchet,
And went with it into the soil to come back at the turn
Of the spade with the carbon and calcium char of the bodies,
The shrines and altars are built anew; the *Aves*
And prayers ascend, and the Holy Bread is broken. (ll. 2115–37)

Ultimately, Pratt rewrites Longfellow. He takes a story of actual French Christian martyrdom (not the myth of separated lovers essential to Longfellow), excised from the problematic context of British-French imperial rivalry (the crux of *Evangeline*), and, to reproduce French missionaries as types of Hebrew faithful and Catholic saints, pits them against ignorant and demonic Aboriginals. Though his narrative indulges, necessarily, in a bifurcation between Christian Europeans and savage Amerindians (and note that, while we do read of a few Native Christian converts, we never read of European malfeasance towards Natives), Pratt is also driven to edge beyond these paradigms. If my suggestion is useful, he at least looks at American literature, specifically Longfellow's *Evangeline*, as a goad to his own work, and he attempts to render French colonialists as reborn classical martyrs and as newfangled Hebrews.

Nevertheless, Pratt's relatively brief epic (or epyllion) fails to provide a useful, national myth. His vision is too racially European, too exculpatory toward imperialism, too triumphalist Christian, and too encased in an Anglo-imperial imperative (despite the French overlay) to be able to provide all Canadian – or even merely Anglo-Canadian – readers with a myth around which all may rally.

## IV  WALCOTT'S *OMEROS*

I do believe, however, that the Caribbean playwright, poet, and Nobel Laureate in Literature Derek Walcott avoids such pitfalls in his epic poem, *Omeros* (1990). Yet, Walcott also must negotiate ontological, racial issues that French philosopher Jean-Paul Sartre establishes in "Orphée Noire," or "Black Orpheus," his 1948 essay introducing a ground-breaking anthology of Black African poetry in French, edited by Léopold Sédar Senghor.

The problem that Sartre forwards for black poets is existential: Our duty is, "[f]rom Haiti to Cayenne, a sole idea – to make manifest the black soul" ("Orphée Noire" 18). Hence, "[n]egro poetry is evangelic, it comes bearing glad tidings – negritude is found again" (18). Worse – or better – than this spiritual prescription is Sartre's searing prophecy, "it is in expressing himself the most lyrically that the black poet attains most surely to great *group* poetry"[14] (21, my emphasis). The black poet must indeed sing Pound's "tale of the tribe"[15] if he or she would be great, and Sartre even proposes that such a poet, "torn between 'civilization' and his ancient black roots" might even go about "abandoning himself to trances" or "rolling himself upon the ground" (21). Moreover, in drafting great poetry, the black poet "must indeed, one day, return to Africa" (20) and allow "the redescent into the bursting Hell of the black soul" (21). Sartre does not propose atavism, per se, but a kind of racial purification: "It is only when they have disgorged their whiteness that [the black poet] adopts [European words], making of this language in ruins a superlanguage solemn and sacred, in brief, Poetry" (26).

Why is it, how is it, that the black poet is called to this reckoning? Well, speculates Sartre, it is "[b]ecause he has, more than all the others the sense of revolt and the love of liberty" (57). In fact, "negritute [sic] is, in its essence, poetry" (64). Fortunately – or unfortunately – the Negro experiences a "tension between a nostalgic Past into which the black no more completely enters and a future where it will give way to new values" (63). For this reason, says Sartre, "[n]egritude fashions itself in a tragic beauty which finds expression only in Poetry" (63).

Moreover, there is, naturally, something sexual and fecund in black expressiveness. Asserts Sartre, "it is ... nudity without color which best symbolizes Negritude" (62). Not only that, but "the black remains the great male of the earth, the sperm of the world" (45).

If there is a future for epic poetry, it is with the black (male), or so Sartre wagers: "Already there is a black *Epic*; first the golden age of Africa, then the era of the dispersion and of captivity, then the awakening of conscience, the dark and heroic times of the great revolts ... then the *fact* of the abolition of slavery ... then the struggle for the definitive liberation" (56). While one might complain that Sartre is too besotted with race to be sensible, it is arguable, if curious, that Walcott's great poem undertakes a catalogue of every black epic trope that Sartre enunciates,[16] while also insisting on a multiracial concept of Caribbean and North American history.

But Walcott's articulation of an "anti-racist racialism" to tell the tale of the Caribbean tribe posits a problem for critics, who, perhaps also, if indirectly, overly influenced by Sartre's colour-coded critique, insist on reading the Laureate "primarily as a West Indian and secondarily as a poet" (*Ambition and Anxiety*, xxii), in the formulation of Line Henriksen. If Walcott is seen as having penned, in Sartre's terms, "a black *Epic*," then the poet is penned into a prison of post-colonial paradox. To cite Henriksen's *Ambition and Anxiety: Ezra Pound's* Cantos *and Derek Walcott's* Omeros *as Twentieth-Century Epics* (2006), "[t]he paradox established between

European classicism and Caribbean identity" (xxii) in Walcott becomes a critical cliché, allowing his work to suffer, generally, from "[a] tendency within some postcolonial criticism to celebrate the texts of the periphery as subversive rather than to analyse them as literary" (xv). Ironically, though, read as an epic poem and not as political anthropology, Walcott's *Omeros* is viewed as a success, while Pound's *Cantos*, due partly to its politics and partly to its form, is noted as a "flawed masterpiece" (xiii), but one that has generated an industry of politicized and formal readings. In contrast, wagers Henriksen, Walcott is "celebrated rather than analysed" (xv, n10).[17]

Still, we must understand how Walcott has succeeded in writing an epic poem that also stands as a true "national" poem of the Caribbean as well as one supportive of Pan-Africanist pride, without resorting to demonization of one ethnicity or another. In other words, how does Walcott succeed at drafting epic where Pound (arguably) – and the Anglo-Canucks Pratt and Dudek (definitely) – fail?

To begin to answer this question, I believe we need to reconsider the early modernist Pound and the mid-twentieth-century Frye. In his beginning as a would-be epic poet, Pound, as we have seen, dismisses heteroglossia and polyphony as constituting discourses of discord that hamper the promulgation of the unified vision that the epic poet must produce. Taking Pound at his word, especially those most poisoned by an appalling racialism, we can say, *pace* Bakhtin, that he has pooled in *The Cantos* monoglossia, thus, as is typical for "poetic epic discourse," he has refused the supposed democratic "openness of the novel" (Henriksen, *Ambition and Anxiety* 122). Critics like John Lauber, who read *The Cantos* as a "fascist" poem, one that offers a "paranoid interpretation of history," and admire "the inseparably associated virtues of the Will, of action, and of hardness" (qtd. in Henriksen 139), view the work as triumphantly wilful in meaning.

However, such a rendering of Pound is "hard to reconcile" (Henriksen 140) with the 1936 critique of the first thirty *Cantos* "put forward by Allen Tate" (140): "*The Cantos* are talk, talk, talk ... Each canto has the broken flow and the somewhat elusive climax of a good monologue: because there is no single speaker, it is a many-voiced monologue" (qtd. in Henriksen 140). Henriksen determines, then, that "Tate's seemingly paradoxical many-voiced monologue" has affinities with Bakhtin's notion of a novelized epic characterized by dialogism: i.e., by diegesis that includes the unidentifiable mimesis of others and may be taken over by such other voices" (142–3). In other words, whatever Pound's stated intent, and given his blatant use of Confucian proverbs, Americana, *Provençal* fragments, translations from various tongues, as well as his typographically produced imitation of forms of accent and speech (sometimes satirical), *The Cantos* must be read finally as heteroglossic.[18]

Frye posits, "the epic of the Renaissance" (Henriksen xvii) is "a narrative poem of heroic action, but a special kind of narrative. It also has an encyclopedic quality in it, distilling the essence of all the religious, philosophical, political, even scientific learning of its time, and, if completely successful, the definitive poem for its age."[19] Keeping this definition in mind, we might question the degree to which Pound's *Cantos* may be said to fail on formal terms, for the very structure of the poem is categorically encyclopedic, even to the point of tedium, given the "slabs" (Pound's term)[20] of American and Chinese prose history that occupy many cantos and what feels like scores of pages. Too, many parts of the poem engage in philosophical, religious, and political discourse, along with observation of science, particularly its military applications. (Henriksen, *pace* Pound, submits, "the epic poem itself is an all-encompassing whole" and Pound saw his role as that of "creating a meaningful whole out of the innumerable pieces and fragments of modern and recent history" [15].)

The "failing" of the verse is not, then, a condition of its form, but rather its thematic harping on the Spenglerian theme of the rise and fall of racialized civilizations or ethnicized dynasties, with their alleged "fall" or decline being blamed on base finances and debased economics, all orchestrated by sly (ethnic) villains.[21] (Because Pratt's *Brébeuf* is not as encyclopedic as Pound's *Cantos*, it is necessarily a slighter poem. Still, its equal failing qua epic is its reductive rendition of a set of Gallic Christian saints and heathen Aboriginal villains, just as problematically limited as Pound's heroic poet[ic]-governors versus treacherous usurers and arms merchants.)

To return to Walcott, then, *Omeros* succeeds as epic, not only because of "the [classically derived] restraints ... placed upon it by a regular metre [mainly iambic] and a division into books, chapters, sections, tercets and lines (largely hexameters)."[22] No, the content, the vision, matter. Walcott produces an encyclopedic, kaleidoscopic, polyphonic poem, one that conjoins African, diasporic African, European, American, Amerindian, and even colonial and imperial histories on a basis of equality and empathy.[23] True: Pound – though not Pratt or Dudek – also juxtaposes elements of these (and Asian) histories, occasionally with aspects of egalitarian respect (particularly in *The Pisan Cantos*).[24] Even so, the chief complaint against it still stands: that it prejudicially privileges Classical/Renaissance

European/Caucasian cultural and aristocratic governorship, though it also looks, ex-"racially," to Confucius and classical China for additional *examples* of such – supposedly good – governance.

Walcott requires no defence and commits no offence. See Book One, Chapter II, Part III (or 1.II.iii), wherein a narrator, presumably the poet himself, recalls – or pretends to – the moment when his title is born – amid a conversation with a Greek woman with "Asian cheeks," a sculptress in a studio attic somewhere in the Americas:

> "O-meros," she laughed. "That's what we call him in Greek,"
> stroking the small bust with its boxer's broken nose ...
>
> I felt the foam head watching as I stroked an arm, as
> cold as its marble, then the shoulders in winter light
> in the studio attic. I said "Omeros,"
>
> and O was the conch-shell's invocation, *mer* was
> both mother and sea in our Antillean patois,
> *os*, a grey bone, and the white surf as it crashes ...
>
> The name stayed in my mouth. I saw how light was webbed
> on her Asian cheeks, defined her eyes with a black
> almond's outline, as Antigone turned and said:
>
> "I'm tired of America, it's time for me to go back
> to Greece. I miss my islands." I write, it returns –
> the way she shook out the black gust of her hair ...
>
> [A]nd [I] felt that another cold bust, not hers, but yours
> saw this with stone almonds for eyes, its broken nose
> turning away ...
>
> But if it could read between the lines of her floor
> like a white-hot deck uncaulked by Antillean heat,
> to the shadows in its hold, its nostrils might flare
>
> at the stench from manacled ankles, the coffled feet
> scraping like leaves, and perhaps the inculpable marble
> would have turned its white seeds away, to widen

the white bow of its mouth at the horror under her table ...

And I heard a hollow moan exhaled from a vase,
not for kings floundering in lances of rain; the prose
of abrupt fishermen cursing over canoes. (14–15)

Walcott's rich, dense language fulfills Henriksen's Frygian maxim: "Literature is allusion; genre is lineage" (*Ambition and Anxiety* xxii). This short but productive fragment of the whole yields a definition of the epic not only as being, as Pound thought, "a poem including history" (qtd. in Henriksen 106), but also as already being epic, because that is what history *is*. In other words, in the *Omeros* fragment cited earlier, Walcott appreciates that the epic form is not only the "poem of poems," but that epic is *intrinsically* epic – i.e., an encyclopedic history – in its smallest particulars. Here his persona interacts with a sculptress who has fashioned a bust of Homer or "O-meros," the reputedly blind first epic poet (or group of singers), assigned authorship of *The Odyssey* and *The Iliad*. By invoking Homer here, Walcott's speaker lays claim audaciously to a lineage reaching back to the Homeric classics. But his Homer – Omeros – also boasts "a boxer's broken nose," which may conjure, for some of us, the many African-heritage pugilists who have dominated the sport in the last century. Hence, not only is Walcott's persona associated with a putatively white – and, here, physically white – culture hero of Occidental civilization, but both he and Omeros are associated implicitly with black boxers.[25]

In the following strophe, the bust looks on while Walcott's persona strokes the white arm of the sculptress and meditates on the name, O-mer-os, and its associations with sea, and bone, thus connecting the Antilles with the Greek archipelago. The sculptress herself seems Caucasian, but she has "Asian cheeks" and black hair (suggesting the possession of some Oriental genes). Too, her name is Antigone and she wants to return to the Greek islands, a fact that hints that she could also be Greek or possess a partially Greek ancestry. Yet, like Walcott's speaker – and, for that matter, like many Greeks and Europeans, Africans, and Asians, in general – Antigone is currently in the Americas, perhaps in the United States itself, as immigrant, exile, tourist, or migrant worker. Here Walcott connects two – or three – diasporas: the African, the Asian, and the European.

Next, Walcott's speaker imagines that Homer's white bust, with eyes that don't see but look like "seeds," may peer beneath the sculptress's floor, imagining it instead as a kind of slave ship, and find therein "horror," that is to say, the bodies of African slaves. In this complex movement, Walcott's speaker suggests the predominantly white woman artist (whose breasts he finds "cold") works out of and celebrates a culture – Western – erected on the horror of the Middle Passage. But, though he offers an archly sexist critique of the sculptress for not responding warmly enough to his "stroking," it is she, even if she represents and replicates the "high art" of the once-enslavers, who suggests for Walcott a poetic model and a poetic hero to emulate, so as to sing – so to speak – not of "[Greek] kings floundering in lances of rain," but "the prose / of abrupt fishermen cursing over canoes."

The further irony here is, though Homer is invoked as a Caucasian, Occidental cultural hero, Homer (Omeros) may also share Black African heritage. (The masculine Greek may be black; the female Greek may be Asian.) In addition, while the Greek bard Homer and his epics are referenced here, the actual form of the poem, *terza rima*, establishes comparison to Dante and his epic poem *The Divine Comedy*, yet another touchstone of Western civilization. While it may be argued that, in 1.II.iii, Walcott privileges African racial history over the European and Asian, it is difficult to offer this perspective unproblematically, given the evident worship of Homer, the speaker's implicit indebtedness to both Homer and Dante, the suggestion of Homer's "black" similarities, and the claim that Omeros would look away in horror from the revealed terrors and stench of the secret slave vessel lurking beneath the cultivated floors and facades of European high art. Furthermore, there is a primal equality between the Eurasian sculptress and the New World African poet (her suitor): Both are migrants.

Though my reading of this short fragment of *Omeros* has been inexcusably epic, it yet fails to encompass the comprehensive and cosmopolitan, world-historical vision of the poem, which certainly exceeds that of Dudek and Pratt, and which is certainly more democratic than that of Pound. Nevertheless, in largely avoiding the traps of ethnic and racial favouritism, and by being encyclopedically inclusive of roughly equalized histories, Walcott provides a way forward for all poets in English who may endeavour to author epic verse. Moreover, his example may be most exemplary for poets of minority backgrounds or for those from multicultural societies. Frankly, African-Canadian *and* all Canadian poets have much to gain by keeping *Omeros* in mind or at hand – should they wish to attempt epic poetry.

## V PHILIP'S *ZONG!*

There is at least one current African-Canadian contender for epic status. The Tobago-born, Toronto-based poet M. NourbeSe Philip (1947–), in

*Zong!* (2007), presents an epyllion – arguably an epic – based on Caribbean (not Canadian) history, and does so in the inclusive terms of Walcott, while favouring Pound-informed postmodernism over the former's pseudo-classical formalism. Philip reveals her acquaintance with Pound and with Walcott in her essay collection *A Genealogy of Resistance* (1997), suggesting her knowledge, then, of both poets' oeuvres.[26]

Philip's brilliant and impossible poem issues from its author's purpose to record "the Song of the untold story of [African slavery]; [what] cannot be told yet must be told, but only through its un-telling" (207). However, "record" is not the right verb; "transcribe" is better, for the text of *Zong!* has apparently been "told to the author by Setaey Adamu Boateng" (i) – an African spirit – whose surname appears as co-author on this hardcover book's title page and dust jacket (though not on its actual spine).

Philip assures us that her text is not only a "found" one, but that its words and tales and voices have been dictated to her, over seven years, from a document related to a true and infamous slaughter: the 1781 drowning of 130 to 150 African slaves, jettisoned from the slaver *Zong*, when its British captain determined that an insurance settlement for the perished cargo might yet earn his employers a profit on what was otherwise a loss-cursed expedition.

Philip names her text a "fugue"[27] (*Zong!* 204) and uses two recent neologisms to describe it: First, its issuance is (she borrows from Jacques Derrida) "hauntological,"[28] and its purpose is (in Philip's spelling) "exaqua" (201, 202) – to recover the African dead from the Middle Passage waters in which they were lost. Hence, the poetry here, especially after the first sixty pages of this six-part, two-hundred-page poem, emerges from a kind of seance, in which Philip, guided by Boateng, inks a text in which every word has been assembled and disassembled from the legal texts of the *Zong!* case. Although one can read the poem – with profound concentration and patience – from left to right and down, the pages look like gibberish, for words are split up, interrupted, spliced with sounds and phonemes from other languages, so that Philip attains the verbal equivalent of both J.M.W. Turner's canvases, where light and water erase forms, and bebop, where sound and rhythm displace melody.

Yet, her method also recovers the linguistic violence of slavery, so that "[w]ords break into sound, return to their initial ... phonic sound – grunts, plosives, labials" (205) and Philip transcribes "this language of grunt and groan, of moan and stutter – this language of pure sound fragmented and broken by history. This language of the limp and the wound" (205). In the end, narrative swirls into a whirlpool of voices. No two readers should ever agree on what they read here, for it is almost impossible to tell just who is saying what when.

Yet the careful reader will "hear" persistently the voice of a guilt-ridden, *white* mariner and husband,[29] who has signed up for the voyage to make money and bring home a slave girl for his wife, "Ruth," but who engages, with other crewmen, in rape, torture, and murder of Africans. He (or another) also ponders blacks, Christianity, and early capitalism, and recalls bits of Homer, Shakespeare, and Dante, often now rendered or positioned ironically. Though the practitioners of African slavery are indicted by their actions and by their own words, here taken apart and thrown up in the air (where some blow back in our collective faces), it is really a *human* story that is told, and the oppression of African people is conveyed through European stutters (mainly English) and African laments, all disrupted by inhumane deeds.

No quotation can do this daunting book justice. Here is a random fragment:

to se  cure our pro / fit we th  row them to res  cue our for / tunes we
do mur t  hey f / all to in   sure our pr  of its ov  / er & o
ver a  gain to sec / ure their re  scue the   y fall o / ver bo  ard to
pre  serve  our profit ... (140)

*Zong!* achieves what Afro-Hispanic-American poet Victor Hernández Cruz cites in his introduction to Adrian Castro's fine epyllion *Cantos to Blood & Honey* (1997): "a Caribbean projection realized," wherein "hermit and popular ingredients dance with each other," a "history of syntheses ...: Andalusian / Mediterranean olive oil, the native people whose energy, foods, and cigars have not disappeared," a "kaleidoscopic noble culture," and "criollo tripolarity and polyrhythmic versing approximat[ing] chant."[30] The form of Castro's verse (unrhymed and free-metred lines set in columnar strophes) is closer to that of Dudek and Pound than it is to that of Pratt and Walcott. Philip may not have read Castro, but her verse does share with his a desire for radical openness in form, while also sharing with Castro and Walcott a Caribbean, egalitarian alignment of peoples. The impediment to her poem becoming exemplary for others is not that it is difficult in content (it is not), but that it is difficult to read, to voice, *to sing*.[31]

To conclude, I think that the unquestionably African-Canadian epic poem, one also dealing with Canada as subject matter/space, to be effective, must bear out a multicultural and multiracial discourse in a barbarous babble – the polyphony of the rabble. Its form must be as raw and as open as the landscapes and seascapes of the Group of Seven and Emily Carr. It cannot be as static as either Pratt or Walcott, but move closer to the conversational tones of Dudek and Pound and Césaire. Finally, as Frank Kermode says of Milton's *Paradise Lost* (1667), it must use "an English of its own choice, for feats beyond normal usage, as great poems, each in its own way, must do."[32]

## VI TWO POEMS FROM "CANTICLES"

Given my conclusion, I offer the following poems, my own compositions, with necessary humility and requisite trepidation. These lyrics are excerpts from my own epic-in-progress, "Canticles," which canvasses – utilizing the info-telegraphic style of Pound's *Cantos* – the image of the "black" in Occidental civilizations, the transatlantic slave trade, and its discontents, and, in passing, the bloody flux and flow of imperialism and colonialism. I follow Walcott in modifying my basic *vers libre* by granting it generic voice as dramatic monologue(s). I acknowledge Philip by presenting, though less radically than she, an epic of phrasing (if not of phrases). I trust that the poems are self-evident (or self-disclosing) in meaning. Assuredly, they are set in a historic framework, exploiting here the presence of Pound in Italy and his adherence to Mussolini (if not explicitly to fascism) as well as the African-American scholar W.E.B. Du Bois's communist and pan-Africanist opposition to fascism, as well as to Italian aggression in East Africa.

### EZRA POUND VISITS RIMINI, 1935 (II)[33]

I.
Now, a black cat ogles me:
The feline eyes a "crypto-Fascist" poet
*or* merely an Americo-Italo poet –
as democratic as is Jefferson
and/or Mussolini?

Well, the cat remains blackly opaque
in its oblique *Recognition* ...

(But cornered in an ecclesiastical corner,
casting a well-fed shadow,
eyeballing the Fascist altar

for Italy's African slain,
there's the rotund, Niggerati inmate –
the profoundly well-rounded Du Bois –
bracingly cerebral –
who, like me, squirted a squib
for Nancy Cunard's seven-seas encyclopedia,
*Negro* [1934].

I cast my hat brim below my brow.
If he spots me, that darkie Commie
will scowl and berate –

play the Harvahd man—
shades of Ol' Possum Tom* –
underrating
a no-name-college Master of Arts.)

II.
Sigismundo – "Sidge" –
bid Alberti build a temple
whose façade is Augustus's Arch,
Tiberius's Bridge,
but also conjuring Greek fashions;

and Sidge was Caesar enough –
man o' war enough –
to steal Pletho's bones outta Greece
and crook em in a marble crypt
on the temple's right
(as ye enter),
so the sacred philosopher
could have his remaining constitution –

the bony alphabet of his corpus –

persist among a people –
the Riminese –

---

\* T.S. Eliot.

as free as the sea's insurgent waves.

(A skeleton's "spelling" signs off
on the vanity of flesh.)

III.
And how else would Ixotta
*not* be an unknown bed-warmer,
if *not* for Sidge's purchasing of portraits –
his cinema as Maecenas –
i.e., pimp-muse –
to painters, poets, architects, eh?

Who else to divulge (Ixotta
as quixotic)
Venus,
if not divine Apollo's heir?

Rain washes saint and sinner alike,
but an *artiste*
gouges out a garden;
he farms precipitation –
and harvests
sunflowers and/or *prosecco* grapes.

IV.
Sidge was "the best loser in all history"
(not counting Nat Turner
or Spartacus);
thus, he forecasts Muss's *Triumph*:

This *condottiere* conducts us to *Il Duce*.

I mean,
Sidge's jaunty suffering prefaces
*Le Grand Guerre* and Muss's services –
surviving the trench holocaust,
the miniature clouds suffocating
or blistering lungs
in *Obeisance*

to Great Power machinations...

It taketh a Great Man to break free
of "free" press (propaganda)
and "free" enterprise (fraud) –
the war boosters and financier bankrupts –

and refute the annual *Fear*
of December 31,
or simply the nightly *Fear*
of tomorrow;

and take even his own tears as arrogant brew!

V.
I laud Muss as a breathing principle –
as commanding and as sculpting
as Moors running Europe
(after overrunning Spain)...

Surely, he feeds *State* enemies
barrels of castor oil,

or baptizes em in gasoline
and lets fire canonize em;

or he chops em into poxy shards;

and/or he torches their redoubts to ash...

Here be a plausible *Canto*:
Muss must be as bloody
as a bullet in the brain

to elevate Italy...

VI.
Sidge was the righteous precedent
for Muss, his successor:

To abort moochers –
*Racailles* –
strip off their fake merit(s) –

peppery or salty *Irreligion* –

and broadcast their gangster screams,
their epic whining

(sounds of hounds).

I feel I'm Sidge's or –
Muss's –
angelically angry companion!

*Si*, to make the world safe for Renaissances
(plural),
and for artist (Dante)
and artisan (Gaudier-Brzeska),

arms traders must be purged –
interest-rate buggerer-uppers must be expunged –

through processes as exhaustive
and stringent
as any *Divorce*.

VII.
To be rid of lice!
To be rid of vipers!
To be rid of slimy parvenus –
cancer-stuffed assholes!
To be rid of the shifty terminology
of plutocrat-purchased "democrats,"
the aristocrats of debasement!

A citizen demands a boss of undoubted *Sovereignty*;
whose popular business is mass *Happiness*;
whose glamorous *Sensibility*
echoes Confucius;

and whose occasions of *Artifice*
are correctly punitive

(thus the *Majesty* of executions).

Regard how all Italy eats out of Muss's hand;
that right hand that delivers seeds, acreage, oxen,
plus wine, milk, honey, fish,

and automobile manufacture even

(by *fiat*).

Regard how gilded foes
get packed into black trenches
and coffined in lye:
Their last sight is dirt.

Sidge / Muss:
These are agile identities.

VIII.
Riminese, as my *Opera Omnia* opens
to *History*,
I add a brace of *Cantos*
to the *Golden Book*
flanking Gemisthus's sepulchre,

and exalt Sidge as the first
Romagnolo man composed of fertile muck,

who buggers bishops and impregnates nuns,

who intuits that Venus, Cleopatra, Bathsheba,
are goddesses resident
in every irresistible beauty,

and that each such vamp is

*settimocielo*.

[Montréal (Québec)–Cornwall (Ontario), VIA train 06 – Car 6, Seat 4C: 21 *novembre* mmxiv]

*À TEMPIO MALATESTIANO (RIMINI)*
by W.E.B. Du Bois

I.
The morbid brilliance of Sigismondo
(World Protector) –
*War*-torn poet –
his demonically sexual lust
for battle –
maketh me cringe.

Larger-than-life, Renaissance rebel –
who did radically smack down Pope
and/or Turks
(depending on *Occasion*),
forecast Mussolini,

this excruciating bandit –
all pretense of *Piety* –
his brain a gunfighter machanism.

II.
Th'adolescent Bishop cometh unto him
to threaten *Damnation*
but Sigismondo offered his own *Salvation*:

ostentatious, public *Buggery*,
to lampoon the lad
with a human harpoon ...

His troop cheered on the frivolous *Violation*,
jeering at the bent over, bottom-fouled Bishop –

jeered as the lad whimpered –

proving the Papacy no untouchable pussy.

III.
Malatesta (Evil-head) plotted to put
his own pontiff
on St Peter's seat.

He'd do remorseless massacres,
experience massive climaxes,

jetting blood from foes' necks,
jetting sperm into ladies' faces,

to enact the fantastic *Policy* –

to present the Papacy
as a common *Commodity*,

thus beautifully degraded.

Raunchy, touchy, a normal "madman,"
He'd be happy to end up eating a Pope –
murdering just to kill,
fucking just to bugger,

to enact his black-shirt seizure of Rome.

IV.
S.M. (Sado-Maso)
ain't one of the kneeling faction,

but is obscenely spleenful,
executing the coal-sparkling skills
of *Assassination*, *Serial Murder*, *Massacre*:

To ply *Rape* and play out *Ruction*
be Sigismondo's *Scripture*
(S.S.) –

to mould flesh into maggot cake,
to be as irreligious as a tiger –

and pounce pon priests
(decrepit mannequins)...

v.
Not to like his face?
Who don't like his face?

Oil, nickel, guns, coffee, chocolate, tobacco,
be comin soon –

plus non-stop campaign of literal backstabbing
and throat cutting –

clearing off Red Chief, Black Chief,

North/South America, Caribbean,
Africa...

The prevailing momentum of Europe's *History* –
from peasants vs. popes
to conquistadors vs. Kings –
is to cannibalize every culture
that got no cannon –

gut every *Civilization*
that got no gunpowder.

That's Sigismondo "Mussolini":
his symbol.

[Rimini (Italy), 8 *novembre* mmxiv]

## NOTES

1 In the end, however, Pound's own epic, *The Cantos*, is dramatically heteroglossic.
2 His *The Lusiads* (1572) relates Portuguese history to both biblical and Greek heroic poetry. Yet, Camões's text is aggressively racist in its effort to justify Portuguese imperialism versus non-whites and non-Christians. In a typical confrontation, the Portuguese – "not men to suffer [Moslem] dogs to

show their teeth," – cannonade the foe, "spreading death all around," and follow up "the victory with more killing and destruction" (52–3).
3 *The Cantos* is exceedingly difficult to date, because, like Whitman's *Leaves of Grass*, it appears in many editions; moreover, it was published in successive chunks, as it was being written. The Faber & Faber Fourth Collection Edition (1987) may be taken as a legitimate conclusion to the work, which ended, definitively, with the author's death in 1972. An initial, experimental "Three Cantos" appeared in *Poetry* in 1917.
4 In his study of *The Cantos*, Peter Stoicheff remarks that Pound makes a "backward glance" – or pseudo-revisionist statements – at the conclusion of his epic, because he seeks to return "to a point in the poem and his career free of their particular overt, and covert, political and racist voices" (8). The insight is intriguing, because it suggests that Pound begins to question (perhaps too little, too late) the ethnic ethics of his text. Stoicheff argues that a similar questioning afflicts "other long poems of the twentieth century" (8). It is not likely the case that Pratt indulges such interrogation in his "Brébeuf." However, Stoicheff's other finding is likely applicable: "the modern long poem is always a poem in conflict with itself, that the characteristic of length creates the limitless potential for the poem's successive stages to contest its earlier mandates" (8).
5 According to WikiAnswers.com, the origins of the compound word "Sehnsucht" come from the German words for "longing" and "addiction" or "insatiable craving." Its usage here may refer to a composition by German composer Georg Schumann (1866–1952).
6 The Polish-born English novelist Joseph Conrad (1857–1924) was christened Józef Teodor Konrad Nalecz Korzeniowski.
7 Marlow encounters a Swedish captain who tells him about "a man who hanged himself on the road ... a Swede, too" (Conrad, *Heart of Darkness* 120). When Marlow asks, "Hanged himself! Why, in God's name?" The captain replies, "Who knows? The sun too much for him, or the country perhaps" (Conrad 120).
8 Alev Lytle Croutier opines, "Orientalism is the Western version of the Orient, created by the Western imagination ... It is the East of fantasy, of dreams" (173). These fantasies include everything from "A man enjoying himself with more than one woman" (176), as in the popular conception of the harem, to "The concept of *keyf* (fulfillment in sweet nothingness)" (177), which can be realized by "Smoking opium and hashish" (177).
9 Djwa and Moyles miss the salient point that it is easier to be a "national poet," i.e., a poet of the people, if one is – as Whitman was – a populist

addressing the popular classes. It is much harder to play that role, *truly*, if one is an academic poet addressing Ivory Tower inmates and their elite acolytes, and that was Pratt's predicament.

10  See Shelley's "A Defence of Poetry" (1821, 1840).
11  A typical, scathing portrait of the results of French imperialism in Martinique runs (in English translation): "Everybody despises the *rue Paille*, where the young are debauched. It is here especially that the sea pours forth its filth, dead cats and dogs." "Shameful," says Césaire's persona, "this *rue Paille*" (54). Certainly, rue Paille is the antithesis of Paris's Panthéon; yet it's a pipeline to Paris's Pigalle prostitution district.
12  Thus, Orientalism tints Pratt, too.
13  Historians dispute the figure, for slavery in Nouvelle-France was multiracial (involving Panis Aboriginals, Negroes from throughout the Atlantic world, and then various and easily confused shades of Métis and Mulattoes). Moreover, it covered a vast swath of North America. In any event, for the territory that is now Quebec, Marcel Trudel settled on a figure of "at least 4,185, of which 2,683 were Panis and 1,443 black," over two hundred years (Mackey 95).
14  In this sentence, Sartre esteems the black poet as spokesperson for his *group*, even if his lyricism is individual. The black poet is, then, a vatic, inspired by occult forces, not, presumably, by his or her studies at La Sorbonne.
15  Qtd. in Terrell, *A Companion*, vii.
16  For instance, in Chapters XXV to XXVIII, Walcott's character Achille suffers a vatic trance, via sunstroke, wherein he returns to Africa by walking along the bottom of the Atlantic, to surface to observe a "natural" – if not paradisiacal, pre-slavery, black homeland, but also to witness the onset of the terror and torture of the transatlantic Slave Trade Diaspora (133–52).
17  Joseph Pivato recognizes that the praise of an "ethnic" writer's vocalization of his or her history can actually enact "another form of marginalization, the reduction of this writing to sociological accounts of past experience" (244).
18  I am tempted to add, following a theory of Linda Hutcheon, that Pound's moments of quotation represent a kind of *adaptation*: an act of decontextualization and reconfiguration. Henriksen, *pace* Bakhtin, holds that "any secondary rewriting of a primary genre is necessarily ideological and involves irony" (xxii). Quotation should be read then as an ironic intervention – a subversive correction or a corrective subversion – of an argument.
19  Frye, *Five Essays*, 3.
20  See, for instance, Tryphonopoulos and Adams (141).

21 See Canto XIV.
22 Henriksen, *Ambition and Anxiety*, xx.
23 See, for instance, XXIX.iii, wherein history is telescoped, but kaleidoscopic, moving from "A Jesuit mission // burned in Veracruz"; to "a Sephardic merchant ... / crouched by a Lisbon dock ... // reborn in the New World"; and from "A snow-headed Negro froze in the Pyrennees, / an ape behind bars, to Napoleon's orders" to "Wilberforce ... struck by lightning, a second Saul / at the crossroads of empire" (ll. 155–6).
24 In Canto LXXVII, Chinese and Persian characters appear alongside French, Latin, Italian, Greek, German, fragments of putatively African-American speech, as well as a seemingly (typographically) Russian-accented sentence, and there is standard English, dialect English, as well as much slang (American and British).
25 Walcott is also conjuring playfully the controversy sparked by Martin Bernal's 1987 work, *Black Athena: The Afroasiatic Roots of Classical Civilization*, which asserts that ancient Greek thought is derived from Egyptian (African) and Phoenician (Asian) sources. So Homer's white bust, with its broken nose, becomes as black-identified as the historical Omeros may have been.
26 For Pound, see 64–5, 95 (albeit only tacitly: Philip uses Pound's Confucian proviso, "MAKE IT NEW"), and 231, n3; for Walcott, see 52, 201–2, 204, and, for two quotations from studies of his work, see 63.
27 Pound uses the same term to describe his *Cantos*. See Kay Davis, *Fugue and Fresco: Structures in Pound's* Cantos (1984).
28 See Derrida, *Spectres of Marx* (1993).
29 Or, says Philip, "someone who appears to be white, male, and European" (*Zong!* 204).
30 Cruz, "Introcaribination," 8–9.
31 In my introduction to my *Whylah Falls* (1990), I insist, "Form is as form does" and "The secret is to sing" (xxiv). Effective epic should be singable.
32 Kermode, "Heroic Milton," 29.
33 These two poems were submitted to this volume as work in progress and can now be found, in their final and polished version, in George Elliott Clarke's *Canticles I (MMXVII)* (Toronto: Guernica Editions, 2017), on pages 377–81 and 374–6 respectively.

## BIBLIOGRAPHY

Anonymous. "The Metre Columbian." Posted 29 September 2000 by Abraham Thomas. http://www.cs.rice.edu/~ssiyer/minstrels/poems/561.html (accessed 15 October 2015, at 7 a.m. EST).

Bernal, Martin. *Black Athena: The Afroasiatic Roots of Classical Civilization.* New Brunswick, NJ: Rutgers University Press, 1987.

Camoens, Luis Vaz de. *The Lusiads.* 1572. Translated by William C. Atkinson. London: Penguin, 1952.

Castro, Adrian. *Cantos to Blood & Honey.* Minneapolis: Coffee House Press, 1997.

Césaire, Aimé Fernand David. *Cahier d'un retour au pays natal.* 1939. *Cahier d'un retour au pays natal / Return to My Native Land.* Translated by Emile Snyder. Paris: Présence Africaine, 1971.

Clarke, George Elliott. Introduction to *Whylah Falls*, [x]–xxiv. 1990. Vancouver, BC: Polestar/Raincoast, 2000.

Conrad, Joseph. *Heart of Darkness.* 1902. In *Modern British Literature*, edited by Frank Kermode and John Hollander, 108–71. New York: Oxford University Press, 1973.

Croutier, Alev Lytle. *Harem: The World behind the Veil.* New York: Abbeville Press, 1989.

Cruz, Victor Hernández. "Introcaribination: The Poetry of Adrian Castro." Introduction to Adrian Castro, *Cantos to Blood & Honey*, 8–9. Minneapolis: Coffee House Press, 1997.

Dante [Alighieri]. [The Divine Comedy]. *Divina Commedia.* Foligno (Italy): Johann Neumeister, 1472.

Davis, Kay. *Fugue and Fresco: Structures in Pound's "Cantos."* Orono: National Poetry Foundation, University of Maine at Orono, 1984.

Derrida, Jacques. *Spectres of Marx: The State of the Debt, the Work of Mourning, and the New International.* 1993. Translated by Peggy Kamuf. London: Routledge, 1994.

Djwa, Sandra, and R.G. Moyles, eds. "Introduction." In *E.J. Pratt: Complete Poems, Part 1.* Edited by Sandra Djwa and R.G. Moyles, xi–xlviii. Toronto: University of Toronto Press, 1989.

Dudek, Louis. *Europe.* 1955. Erin, ON: The Porcupine's Quill, 1991.

– Preface to *Europe*, 9–19. Erin, ON: The Porcupine's Quill, 1991.

Dudek, Louis, and Michael Gnarowski, eds. 2nd ed. *The Making of Modern Poetry in Canada: Essential Articles on Contemporary Canadian Poetry in English.* 1967. Toronto: The Ryerson Press, 1970.

Frye, Northrop. *Anatomy of Criticism: Four Essays.* Princeton: Princeton University Press, 1957.

– "Canada and Its Poetry" (1943). In *The Making of Modern Poetry in Canada: Essential Articles on Contemporary Canadian Poetry in English*, edited by Louis Dudek and Michael Gnarowski, 86–97. 1967. Toronto: The Ryerson Press, 1970.

– *Five Essays on Milton's Epics*. London: Routledge & Kegan Paul, 1966.
Henriksen, Line. *Ambition and Anxiety: Ezra Pound's "Cantos" and Derek Walcott's "Omeros" as Twentieth-Century Epics*. Amsterdam: Rodopi, 2006.
Homer. *The Iliad*. 760–710 BC. Translated by Robert Fagles. New York: Penguin, 1998.
– *The Odyssey*. 800–760 BC. Translated by Robert Fitzgerald. Garden City, New York: Doubleday, 1961.
Hutcheon, Linda. *A Theory of Adaptation*. Routledge: New York, 2006.
Kermode, Frank. "Heroic Milton: Happy Birthday." *New York Review of Books* 56, no. 3 (26 February 2009): 26–9.
Longfellow, Henry Wadsworth. *Evangeline [and the Evangeline Country]*. 1847. Toronto: Collins, 1947, 61–188.
– *The Song of Hiawatha*. London: T. Nelson and Sons, 1855.
Lönnrot, Elias, ed. and comp. *The Kalerala*. Translated by Keith Bosley. Oxford: Oxford University Press, 2008.
Mackey, Frank. *Done with Slavery: The Black Fact in Montreal*. Montreal and Kingston: McGill-Queen's University Press, 2010.
Milton, John. *Paradise Lost*. London: Parker, Boulter, Walker, 1667.
Moody, A. David. *Ezra Pound: Poet*. Vol. I: *The Young Genius, 1885–1920*. New York: Oxford University Press, 2007.
Philip, M. NourbeSe. *A Genealogy of Resistance and Other Essays*. Toronto: The Mercury Press, 1997.
– *Zong!* Toronto: The Mercury Press, 2008.
Pivato, Joseph. *Echo: Essays on Other Literatures*. Toronto: Guernica, 1994.
Pound, Ezra. *The Cantos*. Fourth Collection Edition. London: Faber & Faber, 1987.
– Canto XIV. *Selected Cantos of Ezra Pound*. New York: New Directions, 1948, 1970, 23–7.
– Canto LXXVII. *The Pisan Cantos*, 42–53. Edited by Richard Sieburth. 1948. New York: New Directions, 2003.
– "Three Cantos." *Poetry* 10, no. 3 (June 1917): 113–254.
Pratt, E.J. *Brébeuf and His Brethren*. 1940. In *E.J. Pratt: Complete Poems. Part 2*, edited by Sandra Djwa and R.G. Moyles, 46–110. Toronto: University of Toronto Press, 1989.
– *Towards the Last Spike*. Toronto: Macmillan, 1952.
Sartre, Jean-Paul. *Black Orpheus*. Translated by S.W. Allen. Paris: Présence Africaine, 1976. (First published as "Orphée Noire," in *Anthologie de la nouvelle poésie nègre et malgache de langue française*. Edited by L.S. Senghor. Paris: Presse universitaires de France, 1948.)

Shelley, Percy Bysshe. *Essays, Letters from Abroad, Translations and Fragments.* London: Edward Moxon, 1840.

Spengler, Oswald. *Der Untergang des Abendlandes.* 2 vols. Munich: C.H. Beck, 1918 and 1922.

Stoicheff, Peter. *The Hall of Mirrors: Drafts & Fragments and the End of Ezra Pound's "Cantos."* Ann Arbor: University of Michigan Press, 1995.

Terrell, Carroll Franklin. *A Companion to "The Cantos" of Ezra Pound.* Vol. 1. Berkeley: University of California Press, 1980.

Tryphonopopoulos, Demetres P., and Stephen J. Adams, eds. *The Ezra Pound Encyclopedia.* Westport: Greenwood Press, 2005.

Walcott, Derek. *Omeros.* New York: Farrar, Straus & Giroux, 1990.

Whitman, Walt. *Leaves of Grass.* 1855. Mineola, New York: Dover Publications, 2007.

# Reading Literature through Translation: The Case of Antonio D'Alfonso into Italian

*Maria Cristina Seccia*

This chapter discusses the relationship between literary and translation studies and explores how translation as practice can be a form of literary criticism. The theoretical reflections expressed by Marilyn Gaddis Rose in her seminal work *Translation and Literary Criticism: Translation as Analysis* (1997) guides my analysis of Antonello Lombardi's *La passione di Fabrizio* (2002), the Italian translation of *Fabrizio's Passion* (1995/2000) by the Montreal author Antonio D'Alfonso.[1] My examination is informed by a previous analysis of the source text in light of D'Alfonso's position within the Canadian literary system. The final aim of this chapter is to establish what interpretation of the work Lombardi's translation offers to Italian readers.

As observed by Rose, "translating brings us *into* a literary work":[2] transposing a message into the target language allows translators to enter the text and to become aware of the specific connotations of expressions in the source language. In light of this, the process of translation enables the closest reading of a source text. The translators' resulting interpretation is inscribed in their translation, which is, as a result, the reflection of what the source text meant to the translators themselves.[3] This is confirmed by translation theorist Lawrence Venuti, who argues that translators transform a source text into an autonomous target text by inscribing their own interpretation.[4] The transformation occurs through different translation strategies selected by translators, depending on the facet they want to emphasize. By undergoing a process of transformation, all translations are subject to losses and gains.[5] According to Rose, works of literature can only gain in translation (*Translation and Literary Criticism* 2): through their interpretation, translators can enrich the reading of the source text and add a further layer, which will guide the target-text audience in its reading. From this perspective, translation, like literary criticism, can be an expansion of a literary work and can enhance its understanding (12). This sheds light on the translator's essential role in the interpretation and critical reception of a translated literary work. A talented literary translator is therefore not only the closest reader of a literary work, a cultural mediator and a writer, but also a literary critic. A critical reading of the source text, in fact, entails a theoretical-analytical approach to translation, which is in turn a source of critical reading for the target audience. In view of this, translation "leads, follows and supports" literary criticism, to employ Rose's phraseology (11).

This chapter will be divided into two main parts: it will begin with an introductory discussion of the author, D'Alfonso, showing how he positions himself in the Canadian literary system. This will shed light on my critical analysis of *Fabrizio's Passion*. I will then move on to the examination of the translation, *La passione di Fabrizio*.

The semi-autobiographical novel *Fabrizio's Passion* is a particularly useful source to analyze when considering the relationship between translation and literary criticism, because it deeply reflects D'Alfonso's passion for translation, which he defines as "the most beautiful act of love a writer can offer another writer."[6] Interestingly, the novel was self-translated into French under the title *Avril ou l'anti-passion*, which was published by Montreal publisher VLB in 1990. As explained by the author himself in his essay "There Is No 'Proper' English," he "consciously chose" to publish the French version before the English one for commercial reasons, since his work had rarely received positive reviews in anglophone Canada.[7] In a conversation with Italian-Canadian critic Pasquale Verdicchio, author of the introduction to the Italian translation, D'Alfonso specified that he was "destroyed" by anglophone Canadian literary critics, who did not appreciate the style of his language, while his French version became a bestseller and received several positive reviews.[8] However, it also received negative comments from a reviewer, who interpreted it as a criticism of nationalism.[9] The substantial differences in content and perspective show how the author was influenced by the audience he had in mind and the socio-political as well as cultural contexts in which his works were published. Most notably, it is important to note how D'Alfonso's French self-translation of the English version *Fabrizio's Passion* led to a remarkably different critical reception. The works of D'Alfonso, who is a translator himself as well as a multilingual writer, poet, and filmmaker, offer insightful reflections on the relationship between language, (self-) translation, and cultural and national identity. As a cultural critic and former publisher, he has made a significant contribution to the heated debate on cultural and linguistic diversity in Canada.

As an author of Italian origins who was born in Montreal and spent part of his life in Toronto, D'Alfonso has devoted a considerable portion of his literary and critical writing to reflections on his transcultural identity, as declared in his essay "A Place on Earth": "Within me the Italian, English and French cultures were able to flourish freely and dynamically ... Whatever I have accomplished as a person is largely due to this complex triangulation of cultures."[10]

D'Alfonso's tricultural identity is revealed to be even more multifaceted in a reflection expressed in his "Italicamente," another essay included in his volume *In Italics: In Defense of Ethnicity* (1996): "I am an Abbruzzese/Molisano/Canadian/Quebecois/Italian/European/North American. It is a never-ending list of terms which never completely exhaust my identity, though each term may rightly add a new element to the composite that constitutes me."[11] Through this interminable list of nationalities, D'Alfonso refuses to identify himself with one single culture: he is not only the product of the two conflicting "mainstream" cultures inhabiting the same "country," but he is also "European" and "North American." By associating his cultural identity with the two continents, he seems to stress the opposing cultural values of the "Old World" and "New World," often discussed by Italian-Canadian authors who experienced migration in the early- and mid-twentieth century. Most interestingly, D'Alfonso specifies that he is not simply Italian but "Abbruzzese" and "Molisano," a specification that discloses his strong regional identity, inherited from his parents, and unveils his appreciation of the cultural diversity characterizing Italy. His refusal of the idea of a one-to-one relationship between the country of Italy and its culture also emerges from his use of the term *Italic*, which inspired the title of his volume *In Italics: In Defense of Ethnicity* mentioned above. As clarified in a later essay, "The Future of Italic Culture," this neologism, unlike the adjective *Italian*, emphasizes the detachment of culture from country and goes beyond the geographical borders of the Italian state.[12] In the introduction to *In Italics*, the author explains that he inherited an anti-nationalist feeling from his parents:

> One of the troubles against which I react in a visceral manner is the rise of a nationalistic fervor. This may be due to the fact that my parents, who left a war-ridden Italy, taught me to mistrust any sentiment of nationalism. Perhaps it is because I was born in a minority (Italian) that was dominated by another minority (French) which felt colonized by an overwhelming majority (British). Real and fictitious, whatever the reason, I have become allergic to any blind adherence to an identity which bases itself on a nationalistic sentiment.[13]

D'Alfonso's cultural background leads him to endorse the controversial term *ethnicity*, as disclosed by the subtitle of his volume mentioned above, which denies a one-to-one relationship between country and culture/language.[14] While several transcultural Canadian authors and critics consider this term to be a label adopted by mainstream anglophone/francophone society to marginalize Canadians with different cultural origins (see, for instance, Verdicchio 45; Kamboureli 28; Padolsky 249; Tuzi 8; Ricci 134), D'Alfonso perceives it as a "mark of prestige"[15] and a declaration of non-assimilation into Canadian dominant culture. However, accepting his own "ethnic" identity, which was often a cause for cultural discriminations, in particular during his adolescence, proved to be a "slow and often painful" process for D'Alfonso.[16] He subsequently realized that ethnicity is a "process of awareness."[17] He accepted his ethnic identity only after questioning his Canadian identity: "I thought I was Canadian. But I was soon to learn: even if I wanted to be a Canadian, I couldn't. One is given only one chance to be a Canadian, or for that matter any nationality. And that chance appears in the form of assimilation."[18] D'Alfonso invites his fellow "ethnic" authors to undergo a similar re-analysis of their own cultural origins, without which they "can never find their place in a country," but remain "at the margin of literature."[19]

D'Alfonso's semi-autobiographical novel *Fabrizio's Passion* is the literary expression of the author's analysis of his own transnational identity and offers critical reflections on notions of language, nation, and country, which are a key to a reading of his work. Narrator Fabrizio Notte, a Montreal artist of Italian origins, is in search of his identity, which leads him to recount the salient moments of his family's history. It is the account of Fabrizio's failure as a lover, a writer, and a filmmaker. Most of the twenty-five chapters are narrated by the main protagonist, while others take different forms, such as letters written by Fabrizio's father during his military service, passages from the diaries of his mother, Lina, scripts of his movies, and excerpts from his own diary. A linear narrative thread is replaced by a collection of flashbacks, digressions, and reflections on cultural identity, language, nation, and sexuality. As D'Alfonso has admitted, in a conversation with Verdicchio, the novel "tells the story by the use of fragments" in an unconventional way, often via a lack of characterization, which was cause for a negative reception in anglophone Canada.[20] Most of the narrator's considerations of his transnational identity take place during his sexual encounters with Lea, his Hungarian lover, who is also the wife of his best friend, Mario. Fabrizio associates the idea of love with that of language, since they both help to recognize the "other," while he relates passion, which poses the risk of "blindness" as well as "obsession," with nationalism, which is equivalent to the effacement of the "other." The novel therefore reveals Fabrizio's quest for a balance between passion and anti-passion.

The narrator shares the author's difficulty in accepting his cultural difference. As is typical of migrant and diasporic subjects living in Canada in the mid-twentieth century, Italian origins represent for Fabrizio an obstacle to his integration in Canada. Living in an Italian diasporic environment, "a reality which [he] did not fully understand" (*Fabrizio's Passion* 61), makes him feel different from his peers: "I don't understand why Father and Mother, on the one hand, keep repeating to Lucia and me that the 'others' can do what they please because it is their home here and, on the other hand, that we have to do what we can which, very often simply is never enough" (56). His cultural difference, which he perceives as otherness, is symbolized by his mother's "meatball Panini prepared with Sunday's leftovers" (124) while he was longing for the peanut-butter sandwiches of his Québécois schoolmates. The sense of otherness led Fabrizio to scorn his Italian cultural origins and initially to wish to assimilate into Canadian society: "Being Italian, I dream of changing myself into Canadian. To be simply Italian is an aberration, something that is outdated, something to be ashamed of; whereas the Canadian is the hero I wish to emulate" (61). His cousin's family becomes for him the emblem of Canadian society and a model to follow: "My godfather is a Notte, just like my father, but a Canadian Notte. He represents for me that which I want to become" (61). Fabrizio thinks that emulating his Canadian cousins, who opened "the doors to happiness" (61), would allow his integration into Canadian society, and would help him start a new life. Spending the summer with them made him feel free: "free to eat ground meat fried in butter and served on sliced Wonder bread, free to drink Cream Soda and, just before going to bed, have a glass of milk with Village biscuits" (61). Their wooden wagon, their "magic car," represents for him his "way out of [his] parents' home" (61): "Every day I take a ride across the heavens on my wooden chariot pulled by horses with wings. I see no one. I speak to no one. I am in a dream in which only my cousins are permitted to enter. They laugh their heads off and say: 'Fabrizio is finally able to play with what his parents won't buy him'" (61–2). Fabrizio's desire to integrate into Canadian/Québécois society leads him to undergo a process of "cultural translation" (Bhabha, *The Location*), namely acts of negotiation between his diasporic Italian identity and his Canadian/Québécois one. Like the author who has accepted his Italian cultural difference, the narrator subsequently realizes that assimilation is not the solution to his quest for identity: "Is it my fault if I am different? It's not as though I work at being different. I am myself. Difference is valid only if one's essence is open" (*Fabrizio's Passion* 170). The narrator therefore accepts his cultural difference and realizes that his cultural identity is constructed through a negotiation of his Italian and Canadian ones. His transcultural identity emerges clearly when he challenges essentialist definitions of *culture* and *country*:

> To be Latin: What the hell does it mean? How should we portray, on screen, characters that are neither of British nor French descent? Mine, a film on the chaos of language, on ethnic dissension. What am I? If a Canadian, can I say I'm Italian? If an Italian, can I say I'm Canadian? Or is my identity purely North American? Answers to such ontological questions can never arise from a simplified concept like "country." What is a country? What is a territory? A nation? Or worse, what does the age-old myth known as "roots" truly imply? (163)

The narrator praises the conception that a nation is a group of people who share the same language, ideology, and culture, but not the idea that a nation is confined to the borders of any one country. According to the narrator, who moves across national boundaries and dissolves them, Italian culture – like any other culture – cannot be confined to geographical boundaries. His idea of nation is reminiscent of theorist Benedict Anderson's idea of an "imagined political community," namely an indefinite concept built up on imaginary connections between the members of that assumed group.[21]

The narrator's resistance to any nationalist feelings emerges clearly in the reflections he shares with Lea: "What can I say, Lea, about the nationalist obsession that leads men and women to believe that a piece of land should grow its own particular brand of people?" (*Fabrizio's Passion* 191). His refusal of a one-to-one relationship between language and country is in line with post-colonial cultural theorist Homi Bhabha's idea of hybridity (*The Location*). As observed by Bhabha, the boundaries of a nation are not simple, straightforward, or certain, but shifting and ambivalent, and they "alienate frontiers of the modern nation."[22] Similarly, the narrator rejects the concept of "country," which he sees as a political construction: "There is no such thing as a 'pure' country. We all come from elsewhere" (*Fabrizio's Passion* 89). From his perspective, he shares Bhabha's idea that a nation can never be perceived as whole or pure, but rather as a hybrid ambivalent space constructed by multiple identities (Bhabha, "Dissemination"). As Bhabha explains, hybridity implies a view of the world in which the fixity is continually contested; it dismantles the sense of anything being "pure" or "essential," and stresses the notion of heterogeneity and difference (*The Location*). All cultural systems are constructed in the "Third Space," where the "negotiation of incommensurable differences creates a tension peculiar to borderline existences."[23]

This sort of "in-between space," an interstitial passage between fixed identifications, opens up the possibility of a cultural hybridity that entertains difference without an assumed or imposed hierarchy.[24] Bhabha's observations are clearly embraced by the narrator when he declares himself to be the citizen of a deterritorialized nation-state: "O Lea, how can I tell you where I come from if I haven't said *where I am* at the present moment? I want to be a stateless man. An eternal pilgrim. I want to plant a tree in every city and country I visit" (*Fabrizio's Passion* 193, original emphasis). Fabrizio is clearly unable to define his cultural identity: he wants to be both Italian and Canadian, and yet he refuses to be either as an act of resistance to fixed notions of cultural identity. The metaphor of the pilgrim highlights the length of his journey, which has the "Third Space" as its final destination. He is in a continual movement between the culture of his origins and those of the city and country where he lives.

The narrator is involved in a further process of "cultural translation," this time one conceived in travel writing,[25] when he "translates" his Italian diasporic environment for his Canadian readers. Just like travel writers, the narrator describes, for those reading about his culture, how people of a different culture interpret the world. Through his "foreign gaze,"[26] namely an external perspective, he represents Italian diasporic subjects as the "other," thus contributing to the circulations of cultural stereotypes. The Canadian perspective from which he looks at Italian culture emerges clearly when he refers to the Italian diasporic community as "the Italians" (*Fabrizio's Passion* 55), judges their style as "kitchy" (148), presents the kitchen as "the master room of the Italian household" (43), and ironically calls Italy "Wopland" (107) as a way to exorcise the discrimination he suffered as a child. He emphasizes the conservative nature of his family, which maintained local culinary traditions, such as preparing the homemade sausage every autumn.

The narrator acts as a "fictional translator," to use Rita Wilson's terms ("Cultural Mediation" 236–9), namely a cultural mediator between Italian culture and his Canadian readers, when he explains the Italian tradition of "*La busta*" (*Fabrizio's Passion* 205; original emphasis), an envelope containing a monetary gift for newlyweds. Moreover, he contributes to the construction of gender stereotypical identities when pointing out the importance that "manliness" had in his house, and portrays his mother and grandmother as submissive women, who always served men first at mealtimes. He explains that young women of the Italian diaspora hasten to get married so as not to risk remaining single, and yet, paradoxically, their husbands are as authoritative as their fathers. Through these portrayals, the narrator contributes to the formation of the image of Italian women in need of a dominating male figure and as victims of social conventions, according to which not marrying represents a personal failure. He offers the example of his sister Lucia, who longed to marry her "prince charming," Peter Hebert (132), an anglophone Montreal textile salesman, who represented an escape from her "Father's dictatorship" (129). Peter, however, had to ask for permission to marry her from her father, Guido Notte, who instead wanted his daughter to marry Bruno, an "educated and wealthy" doctor, who represented "the apex of the pyramid of success" (134). Lucia is the stereotypical representation of Italian women of the 1970s, who were still seen as the possession of men, be it of their fathers or of their husbands. Moreover, this family portrayal sheds light on the stereotypical tyrannical Italian father, who wants to impose his opinions on his daughter's life choices and who sees marriage as an opportunity for her to gain economic stability and social status through her husband, who will ideally share her nationality and cultural values.

Italian women in need of a protective male figure are also represented by Fabrizio's mother, who is portrayed as a prudish, reserved, and chaste woman, embarrassed to show her "secret parts" (190) to strangers during her first childbirth. While she "craved for her husband's presence, for his masculine warmth," Guido Notte finds her "beautiful" when she is "lying in her life-giving pain, the same pain suffered by her mother when she gave birth to her many children on one of those hills in Guglionesi" (190). The Italian female figure is therefore mainly depicted in her role as a wife and a mother, while the male figure is portrayed as protective and dominating.

This image is also conveyed through Lea's eyes when she praises Fabrizio during one of their sexual encounters: "You are so typically Mediterranean! ... You are so predictably warm, extroverted and jealous" (104). Through this passage the author contributes to the formation of the stereotypical identity of Mediterranean men as passionate, possessive, and masculine. These examples show the way in which a culture is read and interpreted by another and has to do with the "mythology of stereotyping and representation" linking the respective societies.[27] The narrator's depiction of his family and his translation of Italian culture for his Canadian readers contribute to the circulation of prejudices about Italians in Canada, which had been very common since the 1950s. While men were perceived as sexist, women were seen as submissive and completely dependent on men.[28]

The translational process performed by the narrator is also visible from his several self-translations and metalinguistic reflections. D'Alfonso's dedication to translation emerges clearly when the narrator ponders the equivalent of words: "*Slave* is the English equivalent of *schiavo*. Ah, to be God's slave, love's slave, art's slave" (*Fabrizio's Passion* 127). The author's passion for translation is also revealed by his use of the verb "to translate" meant as "to reproduce" (38) and "to convey" (189), as well as by his comparison of the act of learning to speak a new language with the act of kissing (106) and receiving the Holy Spirit (125). In other cases, the narrator reflects on the differences and similarities between languages and the etymological origin of specific terms: "The *récit*: The English language has no equivalent to describe this genre. On the one hand, we have what we call the novel (*roman*) and, on the other hand, there is the short story (*nouvelle*). The *récit* falls in between" (188). The author's sensitivity to the notion of language emerges clearly when the narrator informs readers about his relationship with his multiple languages and explains that he was sent to anglophone schools by his father because he considered English to be "the language of power and money" (53), as well as the language of the "majority" (54). However, he confesses that "English syntax does not correspond in any way to the things that are fleeting through [him]" (66). He specifies that English is only one of the three languages he speaks, together with Guglionesano – the language he uses at home – and French, the main language spoken in Montreal.

My analysis of *Fabrizio's Passion* will inform the following examination of its Italian translation, *La passione di Fabrizio*, published in 2002 by Cosmo Iannone. The presentation of selected passages will show to what extent translator Antonello Lombardi has managed to "enrich" the reading of D'Alfonso's work, to use Rose's words, and is at variance with Verdicchio's critical introduction to the Italian translation of the novel. As is clear from the very start of the preface, in fact, the Italian-Canadian critic emphasizes D'Alfonso's transnational and hybrid identity: "Antonio D'Alfonso. Canadese, Québécois, Italiano, Guglionesano. Uno, nessuno, centomila" (Verdicchio, "Presentazione" 7). He presents the author as an intellectual, who has contributed to the literary and cultural production of the Québécois context, characterized by cultural diversity and yet often represented by the reductive binarism of anglophone/francophone cultures (7). While he stresses D'Alfonso's resistance to Canadian, Québécois, and Italian nationalism and points out his reflections on cultural identity, nation, and country (9), Lombardi's translation does not prove to be a means of critical analysis, as shown by the examination of the following passages. The items under analysis are highlighted in bold.

*EXAMPLE 1*
Monreale confers on to me the privilege of being three persons in one. Being a strange combination of three cultures, I was able to converge my three views of this city and form a **completely unique triangular (tripartite) worldview** which was not always appreciated by either the francophones or the anglophones who forced me to take sides in their strife for power. (*Fabrizio's Passion* 191)

Monreale mi conferisce il privilegio di essere tre persone in una. Come peculiare combinazione di tre culture, sono stato in grado di fondere le tre visioni di questa città in una **concezione del mondo tripartita**, non sempre apprezzata da francofoni o anglofoni, che mi spingevano a prendere posizione nella contesa per il potere. (*La passione di Fabrizio* 158)

In translating this passage, the result of living in a tricultural environment, namely having "a completely unique triangular (tripartite) worldview," has not been emphasized by Lombardi's omission of "completely unique," which expresses the narrator's "singularity" both for being a diasporic subject and for living in the bilingual city of Montreal (*Fabrizio's Passion* 72). Moreover, while the narrator defines his world view as "triangular" and "tripartite," Lombardi only uses *tripartita*. Although the English "tripartite" is in brackets and might be interpreted as a synonym for "triangular," its use is particularly meaningful because it stresses the connection and the interplay between every single culture moulding his world view. Moreover, D'Alfonso's precision in specifying one word through the other reflects his constant act of translating and the accuracy of his linguistic choices, which has also been pointed out by Verdicchio in his critical introduction to the novel.[29] Italian readers, instead, are not confronted with the narrator's transnational and hybrid identity, which is the result of the process of cultural translation in which he is involved.

Lombardi has also missed the chance to enliven the narrator's acts of translation when reproducing his "foreign gaze" on the Italian diasporic community, as shown by the following passage:

**EXAMPLE 2**
Because we are the children of **immigrants** does not preclude us of being worthy of worldly laurels. The professor says: "They always scream assassins when it comes to pleasure." Many students refuse to write honestly on the topic of ethnicity or on our ignorance in dealing with ethnic issues. (*Fabrizio's Passion* 72)

L'essere figli di **emigranti** non ci impedisce di essere meritevoli di allori temporali. Il professore dice: "Urlano sempre assassini quando si giunge al piacere." Molti studenti rifiutano di scrivere a cuore aperto sull'argomento 'etnicità', o sulla nostra ignoranza nell'affrontare argomenti etnici. (*La passione di Fabrizio* 60)

While the author refers to migrant parents as "immigrants," the translator uses *emigranti*, literally "emigrants." Although they both indicate somebody dislocated from one country to another, they imply a different perspective: while in the source text they are seen through the eyes of the host society, in the target text they are seen from the perspective of the home country they left behind. D'Alfonso's use of "immigrant" suggests that the narrator looks at his parents and other diasporic subjects through Canadian eyes, which is proven by his initial desire for assimilation into his host culture. While D'Alfonso's focus is on the point of arrival, namely Canada, Lombardi's "emigrant" places emphasis on the point of departure: the Italian home country that Fabrizio's parents were forced to leave in search of a job. The two terms therefore register a shift in focus, which is significant, as the migrant experience is a core element stimulating the narrator's creativity. In presenting the narrator's parents as Italians who have emigrated to Canada, rather than as Canadian citizens of Italian origins, translator Lombardi shows that he may have been influenced by the expectations of the target-text readers and their inclination to self-identification. In this way, however, Lombardi leads the target-text audience to read the narrator's Italian perspective as a sign of his belonging to Italy, which is, instead, completely absent in the source text, as shown by the above analysis of *Fabrizio's Passion*.[30] In contrast, the use of the Italian equivalent, *immigrati*, would have stressed the narrator's "foreign gaze" on Italian culture, which clearly emerges through a close reading of the source text.

Lombardi's lexical choice enacts similar mechanisms when translating images of Italian culture through which the author represents Fabrizio's Italian family as the cultural "other," thus contributing to the circulation of Italian cultural stereotypes in Canada.

### EXAMPLE 3

The kitchen is the heart of our family, the master room of **the Italian household**, the place where we eat and discuss, but also quarrel; it is the most sacred part of our home where all gives way and must be mended. (*Fabrizio's Passion* 43)

La cucina è il cuore della nostra famiglia, la stanza principe **di questa casa italiana**, il posto in cui mangiamo e discutiamo, e talvolta litighiamo; è la parte più sacra della nostra casa, dove tutto si infrange e tutto si ricompone. (*La passione di Fabrizio* 40)

In this passage the narrator emphasizes images of the Italian united family, which gives noticeable importance to small daily things, like sharing meals and chatting – sometimes animatedly. Lombardi's translation of "the Italian household" as *questa casa italiana* turns the original stereotypical image into a special quality of the narrator's family only. While the original definite article "the" suggests a generalization made by the narrator, who sees his family as being like other Italian (diasporic) families, Lombardi's use of the demonstrative adjective *questa* – namely "this" – refers exclusively to Fabrizio's home environment. In this way Lombardi's translation does not support the author's external perspective, through which he generalizes and attributes distinctive features to all Italian families. The translator has failed to contribute to the construction of Italian cultural identity through the reproduction of stereotypical images, which is instead a clear result of the process of cultural translation performed by the narrator. Gender stereotypical images have also been diminished by Lombardi, as is shown in the following passage:

### EXAMPLE 4
When **Nonno** Nicola passed away, my father inherited the healthy challenge of being the "man" in a house of strong women. Because I was still a boy, at the time, my **manliness** did not count. It starts to count, however, with Peter's appearance which suddenly invests new significance to the male presence in our family. All these complex ideas make me seriously wonder about Lucia's future. Will Peter be a **replica** of the father she wants to leave so **badly**? This is why I will have to scrutinize Peter minutely, especially those gestures he will have no control over. (*Fabrizio's Passion* 136–7)

Dopo che **nonno** Nicola fu passato a miglior vita, mio padre ebbe a misurarsi con l'arduo compito di essere *l'uomo* in una famiglia di donne forti. Io, all'epoca, ero ancora un ragazzino, e la mia **mascolinità** non contava. Inizia a contare, tuttavia, con l'apparizione di Peter, che investe di nuovo significato la presenza maschile nella nostra famiglia. Tutte queste idee complicate fanno sì che mi interroghi seriamente sul futuro di Lucia. E se Peter fosse un **replicante** del padre dal quale così **cinicamente** vuole staccarsi? È per questo che dovrò scrutare Peter con accuratezza, specialmente in quegli atteggiamenti che non dovesse riuscire a controllare. (*La passione di Fabrizio* 113)

This passage contains some Italian "untranslated words," which have been edited in the target text. While *Nonno* appears with a capital letter in the source text, it is spelled entirely in lower case in the target text, thus toning down the significant role that Fabrizio's grandfather played in his family. The narrator informs his readers about the importance that "manliness" had in his familiar environment. "Manliness" has been translated as *mascolinità*, which in everyday language, unlike its English equivalent "masculinity," is used particularly to refer to physical features typical of men or to describe women with qualities conventionally associated with men. *Virilità*, instead, would have emphasized not only the physical but also the socio-cultural characteristics according to which male subjects should be identified. Although the first definition of *virilità* given by the *Treccani* dictionary refers to men's biological features, a second entry specifies that it is "[l]a qualità propria dell'uomo forte, sicuro di sé e risoluto, coraggioso, che si manifesta nelle sue azioni."[32] Therefore, *virilità* would have referred more accurately to those qualities – such as strength, bravery, self-confidence, and a protective instinct – that the narrator's parents might have associated exclusively with men and expected from their son. The narrator clearly disagrees with these "complex ideas," which make him "seriously wonder" about his sister's future. More specifically, he is concerned that her future husband might be a "replica" of their father, which has been translated as *replicante*, namely somebody who imitates somebody else. The Italian equivalent *replica*, which hints at the repetition of something, instead, would have emphasized that Lucia's "Prince Charming" might be exactly like her father, whom "she wants to leave so badly." Fabrizio's solidarity with his sister, however, has been distorted by Lombardi's translation of "badly" as *cinicamente* instead of *disperatamente*. This adverb, meaning "cynically," implies Fabrizio's disapproval of his sister's desire, while he is clearly empathetic towards her. If we interpret Lucia as one of the several autobiographical characters, her close relationship with the narrator is proven by the fact that the author's sister is one of the addressees of his dedication, unlike their parents. Through this mistranslation, Lombardi presents the narrator as endorsing his father's perspective, thus complying with the values of the Italian diasporic community. As a result, Italian readers are not helped to grasp the narrator's "foreign gaze" on his Italian family and his refusal of their values.

The following two passages show how Lombardi's translation also fails to lead Italian readers' interpretation of the narrator's role as a "fictional translator." Passages 5 and 6 are taken from the second chapter of the novel, consisting of a collection of letters written by Guido – during his military service in the late 1940s in northern Italy – to his future wife, Lina, who at that time was living in the southern village of Guglionesi. These letters were originally written in Italian by Guido and translated by Fabrizio into English, as he reveals in the introduction to his chapter "Father's Military Service," where he expresses his concern about not being able to convey his father's literary style: "My translation of these letters probably does not do justice to Father's unintended literary style. I can only hope that the result of my efforts will shed some light on the kind of person that my father was" (*Fabrizio's Passion* 17). This reflection, which unveils the narrator's dedication to translation, is missing in Lombardi's Italian target text. Overlooking the narrator's role as a translator does not allow Italian readers to grasp the importance of translation as a metaphor for his identity, which is not even highlighted when translating the narrator's clarification below:

### EXAMPLE 5
I have chosen to **translate** the letters he wrote during the month of April 1948 in order to organize what seemed to be, for him at least, a particularly confusing moment in his life. (*Fabrizio's Passion* 32)

Ho scelto di **riportare** le lettere scritte nel mese di Aprile 1948 allo scopo di ricostruire quello che è sembrato, quantomeno a lui, un momento particolarmente confuso della sua vita. (*La passione di Fabrizio* 32)

In Lombardi's translation, the verb "translate" becomes *riportare* instead of *tradurre*. Flagging the narrator's role as a "cultural mediator" between his father and his Canadian readers would have been essential for the target-text readers to understand the presence of some Italian "untranslated words," which make Guido's letters heterolingual, as shown in the following passage:

### EXAMPLE 6
Udine, 25 April 1948

**Amore**,
My Birthday today. It is also the day **Mamma Italia** was liberated from Nazi Occupation ... **Mamma Italia**, your soldiers are not out there toasting your liberation. They are drinking to forget the families and fields waiting for them back home. (*Fabrizio's Passion* 32)

Udine, 25 Aprile 1948

**Amore**,
Oggi è il mio compleanno. È anche il giorno della liberazione di **Mamma Italia** dall'occupazione nazista ... **Mamma Italia**, i tuoi soldati non sono lì fuori a brindare alla tua liberazione. Bevono per dimenticare le famiglie ed i campi che li aspettano a casa loro. (*La passione di Fabrizio* 31-2)

In light of the narrator's role as a "fictional translator," it is clearly no coincidence that he left these Italian words untranslated. *Amore*, namely "my love," which Guido uses to address Lina, shows how language operates on an affective level. As the narrator reveals later in the novel, his parents' relationship was a model for him: "I wanted to imitate the love my parents had for one another. Impossible. Unfortunately, it soon occurred to me that I was the product of social anguish, disgust, and hatred" (152).[33]

In the case of *Mamma Italia*, instead, the Italian language emphasizes the sarcasm that the narrator perceived in his father's words. In light of his father's anti-nationalism, the word *Mamma* ("Mom"), which usually has an affective connotation, clearly clashes with the idea that Guido and Fabrizio have of Italy as a country. Through this "untranslated word" the narrator ridicules the idea of *madrepatria* ("motherland"), and instead depicts Italy as a bad mother, who forces her soldiers to stay away from their families, even on important occasions, like their own birthdays. Guido's frustration in fighting for his motherland is proven when he compares the importance of his birthday to that of the anniversary of Italy, which was liberated three years before from German occupation, thus revealing his indifference to the events affecting his home country.

In Lombardi's target text, however, the original emphases on the "untranslated words" are toned down, both in the case of *Amore*, which does not unveil the crucial importance of the narrator's cultural origins, and *Mamma Italia*, which fails to convey his resistance to any kind of nationalism. Lombardi's suppression of italics does not signal that the "untranslated words" were spoken in Italian in the source text and does not draw the target-text readers' attention to them, although they are vibrant linguistic signs of Guido's migrant identity and of the narrator's role as a "fictional translator." Retaining these "untranslated words" in italics would have helped the Italian audience to interpret Guido's letter and grasp both his relationship with his country and Fabrizio's attachment to his family.

Finally, Lombardi opted for similarly debatable lexical choices when translating the term "language" in the last passage analyzed:

### EXAMPLE 7
But the power of a country can't be saved only for the members of any one tribe; nor should culture confine itself to one sole **language**, or civilization be propelled by one ideology alone. (*Fabrizio's Passion* 89)

Ma la potenza di un paese non può essere consacrata ai membri di una sola tribù; né la cultura dovrebbe essere confinata ad un solo **linguaggio**, o la civilizzazione essere promossa ad una sola ideologia. (*La passione di Fabrizio* 73–4)

The term "language" has been translated as *linguaggio*, instead of *lingua*. Although they share the same English equivalent, the difference between these two Italian terms is substantial in light of the focus on language in this novel. While *linguaggio* has a generic meaning, and refers to any kind of communication, *lingua* indicates the system of communication conventionally shared by people belonging to the same cultural community. The translator's lexical choice does not help Italian readers to interpret the narrator's sensitivity to the concept of language.

The analysis of these passages shows how Lombardi fails to lead Italian readers to grasp the narrator's transnational identity, which is a key element in reading D'Alfonso's work. This has happened because of different debatable translation strategies, like the omission of specific words, which signify the narrator's position between different cultures (see example 1). The same translation strategy, together with the suppression of italics, has also diminished the narrator's role as a "fictional translator" (see examples 5 and 6). The narrator's "foreign gaze" has not been retained either (see examples 2, 3, and 4), and a non-accurate translation has failed to do justice to Fabrizio's sensitivity to the concept of language (see example 7). Lombardi's debatable lexical choices suggest that his translation lacks a previous critical reading of the source text informed by D'Alfonso's position in the Canadian literary system. As a result, the translator fails to offer a critical reading of the novel to his Italian audience, who do not have access to the source text. This sheds light on the essential link between translation and literary criticism: a critical reading would have allowed Lombardi to opt more consciously for specific translation strategies, thus advancing his Italian readers' understanding of the text. In conclusion, this analysis stresses the crucial role played by translation, not only in the circulation of literary texts from one literary and cultural system to another, but also in the understanding of the relationship between different literatures. Rose's observation that translation is a critical method for analyzing literature elucidates the pivotal role that literary translators play in the study of comparative literature. As stated by the scholar, literary criticism is dependent on translation, which, in turn, gains from the scrutiny of the latter.[34] They are closely interrelated, as together they enhance the understanding and appreciation of literature.

## NOTES

1. The novel was first published in 1995 by Guernica and republished in 2000. The passages under analysis are taken from the second edition of the novel.
2. Rose, *Translation and Literary Criticism*, 2, original emphasis.
3. Ibid., 7.
4. Venuti, "World Literature," 180.
5. Ibid.

6 D'Alfonso, "Ten Questions."
7 D'Alfonso, "There Is No 'Proper' English," 249.
8 Verdicchio, *Duologue*, 29.
9 D'Alfonso, "There Is No 'Proper' English," 250.
10 D'Alfonso, "A Place on Earth," 160.
11 D'Alfonso, "Italicamente," 187.
12 D'Alfonso, "The Future of Italic Culture," 46.
13 D'Alfonso, "Introduction," *In Italics*, 13.
14 D'Alfonso, "Unmeltable Ethnics," 150–1.
15 D'Alfonso, "The Enduring," 198.
16 D'Alfonso, "The Road," 25.
17 D'Alfonso, "Italicamente," 186.
18 D'Alfonso, "The Path," 121.
19 D'Alfonso, "A Literary Culture," 62.
20 Verdicchio, *Duologue*, 29.
21 Anderson, *Imagined Communities*, 6.
22 Bhabha, "DissemiNation," 315.
23 Bhabha, *The Location*, 218.
24 Ibid., 4.
25 See, for example, Cronin; Polezzi, *Translating Travel*.
26 Polezzi, "Reflections," 30.
27 Carbonell, "The Exotic Space," 80.
28 On this topic, see for instance Jansen 1988, Iacovetta 1992, DeMaria Harney 1998.
29 Verdicchio, "Presentazione," 9.
30 The nostalgia and sense of belonging conveyed by the use of *emigrante* is confirmed by its appearance in Italian-language literary works by first-generation migrant women Anna Moroni Parken (1896; 1907), Elena Maccaferri Randaccio (1979), and Maria Ardizzi (1982; 1984). As is clear from the eloquent titles of their literary works *Emigranti: quattro anni al Canadà* (1896/1907) and *Diario di una emigrante* (1979), Moroni Parken and Randaccio see themselves as emigrants and implicitly express their sense of belonging to that home country they left as adults. Nostalgia makes the integration into the host country difficult also for the protagonist of Ardizzi's *Made in Italy* (1982), who confesses to be unpleasantly impressed by the meaning of *emigrante*: "Il significato della parola emigrante mi ha sgradevolmente colpita solo dopo aver emigrato: e mi ha colpita per le implicazioni che balzano alla superficie solo quando sei emigrante" (15). The sense of belonging is shared by the female character of *Il sapore agro della mia terra* (1984), who feels split between her two countries: "Io,

chi sono? ... sono un'emigrante. Non sarò mai separata dal mio vecchio mondo, ho pensato, potrò sottrarmi al nuovo mondo? Rimarrò qualcosa di mezzo, che non sta né da una parte né dall'altra?" (175). In all of these cases, it is clear that the writers see themselves through Italian eyes, namely through the eyes of the relatives they left in Italy.

32 See entry for "virilità" in the online dictionary *Treccani.it. L'enciclopedia italiana*: http://www.treccani.it/vocabolario/virilita. (Accessed 1 September 2015.)

33 On the relationship between language and emotions in heterolingual memoirs, see Mary Besemeres, "Language and Emotional Experience," 2006.

34 Rose, *Translation and Literary Criticism*, 11.

**BIBLIOGRAPHY**

Anderson, Benedict. *Imagined Communities: Reflections on the Origin and Spread of Nationalism*. London and New York: Verso, 1983. Revised edition, 2006.

Ardizzi, Maria Jose. *Made in Italy*. Toronto: Toma Publishing, 1982.

Besemeres, Mary. "Language and Emotional Experience: The Voice of Translingual Memoir." In *Bilingual Minds: Emotional Experience, Expression and Representation*, edited by Aneta Pavlenko, 34–58. Clevedon: Multilingual Matters, 2006.

Bhabha, Homi K. "DissemiNation: Time, Narrative, and the Margins of the Modern Nation." In *Nation and Narration*, edited by Homi K. Bhabha, 291–322. London and New York: Routledge, 1990. Reprint 2000.

– *The Location of Culture*. London and New York: Routledge, 1994.

Carbonell, Ovidio. "The Exotic Space of Cultural Translation." In *Translation, Power, Subversion*, edited by Román Álvarez and María Carmen África Vidal, 79–98. Clevedon: Multilingual Matters, 1996.

Cronin, Michael. *Across the Lines: Travel, Language, Translation*. Cork: Cork University Press, 2000.

D'Alfonso, Antonio. *Avril ou l'anti-passion*, Montreal: VLB, 1990.

– *Fabrizio's Passion*. Toronto: Guernica Editions, 1995/2000.

– *In Italics: In Defense of Ethnicity*. Toronto: Guernica Editions, 1996.

– "A Literary Culture in Search of a Tradition." In *In Italics: In Defense of Ethnicity*. Toronto: Guernica Editions, 1996, 59–62.

– "A Place on Earth." In *In Italics: In Defense of Ethnicity*. Toronto: Guernica Editions, 1996, 159–64.

– "Italicamente." In *In Italics: In Defense of Ethnicity*. Toronto: Guernica Editions, 1996, 181–90.

– "The Enduring Writer." In *In Italics: In Defense of Ethnicity*. Toronto: Guernica Editions, 1996, 191–200.

- "There Is No 'Proper' English." In *In Italics: In Defense of Ethnicity*. Toronto: Guernica Editions, 1996, 249–52.
- "The Path to Hope." In *In Italics: In Defense of Ethnicity*. Toronto: Guernica Editions, 1996. 117–22.
- "The Road Between." In *In Italics: In Defense of Ethnicity*. Toronto: Guernica Editions, 1996. 23–42.
- "Unmeltable Ethnics." In *In Italics: In Defense of Ethnicity*. Toronto: Guernica Editions, 1996. 145–58.
- *La passione di Fabrizio*. Translated by Antonello Lombardi. Isernia: Cosmo Iannone Editore, 2002.
- "The Future of Italic Culture." In *Gambling with Failure: Essays*, 46–55. Toronto: Exile Editions, 2005. Reprint 2006.
- "Ten Questions with Antonio D'Alfonso." *Open Book Toronto* (2009). http://www.openbooktoronto.com/news/ten_questions_with_antonio_d_alfonso (accessed 1 September 2015).

D'Alfonso, Antonio, and Pasquale Verdicchio. *Duologue: On Culture and Identity*. Toronto: Guernica Editions, 1998.

DeMaria Harney, Nicholas. *Being Italian in Toronto*. Toronto: University of Toronto Press, 1998.

Iacovetta, Franca. *Such Hardworking People: Italian Immigrants in Postwar Toronto*. Montreal: McGill-Queen's University Press, 1992.

Jansen, Clifford. *Italians in a Multicultural Canada*. Lewiston, New York: E. Mellen Press, 1988.

Kamboureli, Smaro. "Canadian Ethnic Anthologies: Representations of Ethnicity." ARIEL: *A Review of International English Literature* 25, no. 4 (1994): 11–52.

Maccaferri Randaccio, Elena. *Diario di una emigrante*. Bologna: Arti Grafiche Tamari, 1979.

Moroni Parken, Anna. *Emigranti: quattro anni al Canadà*. Milan: Somi, 1896; 1907.

Padolsky, Enoch. "Italian-Canadian Writing and the Ethnic Minority/Majority Binary." In *Social Pluralism and Literary History: The Literature of the Italian Emigration*, edited by Francesco Loriggio, 248–68. Toronto: Guernica Editions, 1996.

Polezzi, Loredana. "Reflections of Things Past: Building Italy through the Mirror of Translation." *New Comparison* 29 (Spring 2000): 27–47.
- *Translating Travel: Contemporary Italian Travel Writing in English Translation*. Aldershot and Brookfield: Ashgate Publishing, 2001.

Ricci, Nino. "Questioning Ethnicity." In *Roots and Frontiers/Radici e Frontiere*, 122–35. Turin: Tirrenia Stampatori, 1992; 2003.

Rose, Marilyn Gaddis. *Translation and Literary Criticism: Translation as Analysis*. Manchester: St Jerome Publishing, 1997.
Tuzi, Marino. *The Power of Allegiances: Identity, Culture, and Representational Strategies*. Toronto: Guernica Editions, 1997.
Venuti, Lawrence. "World Literature and Translation Studies." In *Routledge Companion to World Literature*, edited by Theo D'haen, David Damrosch, and Djelal Kadir, 180–93. London: Routledge, 2011.
Verdicchio, Pasquale. *Devils in Paradise: Writings on Post-Emigrant Cultures*. Toronto: Guernica Editions, 1997.
– "Presentazione." *La Passione di Fabrizio*, 7–11. Translated by Antonello Lombardi. Isernia: Cosmo Iannone Editore, 2002.
Wilson, Rita. "Cultural Mediation through Translingual Narrative." *Target* 23, no. 2. (2011): 235–50.

# Exile, Media, Capital: Interpreting *Calendar*'s Systems of Exchange

*Monique Tschofen*

In the American Comparative Literature Association's 2014–15 *State of the Discipline Report*, in an entry titled "Comparative Non-Literature," Scott Kushner argues that non-literary media provide an opportunity to "reimagine what the discipline of literary studies takes as its object of study and its raison d'être." His focus is on how non-literary media can help the literary scholar attend to the materiality of texts, appreciate the variety of reading strategies they solicit, and also force a reconsideration of core concepts such as "author, text, and genre – but also edition, audience, character, and narrative" in addition to "generic categories such as novel, poem, and play." However, what Kushner does not say is that once the discipline's doors open to consider electronic texts, films, photographs, fashion, social media, and the like, alongside print literature, the complexity of the project of comparison becomes fractal, and yet its mission all the more important to get right. In order to trace the travelling of cultural practices over time, across national boundaries, in and out of languages, through genres, across media, and into and out of everyday life, comparatists today require multiple intersecting literacies. They must understand intertextuality as well as intermediality and transmediality. They must have deep knowledge of print and oral cultures, as well as visual cultures. They must appreciate the symbolic, ideological, and the material determinants of culture. They must remain conscious at all times of the ethics of comparison, aware of the perils of mistranslation and the dangers of cultural appropriation, and simultaneously reflexive about the forces that govern their own interests in seeking knowledge about the other. Yet the contemporary comparatist knows that, with this expanded body of texts in literary and non-literary media to study, often comes expanded intellectual resources – new guiding metaphors, refocused sets of research questions, and elaborated models for research methods that together make this new century's cross-cultural and cross-medial work ever more rich and meaningful.

In this chapter, I turn to a singularly rich text, *Calendar* (1993), an early film by one of Canada's premier directors, Atom Egoyan, as one such resource. The short, experimental art-house film traces the journey of an Armenian-Canadian couple back to Armenia. I have long been drawn to the work's remarkably complex formal symmetries, its dark, humorous tone, and have insisted upon the important role it played in extending Canadian cinema beyond a two-solitudes model. However, for me, the film has condensed a complex of issues that pertain to my own sense of the aspirations and perils of our discipline in Canada. Like a *Pilgrim's Progress* for its time, *Calendar* lays out in allegorical form the fraught journey that contemporary comparatists today commit to undertake.

The film traverses geographical territories and spoken languages, but also moves through the fields of visual representational media, including photography, video, and film, in addition to everyday media, such as the wall calendar, diary, letter, television, and telephone call. In so doing, the film brings into view the forces of capitalism's global flows, that is, of the complex and uneven movement of goods and persons, representations and concepts, through pathways dictated by capital. It exposes the persistence of ideologically conscripted media-embedded "ways of seeing" that implicitly govern the terms of cross-cultural encounters, due to their embeddedness in the technological apparatus as well as in symbolic systems of representation. It persuasively suggests the fact that *misunderstanding*, rather than understanding, is the a priori of cross-cultural encounters, and that to genuinely reach for an understanding of the other requires not only listening more closely but also going off script – a crucial lesson for the scholar whose critical explorations of identities in the contemporary world are often carried from what the film would identify as fundamentally narcissistic identity politics. Read as a parable of the complexity of comparative inquiry in an age of global "scapes," *Calendar*'s almost twenty-five-year-old filmed scenarios are teeming with the kinds of critical insights that can take comparative literature forward twenty-five more years.

*Calendar* has already been written about extensively. In his book *Atom Egoyan*, Jonathan Romney situates the film alongside Peter Greenaway's films, which are frequently built around series or catalogues. Looking at the way the film is organized around a structural grid, Romney then analyzes the places where this rigid structure breaks down to show how the film draws out tensions between rigidity and flexibility. Katrin Kegel, in her brilliant essay "The Thirteenth Church," delves more deeply into the film's complex structure, arguing that it is an analogue to the form of the musical exercise, the baroque theme and variations, and finally the sonata. In his two essays on *Calendar,* "Allegory" and "Montage," Sourayan Mookerjea examines *Calendar* in relation to its form of social critique. He argues that the film must be read as an allegory of larger sociological issues around overdevelopment and underdevelopment in sociology. Constructing a particularly filmic solution to the problem of global flows, the film, Mookerjea argues, offers cultural studies a model for critical self-reflexivity. Tolof Nelson takes still another approach in "Passing Time in Intercultural Cinema: The Exilic Experience of the Time Passer in Atom Egoyan's *Calendar.*" Departing from Homi Bhabha's question about whether the experience of exile yields a unique temporality, Nelson argues that the film's temporal traces, materially recorded in the durational rhythms of images, reproduced through various media such as photography, film, and video, are integral to the film's articulation of exilic experience.

What I offer here extends these discussions by bringing them into an even wider framework. I take up the question about what the film tells us about circuits of exchange in two ways. On one hand, I ask how it identifies the core determinants of the production, reproduction, circulation, and internalization of culture across cultures and media in a globalized world. I look at its construction of belonging and exile, connection and rupture, remembering and forgetting, in relation to the social, economic, and historical contexts that the film exposes and critiques. On the other hand, I ask about how the film invites us to take a journey into comparison that parallels its own journey, warning against the dangers of binaristic models of understanding media and culture.

To begin, it is necessary to understand how Egoyan's film set itself up as a study of how the experience of geographical displacement affects circuits of knowledge exchange within networks of overlapping and intersecting media. It does so by casting only three characters, each of whom represents a different position in the global diaspora. The film's central character is a photographer (Atom Egoyan). He represents the immigrant who has fully assimilated into English culture. In the film, he returns to his homeland of Armenia, tasked with taking a series of photos of old churches for the kind of nostalgic decorative calendar that reminds migrants of the beauty and history of their ancestral homeland. His relation to this journey is purely instrumental, and the products of his translation of the landscape into photographs empties it of its meaning, rendering it into a purely visual – beautiful and yet kitchy – signifier. However, in a supplement to his photography, which flattens the multi-dimensionality of homeland, he videos the journey and the very human exchanges that happen in it, logging a history of the present rather than the past. His wife, who serves as his translator/interpreter (Arsinée Khanjian), remains closer to her homeland than to her new land, and in fact has retained her accent – the linguistic signifier of her double-consciousness. Her job is to facilitate the photographer's access to the photo-shoot locations. Still, she wants to probe these landscapes to retrieve deeper registers of meaning, understanding its history through storytelling as well as deeply embodied experience. In so doing, she is excluded from the photographs, but features prominently in the video history of the travels. The third character is their driver and guide (Ashot Admian), who is primally and organically linked to the homeland. He inhabits the margins of the video documentary and is absent from the photographs. Each in the triad needs the other to bridge the gaps in their knowledge and experience shaped by the broader forces of migration.

Despite the efforts of the three parties to find ways to translate, interpret, and mediate among their positions, the translator becomes traitor, and she eventually retreats from her bridging role. The triad devolves into a new dyad that excludes the photographer. Throughout the journey, the photographer logs how the conversations of his wife and the interpreter about the landscape, the churches, and their history become more and more intimate. It eventually becomes clear in the film's present tense that the marriage has crumbled. His wife stays in the homeland with the driver, leaving Armenia itself an alien and unknowable territory.

Over twelve calendar months, we see the photographer attempt to review what happened. His efforts to interpret the interpreter/translator's betrayal very much resembles the labour of scholars: they involve pouring over the documented evidence – work he compares to the rewind function of the medium of video tape – and writing about it. However, his efforts draw from the theatrical arts, such as scriptwriting and directing. He scripts scenes with a series of paid call girls from around the world, each of whom resembles his wife in one key dimension: they speak a language he cannot understand. The scene is always the same. He invites them for dinner, and, on cue, they are to turn their backs to him to take a phone call, during which they are to speak in their mother tongue. He seems to hope that simulating *and* controlling his experience of bewilderment will allow him to better understand it. The clear problem is that, in this transaction, he repeats his own error of othering, and can come to no understanding. Only at the end of the film does he give up his twinned urges to investigate and to direct. He finds authenticity in a friendly, unscripted conversation with a call girl, seemingly prepared to abandon the rigid grip of the self-other dichotomy.

Two intersecting journeys thus dictate the movement of this film. One journey through geographical space engages with issues around migration, such as translation, cross-cultural understanding, and the preservation of identity, language, and culture across generations. The other journey into inquiry engages with problems around interpretation itself. It should be clear from my discussion how relevant *Calendar*'s central issues are to the comparatist's own interpretive project. When the film presents different perspectives one might take within this contact zone, ranging from Othering to fetishizing to, finally, understanding difference from within an ethical frame, it is offering a meta-commentary on common pitfalls in comparative literature.

One of the most important contributions the film makes relates to the way it exposes and then undermines binary thinking and in its stead offers almost fractal ways of understanding relationships in complex systems. The film at first glance appears to be rigorous about setting up a grid of comparison according to rigid sets of binary oppositions. Since the core of the narrative is a journey from a new home to the homeland, many of the binaries are overlaid onto a geographical/affective topography. In the visual language of the film, the new world could not be more distinct from the old world. North America is bland and generic. Its placeless interiors are tight, geometric, and claustrophobic. Its tone is panicked and profane. Armenia's landscapes are fluid and organic. Everything in the mythic homeland is pastoral, serene, sensual, and sacred. However, I argue, the film seeks to explode the seemingly stable valences of the two poles by showing how they are highly mediated, and thus subject to interpretation.

The central iteration of the film's treatment of interpretation involves translation. Much of the film is *not* translated. At various times, the film presents English and Armenian, English and Arabic, English and Macedonian, among other pairings. In these bilingual scenes, the voices are estranged, and do not interanimate, or interilluminate, but neither does one dominate the other (Bakhtin 49). The portions of the film that are translated are all mediated through the interpreter. She bridges the delineated geographical spaces of the motherland and the place of exile. Still, her translations often seem to be inadequate. Sometimes the driver offers a long excursus that she will translate into a short sentence. Sometimes she offers a lengthy translation of what seems to be only a curt remark. Her accented speech, moreover, is often confused and confusing. As an example, in the pivotal scene, in which the director comes to understand that the driver has desires for his wife, convolutions are rampant and questions lead to other questions. She relays a message from the driver to the director: "He wants to know if you wish to exactly know how he feels about me, if he has any desire towards me or not. Is that what you want to know?" The photographer answers: "Yes, I want to know where this is going to lead. I've obviously lost something very close to me, and I want to know how he feels about that." She translates the driver's response awkwardly: "He feels that you are a too adventurous –" The photographer interrupts: "That I'm too adventurous?" She answers: "No, that the two of you are adventurous men."

Then the conversation seemingly veers off topic. She continues talking to her husband about what the driver purportedly has said: "He says, because we know that we're talking about something and within it, you can find many other things, such as evil and the divine." The sudden intrusion of metaphysics in a conversation about feelings of betrayal reveals something about the film's position on the search for meaning and meaningfulness. *Translation* and its quest for equivalencies falters. *Interpretation*, which can mean reaching into unintelligibility and pulling out something terrifyingly yet deeply meaningful, has the potential for far greater rewards.

The next iteration of the film's treatment of interpretation involves mediation. Throughout his career, Atom Egoyan has made a persuasive case for the importance of understanding media by drawing attention to the materiality of media, as well as their capacities to serve as storage devices for memory, time, and affect. If spoken language reaches for meaning and sometimes falters, technological media frame it. They yield "ways of seeing" and, with them, generate blind spots.

The film focuses on three visual media. Film is the ur-medium that provides the substratum of the narrative, and is the only container capable of representing other media. For Egoyan, film records action impassively and with objectivity. In this way, it is an analogue to the novel's third-person objective mode of narration. Its chief capacity is to capture the movement of the continuous present. Only through editing can film separate time from itself and rearrange it in any way.

Photography works differently. Egoyan's protagonist photographs ancient ruins and monuments. The photographs are objective, anonymous, and idealized. They freeze the moment. In so doing, they render the photographed objects under-meaningful by separating them from lived and living history. Yet the photographs are also charged. Affixed to calendars in the homes of exiles, they serve as monthly triggers for the very nostalgia that keeps cultural identity in the diaspora alive.

Video, in turn, has yet another logic derived from its medium-specific qualities. Video is a first-person mode of narration that captures immediate, lived experience from a purely subjective lens. It is the most distorting medium, with the texture of dreams, and thus projects the landscapes of fantasy. Its treatment of time is the most complex. With its unique capacity for rewinding, the medium is able to locate "pastness" in a perpetual present.

When the film jumps back and forth among these three media, each with its own temporality and texture, it brings into view some of the many ways the contemporary world *frames* experience and dictates *perspectives on* it. More importantly, as the film travels among media, it disorients the viewer, whose estrangement echoes that of the exile.

What do media do? According to the art critic John Berger, they produce "ways of seeing." Ways of seeing occur at the confluence of vision technologies, histories of practice, and socio-political formations. For Egoyan, media's ways of seeing inevitably generate blind spots. The blind spot of the film's photographer is the world of depths. Paul Virilio cites a passage from a filmmaker, François Reichenbach, that might also be spoken by Egoyan's photographer: "From the moment I owned a camera," Reichenbach says, "I no longer felt the slightest interest in being with people, in living among them, unless I could get them on film" (Virilio 9). Virilio comments on the passage: "The camera would forever after come between him and all things; the miracle of industrial cinema lay in reproducing [a] primordial communication breakdown by the million" (9). The photographer's problem is that his camera lets him, or makes him, relate to the world from a distance. At one point, observing the photographer's disinterest in being with people, the driver asks through the translator-interpreter, "Don't you feel the need to come closer, to feel, like actually touch and feel, realize how it's made?" The photographer responds with bewilderment and a hint of disgust: "Touch and feel? Touch and feel the churches?" When she says "Yeah," his tone becomes sarcastic: "It hadn't occurred to me." She asks, "It hasn't occurred to you?" and he answers bluntly, "No." Again she asks, "You didn't feel the need?" He suggests that he finds the question perverse: "What, he'd like me to caress them, or ... ?" She tries to chide him: "You know what he means." But the photographer's knowledge is limited, tentative; he does not really see. He explains: "No, I don't really." She explains, "He says if you had seen someone else's photography of these places you wouldn't have wondered what it was inside, what it looked like inside?" The photographer's response reflects how his own personal blind spots are intricately related to his medium's: "No, I would think that they were beautiful places, and I'd think they were very well-composed and beautifully lit and very seductive. Is that what he wants to hear?" Of course, this is not what she wishes to hear.

The film's treatment of the medium of video further illuminates the media's "ways of seeing." If photographic ways of seeing remain superficial and cold, videoed ways of seeing are abstracted and abstracting. They fixate on stereotype and archetype rather than the real. The photographer returns obsessively to one of the segments of the journey, shot on video, of a huge flock of sheep. In one part of the sequence, the sheep's bodies, moving in tandem, are so close to each other that they create the impression of one giant, mobile, articulating body. The camera pans slowly, with and against the flow of the herd. The scene is shot through the window of a car – in other words, through a technological frame – but everything in it would appear to connect a mythical Armenia to the pastoral and the organic.

His wife is featured in the other segment of the sheep footage. She runs and runs towards the camera, which separates her from him. Even though she moves in space, the zoom on the camera makes it seem as though the distance between her and the camera is constant and unchanging. Finally, when she is close enough to be framed in no more than a middle shot, she opens her arms and hugs herself. Looking into the camera, she mouths the words "Touch me." She is thus linked to the material world, to nature, to the collective body, and to desire and intimacy. Viewed compulsively as the photographer rewinds and replays the video footage, it becomes a profound allegory of loss – loss of the beloved and of the homeland of which she is the archetype.

However, this scene is *re*interpreted at the end of the film, in a message left by the translator/interpreter on his answering machine. She says:

It's strange, but the strongest memory I had is not of any of the churches, but of the time we drove into that huge flock of sheep. You took your camera out, and as you were taping, he placed his hand on mine. I remember as I gripped his hand, watching you grip your camera so tightly, like you knew what was happening behind you. Did you know? Were you there? Are you there?

Her verbal description of this scene is cinematic, presented in a series of shots and countershots made up of close-ups of hands gripping. His hands are attached to his camera. Hers make contact with her lover's hands. Her betrayal of him, in other words, is the product of the disconnected way he views her and his homeland. His optic is superficial, and traffics in archetypes and stereotypes that cannot generate real knowledge; technological modernity has given him such a limited perspective that he is incapable of seeing her distance herself from him right before his very eyes.

The medium of the handwritten word appears to belong to a different order than the technological media of film and photography, but it too frames the world and anchors a perspective on it. We might say that instead of framing ways of seeing, writing frames being. Throughout the film, the photographer is shown with a pen in hand, trying to find something to write. The writing has been solicited from the translator/interpreter to help her interpret his actions, and so it parallels his attempts to review visual footage to interpret hers.

The solicitation comes through a message left on the photographer's answering machine. She says:

> I finally received the calendar. I was upset you sent it without a letter. What's going on in your mind? We've known each other too long to play these games. We've loved each other too long. You are mean to send me without letting me know how you feel about it. You must be very angry with me. But I tried not to be cruel to you. Why are you being so cruel? Just share with me whatever there is to share. Please, please write to me. I do miss you.

Initially, the photographer refuses to undertake her request. After months of silence pass, in another message on his answering machine, she implores him again: "Have you received my letters? Have you received my messages? Are you receiving this? Why aren't you answering? Don't you feel like letting me know what you're feeling? Why aren't you writing?"

It is clear from her request that she wants a particular kind of epistolary writing. A love letter that exposes his feelings and reveals his inner self would compensate for the coldness and abstractness of his visual cultural ways of seeing and simulate closeness despite the distance between them. Given his limited perspective, this is not an exercise he can undertake easily.

When the photographer finally agrees to write, he responds to her in a message recorded on an answering machine – his own, not hers, addressed to anyone who calls: "Yes I've received all your letters, yes I've listened to all your messages, and yes, I feel like I can finally begin to write to you. It's May 23 and I've been in the darkroom all day." The message jars. His first sentence seems too personal to be addressed to anyone but its intended recipient. The final sentence veers sharply toward the impersonal.

However, if we think about the answering-machine message not as a deflection but *as* the epistle she has solicited from him, it makes more sense. As Janice Gurkin Altman argues, epistolary discourse is designed to map distances:

> The *I* of epistolary discourse always situates himself vis-à-vis another ... To write a letter is to map one's coordinates – temporal, spatial, emotional, intellectual – in order to tell someone else where one is located at a particular time and how far one has travelled since the last writing. (119)

The photographer's message very clearly identifies his temporal, spatial, emotional, and intellectual coordinates.

The conflicts about writing make a key point in the film about understanding media. Her solicitation of a love letter is a request for intimacy that rejects practicalities, formalities, and authoritarian exchanges. She thus expresses the fantasy that the medium of exchange does not matter. He quells that fantasy by suggesting that media *mediate*. He counters her hope that writing might provide the clearest translation of their minds and lead to the meeting of authentic selves with the more pragmatic view that such factors as genre or the materiality of media always dictate the terms of exchange. Against her belief in an authentic self, he presents a purely functional *narrator*.

As I have said, though, Egoyan links issues around mediation to issues that concern interpretation. In French, we call a performance an "interprétation." We say that an actor has "interpreted" a scene. The next item in the list of media and their forms of mediation that Egoyan's film explores as it studies the processes of translation/interpretation/mediation is performance, with its cognates of scripting, directing, and acting. Performance imposes frames that, like the visual technologies, distance the observer from the observed, and this, in turn, separates self and other. When the photographer stages the scenes with the call girls, he "interprets," in the theatrical sense of the word, a scenario that he wants to interpret in the analytic sense. He does this by directing and acting in a scene he has also scripted.

His dramatic interpretation is transmedial, and relies on a series of relays and translations across other media. In order to trigger his letter writing, he instructs the "call" girl to follow a cue. She must leave an improvised conversation to engage with technological media. This segment of her performance echoes his own, when holding the camera in Armenia made him retreat from a world of depths and interactions. Then, with her back turned to him, she is to pretend to have a telephone conversation in her mother tongue. This allows him to replay the scenarios in which he was forced to listen to his wife speak to the driver without understanding what they were saying. Nobody is on the other side of the staged call, though. The photographer's scenario punishes the call girl, who is the body double for his wife, with monologue, thereby preventing her from speaking with authenticity to another.

As in the scenes around verbal translation, these sequences bring the film back to the question of unintelligibility. Egoyan highlights the discomfort of the comparatist who is seeking to interpret what resides at the limits of his or her knowledge. He signals the pathologies and fetishes and even sadism that can underwrite interpretation under these scenarios. He draws further attention to the many frames that limit how we see. In the film's final scene with a call girl, the photographer provides the cue for the call girl's performance, but then summons her back. Dropping all of the layers of artifice, he goes off-script and has a simple, direct conversation, in which they act as equal partners. It is not the case that Egoyan has dreamt of a way to circumvent all the mediations I have described. Rather, he has shown how to proceed despite them.

The film clearly uncovers the complex systems that govern translation, interpretation, and mediation. What does it say about inquiry? A consideration of the film as a kind of detective narrative is useful. From the perspective of the photographer, a body is missing. Although the film would seem to suggest that it is the husband's body that is missing, as it is cut off from an entire realm of authentic experience and instead involved in highly distorted behaviours, from his limited perspective, the wife's body is the one that must be sought, because she is the one who has disappeared from the relationship, and she is the one whom he misses.

The photographer's pouring through photos and videotapes searching for signs of guilt, condenses a number of issues around modernity and its practices of production and circulation. In "Tracing the Individual Body: Photography, Detectives, and Early Cinema," Tom Gunning explains that

> [t]he detective story maps out two positions in this dialectical drama of modernity: the criminal, who preys on the very complexity of the system of circulation; and the detective, whose intelligence, knowledge, and perspicacity allows him to discover the dark corners of the circulatory system, uncover crime, and restore order. (20)

When he watches his own video footage and re-enacts scenes with the call girls, the photographer in *Calendar* returns to the scene of the crime like the guilty criminal who has made a body disappear, but he also acts like the detective who wants to interpret it.

That the photographer's primary medium is photography is significant because, as many writers have pointed out, the development of photography is frequently referred to in early detective narratives (Thomas, *Making Darkness Visible*). Not only does the development of photography coincide historically with the development of the detective genre; the conceptions of what a photograph can and should do form a kind of template for/ analogue to the genre. Early on, photography became essential to policing practices of criminal identification based on the medium's indexical nature. Rogues' galleries, for example, were used as "wanted" lists, as well as for purposes of witness identification. That the photographer does not ever photograph his wife is significant. Any images he has of her are simply stills from moving pictures – attempts to freeze time and halt her movement away from him. The photographs, in other words, poignantly anticipate and even capture her absence.

There is another connection between the detective narrative and photography alluded to in the film that has to do with economics and systems of exchange. Despite its use as a mechanism to identify individuals, photography must be understood as a standardized product that gets used as a kind of universal form of currency in the late-nineteenth century through to today. Linking media to the global networks that force the individual to be lost in the crowd, Jonathan Crary explains: "photography and money become homologous forms of power ... equally totalizing systems for binding and unifying all subjects within a single global network of valuation and desire" (13). In the photographer's media-saturated environment, the search to locate the missing body and affirm its identity is in other words symptomatic of, as well as a product of, the logic of capitalism. In this context, the detective-figure's dual role of prompting and investigating the body's disappearance within a context where he himself elaborates complex systems of equivalences and exchange has the function of illuminating another kind of perversity complex system.

The film strongly connects the photographer to the alienating effects of capital. Money both generates absences and compensates for them. One of the core myths of money-systems is that empty signs can be exchanged for presence. In *Calendar*, the steady stream of call girls from all over the world who come for dinner at the photographer's Toronto home are there to compensate for the missing wife. As double signifiers, then, the call girls connect the modern experience of geographic circulation to economic circulation. The madam's messages on the photographer's answering machine make the connection between geographic and economic circulation most explicit. She asks only two sorts of questions, but both are about exchange. First, because her exotic call girls are able to speak several languages, she asks about whether they should speak one foreign language instead of another. Second, because she provides these call girls in exchange for money, she asks about the photographer's "account."

Beyond the obvious example of his transactions with the escort service, there are clues to indicate that the photographer conducts all his social relations according to a paradigm that centres on financial exchange. Early on in the film, prompted by his lack of interest in the histories that she is providing, his wife asks him whether her services as a translator are only "practical." His answer, "I guess," though weak, indicates his tacit recognition that he relates to her through a social contract that positions him as the purchaser of services she provides. While, for the wife, the journey to Armenia is intensely personal and metaphysical, and reconnects her to sacred places with specific energies and fascinating histories, for the photographer, the journey is purely practical. When he admits that he has not done research into the places he is photographing, because "I am doing this as a job. It wasn't my idea," he clearly indicates his desire to keep the journey professional. He also confesses that he would not have come to Armenia, his mother country, unless he "had some reason to come."

The practical, for the photographer, is thus bound with an economy where labour is exchanged for money. The foreignness and strangeness of his reluctance to let go of the cameras and wander freely in the landscape reflects his inability to not work. In the scene where he finds out that he is taking photographs of a place that is not a church but rather a pagan temple, the photographer quips that it "looks like a bank." His comment prompts him to attack the driver. By suggesting that the driver is involved in some kind of deception motivated by greed, the photographer cheapens his penetrating comments on the histories of the area: "Listen, um, before he keeps talking, I mean, is it possible that we make it clear whether he sees himself as a sort of guide or just a driver, because I have this impression –" His wife interrupts: "What do you mean?" He elaborates: "Well, he keeps telling these stories, and they're great stories, but I just want to know whether at the end of this he expects more money or something like that?"

The photographer's question is legitimate within his own cultural economy, where the labour of making art, whether images or narratives, is always defined in relation to its exchange value rather than its use value. The driver and the wife are, however, both terribly upset by his implication that their transactions are motivated by money. Stories are being exchanged, she urges, as if he would understand: "He's explaining that the place has a history, he knows that history, nothing more." The photographer apologetically explains that he just wanted to "clarify the situation," but no clarity ensues.

Even in his conversations with the call girls, which are unequivocally framed in a situation where money is exchanged for services rendered, the photographer shocks the women with his insistence on the presence of capital at the heart of intimate transactions. When he discovers that one of the call girls he is eating with is an oriental dancer, he tells her about the first time he touched a woman, also a dancer. His intimate touching involved the mediation of cash:

> My father had taken me for my birthday to this restaurant. At a certain point, he gave me this two-dollar bill and said, "You're supposed to put this in her waistband." I waited until the dancer came to the table, and I pulled back her waistband, and she wasn't wearing anything underneath. I remember that she wasn't wearing anything. It was actually kind of odd, and I took the two-dollar bill and kind of lingered there. I don't know, it just kind of left an impression on me I guess.

The dancer he has hired as his call girl promptly ruptures his fiduciary fantasy by speaking from the position of the exchanged other. She blurts out: "I hate it when people touch me. When I dance. I find it very intrusive. I think if they want to give me money, they should shower it on my head. It's a compliment." Unable to respond to her outburst, he pours the last drop of wine, and thus gives her the cue to get up and walk away from him.

The photographer is so immersed in a capitalist system of exchange that he brings the issue of money even to the question of reproduction and children. When he shows pictures of his foster child, Lucinée, to one of the call girls, he appears to be more fascinated with the photo-reproduction than with the child. His call girl asks him questions about the foster plan: "How much does it cost you?" He answers: "Well it just went up. It used to be twenty-eight, and now it's thirty." She invites him to talk about what his parenting is worth to him. Her language, however, is the language of accumulation: "And what do you get, a picture, and what else?" His answer indicates that he measures value by the number and types of copies and representations, not by any kind of deeper meaning. He specifies: "They send a picture. Yeah, I've got a video tape. Yes, it's nice, I like it, I like the …" He breaks off to explain that he wrote Lucinée a letter. He does not tell the call girl what he says in the letter. As with the photographs of the child, the medium is more important than the message. He explains that Lucinée wrote back. Her letter thus merely contributes to the swelling of his list of items he got for his investment. The photographer then turns the questions back on the questioner, and asks the call girl whether she has children, and how much they cost her. She responds with outrage: "It's a ridiculous question, you don't think about those things." When she refuses to provide a "ball-park" figure that could be compared to his twenty-eight or thirty dollars, the photographer again pours the last bit of wine, which is her cue to stand up and leave him.

If we consider that the detective figure has also often been an emblem of the scholar/researcher who similarly sifts materials for evidence that confirms or rebuts intuitive guesses, it is possible to see that the photographer is engaging in a kind of inquiry/system of exchange that instrumentalizes its object.

An alternative to this instrumentalizing system of exchange is presented through the translator/interpreter, who models a productive, rather than suspicious, mode of interpretation. Even though she is the mediator, the translator, the one in the film who has access to both worlds, she does not wish to participate in the commercial system that the photographer is swept up in. She wants real children, not purchased photographic and videotaped evidence of them. She wants an exchange of stories and histories that has nothing to do with jobs or practicalities. When she chooses to leave the photographer and her life in Toronto for a life with the driver in Armenia, she remains remarkably guilt free.

And yet, in the economy of the film, she does not really get to step out of the system of exchange she deplores, because it seeks to contain her. In a remarkable scene, communicated more through body language and looks than words, the driver for whom she leaves her husband appears to acknowledge his complicity in the system. The initial premise of the scene is a visual joke. She rushes to the camera laughing, and explains that the driver knows how to "do a KGB thing, checking your passport." The photographer inquires what that means, and asks them to show it. Initially, the interpreter and driver arrange themselves to act out the scene together. Operating the video camera, outside of the film frame, the photographer is a passive spectator. The driver grabs her passport, opens it up, and looks at it sternly. The intimacy of their postures makes the photographer an outsider, so he asks them to rearrange things: "Let him do it to me, let him do it to the camera," he urges with a false laugh. She hesitates, and then asks the driver to do it to the camera. With her passport still in his hand, he looks directly into the camera, nodding at the passport in his hand. "He wants your passport," she interjects. From behind the camera, the photographer hands over his passport. The driver examines both passports in his hand, opens up the photographer's, and then with a sleight of hand, passes the photographer's passport over to her while retaining hers, now opened to her photo image. The driver peers at her image slowly, and then looks directly into the camera, finally lowering his eyes introspectively. His look seems to avow to the photographer that he too fetishizes her image. It also seems to avow that she (and her image) is changing hands – exchanged between men in a formal ritual with authoritarian overtones. All of the laughter has evaporated, and she becomes unusually silent. The crime of the missing body in the film, then, is attached to the experiences of geographic and economic circulation that characterize late capitalism's flows, and is informed by a practice of exchange which works by staging equivalencies that "transform traditional beliefs in solidity and unique identity" (Gunning 18). The challenge is to be able to inquire about this phenomenon without perpetuating its logic of instrumentalization.

I began this paper by pointing out that the film presents binary structures and then refutes them by uncovering more complex models of exchange. What I have not yet talked about is how the film's presentation of a binary of effects laid onto the film's geographical and imaginary spaces lays the ground for explicit modes of critique. Read this way, it is possible to see the interpreter and driver's relationship to Armenia as the pathological and inauthentic one, and the photographer's relationship to the urban mediascape as the one that has the greatest authenticity. In the film, it is this latter relationship that is used to represent a truer understanding of the circumstances and consequences of migration in a globalized world.

It is important to pause here to think about the romanticism inherent in the representation of Armenia and the interpreter and driver who "belong" to it. The film appears to encourage us to understand their organic, pure relationship to the land as archetypal and primal. But there is another way of thinking about this, because to attend to the archetypal nature of their experience of homeland is to neglect the insight that home and homeland always have particular meanings to the individuals who stay and leave it. What is unique about the characters' migration from this particular homeland? Just as the film makes a point about photography's relationship to social intimacy by *not* representing the wife in the calendar photographs, the film makes a point about historical context through its total silence about what is perhaps the most important event in Armenia's history. Despite its survey of the major archaeological sites in Armenia, the film never once speaks about a cause of the Armenian diasporas. Beginning in 1915, the Ottoman Empire began a program of systematically exterminating between 0.8 and 1.5 million ethnic Armenians in what is now modern-day Turkey. The Armenians who survived became part of a global diaspora, whose memories of trauma were passed on from generation to generation. The experiences of both leaving and returning home, for each generation since then, have been sculpted by the legacy of a genocide that has yet to be acknowledged by Turkey.

And so we need to see that, on one hand, the tour of Armenian monuments registers a collective desire to remember the past, pre-genocide. The translator/interpreter's journey into the landscape, aided by the driver's storytelling, can be understood as a quest for a sort of "transgenerational stability of knowledge," as Arjun Appadurai puts it, and for the creation of a "community of sentiment" (43, 8). In cases where the exile's experience is traumatic rather than neutral, both forms of reaching for forms of connection are understandably important to the exile's sense of groundedness and belonging, since the history of this particular homeland has made many of its citizens essentially homeless.

On the other hand, however, the driver's tour and the translator/interpreter's response to it aestheticize, poeticize, and thus conceal a history that is already characterized by denial. Despite being connected to the body, to touch, to immersive and intimate experience, the film's representations of Armenia can be understood as being involved in the construction of a kind of depthless nostalgia. The pastoral imagery, which contrasts sharply to the stark imagery associated with Toronto – the place of exile – thus must be seen as belonging to the imaginary. This imagery represents the *invention*, rather than merely the *recollection*, of a tradition that mobilizes utopian tropes not specific to Armenia, but rather apolitical and trans-historical. They are thus ideological, participating in the creation of a kind of false consciousness through a remembering that is actually a kind of forgetting.

And what of the photographer's presentation of a set of pathological symptoms for which Armenia seems to be the antidote? His highly mediated, essentially capitalistic, instrumentalizing mode of engagement with the world lets us rewind and replay something that is important to explicitly witness. For the film's audience, what the photographer's narrative yields about the modern North American geography is the opposite of false consciousness. It offers a sociological history of the present by showing, as in a slide show, the often pathological but entirely real dimensions of global cultural flows that Arjun Appadurai describes in his work on modernity and globalization. They make many of the co-factors involved in the experience of diaspora visible and thus available to critique.

Appadurai argues that the contemporary world must be conceived of as an unstable interrelating set of building blocks that he terms ethnoscapes, mediascapes, technoscapes, financescapes, and ideoscapes, which overlap and intersect and through which the individual must navigate. Appadurai's ethnoscapes refer to "the landscape of persons who constitute the shifting world in which we live: tourists, immigrants, refugees, exiles, guest workers, and other moving groups" (33). Appadurai's technoscapes refer to the "global configuration of technology, both high and low, both mechanical and informational," while financescapes refer to the "disposition of global capital" (34). Mediascapes, in turn, "provide large and complex repertoires of images, narratives, and ethnoscapes to viewers throughout the world" (35). They tend to be "image-centred, narrative-based accounts of strips of reality, and what they offer to those who experience and transform them is a series of elements (such as characters, plots, and textual forms) out of which scripts can be formed of imagined lives" (35). Finally, ideoscapes refer to the global flow of ideologies – metanarrative-level ideas with staying power, such as the Enlightenment values like democracy that can still find purchase in a contemporary environment.

Thinking about these "scapes" helps make it clear that, in *Calendar*, the *behaviours* of the photographer may reek of inauthenticity, but their *representation* possesses a degree of authenticity not associated with the more archetypal and ahistorical presentation of the wife and driver's narratives. Taken together, his vexed relationship to his long-ago abandoned motherland, his immersion in a machine world that cuts him off from communication and intimacy, his generation of systems of exchange that tie up with capitalism's alienating logic, his production of a variety of mediascapes through his compulsive use of cameras as prosthetics, and the way his mode of being condenses some of the central ideological impetuses of modernity, make available a diagnosis – untainted by nostalgia – as much as they betray a set of symptoms.

However, in *Calendar* there is a third set of characters who deserve still more attention than I have thus far given them, because they also provide a line on the "scapes" that shape the contemporary world. The series of call girls who are indistinct as characters are easily subsumed under the same category of North Americanness and its modernity, yet they are used most powerfully to comment on the social realities of an age of media and mobility. Just like the elision of the history of Armenia says so much through the film's silence about relationships of the three main characters to it, the silences around the call girls' socio-cultural realities condenses a number of important issues about the present. In essence, what they represent to the audience is a way of linking the worldwide experience of diaspora to class.

While the photographer and madam speak about the transactional nature of the relationship, we must see that these women seem far more like new Canadian citizens than guest sex workers, but that they share with the sex worker a need to leverage their foreignness and femaleness in their new environment. The film disconnects them from their "community of sentiment" by not even naming the language they speak as they turn to the telephone on cue from the photographer. Yet from an optic attuned to the way North America, attached to the photographer's story, makes available an astute critique of the global "scapes," these women's phone calls, designed to perform the photographer's experience of betrayal, must be understood as calls *home*, rather than just as random exotic/erotic sweet talk in which the essentially monolingual photographer is unable to participate.

The contrast between the translator's actual *journey* home, the photographer's *visit*, and the call girls' *calls* home, then, makes the translator's return to her homeland and the photographer's quick tour *both* seem somewhat touristic, that is, made possible by class privilege. The call girls' highly mediated connectivity, in turn, captures an experience so common in the worldwide diaspora of individuals for whom phonecards are the primary mode of reaching home, because travel would be either too expensive or too dangerous. They represent, in other words, the experience of diaspora in a politically inflected and class-based world. Even though they take us beyond the romanticized affective geography of Armenia, or really of any place in particular, then, these characters are not archetypal as much as representative.

At the end of the film, something important happens. The photographer puts down his pen and begins to talk to the final call girl in his series as if she were his guest instead of someone he pays for services. The woman becomes individualized, and she is permitted to freely speak her mind, as is he. Everyday communication, with no romance attached, unhindered by the prosthetics of mass media, outside of the framework of capital, anchored in the present, is offered as the cure for the modern condition – as that which allows the faulty process of mourning to be resolved, such that the global subject may move forward. The utopian possibilities imagined in connection with the pastoral mode and the dystopian possibilities imagined in connection with the realist mode, the film finally says, are not as strong as the practical possibilities proposed in connection with *everydayness*. *Calendar* thus finds in routine practices a way for the modern subject to better inhabit the larger social, economic, and historical factors that the film exposes and critiques. The representation of these routine practices takes the viewer back to the space outside the film where they will see the tremendously liberating power of open eyes and small gestures.

To return, then, to where I started, I want to underline what it is that *Calendar* treats that is relevant to contemporary comparatists. The film's chief focus, as I said, is interpretation itself. Indeed, its most charismatic and enigmatic character is an interpreter, tasked with making a now-foreign homeland legible to one of its exiles. When she stops interpreting for him by leaving the marriage, the photographer-in-exile then undertakes a separate task of interpretation and translation. Trying to understand why his wife left him, rather than to understand the world and language she left him for, he decides to compulsively sift through a mountain of textual matter, comparing images, video and audio recordings, letters. However, he does not only seek to read the evidence; he seeks to produce more, scripting encounters that stage his pathological fixations with the other. Both of the characters then launch an ethical question: how, amidst the destabilizing global flows of persons and commodities and concepts, is it possible to interpret without instrumentalizing the knower or the known?

Travelling across geographical boundaries but also boundaries between media, trafficking in stereotypes and archetypes, Egoyan's film delineates between possible structures of comparison and inquiry. One is a binaristic paradigm that exoticizes or romanticizes the other, or alternately controls and contains it. Against this binaristic model, it presents a paradigm that is less instrumentalizing, one more comfortable with the destabilizations of meaning that cross-cultural and cross-medial encounters invariably produce. The film shows why, since languages move across and are stopped at borders and checkpoints, mistranslations are fundamental to cross-cultural experience. It reveals that the untranslatable need not pose an insurmountable obstacle in the movement toward understanding; misunderstanding and not understanding can launch more genuine inquiry (Apter, *Against*).

But *Calendar* offers more that is relevant to our own hermeneutic exercises when it draws attention to the materiality of media. When the film presents the differences between photography, video, film, epistolary writing, and scripted as well as improvised face-to-face dialogue or monologue mediated by telephone answering machines, it wants us to ask how media provide frameworks for social experience, and dictate "ways of seeing." It signals that media are intrinsically related to the production and global circulation of imagined communities, as they are related to the production of identity and subjectivity. We must thus understand *media* as having specific material constraints, a specific social history, and specific effects for its users.

Finally, *Calendar* cautions against the simplistic desire to idealize the ethnic and celebrate the homeland in the spirit of embracing diversity. This is important, because when we step back from our texts in order to better understand how they work in wider global contexts, when we tune in to not only the personal and community narratives that stories offer, but also their ideological – that is social, political, and economic – dimensions, we are able to gain a much more nuanced understanding of how representations do not just mirror experience but also open it up to critique. In short, this one Canadian film that embodies the spirit of comparison through its staging of cross-cultural encounters invites reflection on the scope and methods of the discipline of Comparative Literature, and as such, could be seen as "required reading."

## NOTES

Author's note: Portions of this chapter are taken from my unpublished doctoral dissertation, "Anagrams of the Body: Hybrid Texts and the Question of Postmodernism in Literature and Film of Canada" (University of Alberta, 1999).

Editor's note: Canadian actor Arsinée Khanjan also appeared in *The Lark Farm*, a 2007 Italian film about the Armenian tragedy based on the 2004 novel *La Masseria delle allodole* by Antonia Arslan.

## BIBLIOGRAPHY

Altman, Janet Gurkin. *Epistolarity: Approaches to a Form*. Columbus: Ohio State University Press, 1982.
Anderson, Benedict. *Imagined Communities: Reflections on the Origin and Spread of Nationalism*. London: Verso, 1991.
Appadurai, Arjun. *Modernity at Large: Cultural Dimensions of Globalization*. Minneapolis: University of Minnesota Press, 1996.
Apter, Emily. *Against World Literature: On the Politics of Untranslatability*. London: Verso, 2013.
Bakhtin, Mikhail. *The Dialogic Imagination*. Edited by Michael Holquist. Translated by Caryl Emerson and Michael Holquist. Austin: University of Texas Press, 1981.
Berger, John. *Ways of Seeing*. London: Penguin Books, 1972.
Crary, Jonathan. *Techniques of the Observer: On Vision and Modernity in the Nineteenth Century*. Cambridge, MA: MIT Press, 1990.
Desbarats, Carole, Danièle Rivière, Jacinto Lageira, and Paul Virilio. *Atom Egoyan*. Translated by Brian Holmes. Paris: Dis Voir, 1993.
Egoyan, Atom. Interview with Douglas Cooper. *Sundance Filmmaker Focus*. 25 Jul 1998. http://www.sundnacechannel.com/focus/egoyan/intl.html (accessed July 1999).
Egoyan, Atom, dir. *Calendar*. With Arsinée Khanjian and Ashot Admian. Zeitgeist Films, 1993.
Gunning, Tom. "Tracing the Individual Body: Photography, Detectives, and Early Cinema." In *Cinema and the Invention of Modern Life,* edited by Leo Charney and Vanessa Schwartz, 15–45. Berkeley: University of California Press, 1995.
Harcourt, Peter. "Imaginary Images: An Examination of Atom Egoyan's Films." *Film Quarterly* 48, no. 3 (1995): 2–14.
Kegel, Katrin. "The Thirteenth Church: Musical Structures in Atom Egoyan's *Calendar*." In *Image and Territory: Essays on Atom Egoyan*, edited by

Jennifer Burwell and Monique Tschofen, 79–100. Waterloo, ON: Wilfrid Laurier University Press, 2007.

Kushner, Scott. "Comparative Non-Literature and Everyday Digital Textuality." http://stateofthediscipline.acla.org/entry/comparative-non-literature-and-everyday-digital-textuality-0 (accessed 5 May 2015).

McLuhan, Marshall. *Understanding Media: The Extensions of Man*. Edited, with Introduction by Lewis H. Lapham. Cambridge, MA: MIT Press, 1995.

Mookerjea, Sourayan. "Allegory, Stereotype, and the Local Mode of Construction: *Calendar*'s Filmic Concept of Global Flows." *Space and Culture* 5, no. 2 (2001): 103–23.

– "Montage in Spatial Ethnography: Crystalline Narration and Cultural Studies of Globalization." *Symploke* 9, no. 1–2 (2002): 114–33.

Nelson, Tollof. "Passing Time in Intercultural Cinema: The Exilic Experience of the Time Passer in Atom Egoyan's *Calendar*." *SubStance* #106, 34, no. 1 (2005): 129–44.

Romney, Jonathan. *Atom Egoyan*. London: BFI Institute, 2003.

Szeman, Imre. "Review of *Modernity at Large: Cultural Dimensions of Globalization* by Arjun Appadurai." *Public Worlds*. Vol. 1. Minneapolis: University of Minnesota Press, 1996. http://clogic.eserver.org/1-1/szeman.html.

Thomas, Ronald R. "Making Darkness Visible: Capturing the Criminal and Observing the Law in Victorian Photography and Detective Fiction." In *Victorian Literature and the Victorian Visual Imagination*, edited by Carol T. Christ and John O. Jordan, 134–86. Berkeley: University of California Press, 1995.

Virilio, Paul. *Art of the Motor*. Translated by Julie Rose. Minneapolis: University of Minnesota Press, 1995.

SECTION THREE

# INTERNATIONAL COMPARATIVE STUDIES

In order to explain why we have collected this diverse set of chapters under the heading of "International Comparative Literature," we point out that all the literary texts discussed are by authors with ethnic minority backgrounds. We would like readers to view these contributions as examples of Comparative Literature that can serve as models to students and scholars in many different parts of the world. We see this work on multicultural writers as promising future directions for Comparative Literature. To support this approach, we would like to quote from the chapter "Anonymous" by Sneja Gunew, included in this collection:

> In my own work I have reconceptualized so-called multicultural writers as mediators between national literatures and a world literature. While the nation state and its anxious reiterations continue, there are competing terrains, such as the diasporic, and the latter often comes together in the metropolitan city – the microcosm as macrocosm or possible model for a differing conception of the literature of the world. In this vision, world literatures are not stratified into nations, and their supposedly evolutionary histories into a progress towards modernity, but consist of the coeval existence of many histories, languages, and forms of the human and posthuman coexisting and sometimes interacting across borders. (34–5)

This view is consistent with practices in Comparative Literature programs in Canada, as the three examples below illustrate. One of the first MA degrees in Comparative Canadian Literature was earned by bilingual student Max Dorsinville at the Université de Sherbrooke in 1968. His thesis on Quebec, Black American, and Caribbean writers was the basis for his book *Caliban without Prospero: Essays on Quebec and Black Literature* (1974). This is the first Canadian study that combines comparative methodology with post-colonial theory. A former MA student from Sherbrooke, Francis Macri earned a PhD in Comparative Literature at the University of Alberta in 1980 with a thesis solely on Canadian and Quebec writers:

Gabrielle Roy, Margaret Laurence, Anne Hébert, and Margaret Atwood. At the University of Toronto, there are on record several PhD theses in Comparative Literature based solely on English and French-Canadian texts. Trilingual student Winfried Siemerling earned a doctorate in 1991 with a thesis on Canadian texts, which later became the basis for his book *Discovering the Other: Alterity in the Work of Leonard Cohen, Hubert Aquin, Michael Ondaatje, and Nicole Brossard* (1994).

**BIBLIOGRAPHY**

Dorsinville, Max. *Caliban without Prospero: Essays on Quebec and Black Literature*. Erin, ON. Press Porcepic, 1974.

Siemerling, Winfried. *Discovering the Other: Alterity in the Work of Leonard Cohen, Hubert Aquin, Michael Ondaatje, and Nicole Brossard*. Toronto: University of Toronto Press, 1994.

# A Many-Tongued Babel: Translingualism in Canadian Multicultural Writing

*Deborah Saidero*

> And Saida sang: Negema wangu binti
> mchachefu wa sanati / upulike wasiati
> asa ukazingatia.
> M.G. Vassanji (53)

When Rohinton Mistry uses Gujarati in *Such a Long Journey* (1991), Hiromi Goto uses Japanese in *Chorus of Mushrooms* (1994), Antonio D'Alfonso uses Italian in *Fabrizio's Passion* (1995), and M.G. Vassanji uses Swahili in *The Magic of Saida* (2012), they join a growing number of writers who freely include phrases and sentences from their heritage languages to introduce a different cultural perspective into their narratives. Because of their peculiar position in between languages, Steven Kellman defines them as "translingual writers," that is, authors "who write in more than one language or in a language that is not their primary one," arguing that "by expressing themselves in multiple verbal systems, [they] flaunt their freedom from the constraints of the culture into which they happen to be born" and are able "to cross over into a new linguistic identity" which endows them with alternative perspectives of the world.[1] Among them are writers for whom the medium chosen for artistic expression is the language of imposed colonial domination, as in the case of post-colonial authors like Mistry or Vassanji, and writers for whom it is the language of assimilation and acculturation, as in the case of immigrants like Goto and Michelut. For all, translingualism is a performative act of resistance and a self-reflexive tool for crossing and bridging cultural boundaries.

Within Canada's vibrant literary scene, translingual writers of various ethnic origin are certainly making their presence felt through a large body of works that interrogates cultural differences. Like their counterparts in the US and around the world, by self-consciously engaging with different tongues, they promote a transcultural model of communication that shatters the limits of monolingual perspectives of reality, and thereby opens up a dialogic contact zone between and beyond languages and cultures. In this dynamic and productive zone, the interplay of linguistic and cultural intersections prompts a broadening of what Vassanji calls "the substrata,"[2] the knowledge, that is, of both the self and the other, which necessarily affects the author-reader relationship. By demanding that the reader be engaged in the contact zones of the text, translingual writers usher their monolingual and polyglot readers into the liminal spaces between cultures, where they are not only called to participate actively in the encounter with the Other, but also to renegotiate their perception of self and the world. In other words, plurilingual texts invite readers, as Tina Steiner has noted, to engage in a process of "cultural translation," which multiplies their interrelations and "opens up pockets of resistance to dominant discourses."[3]

One form of resistance that translingualism opens up for Canada's "ethnic minority writers" is vis-à-vis the mainstream literary canon. The incorporation of heritage languages challenges, in fact, the linguistic, cultural, and literary hegemony of English and French in Canadian literature and sanctions the legitimacy of reclaiming other languages to give voice to multi-faceted experiences. What was initially a bilingual duologue between the country's two solitudes has now become a translingual polylogue among its many ethnic communities, which seeks to disrupt mainstream *vs.* minority writing dialectics. In her survey of Chinese-Canadian literature, Lien Chao argues, for instance, that Asian-Canadian writing "raises a resistant voice against European cultural hegemony in Canadian literature," much like the literary contributions of Black or Native writers do.[4] African-Canadian author George Elliott Clarke acknowledges, on the other hand, the exemplary role played by Italian-Canadians in making their subaltern community visible in the vertically aligned mosaic, thereby offering "a useful model for scholars of other minority or ethnic Canadian communities who seek to affirm and reconceptualize these literatures."[5] In Quebec, writers like Filippo Salvatore and Dany Laferrière, who are part of Montreal's stimulating multilingual milieu, shift between French, English, and their heritage languages and dialects to destabilize any identification with a single language position, or a single literary canon.

Quebec is also home to a number of Arabic writers, who work in French, but are always conscious of the Arabic language and regional dialects from their countries of origin. They include Saad Elkhadem, Naïm Kattan, Abla Farhoud, Wajdi Mouawad, Hédi Bouraoui, and others. F.

Elizabeth Dahab has made several studies of these French-language authors in terms of their different adaptations to literary culture in Canada and in *la Francophonie*.[6]

Because of their exotic flare and the challenging demands they make on the reader, translingual texts are often discarded by those who do not belong to the same linguistic community as the writer and are relegated to a liminal position within the literary polysystem. They are situated, that is, on the edge of Canadian writing. To avoid the effects of pigeonholing, authors like Aritha van Herk and Janice Kulyk Keefer refuse to use their heritage languages (Dutch and Ukrainian respectively), without, nonetheless, neglecting their ethno-cultural backgrounds. Keefer, for instance, engages with her ethnicity in the novel *The Green Library* (1996) and in her family memoir *Honey and Ashes* (1998), while van Herk discusses her conflicted relationship with her Dutch heritage in the essay "Of Dykes and Boers and Drowning":

> And oh, the mouth so full of words that never say themselves, bundled up in a backwash of that other language, forbidden, choking, the one that everyone laughs at: Dutch, Dutch, Dutch, as ugly as it sounds and as throaty guttural of its pronunciation. Full of connotations of lowness, levelity; Netherlandish the bottom, like the bottom of the throat where words fathomage, clogged, choking, thick with *draskestijn* and drunkeness, their derogatory dungeons clanking in chains around the duplicities of Dutch concerts, and Dutch courage.[7]

There is no overt sentiment of nostalgia for the mother tongue here, but we also detect that this writer protests too much over the rejection or loss of the heritage language of her parents, as if she is actually trying to hide her true feelings.

The rapid growth of translingual literature in Canada witnesses, however, a widespread commitment to questioning the premises of Canadian multiculturalism through a heightened multilingual perspective. In this chapter I will analyze the occurrence of translingual practices, such as codeswitching, heteroglossia, and self-translation, in the works of some multicultural Canadian writers, to show how these practices are inserted within a transcultural paradigm that promotes a transnational reimagining of belonging in cosmopolitan terms, as well as a reconsideration of literary polysystems that debases simplistic categorizations of "national literature." By relying on multiple cultural and linguistic traditions, these writers embrace, in fact, a comparative model of literature and claim access to the broader canon of "world literature."

Often a by-product of migration or colonial domination, translingual writing practices stem from a peculiar hyperconsciousness of language, from an awareness that "no language is neutral," as Dionne Brand says (1990). Every language conveys its own set of meanings, and words carry the cultural and ideological values of their speakers. Multilinguality is thus intimately bound to different cultural identities. In *The Translingual Imagination*, Kellman highlights how literary translingualism becomes a privileged site for investigating identity, both personal and collective, since it counters the restricted visions of self, society, and the universe inherent in monolingualism. And, since identity is shaped by language, translingualism is also linked with transculturality, a concept put forward by the philosopher Wolfgang Welsch, which questions understandings of cultural categories as stable, monological, given, and self-contained, emphasizing instead the interactions and permeations among cultures that transcend cultural boundaries.

In his novels, African-Asian-Canadian writer Moyez Vassanji shows an ongoing commitment to investigating how language operates in relation to culture and identity. Born in Kenya into a family of Indian origin, Vassanji grew up in Tanzania and then moved to the United States and Canada. His peculiar experience of in-between-ness in societies where colonial legacies have produced cultural-linguistic hierarchies permeates his narratives, which most often include both African and Indian languages in the flow of the English text. In an interview he comments on how "natural and easy" it is for him to mix languages, as Jewish writers have also done: "I use Swahili-like inflexions for Swahili dialogue; sometimes I insert something completely in Swahili; the meaning is evident in the context or is suggested by the rest of the text without being intrusive. The same thing when I insert a dialogue or speech in an Indian language. These techniques have been used by Jewish writers."[8]

The multilingualism of his narratives is never decoupled from his portrayal of East-African Indians and the transcultural dimension of his African homeland. As Mikhail Gromov points out in his discussion of *The Gunny Sack* (1989) and *The In-Between World of Vikram Lall* (2003), language-mixing devices are masterfully used to represent East Africa "as a contact zone of various cultures, mentalities and attitudes," and to embody their speakers' search for a new identity in the interstices of these cultures (62). The use of non-English words and expressions, mainly from Swahili, Cutchi-Gujarati, and Punjabi (and occasionally from other

Indian tongues) thus serves various functions that go well beyond the "needs of reproducing the local colour or specific cultural realities" (73) of Tanzania and Kenya with their mixed European, Indian, and African societies. Being an integral part of the text, the mingling of languages draws attention to their role as "powerful factors in the social life of characters ... assisting them in expressing and ... constructing their varied identities" (69). At the same time, it also draws attention to their importance in the construction of a new collective identity in these post-colonial African states. For both Salim and Vikram, the Indian-African protagonists of the two novels, the Indian languages of their ethnic communities mark their in-between state amidst the whites and Africans and their ranking within the colonial hierarchy – inferior to the white colonizers, but superior to the Africans. Swahili, on the other hand, is the language that marks their "in-ness" (72), for its acquisition allows them to forge their new identity as true Africans and true citizens of the new country. Since it is used by both the Indians and the Europeans in their everyday interactions with the local Africans, Swahili is the language that bridges races and communities in the emerging independent African states, thereby allowing for a renegotiation of identities and settler positions. An example of this bridging is found at the back of Vassanji's novel *The Book of Secrets*, where he provides a glossary of terms, with this explanation: "[t]he symbols * and + following definitions indicate Swahili and Indian words respectively. These words, especially Swahili, may have origins in Arabic."[9]

By posing Swahili as a symbol of the new African states and their distinctive identity after colonial domination, Vassanji undermines the status of English as the colonizer's language. The incorporation of Swahili words thus enacts an effort to cross-culturally re-appropriate, criticize, and reinvent the English language. Other writers from former non-settler British colonies similarly use translingualism as a discursive strategy to subvert colonial relationships. Writers of the Indian diaspora like Mistry and Anita Rau Badami, for instance, incorporate a variety of Indian languages (Urdu-Gujarati-Hindi-Parsi) to celebrate the richness of multilingual India and emphasize the distinctiveness of Indian English as a legitimate geographical dialect. Irish-Canadian author Jane Urquhart inserts Irish Gaelic words and phrases in her novel *Away* (1993) to reclaim an ancient folkloristic and mythological tradition that was suppressed by Anglo-Irish colonial relations. In her novel *In Another Place, Not Here* (1996), Trinidadian writer Dionne Brand creates a heteroglossic continuum between standard English and Caribbean-English to counter the muting of the Afrosporic subject by the hegemonic politics of colonial oppression. The use of the demotic, which is itself a hyphenated inter-language deriving from the fusion of English and West African languages, is aimed at disrupting hierarchical power relations and creating a dialogic discursive space where the polyvalent and polyrhythmic elements of West Indian culture may coexist alongside standard English ones. Code-mixing thus becomes for these authors a tool through which they may alter the English language and assert cultural differences. In Steiner's words: "For the postcolonial writer, to conquer English is precisely to re-translate structures of domination and oppression of the language into new modes of creation"; it is a mechanism "for engendering new meanings and forms."[10]

Joining other Caribbean writers, such as Marlene NourbeSe Philip, Edward Brathwaite, and Edouard Glissant, Brand exploits the potentialities of Caribbean linguistic plurality to portray the multiple levels of physical, emotional, psychological, cultural, and linguistic displacement caused by the diaspora of the Afro-Caribbean peoples. Her use of the Caribbean demotic is, however, equally directed toward debasing the colonial subjugation of Black women in patriarchal societies. In *In Another Place, Not Here*, the demotic is, in fact, used to give voice to Elizete and her quest for selfhood, from slave-like cane-field worker who has to put up with her husband's aggressive lovemaking to lesbian lover with Verlia, the other questing female hero. Dictated by the wish to empower the triply silenced and marginalized Black lesbian woman, Brand's linguistic endeavour to recreate Elizete's thick, poetic island drawl exploits the imagistic and metaphoric richness of Afro-Caribbean folklore, its mythical archetypes, rhetorical vigour, oratorical energies, tonal accentuation, and musical rhythms reminiscent of the calypso, to create a female code of resistance, challenge, and survival. In particular, in Brand's text the demotic becomes a transformative mode of expression, which relies on the subversive techniques rooted in African languages to destabilize both the linguistic hegemony of the standard tongue and the oppressive patriarchal logic inherent in both Eurocentric and Caribbean cultures. The musical and lyrical cadences of the oral Caribbean nation language functions, in fact, to deconstruct the dominator's racialized and genderized language:

> I see in she face how she believe. She glance quick as if unimportant things was in her way, like Oliviere, like fright. She eyes move as if she was busy going somewhere, busy seeing something and all this cane all this whipping and lashing was a hindrance. Then like a purposeful accident she eyes rest on me, and she face open, them big teeth push out to laugh for me, sweat flying, she fall again to the cutlass.[11]

At the same time, the demotic text is also infused with feminist imagery and body language and becomes the discursive site where the language of lesbian desire is articulated. Abundant, for instance, are water-related images to signal the women's sexual intercourse and mouth/tongue-related imagery to portray the resistant female body. The linguistic dynamics of Brand's demotic, thus, result from a complex intermingling of indigenous Afro-Caribbean features and imported (mainly North American) elements, from a creolization, that is, of linguistic, stylistic, and cultural traditions. This creates a heteroglossic continuum, or "polyphonic collision of competing languages," as Jason Wiens calls it,[12] which deconstructs binary oppositions (i.e., self/other, white/black, heterosexual/homosexual, standard/dialect, formal/informal, monophonic/polyphonic, poetic/colloquial, written/oral, etc.) and achieves a polyvocal synthesis of languages that allows for multiple modes of self-expression.

For many migrant and diasporic writers, the translingual experience involves living between languages and engaging in a conscious, but nonetheless painful, process of translating their world views, experiences, and perceptions from one medium to the other. Code-mixing and code-switching devices may, thus, also signal the fragmentation of the self that individuals experience when forced to choose between systems of representation, often by relinquishing one language in favour of another. In *The Magic of Saida*, Vassanji dramatizes the tension inherent in assimilating to a new identity through his interplay of languages. For Kamal, the half-blood, half-caste "chotaro" (194), who must give up his mother's African community to become part of his father's Indian family, language – like race and religion – intensifies feelings of unbelonging and non-identity. While living in Kilwa with his mother, Swahili initially conveys his sense of belonging to that community, even if he is perceived by others as an Indian. For example, when local poet Mzee Omari gives him an Indian coin and says, "It's from your country," Kamal responds in Swahili to prove his African-ness: "Kwangu ni hapo ... I am from here" (68). Swahili is also used to convey the clash of identities he feels amidst the Hindu community in Dar es Salaam, where "he was caught in a crossfire between several voices babbling loudly in Kihindi all around him ... Slowly, slowly he learned to bend his tongue to utter Kihindi ... He spoke it with a certain lilt, a musical accent, and he would tend to put vowels at the end of words, the Swahili way" (194). Paradoxically, even when he learns and becomes fluent in "Kihindi," the Swahili word for Hindi, the Indian community continues to call him "Golo," a pejorative nickname that constantly reminds him that "[h]e was a descendant of a Matumbi slave" (52). Translingualism thus dramatizes Kamal's psychic and emotional split vis-à-vis his multiple identities and the loss of self, deriving from his inability to accept his hybridity. The retrieval of Swahili many years later when he returns to Kilwa as a successful Edmonton doctor signals, however, how language is a determining factor in the process of coming to terms with binary identities.

In order to recover his lost African-Indian history, Kamal hopes to write his family history. This project is not supported by his wife, Shamim, who dismisses it as a passing African obsession. At one point, Kamal shows his son, Hanif, the only photo he has of himself as a child with his African mother and Indian father: "The shock on Hanif's face – he was eleven then – was cataclysmic. 'Me African? That black woman in that weird outfit, my grandmother? You're lying. No way.' Utter rejection by his private-school son" (29).

The trauma inherent in reconciling with one's various linguistic, cultural, and ethno-racial subjectivities recurs in the works of Dôre Michelut and Marisa De Franceschi, two migrant writers from the Friuli region in Italy. Like Vassanji, they are in the unusual position of having to balance between their three languages: their Friulan mother tongue; standard Italian, which they learned either at school, at home, or within the Italian-Canadian community; and English, the language they mastered in Canada. In her autobiographical essay "Coming to Terms with the Mother Tongue," Michelut describes the psychological effects of her translingualism in terms of both loss and fragmentation and as opportunity and mediation. As I have argued elsewhere,[13] Michelut's account of her conflictual relationship with her three languages echoes the sociolinguistic findings reached by Aneta Pavlenko and James P. Lantolf in "Second Language Learning as Participation" (2000) on how bilingual or multilingual individuals renegotiate their sense of self only after overcoming the initial phase of displacement/continuous loss caused by dislocation and engaging in a process of recovery/(re)construction of identity, which entails constructing meaning and experience in all their languages. Upon arrival in Canada as a young girl, Michelut suffers the loss of Friulan and is obliged to relocate herself in two alien linguistic mediums: Italian, the more prestigious language her parents chose to use in the new country, and English. Such a loss of the mother tongue occasions a split sense of self, which urges her to erroneously attempt to relinquish her Friulan identity, just as Kamal had tried to do when he neglected his African-ness to become Indian. As an adult, Michelut realizes, however, the impossibility of denying her linguistic identities, each of which conveys different experiences and expresses a different subjectivity. She thus engages in a process of self-translation, which allows her to go "from English to Furlan and back, from Furlan to Italian or Italian to English and back," so that "each language still speaks me differently, because it must, but each speaks me more fully."[14]

Self-translation is, indeed, the privileged translingual practice used by Michelut in her poetic collections, *Loyalty to the Hunt* (1986) and *Ourobouros: The Book That Ate Me* (1990), in which she creates a fluid heteroglossic continuum among her three tongues as part of her quest to negotiate her plural identities. It is also the strategy employed by Italian-Canadian poet Gianna Patriarca in *My Etruscan Face* (2007), where the two parallel versions of the poem "i am ciociara," one in English and the other in the ciociaro dialect spoken in the Lazio region, represent the climactic moment of her attempt to come to terms with her Roman background and her Mediterranean phenotypical traits. Through the self-translated poems, both poets re-appropriate their mother tongues, acknowledging that this enables them to initiate a process of healing and recovery from the trauma of linguistic and cultural displacement and to begin "generating a dialectical experience that [is] relative to both languages."[15] It is, in fact, in the polyphonic and dialogical space created between the texts that they manage to achieve a unification of identities within their fractured and hybrid selves. As Patriarca acknowledges, by writing in the interface between English and "*ste dialet mezz stuort e sturdit*" ("this half drunk and broken dialect"),[16] she is empowered with the awareness that "i am the words i speak."[17] The translingual experience allows her, thus, to accept both her cultures and languages as part of a transcultural identity that is necessarily mercurial, an ongoing invention and reinvention of past and present selves.

For polyglot writers like Filippo Salvatore and Antonio D'Alfonso, who are based in Quebec, self-translation takes on the additional role of drawing attention to the power dynamics between anglophone and francophone Canada. By translating some of their works from French into English, they attempt to bridge the cultural divide between Quebec and the rest of Canada, but also to destabilize the hegemony of English, by laying bare structures of inequality and enriching it with their peculiar visions and affiliations. In his trilingual poem "Nous les Rapailles," Salvatore, for instance, encodes his plight to accept difference as part of Québécois identity in French, English, and Italian. The three versions, however, are rewritings, rather than faithful translations of the original French poem dedicated to Gaston Miron, and they articulate Salvatore's political views to different audiences with different registers. Thus, in the English poem, he deliberately inserts both formal, archaic terms like "harlot" and colloquial ones like "teeny-hopper" to mock the supremacy of English and to show that English domination in the country is both old and new. In the Italian version, the use of English loan words like "penthouses" and "downtown" likewise summons a reflection on the threat posed by the spread of English in Quebec and around the world – a spread that is synonymous with economic domination. On the other hand, the choice to leave the French title untranslated in all three versions strategically draws the reader into an encounter with the other, which obliges them to become aware of a different reality.

Writing in different languages also represents for many diasporic authors an effort to relocate their ethnicity outside the motherland's borders. The use of the Sicilian dialect in some of the English poems contained in the anthology *Sweet Lemons 2: International Writings with a Sicilian Accent* (2010) signals, for instance, the tension these writers feel for the loss of their primal language, owing to the immigrant experience. Yet, as Kenneth Scambray writes in his preface to the volume, instead of conveying "a sentimental reconstruction of a lost past,"[18] code-mixing is here a strategy of resistance to the historical erasure of ethnicity that comes as a consequence of assimilation in the new land and the adoption of another language. Embedding Sicilian in the English text counters the problematic disappearance of the immigrant experience in North America and is "a sign of the relocation of the Sicilian immigrant experience into another idiom."[19] Marisa De Franceschi's retrieval of her native Friulan tongue in *Random Thoughts* (2010) performs a similar act of resistance, in this case to the gradual disappearance that this minority language is undergoing. In the poem "International Cuisine," for instance, she creates a plurilingual feast, in which the Friulan names of rural dishes are given equal status alongside Italian, English, and Spanish ones. The heteroglossic space in which she positions Friulan relocates it beyond geographical confines, so as to ensure its survival outside of Friuli, where it is progressively losing ground to Italian.

Caterina Edwards also uses codeswitching as a strategy of resistance against forgetfulness and the denial of ethnic identity in her creative autobiography *Finding Rosa: A Mother with Alzheimer's, A Daughter in Search of the Past* (2008), in which the use of words from Italian and Venetian and Istrian dialects is both part of a personal quest to re-appropriate her mother's lost Venetian-Istrian lineage, and of a collective quest to reconstruct the troubled and neglected historical vicissitudes of Istria and the Italian *istriani* during the wars. Here the heteroglossic mixing of languages serves, in fact, multiple functions. First, it signals the surfacing of Rosa's forgotten childhood memories through the cracks of her growing dementia, as witnessed, for instance, by the line "*Ciribirin ch'bel Nasin, chi bel bocchin*" (80) from the song her father used to sing to her, or by words like "*ciaparse*" (77), the game of catch Rosa used to play as a child in the "piazza" (77) she would go to with her dad to eat "gelato" (79). Secondly, it counters the historical erasure of identity suffered by the Italian minority in Istria and Dalmatia as the regions passed under various regimes in a relatively short time span. And thirdly, it enacts Edwards's own reclaiming of her Istrian-Veneto identity. In Chapter 6, for instance, entitled "What Remains," the author's return to Mali Losinj/Lussinpiccolo, now part of Croatia but once part of the Kingdom of Italy, spurs an instinctive retrieval of the Istro-Veneto dialect, an idiom she acknowledges as her mother tongue. Despite her husband's attempts to correct her "mistakes" and encourage her to use standard Italian, she realizes, in fact, that "the first words that come to me, the grammatical constructions that feel right to me, are the ones I learned from my mother, before I began to speak English." Her language is thus, "not broken Italian but correct Istro-Veneto," a language that seems "natural and proper" (58–9) for her to use with a fellow *lussignano* of Italian origins like herself, one of the few *rimasti* who did not leave Istria when it fell under the Slav regime, despite the policy of ethno-cultural and linguistic erasure put into action by the new government. As she writes: "Switching into dialect became my magic wand ... I had found one of the *Rimasti* (or their children or grandchildren). The wand exposed not just their true selves, but mine, I was changed from a stranger to a daughter of the exile" (63). The use of dialect allows her to be identified – and to identify herself – as "*Vera, Lussignana*" (59), to establish, in other words, a connection with her past. Edwards's efforts to use the Istro-Veneto dialect are, thus, situated within her endeavours to re-appropriate the silenced history of her people and to legitimize their recognition as Italians, both by Italy, the mother country who dismissed them, and Croatia, the country that repressed their ethno-linguistic identity "as a subversive act" (63).

The creation of a Bakhtinian polyvocal and dialogic space, which we find in translingual texts such as those discussed above, destabilizes hierarchies among languages and subverts the master narrative of a monolingual pre-Babelian world. Their linguistic pluralism welcomes, instead, difference and a respect for multiple modes of being, belonging, and communicating. It thus functions to reinforce the transcultural re-envisioning of identity as intersubjective and interrelational, which is embraced by many Canadian writers (translingual and non) as an appropriate model for a multicultural nation like Canada, where the presence of multiple ethnicities, races, and languages requires a crossing of borders between different selves, in order to establish a respectful cohabitation and connection with others. Implicit in this new model of identity is also the awareness that cultural identity can no longer be defined in unitary terms or associated with a single homeland, but must be conceived of as transnational. The idea of "home," like those of "nation" and "citizenship," become, for many writers, imaginative spaces that transcend political and geographical confines. They are, in other words, spaces where history, memory, and place cohabit and intermingle, thereby prompting a sense of non-belonging to any place specifically and of co-belonging to multiple spaces at once.

Translingual texts emphasize how language represents a discursive space in which to imagine and reclaim one's sense of home and to accept multifaceted aspects of belonging. Edwards's plurilingual effort to establish connections with her multiple familial alliances – the Venetian, Istrian, English, Canadian, and American – enacts a desire to belong to a variety of ethnic, national, and transnational collectivities and to thus reconfigure her citizenship in cosmopolitan terms. The Caribbean demotic used by Brand in her novel is the only discursive space in which her displaced protagonist can feel a sense of belonging in an otherwise uprooted existence. Being the language of the African slaves who suffered the Middle Passage, it allows Elizete to reclaim a bond with her ancestral homeland and people, which transcends physical and geographical boundaries. In her historical novel *Half-Blood Blues* (2011), Ghanaian-Canadian novelist Esi Edugyan similarly mixes French, German, and English to explore the meanings of home and belonging in relation to both ethnic identity and racism in Nazi Germany. Much like Edwards and Brand, identifying with multiple languages (including, in her case, the language of jazz music) allows Edugyan and other writers of the African diaspora to embrace what Robert Bromley has called a nomadic, "post-national model of belonging"[20] in which individuals can belong "simultaneously, mentally, psychologically and experientially, to a diversity of cultures."[21]

A sense of home and belonging is explored in Hiromi Goto's *Chorus of Mushrooms*, in which Muriel, a young Japanese-Canadian woman, tries to recapture the Japanese language and culture that have been rejected by her mother, Keiko. Muriel's grandmother changes her name to the Japanese Murasaki and tries to teach her the heritage language and culture through stories.²² By the end of the novel, Murasaki is surprised to realize that Japanese has become the language of intimacy with her new boyfriend. He tells her, "[b]ut when I speak with you, I only speak in Japanese. Jibun de wakaranai no? Itsumo Nihongo de hanashiteiru noni."²³ In contrast to this recovery of the lost language, we have the example of Naomi and her aunt Obasan in Joy Kogawa's Japanese-Canadian novel *Obasan*, in which silence about the internment of the Japanese community becomes the dominant experience. Only as an adult does Naomi return to recover her lost history.

Such a nomadic sense of belonging to a plurality of cultures and languages necessarily destabilizes any notion of identification with a single literary canon, tradition, or readership as well. With their mixing of languages, registers, cultures, and literary traditions, translingual texts are a privileged space of translation and negotiation, wherein multiple subjectivities and world views may coexist and dialogue and where a symbiosis of cultures may be achieved. As Sudanese-British writer Jamal Mahjoub puts it, these texts have a potential to open up "the thin crack of light" between people that gradually grows wider so that "where there was once only monochrome light, now there is a spectrum of colours."²⁴

Lien Chao concludes her original seminal study of Chinese-Canadian literature with an observation that can also be applied to the groups of diverse writers I have examined here: "'A thousand-li journey starts from beneath the feet.' This well-known Chinese proverb describes the current stage of Chinese-Canadian literature. Ahead and beyond the stage of breaking through the hundred-year silence endured by the community, a much longer journey is awaiting the contemporary and future generations of writers."²⁵

## NOTES

1 Kellman, *Switching Languages*, ix.
2 Kanaganayakam, "Interview with Vassanji."
3 Steiner, *Translated Peoples*, 1.
4 Chao, *Beyond Silence*, xiv.
5 Clarke, *Odysseys Home*, 325.
6 See her *Voices of Exile*, and also *Voices in the Desert*.
7 van Herk, "Of Dykes and Boars," 279.
8 Reynolds, "M.G. Vassanji: Interview," 2013.
9 Vassanji, *The Book of Secrets*, 334.
10 Steiner, *Translated Peoples*, 12.
11 Brand, *In Another Place*, 16.

12 Wiens, "'Language Seemed Split in Two,'" 14.
13 Saidero, "Plurilingualism and Self-translation," 2008.
14 Michelut, "Coming to Terms," 170.
15 Ibid., 166.
16 Patriarca, *My Etruscan Face*, 25–7.
17 Ibid., 13.
18 Fazio and De Santis, *Sweet Lemons 2*, 18.
19 Ibid.
20 Bromley, *Narratives*, 4.
21 Ibid., 7.
22 Goto, *Chorus of Mushrooms*, 15.
23 Ibid., 187.
24 Mahjoub, "The Writer," 5.
25 Chao, *Beyond Silence*, 189.

## BIBLIOGRAPHY

Brand, Dionne. *In Another Place, Not Here*. Toronto: Random House, 1996.
– *No Language Is Neutral*. Toronto: McClelland & Stewart, 1990.
Bromley, Roger. *Narratives for a New Belonging: Diasporic Cultural Fictions*. Edinburgh: Edinburgh University Press, 2000.
Chao, Lien. *Beyond Silence: Chinese Canadian Literature in English*. Toronto: TSAR, 1997.
Clarke, George Elliott. *Odysseys Home: Mapping African-Canadian Literature*. Toronto: University of Toronto Press, 2002.
Dahab, F. Elizabeth. *Voices of Exile in Contemporary Canadian Francophone Literature*. Lanham: Lexington Books, 2009.
– ed. *Voices in the Desert: An Anthology of Arabic-Canadian Women Writers*. Toronto: Guernica, 2002.
D'Alfonso, Antonio. *Fabrizio's Passion*. Toronto: Guernica, 1995.
De Franceschi, Marisa. *Random Thoughts*. Montreal: Longbridge Books, 2010.
Edugyan, Esi. *Half-Blood Blues*. Toronto: Thomas Allen, 2011.
Edwards, Caterina. *Finding Rosa: A Mother with Alzheimer's, A Daughter in Search of the Past*. Vancouver: Douglas & McIntyre, 2008.
Fazio, Venera, and Delia De Santis, eds. *Sweet Lemons 2: International Writings with a Sicilian Accent*. New York/Ottawa: Legas, 2010.
Goto, Hiromi. *Chorus of Mushrooms*. Edmonton: NeWest Press, 1994.
Gromov, Mikhail D. "Facing the Language Border: Multilingualism in Two Novels of M.G. Vassanji." *Swahili Forum* 21 (2014): 60–75.
Kanaganayakam, Chelva. "Broadening the Substrata: An Interview with M.G. Vassanji." *World Literature Written in English* 31, no. 2 (1991): 19–35.

Keefer, Janice Kulyk. *The Green Library*. Toronto: HarperCollins, 1996.
– *Honey and Ashes: A Story of Family*. Toronto: Harper Perennial, 1998.
Kellman, Steven G. *Switching Languages: Translingual Authors Reflect on their Craft*. Lincoln and London: University of Nebraska Press, 2003.
– *The Translingual Imagination*. Lincoln and London: University of Nebraska Press, 2000.
Kogawa, Joy. *Obasan*. Toronto: Lester & Orpen Dennys, 1981.
Mahjoub, Jamal. "The Writer and Globalism." *Djembe Online Magazine* 40 (April 2002). www.libhel.fi/mcl/articles/mahjoub.htm (accessed January 2016).
Michelut, Dôre. "Coming to Terms with the Mother Tongue." In *Collaboration in the Feminine: Writings on Women and Culture from TESSERA*, edited by Barbara Godard, 162–70. Toronto: Second Story Press, 1994. First published in *Tessera* 6 (1989).
– *Ourobouros: The Book That Ate Me*. Laval, QC: Édition Trois, 1990.
– *Loyalty to the Hunt*. Montreal: Guernica, 1986.
Mistry, Rohinton. *Such a Long Journey*. Toronto: McClelland & Stewart, 1991.
Patriarca, Gianna. *My Etruscan Face*. Thornhill, ON: Quattro Books, 2007.
Pavlenko, Aneta, and James P. Lantolf. "Second Language Learning as Participation: (Re)constructing a Self." In *Sociocultural Theory and Second Language Learning*, edited by James Lantolf, 155–77. Oxford: Oxford University Press, 2000.
Reynolds, Clarence. "M.G. Vassanji: Interview." *Mosaic Magazine*. 9 April 2013. http://mosaicmagazine.org/2013/04/09/m-g-vassanji-interview (accessed 7 January 2016).
Saidero, Deborah. "Pluriliguismo e autotraduzione in Dôre Michelut." In *Itineranze e transcodificazioni: scrittori migranti dal Friuli Venezia Giulia al Canada*, edited by Alessandra Ferraro and Anna Pia De Luca, 87–95. Udine: Forum, 2008. Also: "Plurilingualism and Self-translation in the Works of Dôre Michelut." http://canadian-writers.athabascau.ca/english/writers/dmichelut/dmichelut.php.
Salvatore, Filippo. "Nous les Rapailles." In *Quétes: Textes d'auteurs italo-québécois*, edited by Fulvio Caccia and Antonio D'Alfonso, 138–9. Montreal: Édition Guernica, 1983.
Steiner, Tina. *Translated Peoples, Translated Texts: Language and Migration in Contemporary African Literature*. London: Routledge, 2009.
Van Herk, Aritha. "Of Dykes and Boers and Drowning." In *Making a Difference*, edited by Smaro Kamboureli, 422–6. Toronto: Oxford University Press, 2007.
Vassanji, M.G. *The Book of Secrets*. Toronto: McClelland & Stewart, 1994.
– *The Gunny Sack*. London: Heinemann, 1989.

– *The In-Between World of Vikram Lall*. New York: Doubleday, 2003.
– *The Magic of Saida*. Toronto: Doubleday Canada, 2012.
Welsch, Wolfgang. "Transculturality – the Puzzling Form of Cultures Today." In *Spaces of Culture: City, Nation, World*, edited by Mike Featherstone and Scott Lash, 194–213. London: Sage, 1999.
Wiens, Jason. "'Language Seemed Split in Two': National Ambivalence(s) and Dionne Brand's *No Language Is Neutral*." *Essays on Canadian Writing* 70 (Spring 2000): 81–102.

# "Like a Dancing Gypsy":
# A Close Reading of *Cockroach*

F. Elizabeth Dahab

Franz Kafka is one of the most influential writers of the twentieth century. Among the authors who have followed his literary example are: Albert Camus, George Orwell, Jean-Paul Sartre, Gabriel García Márquez, Eugene Ionesco, Jorge Luis Borges, and J.M. Coetzee. To this list we can now add the Lebanese-Canadian writer and photographer Rawi Hage and his novel *Cockroach*. Because of these broad international influences, Kafka is often the subject of Comparative Literature research projects and theses. Kafka is also the subject of Gilles Deleuze and Félix Guattari's essay *Kafka: Toward a Minor Literature* (1986), which has become an important source for the study of ethnic minority writing in North America and Europe. This is the context in which we will read Hage's *Cockroach*, a surreal narrative in which the main character reminds us of Kafka's short story, "The Metamorphosis," the transformation of a man into a monstrous insect. Like many of Kafka's characters, Hage's protagonist gives us a minority or marginal perspective on society. In some scenes we literally get a photographic point of view from the ground up.

*Cockroach* is a first-person narrative told by an unnamed narrator/protagonist in a colloquial style full of profanities, sprinkled with French expressions (and entirely devoid of quotation marks to signal dialogue). A recent immigrant and a petty thief in his early thirties, the protagonist is hungry and destitute, struggling for survival in a cold Montreal winter, in what he calls "a shithole of a rundown place," where "windows whistled and freezing snow drifted through cracks" (17). Even though his country of origin is never named, and is always referred to as "back where I came from" (128), it is Lebanon in the 1980s, because of the regular mention of bombings and the presence of a militia and because of the Arabic names of characters – Mona, Suad, Naim – that evoked "back home" (143).

The humanity of the narrator-protagonist is ambiguous, as is suggested at the outset by the title, as well as the first epigraph to the novel: "what we call species are various transmutations of the same type," a telling quote from the nineteenth-century French zoologist Étienne Geoffroy Saint-Hilaire, who believed in the transmutation of species in time.[1] It is under the auspices of this ambiguous *transmutative* devolution, half cockroach and "half human" (5, 245), as he describes himself, that the protagonist-narrator engages the reader. The narrator's dual nature in *Cockroach* provides him with a viable trope to deliver his own experience, as well as the experience of a *segment of immigrants* that represent the underprivileged and the underdog, "the Montréal most Canadians fail to see," to quote a critic (Tabar). As one of the characters points out: "Montréal, this happy romantic city, has an ugly side to it, my friend. One of the largest military-industrial complexes in North America is right here" (281). This socio-political criticism levelled at the city makes the latter a witness/accomplice to other dimensions of ugliness embedded in those who live in it.

In my close reading, I argue that Rawi Hage's portrayal of an Arab antihero in a post-9/11 text belonging to Arab-Canadian literature is a move away from political correctness toward freedom of contestation, artistic liberation, and political satire. The protagonist-narrator may have been conceived after all as a reflection of a *mal de vivre* experienced by vulnerable foreign nationals from the Arab world in a Canada whose new multicultural legislations in the wake of 9/11 became all too subservient to the United States's global war on terror. If this reading is viable, then Hage's text can be said to be unique within the Anglophone Arab-Canadian novelistic tradition, in that it allegorizes superbly the failure of Canadian multiculturalism.

With regard to the protagonist-narrator himself, the patently overarching theme – "I feel like an insect, therefore I am an insect" – colours the ubiquitous *cockroachness* of the outward and inward elements of the entire novel, its atmosphere, style, tone, and the portrayal of some of its characters, "new comers to this land dragging their frozen selves" (79). The main antagonist of this compellingly morose account is in fact the setting itself, Montreal, or rather, the unrelenting cold weather of "this city with its case of chronic snow" (17), as the narrator quips. In a moment of bitter introspection, worn out and famished, he poses a question about his new whereabouts: "How did I end up trapped in a constantly shivering carcass, walking in a frozen city with wet cotton falling on me all the time? And on top of it, I am hungry, impoverished, and have no one, no one" (8-9). This state of dire lack, with the protagonist barely eking out a living on welfare cheques and work cleaning a restaurant on weekends, does not even allow him as much as the proper gear to shield himself against the elements. For instance, witness the regular ordeal experienced in the course of the otherwise trivial, banal act of being a pedestrian in Montreal: "The ground was frozen bumps of ice. Slippery glass. Thick and transparent. My fucking shoes, however, were totally flat on the bottom. No grip left on the soles, and in any case the soles were smooth to begin with, which made them even more slippery" (147). One day, when he is in possession of newly stolen boots and warm socks to replace his perpetually half-wet pair of socks, which he dries under his mattress every night, the narrator suddenly feels dignified, warm, and stable, almost self-confident and joyful (253). We can also see here how Hage captures the visual details to make the scenes cinematic.

The bulk of this confessional novel resides not so much in the plot, episodic at best, nor in character development. The heart of *Cockroach* showcases a slice of daily life with various events it has unfolded in a recent past, punctuated by figures and incidents of varying impact in flashbacks to the narrator's more-distant past, prior to immigration. The novel is divided into six chapters of unequal length, with the first sentence of each one entirely capitalized. The narrative present is the last leg of a three-tier episode on which the novel opens: the protagonist has just tried to commit suicide; he is committed thereafter to a psychiatric ward; he undergoes psychotherapy. Chapters 2 to 6 each open with the weekly compulsory meetings with Geneviève, the analyst who assesses his progress – on taxpayers' money, she points out – after he is released from the mental hospital following his failed suicide attempt on the branch of a tree in the park. He is regularly reminded that any regression on his part would mean being recommitted to the mental hospital, and he is invited to disclose his daily undertakings. This narrative device of the weekly meetings on an "interrogation chair" (47), as he calls it, sets the confessions in motion, allowing the narration to expose the main events of his troubled life in Lebanon, as he answers persistent probing about his family life in his native country. Two main turning points thus unfold: in Beirut: his sister's unhappy marriage, then her death (prior to his immigration), a death for which he is indirectly – albeit unwittingly – responsible. It is his grief over this loss that prompted him to exile himself *as cockroach*: "I wept until I heard echoes in the drain, like the fluttering of sails, telling me to leave. I shaved and then I sailed away from that room, that land, thinking that all was past, all was buried, all would come to an end" (300).

The novel's dénouement occurs in Montreal, the culmination of a sudden revenge mission in which the protagonist gets involved towards the last third of the novel. It features him murdering his lover Shoreh's former rapist and jailer, Shaheed. This happens in The Star of Iran, the upscale restaurant where the ex-torturer is a patron and where the protagonist works. The murder constitutes the penultimate scene of the novel, followed by the definitive, intended disappearance of the narrator-protagonist into the underground through the kitchen sink, in a picturesque and vivid closing passage, worth citing in its entirety:

> The bodyguard had his back to me. I stuck the knife in his liver ... The gun fell from his hand. I picked it up and aimed it at Shaheed. I shot him twice. I shot him right in the chest and he fell beneath the tablecloth. I dropped the gun and walked back to the kitchen. I looked at the water that gathered and rushed towards the drain. Then I crawled and swam above the water, and when I saw a leaf carried along by the stream of soap and water as if it were a gondola in Venice, I climbed onto it and shook like a dancing gypsy, and I steered it with my glittering wings towards the underground. (305)

This victorious final exit down the drain is obviously told from the viewpoint of the cockroach, to which the perspective has abruptly switched after the description of the murder. Throughout the novel, there are no fewer than twenty such narrative instances where the point of view switches from that of a person walking to that of an insect crawling (17, 26, 27, 30). This *dédoublement*, doubling or twinning, sometimes occurs in the middle of a sentence, or in the space between one sentence and the other. It can occur in the same descriptive paragraph or in the one immediately following, as in the closing scene just quoted. In this dramatic revenge scene, Hage focuses on the visual elements making the action cinematic.

The *shifting perspective* fulfills an important purpose. From a narrative standpoint, the subjective cockroach point of view provides a convenient vantage point, an underbelly position from which to observe the Montreal wealthy, the "Third World elite," Francophones or Anglophones alike, in whose lives the protagonist can enter uninvited, crawling with ease under their doors, along their walls, or into their food-stacked refrigerators to satisfy his hunger or steal their belongings. The following example illustrates the shifting viewpoint (within the same narrative passage) in the presence of the wealthy, against whom he retaliates in his own way: one day, hungry as usual, he is in front of an upscale restaurant on St-Laurent Street, "leaning on a parked car, watching a couple eat slowly" (86). He is asked to leave by a security guard, and refuses to obey. A police offer comes, checks his papers, and repeats the order. The couple finally come out and get into a BMW, but he manages to follow them as a cockroach: "I crawled to the edge of the pavement, rushing with my many feet, my belly just above the ground" (88). The couple drive off with him in the car. The woman makes a comment on the fact that St-Laurent Street is "becoming too noisy and crowded with all kinds of people," and the remark makes the protagonist cringe, for he feels it is directed at the likes of him, but he has to remain still: "The man must have nodded or not responded. / He was the driver. / She was the driven. / I was the insect beneath them" (88–9).

The low camera angle gives us a point of view from the ground, so that we too feel like an insect crawling on many legs: "At the couple's home I stole his gold ring, his cigarettes, a Roman vase, his tie, and his shoes (*I took time to carefully pick clothes that suited my dark complexion*). Once I had finished checking myself in the mirror, I slipped under the garage door. And I crawled, glued to the wall, my insect's wings vertical now and parallel to the house's living room window" (90). In this evocative visual scene, the switching viewpoint, occurring as it does three times within the same narrative instance (twice within the closing paragraph), brings out two elements: namely, the need for the protagonist to get even with a wealthy white sample of Montreal suburbia – a constant reminder of his own contrasting degradation – and the need to do so precisely by revamping his own self-image as one able to rise likewise to elegance and classiness when appropriating the white man's choicest apparel, which incidentally has the power to enhance his own dark complexion and to become subservient to his needs.

That he was "the insect beneath them" when riding in the couple's car, hungry, destitute, and listening to depreciatory comments about the likes of him, is subsequently offset by his victorious exit along the garage wall, carrying some accessories of wealth, crawling majestically, not humiliated as usual, but proudly so, *precisely* with his "insect wings vertical now." As the protagonist puts it, in a moment of anger towards the injustice he was subjected to by Maître Pierre, who refused to hire him on account of his dark complexion, "no one can barricade against the powerful, fleeting semen of the hungry and the oppressed" (90). The semen of the hungry, ubiquitous as it may be, would also become the plight of the powerful of the earth, invading and infecting them by the same token that the poor and the destitute have to suffer in their close proximity. Sometimes the protagonist will likewise use his mutative skills to get even with his own companions in misery in what makes for a metastasis, so to speak, of his spite against his contemporaries, regardless of colour. What is surmised here is that the targets of his hatred are injustice, sham, and capitalist disparity of wealth. Hage's cockroach protagonist is reminiscent of Kafka's characters, who face dire inequalities in their contemporary societies.

The cockroach's jaundiced vision of his contemporaries, Canadians and refugees alike, is that of the misanthrope, irritated *once and for all* with humanity. Even though he affirms that he "only loved those who suffered" (143), in point of fact, with the exception of his attractive lover, Shoreh, and one or two other characters, his spiteful gaze does not spare most of his own *compagnons de misère* either, "brownies and darkies ... on the run from dictators and crumbling cities" (58). Of the colourful panoply of characters portrayed in *Cockroach*, some are encountered in smoky cafés on St-Laurent Street or in parties packed with Iranian exiles described as "runaway artists, displaced poets, leftist harsh-rollers, and ex-revolutionaries turned taxi drivers" (13), with background stories marked with violence and trauma, a sad legacy of Third World modern dictatorships. The following examples will illustrate the unforgiving *cockroachness* of the portrayal of his Montreal acquaintances by the protagonist-narrator: first in line is Reza, "the Middle-Eastern hunchback" (11), a cocaine snorter and a freeloader, a restaurant sitar-player, who had a finger broken by the Ayatollah Khomeni's guards. He is described as "a master charlatan who for years had managed to couch-surf in women's houses, bewitching his hosts with his exotic tunes and stories of suffering and exile" (24–5). There is also the pathetic figure of "Professor Youssef," described as an "empty container" (271) and a "lazy, pretentious, Algerian pseudo-French intellectual" (10), whom he met at the St-Laurent Street Artista Café, where "he sits all day ... and talks about 'révolution et littérature.'" Then he found out one day, when he crawled into the professor's apartment, that he is actually on welfare just like himself, albeit too proud to admit it, and that he was tortured in his native Algeria. A target of the protagonist-narrator's contempt is also the wealthy Iranian owner of the upscale restaurant where he is employed as a general factotum. He is portrayed as greedy, obsequious to his rich patrons, and a slave driver to his own personnel: "The Third World elite are the filth of the planet ... Filth!

They consider themselves royalty when all they are is the residue of colonial power" (159).

If the above-mentioned Iranians are portrayed with spite and negativity, either because of their complacency, their hypocrisy, or their wealth, the following characters, two of whom are women, are spared the narrator's wrath, a significant fact that unveils a compassionate side to the protagonist, for what they have in common is either their vulnerability or a past marked with intense suffering. They are: Shoreh, who was tortured in her native Iran and whom he mentions in the very first sentence of the novel, since he is in love with her (3); Majeed, the fine Farsi poet-turned-cab-driver, a friend of Shoreh's late uncle, who was executed in Iran because he refused to release the names of his comrades in the resistance movement; the compelling figure of Farhoud, the gay man, who was persecuted, jailed, and raped in Iran by the mullahs before making a narrow, quasi-miraculous escape to Afghanistan, India, then Canada, with the help of a bisexual Canadian diplomat he met on an Indian beach; and finally Sehar, the restaurant owner's pretty teenage daughter, with whom he flirts whenever her father is out of sight.

The negative portrayal of his fellow Iranian refugees evoked above is echoed by a parallel spiteful characterization of a collection of white Canadian characters, whom the protagonist comes across in a counterpoint that provides perfect balance to the narrative and adds credibility to his spiteful vision. Their wealth, egoism, lack of compassion, and racist outlooks toward immigrants with dark complexions may be what they have in common, and the reader may wonder at times who is the cockroach here after all. Worthy of mention is *la gang*, Sylvie and her friends, Francophone *Montréalais* – with sham claims to spirituality, beauty, and exoticism – characterized as "corrupt, empty, selfish, self-absorbed, capable only of seeing themselves in the reflection from the tinted glass in their fancy cars" (185). The protagonist provides the group with cocaine and is admitted to their parties, which he detests, for he represents for them, in his own words, "the fuckable, exotic, dangerous foreigner" (185). As for the Anglophone Canadians, the McGill University graduates, "sons and daughters of the wealthy" (228), they are not spared the narrator's biting prose either, portrayed as they are as fakes who like to conceal their "old money, their future corporate jobs," and who, meanwhile, camouflage themselves in seedy St-Laurent Street cafés to complain about money and to "sit, drink, and shoot pool" (228). There is also the minor figure of Maître Pierre, the owner of a fancy French restaurant on Sherbrooke Street, incidentally called Le Cafard (The Cockroach), where the protagonist himself once worked as a busboy, quitting when the owner – described as a "filthy human with gold braid on his sleeves and pompous posture!" – refused to promote him to waiter on account of his being too dark, "too well done for that" ("un peu trop cuit pour ça") (29).

In the movement that switches the setting back and forth from Montreal to Beirut and vice versa, the main figures that are evoked from "back home" are the protagonist's sister, the beautiful Souad, with the sentimental voice, who eloped with and married a member of the militia, Tony, eventually being killed by him on suspicion of adultery. If the narrator detested Tony even before he murdered his sister, that is not the case with Abou-Roro, the neighbourhood thug and fearless bandit, whose motto was "when one is hungry one should steal" (55). He took the then-adolescent narrator under his wing, initiating him into his ways, and glorifying their merits in the following terms: "The underground, my friend, is a world of its own. Other humans gaze at the sky, but I say unto you, the only way through the world is to pass through the underground" (55).

Herein lies the key to *Cockroach* as a sequel to Hage's debut novel, *De Niro's Game*: the convergence with the subversive and possibly the illicit in historical moments when life becomes a matter of mere endurance and resilience in societies steeped in various forms of violence. A critic has noted that a traumatic quality permeates both novels stylistically; she qualifies *Cockroach* as "grippingly cinematic and blending an almost obsessive figurative energy with cynically dark humour and rawly violent prose that bombards the reader with 10,000 images – the stylistic equivalent of the 'ten thousand bombs' that haunt Beirut and the narrator in *De Niro's Game*" (Sakr 345). Since the underground (understood in the above quote as the illicit and the violent as opposed to the religious and the mystical) was familiar ground to the protagonist as early as his youth in his native country, it is attractive enough for him to continue dwelling in it after his exile, albeit in a different context, with different means, in what unlocks a variation of the species of *undergroundedness*, to evoke the law of "unity of composition" implied in the epigraph to the novel (Saint-Hilaire). I have also pointed out some of the "grippingly cinematic" scenes in *Cockroach*.

The rapprochement here is between a city under siege and a city where one is a despised minority. This minority comes under siege, and is as vulnerable as any population living in a war zone. The coping mechanisms would be the same, mere means of survival in an otherwise unbearable existence. Was that indeed what Hage set out to convey? In a 2009 interview on a CBC cultural show, *Q*, shortly after the publication of his second novel, when asked if *Cockroach* is a metaphor for the assimilationist experience, Hage answered, "it is a metaphor for something wider ... My protagonist was torn between staying human or joining that movement of the underprivileged and eventually act in a violent way and take power." It is in this light that we could interpret the retaliation and revenge mission the protagonist undertakes on behalf of his lover before descending to the literal underground down the kitchen drain. When repeatedly questioned by the insistent interviewer about precisely "why a cockroach?" Hage deftly counters, "I made it a political statement," an allusion to the mounting suspicion that marks the rapport between East and West, between the whites and their brown counterparts living in that same West that drove the latter to leave their own countries in the first place. Says Majeed, the highly educated poet/cab driver in *Cockroach*: "we come to these countries for refuge and to find better lives, but it is these countries that made us leave our homes in the first place" (223).[2]

I referred earlier to the function of the cockroach's point of view from a narrative perspective. On an allegorical level, the cockroach's point of view drives home an important trope, one possibly related to the "landed refugees" (ironically mimicking the phrase "landed immigrants," the Canadian equivalent of the US "permanent residents"), as Hage's narrator calls his fellow exiles (44). It refers to those who endure a sordid existence in "rich, lovely, joyful Canada" (Elkhadem 35), as the protagonist of the trilogy by the Egyptian-Canadian writer Saad Elkhadem would say; an existence aggravated by the mounting racism against Muslims (in the aftermath of 9/11), some of whom survive in the host country in a status of "identity in negation, a hijacked identity," to borrow a critic's apt phrase (Gana 22). If a "cockroach" literally refers to the vermin symptomatic of poverty and filth, it symbolically could be construed as the negation of a negation, whose terms run as follows: "I am not a despicable insect. I am a human being. Not quite: I am half-vermin, half-human. I am a cockroach of human size." The first negation (the thesis) being that one is not a human being (in the white acceptance of the word); the second negation (the antithesis) being that it is not true that one is not a human being; the synthesis (the negation of the negation) being that one is not a human being, but rather a special case of a cockroach/human, and a force to reckon with. "They shall inherit the earth" (53), affirms the protagonist of *Cockroach* about his fellow insects, in what makes for a twisted ironic echo of Jesus's pronouncement on the meek of the earth in the Beatitudes, and an obvious rapprochement. In fact, this view is supported by the ultimate scene of the novel in which the protagonist faces a human-sized fellow bug, a "striped albino cockroach standing on its two feet, leaning against the kitchen door" (200–1), which is tantalizing and claiming him as a member of his own species.

By giving his mentally deranged protagonist the lowest denominator's vantage point, Hage cleverly manages to co-opt the image of the dangerous Other with the various stereotypes it entails, giving it back full-fledged, in the shape of the underground man, the insect-protagonist, with perverse antisocial attributes highly reminiscent of Fyodor Dostoyevsky's novella *Notes from the Underground* (1864), in which an unnamed narrator attacks moral vacillation, inaction, and the illusion of optimistic philosophy.

In what stands for a mere instance of the politics of writing an English novel to an Anglophone readership, the cockroach metaphor for Hage serves as an incubator of identity, a transnational allegory for the diasporic wretched of the Western world, and one which is geared to raising sympathy, not offence, in readers not accustomed to such views *from the edge*. In my view, part of the originality of Hage's novel, and what is unprecedented on the Canadian-Arab novel-scape in English, is precisely the inherent social-activist awareness the novel exhibits toward the underdog in general, without distinction of national origins: "*Cockroach* is deeply concerned with class, economic disempowerment, unemployment, and misery among various groups of immigrants" (Sakr 349). What Rawi Hage communicated through his cockroach allegory he subsequently paraphrased when questioned about the future of migrant communities and host nations: "Integration is fragile and fake if egalitarian values are not unequivocally established" (Sakr 343). Moreover, in the 2009 CBC interview mentioned above, Hage deftly contended, when questioned on authorial intention, that he mainly wanted to explore human nature, poverty, class, displacement, and religious fundamentalism (Ghomeshi).

Irrespective of authorial intention, it is conceivable that Hage's portrayal of an Arab anti-hero is unique among Arab-Canadian and Arab-American novels in the way that it allegorizes the failure of Canadian multiculturalism and represents the negation of a negation in celebrating the lowliness of the cockroach. It is a satire of multiculturalism. As Mohamed Lotfi suggests: "Beneath its image as a noble protector of the rights of 'minorities,' the Canadian government creates a cultural communitarianism with its multiculturalism policy; this means that even immigrants who don't want to fit into the mould are forced to" (Lotfi). The same critic attributes the discomfort felt by Lebanese-Canadian Francophone writer Wajdi Mouawad in presenting his film *Littoral* as part of the Festival du Monde Arabe de Montréal to this *malaise*. That also explains why Mouawad's film was criticized for the use of Québécois actors to play Arab roles. Lotfi concludes: "Racism in Quebec is also fuelled by this ambiguity between diversity and cultural communitarianism" (Lotfi).

This view seems consistent with Hage's stance as well. When asked in the CBC interview about his national allegiance as a successful writer, Hage responded, "I am not an ethnic writer. I am a cosmopolitan writer" (Ghomeshi). He also insisted that his portrayal of a "bleak" picture of Montreal was one necessitated by his clear vision and his lack of naïveté about nations and cities. Hage seems to share the predicament of the writer caught in the stifling constraints of the politics of writing, the writer who happens to portray the underground world of the metropolis, and who risks being taxed with ingratitude. In fact, on the same occasion, Hage was quick to express his indebtedness to the Canadian "egalitarian social programs" for the creation of his two novels (Ghomeshi). When probed about the immigrant experience in Canada and the meaning of his novel, Hage cringed, contending that *Cockroach* was not an immigration novel after all, and that "it so happens" that the protagonist is an immigrant and the characters are likewise immigrants — "it could have been anybody else who is living hardships and maybe the tone would have been the same" (Ghomeshi). Certainly, with regard to the Arab-Canadian Anglophone novel, *Cockroach* strikes a new chord, unique, vibrant, and of current significance, tapping into the global dialogue of culture, power, and politics.

*Cockroach* conveys a sample of the hardships of daily life – not in Beirut this time, as in the author's debut novel, *De Niro's Game* (2006), but in some of Montreal's struggling communities. The topology of this metropolis, from the student ghetto around McGill University to the wealthy neighbourhood of Mount Royal, is brilliantly portrayed in this novel, which brings into collision the opposing layers of stereotype versus reality by portraying the hardships and violence experienced by some (mostly members of a marginalized, Anglophone enclave of Iranians) in a Montreal unfamiliar to those who connect it solely with beauty, charm, and culture. In this novel, the metaphor of the global positioning system encompasses transnational, as well as socioeconomic, linguistic, and racial boundaries, in a city that delineates the geography of despair. Hage's 2012 novel, *Carnival*, goes a step further.

*Carnival* taps into the compassionate stance toward the down-and-out, except that here it does so more intensely and in a more focused manner than in *Cockroach*, occasionally in eloquent, heated, lyrical diatribes.

In *Carnival*, we are in the presence of a transplanted Orient locally experienced within a cosmopolitanism wrought with tension. Hage has managed to deftly establish some reconciling correspondences between exile, transnationalism, and migration in the otherwise seemingly chaotic universe he has created.

As a comparatist I have studied and written about Arab authors writing in French in Canada. In *Voices of Exile* (2009) and *Voices in the Desert* (2002), I have explored the development of this French ethnic minority literature outside the larger canon of Quebec literature. Rawi Hage is one of the Arabs in Canada who writes in English, and thus contributes to an ethnic minority literature outside of the English-Canadian canon. In their essay *Kafka: Toward a Minor Literature*, Deleuze and Guattari argue that a minor literature has these three characteristics: "But the first characteristic of a minor literature ... is that in it language is affected by a high coefficient of deterritorialization ... The second characteristic ... is that everything in them is political ... The third characteristic ... is that in it everything takes on a collective value" (16–17).

In my close reading, Hage's novel *Cockroach* meets these criteria: the author is a displaced Arab writing in English about a reality beyond the experience of most Canadian readers. He explains some of his political intentions behind his writing, and he speaks for many displaced people who cannot speak for themselves. With other Arab-Canadian writers, such as Abla Farhoud, Wajdi Mouawad, Andrée Dahan, and Marwan Hassan, Rawi Hage is creating an ethnic minority literature outside the canon of Canadian literature. From the margins, in many different ways, *Cockroach* is writing back to the centres of power.

Some readers have pointed out that *Cockroach* has been a finalist for a number of literary prizes: the Scotiabank Giller Prize, the Governor General's Literary Award, the Rogers Writers' Trust Fiction Prize, and the CBC Canada Reads Award. It did not win any of these, but received two smaller local prizes: the Paragraphe Hugh MacLennan Prize for Fiction and the Grand Prix du Livre de Montréal. Despite this recognition, I maintain that the novel is still outside the literary canon. How many copies were actually sold? How many bestseller lists did it make and for how long? The numbers here are not significant.[3]

Maybe this is due to the subject matter of a cockroach's view of the world. Only time will tell if this peculiar Arab novel will be embraced by a broad group of Canadian readers. And I might add that, with the 2017 Trump administration's systematic attacks on Muslims, the progress of Arab-Canadian authors may be difficult.

## NOTES

1 Étienne Geoffroy Saint-Hilaire (1772–1844). He coined the principle of "unity in composition." The quote comes from the biography written by his son Isidore Geoffroy Saint-Hilaire (1805–1861). Etienne Saint-Hilaire took part in the Napoleonic scientific expedition to Egypt in 1798. In a telling gesture, Balzac dedicated his multi-volume *Comédie Humaine* (1842–55) to him.
2 In the CBC Q interview, Hage was asked a question about this quote, and he pointed to the fact that Mossadeq, who was democratically elected in Iran in the early 1950s, was overthrown in a coup backed by the US, following which the autocratic Shah (Mohamed Reza Pahlavi), emperor of Iran since 1941, returned and remained in power until his overthrow in 1979.
3 Despite its lack of popular appeal, some critics maintain that Hage's novel is frequently identified and taught in university courses as a major contemporary urban novel from Montreal that represents marginal views and talks back to the centres of power, which makes it an emergent canonical text with minority sensibilities.

## BIBLIOGRAPHY

Dahab, F. Elizabeth. "The Arab Canadian Novel and the Rise of Rawi Hage." In *The Rise of the Arab Novel in English: The Politics of Anglo Arab and Arab American Literature and Culture*, edited by Nouri Gana, 362–403. Edinburgh: Edinburgh University Press, 2013.

– ed. *Voices in the Desert: An Anthology of Arabic-Canadian Women Writers*. Toronto: Guernica Editions, 2002.

– *Voices of Exile in Contemporary Canadian Francophone Literature*. Lanham, MD: Lexington Books, 2009.

Deleuze, Gilles, and Félix Guattari. *Kafka: Toward a Minor Literature*. Minneapolis: University of Minnesota Press, 1986.

Elkhadem, Saad. *Trilogy of the Flying Egyptian* (*Canadian Adventures of the Flying Egyptian*, 1990. *Chronicle of the Flying Egyptian in Canada*, 1991. *Crash Landing of the Flying Egyptian*, 1992.) Translated by Saad El Gabalawy. Bilingual edition (English-Arabic). Fredericton: York Press, 1990–92.

Gana, Nouri. "Everyday Arabness: The Poethics of Arab Canadian Literature and Culture." *CR: The New Centennial Review* 9, no. 2 (2009): 21–44. hu.edu/login?auth=0&type=summary&url=/journals/new_centennial_review/v009/9.2.gana.pdf.

– "Review of *De Niro's Game* by Rawi Hage." *International Fiction Review* 34, no. 1–2 (2007): 196–8.

Geoffroy Saint-Hilaire, Isidore. *La Vie Etienne Geoffroy Saint-Hilaire*. Paris, 1847.
Ghomeshi, Jian. Interview with Rawi Hage. QTV. 26 February 2009. http://www.youtube.com/watch?v=srlHTSxX8mo (accessed 22 October 2010).
Hage, Rawi. *Carnival*. Toronto: House of Anansi Press, 2012.
– *Cockroach*. New York: W.W. Norton, 2008.
– *De Niro's Game*. Toronto: House of Anansi Press, 2006.
Hammoudi, Rima. "Interview with Rawi Hage." *Tadamon*. 1 October 2009. http://www.tadamon.ca/post/4842 (accessed 20 October 2010).
Harel, Simon. *Braconnage identitaire. Un Québec palimpseste*. Montréal: VLB, 2006.
– "La parole orpheline de l'écrivain migrant." In *Montréal imaginaire: Ville et littérature*, edited by Pierre Nepveu and Gilles Marcotte, 373–418. Montreal: Fides, 1992.
Lotfi, Mohamed. "Racism, Made in Quebec." 9 January 2009. www.citoyen.onf.ca/extraits/media/racism_quebec.pdf (accessed 20 October 2010).
Sakr, Rita. "Imaginative Migrations: An Interview with the Lebanese-Canadian Writer Rawi Hage." *Journal of Postcolonial Writing* 47, no. 3 (2011): 343–51.
Tabar, Tania. "Rawi Hage's Book *Cockroach* an Existential Arab Immigrant Romp," *Menassat*. 5 February 2009. http://www.menassat.com/?q=en/news-articles/5935-rawi-hage-s-book-cockroach-existential-arab-immigrant-romp (accessed 12 October 2006).

# The Power to Narrate: Representing Italian Migrant Working-Class Experiences in Two Steel Cities in Australia and Canada

*Gaetano Rando*

Emigration can be seen as the quintessential experience of our time that fragments families and identity, creates dislocation, and imposed silence. An important function of literature written about migration is to break that silence, giving voice to the invisibility of such experiences.[1] Similarly, working-class literature functions to break the silence related to working-class experiences and the invisibility of class,[2] class being considered a shaping force "inseparable from other markers of identity," among them ethnicity.[3]

This chapter proposes to examine two novels by writers of Italian working-class origins: Pietro Tedeschi, who writes about his initial experiences in steel-producing Port Kembla in Australia from the perspective of a first-generation working-class migrant, and Frank Paci, a second-generation migrant from a working-class family, who writes about an Italian family's long-term experiences in steel-producing Marionville in Canada. It can be posited that these novels challenge to an extent the sanitized history of the Italian migrant working class in the two countries.

By way of background, it can be observed that Italian migration to Canada began earlier and historically involved greater numbers than Australia, with Italian communities becoming firmly established in the early decades of the twentieth century in both countries. Post–Second World War emigration from Italy resulted in considerable additions to the numbers of Italians already present with about 450,000 migrating to Canada and approximately 230,000 to Australia by 1961. Both countries had embarked on mass immigration programs to build up their "white" population (Australia particularly so, in view of the then-current White Australia Policy) and, despite a preference for persons of British stock or from Northern Europe, they soon realized that, to meet targets, they needed to accept persons of other origins, including Italians. Among the reasons for requiring large numbers of immigrants were: 1) the need to protect the Pacific Rim from substantial Asian immigration for Canada and, for Australia, the need to protect itself from a perceived "yellow peril" from the north – Australia had significantly coined the slogan "populate or perish" – 2) the need for workers for large infrastructure projects and for developing industries – the influx of immigrants was to a large extent initially used as industrial cannon fodder. However, the stories of these working-class migrants remain largely untold.

It is precisely the theme of the engagement of Italian migrant workers in heavy industry that provided the initial inspiration for the novels *The Italians* (Ottawa: Oberon Press, 1978) by Frank Paci and *53B* (Wollongong [NSW]: The Author, 1993) by Pietro Tedeschi. Each novel can be considered as having a considerable overt and transparent biographical basis in theme, characterization, and structure. Both writers seem to adhere to the concept expressed by Paci that "[i]n this world we live on a bumpy road of surface reality and abstract reality ... Reality in the novel ... includes all differences — all parts — because it sees that only the whole is truth."[4]

The "realities" referred to here are, of course, those of the experience of migration and, especially in the case of Paci, of its long-term effects. In a sense, this can be linked to the theoretical issues raised by Joseph Pivato (*Echo*) and Sneja Gunew ("Denaturalising Cultural Nationalisms," "A Conversation," and *Haunted Nations*) regarding the way in which writers engage in the attendant geographical and cultural dislocations of the migration process and propose a return to questions of both origins and belonging, thus giving voice to common experiences that remain largely silent. Given that interrogations of the national emerge from both local communities and global diasporas, Homi Bhabha's concept of the ambivalent nature of national culture that is "neither unified nor unitary in relation to itself,"[5] and his argument that cultural contestation posited by cultural difference has the ability to shift the ground of knowledges,[6] can also be considered relevant to the topic elaborated upon in this chapter.

As well as migration, the two novels present another set of common, but largely unvoiced, realities – those of the working class. In her fundamental work on American working-class literature, Janet Zandy (*Hands*) examines how writings created by working-class authors express the costs the body must bear when exposed to the risks of certain types of work, how these texts help recover submerged labour histories, and the important function of these works as creators of culture. One of the themes explored is that of the need for workers to move from place to place in order to find work and engage in coping with a new environment, an aspect that is fundamental in the case of Tedeschi's and Paci's protagonists, who must leave their native land for this purpose.

It can be posited that both Tedeschi and Paci engage in cultural creation, and also subtly engage to an extent in cultural contestation that challenges sanitized history. Their narratives "give space and voice to the excluded and dispossessed ... [as well as] ... raise the issues of what the world looks like from the margins,"[7] revealing "a richness of understanding not usually available in sociological studies."[8] Edward Said has argued that the "power to narrate, or to block other narratives from forming and emerging is very important to culture and imperialism, and constitutes one of the main connections between them."[9] Extrapolating from this, it can be considered that, in the context of Italian-Australian and Italian-Canadian narratives, the power to narrate constitutes an important connection between the dominant host Anglo-Australian or Anglo-Canadian society, Italian migrants, and their children.

Deleuze and Guattari's observation that the migrant goes principally from one point to another, even if the second point is uncertain, unforeseen, or not well localized,[10] has been contested and amplified by later studies. Ben Rogaly, for example, has argued, on the basis of his research, that mobilities and fixity interrelate with respect to the "end point," and often coexist at the same moment for the same person as a result of the process of migration and its long-term effects.[11] Writing about migrant experiences can be seen as one way of attempting to make sense of this trajectory through the creation of myths, including narratives, that engage with the imperative to preserve traditional practices from host-society expectations of assimilation, and the issues arising from living between the old world and the dominant hegemony of the social and cultural institutions of the new world. In Tedeschi's case, this involves the transition from the well-established industrial cultural traditions of his protagonist's hometown, which include clearly articulated concepts of worker solidarity to the embryonic industrial culture of the new country. For Paci's protagonist, the transition is from the agricultural setting of central Italy to the industrial environment of Canada.

One of the ways of creating myth/narratives that engage with these issues is through the production of narrative works by Italian-Australian and Italian-Canadian writers that are based more or less explicitly on biographical or autobiographical experience.[12] In certain Italian-Australian narrative texts, this basis can be obvious and transparent, in that the characters and events represented have an explicit identification with the experience of the author.[13] Usually this type of writing covers episodes in the life of the writer over a period of one or two years, which are seen as particularly significant and life-changing and which are related to migration, as well as, in some cases, to new workplace experiences.

In the case of Pietro Tedeschi's *Senza camicia* (1986), it is the difficult and indeed desperate life experience of the writer/protagonist in his home town of Reggio Emilia that leads to his decision to emigrate, a situation that can be directly correlated to Tedeschi's own real-life experience. The sub-proletarian protagonist of Rosa Cappiello's *Paese fortunato* (1981) can to some extent be identified with the author, and some of the other characters can also be identified with living people, but the characterization and the thematic presentation tend to transcend a strict adherence to the (auto)biographical genre, thus making this element less central to the development of the work. Giovanni Andreoni's *Martin Pescatore* (1967), although not so transparently autobiographical, deals in part with the writer/protagonist's metaphysical travail, based on his life experience, in his transition from the old country and culture to the new. Charles D'Aprano's novel *Tears, Laughter, and the Revolution* (1998) also has a number of elements in common with the foregoing, but it additionally presents an aspect that is substantially developed by second-generation writers – the re-evaluation of home society and culture which takes place after the consummation of the migration and settlement process. In D'Aprano's case this leads to the positing of a new and unique "Italian-Australian" cultural identity with strong identification with the working class. However, the other side of the coin is presented too, when, in *Cenere* (1982), Andreoni posits the practical impossibility of the emergence of this desirable and positive new identity, since it is stifled by the racism and cultural conservatism incipient in the host society.

These writings can be thus seen as one way in which migrants deal with the impact of separation from their previous symbolic order by devising narratives that can assist in overcoming the psychological effect of such life-changing events. Gerardo Papalia, in fact, points out that Italian-Australian literature in general is one mechanism used to confront cultural bereavement.[14] Papalia's observation can be linked to Ross Gibson's claim that we desire our myths and need our histories, since the creation of myths is a way of resolving contradictions narratively rather that rationally, whereas histories help to analyze persistent contradictions to avoid being lulled by the myths used to console and enable.[15]

Migration is a substantial, life-changing experience. Accounts of this experience relate the anger and frustration, the hopes and disappointments, lived by migrants. For the first generation, this includes the traumatic process of leaving one's native land and of having to begin all over again, adapting to a new country. For the second generation, there is the attempt to "find one's place" at a point somewhere between two different cultural contexts that present some irreconcilable elements. For both the first and second generation, writing about such experiences is one way of making sense of this process, of attempting to understand where one is coming from and where one is heading.

Pietro Tedeschi reports that writing about such experiences has been a sort of liberating therapy, whereby "attraverso voli di fantasia pindarica, più o meno creativa o valida, mischiando futuro e passato, allegorie, situazioni immaginarie, riprendevo contatto con la realtà del vivere quotidiano." (By means of flights of Pindaric fantasy, more or less creative or valid, by mixing the future and the past, allegories, imaginary situations, I regained contact with the reality of everyday living.)[16] When asked why he chose to relate his experiences in a fictional form, Tedeschi replied that he was not sure about dates, and that, over time, he had lost track of a number of precise details and information about people. However, his intention of representing a "real life" situation is quite explicit:

> Di fronte a questo spettro universale a questo fascio di nuove impressioni, dal fondo della mia mente a barlumi, riprendeva forma il desiderio, l'urgenza di registrare di cronicizzare questi fatti, queste nuove esperienze irripetibili. Il desiderio di far partecipe anche i "non presenti" a queste nuove sensazioni. La descrizione dell'ambiente, il momento storico di questo grande paese, di questa nuova frontiera aperta al mio e al futuro di tanta gente. E qui ancora la frustrazione, l'ostacolo della mia impotenza a tradurre il pensiero, le sensazioni in parola scritta in maniera idonea comprensibile.
> [Faced with this universal specter and this bundle of new impressions, from flashes at the bottom of my mind the desire, the urgency of registering, of relating these facts, these new unrepeatable experiences, the desire of allowing the participation in these new sensations of "those who were not present" regained form. The description of the environment, of the historical moment of this great country, of this new frontier opened up to my future and

that of so many people. And also the frustration, the obstacle of my impotence to translate thoughts, sensations, into the written word in an understandable and suitable manner.][17]

For Frank Paci, writing about such experiences reflects the process of achieving "a form of integration without being swallowed by the anonymous forces of assimilation," as well as struggling with issues of identity and the shame of being ethnic.[18] Specifically, Paci states:

> I reacted strongly against my family, wanting to be exactly the opposite of what they were. In my adolescent years I experienced some sort of Cartesian turn of consciousness when my safe secure worlds came crashing down on me ... You can make a pretty good argument that writing is a form of mythologising to compensate for the loss of the old myths. Another factor has been my lifelong fascination with language, the power of language to give meaning and to transform factuality. But the ultimate reason for my turning to writing was that for me it seemed the only way to find out who I was and why I was on earth. These things build up slowly, of course, but by my second year in university, when I wrote my first story and carried it around in my back pocket, I seemed to jump from one level into another – and the path opened up for me.[19]

This statement has a direct correlation with the narration of Marco Trecroci's (a character in a number of Paci's novels) development as a writer and intellectual.

Pietro Tedeschi migrated to Australia from Reggio Emilia in 1952 at the age of twenty-seven, after obtaining trade qualifications as a fitter and turner and working at the Officine Reggiane. He initially found employment at the Port Kembla Steelworks, subsequently passing the English Placement Test (EPT) upon recognition of his Italian trade qualifications. After his retirement in 1979, he was an active participant in Italian community activities until his death in 1998. For over thirty years, he wrote reports on local Italian community events, essays, and short stories for the Sydney-based Italian-language newspaper *La Fiamma*. His literary production includes two collections of poetry that significantly focus, often in ironic terms, on the industrial environment of his workplaces and two novels. The first novel, *Senza camicia* (1986), set entirely in Italy and significantly written in Italian, relates the events leading to the central character's decision to migrate to Australia from Reggio Emilia in the early 1950s. The second novel, *53B* (1993), set entirely in Australia and understandably written in English, describes the central character's first year in Australia. Although the names of the protagonists – Morcia in *Senza camicia* and Reggio in *53B* – are different, there is a strong, implicit sense of continuity in their narratives, suggesting that they are in fact the same character.

In the two novels, Tedeschi traces the central character's physical and metaphysical journey from unsettlement in Reggio Emilia, an industrial city that is down but not out in the years immediately after the end of the Second World War, to potential resettlement in Port Kembla, a developing industrial city without the technological sophistication and worker awareness and solidarity of Reggio Emilia. *Senza camicia* begins with the worker occupation of the Officine Reggiane, Morcia's subsequent unemployment and struggle to make ends meet, his decision to emigrate, with the accompanying condemnation of the Italian Christian Democrat government policy on emigration (the government treats Italian workers and peasants like two-legged animals), and ends with Morcia boarding ship to leave for Australia. The second novel, *53B*, begins with Reggio's arrival in Wollongong, the ups and downs of life in the migrant camp, and his experiences as an unskilled worker beginning his Australian career at the Port Kembla steelworks.

Frank Paci migrated to Canada from Pesaro with his parents in 1952 at the age of four and grew up in steel-producing Sault Ste Marie (Ontario), becoming a high-school teacher and obtaining an MA in English in 1980. His first novel, *The Italians* (1978), was followed by twelve other novels. *The Italians* became a bestseller and has also been published in a French translation (1990), but it is his second novel, *Black Madonna* (1982), that has so far proved to be his most popular book. Most of Paci's novels feature the central character Marco/Mark Trecroci as he progresses from childhood experiences in a working-class Italian migrant family in a steel-producing Canadian city to university graduate and aspiring writer.

Marco Trecroci's family came from the gentle countryside of central Italy to settle in an industrial Canadian town characterized by cold, ice, and steel. Paci's series of novels represent a mainly metaphysical journey about the central character's acquisition of intellectual and ethnic wisdom. His progression through school and university, his activity as a writer, and his journey back to Italy represent a cycle of uncertainty-rejection-reacceptance of dual ethnicity. This process internalizes the dialectic of the two cultures (the Italian *contadino*, or "peasant," cultural traditions from his parents, and the Canadian culture around him outside the home), while at the same time coming to grips with the Western cultural tradition (particularly philosophers and literary critics) also ending in cultural duality – identification with high culture and with the *contadino* culture of his ancestral homeland (Novilara in the Marche region). To an extent, there are some interesting parallels between the trajectory followed by Marco Trecroci and that of Jim Romano, the central character in D'Aprano's *Tears, Laughter, and the Revolution*.

But it is Paci's first novel, *The Italians*, that sets the tone for his subsequent production, and it is the one that most strikingly represents the relationship between the migrant worker and the host country's industrial culture. *The Italians* narrates the story of the Gaetano family from the standpoint of Lorianna, the daughter; Alberto, the father; Bill, the youngest son; and Aldo, the eldest son. Giulia, the mother, has no part in the narration, although she is distinctly present as a character. Some twenty years after migrating from Romagna to the steel-producing town of Marionville in northeastern Canada, Alberto has achieved some of the goals that led him to leave the old country. At the cost of forsaking his talents as a musician and an *artigiano* (craftsman), he has become a leading hand and valued worker at the local steel plant. The *miseria* (extreme poverty) he and Giulia had experienced in the old country is a thing of the past, though it is still a shadow on the present, despite their well-stocked cellar and their proud ownership of the house painstakingly renovated and refurbished by Alberto. Their children are well on the way to being *sistemati* (taken care of) (Lorianna through marriage, and the two sons in contexts that promise to take them away from a working-class future), despite some worrying interferences and considerable generational friction in the process. All this, however, changes when Alberto has a life-threatening accident at the plant, bringing the members of the family to confront both their essential selves and their relationships with each other. Here, the correlation with Zandy's analysis regarding the treatment of the physical dangers to which workers in industry are exposed is quite striking.

By contrast, Tedeschi's *53B* tells the story of Reggio, a single man in his mid-twenties, who emigrates from Reggio Emilia to Australia in the early 1950s to escape the long-term unemployment he had experienced as a result of adverse socio-economic conditions. He is initially sent to the migrant camp at Bonegilla, where he participates in the Italian migrants' revolt against bread rationing and is subsequently assigned to the labour force at the Port Kembla steelworks as an unskilled worker, despite the fact that he had obtained trade qualifications in Italy. Reggio needs to create his space, both in the Berkley migrant camp and in the steelworks. His space at the migrant camp, a place of transition until he can find more permanent accommodation, is marked both by his association with his Italian friends, all young single men, and by the attempts he and his friends make to establish a rapport with some of the other migrants at the camp, mostly made up of English families. In Reggio's case, this leads to a passionate but discreet affair with a young English married woman. On the work front, Reggio finds that he has to start from scratch in conditions that are decidedly inferior to those he had experienced in Italy. However, despite his lack of English and his somewhat bemused puzzlement at the primitive working environment, he manages to establish a good working relationship with his Australian foreman.

Although there are references to the environment and to the protagonists' rapport with their respective workplaces (as discussed in the following paragraphs), the two novels do not contain enough specific details of the industrial processes and workplace practices in their respective steelworks to indicate to any great extent similarities or differences in environment, working conditions, and relationships. While it could be posited that in the respective real-life situations there would be differences at a micro level (to determine these differences would involve a separate research project), there is substantial commonality in the way the two protagonists relate to the industrial environment. For both Alberto and Reggio, the dictates and constraints of the industrial process are determining factors in their life experiences in their respective host countries. Both find that a considerable part of their lives is controlled by the steel plant, and for both this situation sometimes leads to mindsets and behaviour that are to some extent contradictory.

Despite Alberto's twenty-year association with the steel plant, the environment has remained to some degree unfamiliar and potentially alienating:

> During spring and summer he'd always stare at the water while walking to work. It reminded him of the Adriatic. But in the winter ice covered the whole channel from Lake Superior, and the warm waters of his home were even harder to call to mind. The plant was like a giant fortress rising squarely from a bend on the northern bank of the river. He never lost his amazement at how such a structure could function, let alone exist, in the limitless expanse of snow and ice. Past the gate and administration buildings its mills of dull red and turquoise formed a gigantic maze.[20]

Reggio's first impression of the Port Kembla steelworks, located on the coast in a sandy landscape, is that of a desolate, barren, and chaotic environment very different from his native Reggio Emilia:

> The view was impressive ... interlacing of trestles; girders; pipes of all sizes; corrugated iron; steel hoppers generated a forest of vertical structures painted in the same reddish brown tint of the mineral stockpile on the right flank. Further on, in the same direction, another set of black dunes, presumably coal, was topped by clouds of steam coming from a stumpy chimney ... At the centre of the view, between the foreground and the two toned blue ocean, a large strip of sandy marsh, patched with still water, dry trees and dusty brushes, gave the impression of a colourless no-man's land.[21]

For Alberto the steel plant has become a way of life, albeit quite separate from his life at home with his family, even though it is through his work at the steel plant that Alberto has been able to realize the goals that had led him to migrate to Canada. Work at the plant is a means to an end: "He had worked hard to get up the rungs of the ladder of seniority since he felt it was a father's duty to make the best money possible so his wife and children should not live like animals ... he wholeheartedly subscribed to the saying in the plant that half of one's life was wasted in working so the other half could be enjoyed with some degree of comfort."[22] Over the twenty years he has worked there, Alberto has come to identify with and take pride in the production process,[23] to the point that he refuses to participate in a union-instigated strike for better pay and conditions, an attitude motivated by a sense of loyalty to his workplace (although he believes in union solidarity, he questions the decision to implement a wildcat strike, since it was "something close to anarchy of which he had seen the consequences in the old country" (*The Italians* 115). However, over the years the work has become wearing and unpleasant: "That first contact with the smell [of the plant], along with the pounding noise of the huge blowers and hot stoves, never failed to make him shudder with revulsion" (122), to the point that it is wearing him down: "[H]e felt his body giving way more and more recently. The old tasks which he used to perform with ease he now found too much of an exertion ... After particularly arduous shifts he had even found it difficult to walk to the car from his locker-room" (128).

Reggio has mixed feelings about his work at the steel plant, which is about ten times bigger than the one in Reggio Emilia. He is appreciative of the fact that it offers him the opportunity to become "an active producer once more" (Tedeschi, "The Steelworks" 186) and to regain his self-esteem after years of forced unemployment. However, he is somewhat uneasy with the chaotic and reminiscently Dantesque inferno-like atmosphere of the place: "[A]head was a steel jungle submerged in smoke, dust, fire, and the roars and bangs filling the air, where people entered in hundreds as if swallowed by the giant jaws of hell" (183), an interesting parallel with Zandy's[24] comments about industry as the devouring minotaur of labour.

Reggio is equally somewhat dismayed at the primitive work methods used in clearing a flooded area: "Both teams were going to dig a metre-deep ditch to reach lower ground seventy meters away. 'How original! And what about water pumps?' I asked myself. 'Leonardo invented them four or five hundred years ago'" (193). However, he is prepared to shed his cultural high ground and adapt to local work practices by proposing a quicker and more practical way of clearing the flooded area. His contribution to the gang's effort earns him the praise of Fred, his Australian foreman, and gives him a feeling of being accepted: "He pointed at me with a grin. 'I couldn't have done it without the help of me mate here' ... I didn't understand one word Fred had exchanged with his compatriots, but I had grasped the real meaning of the definition 'mate' for the first time ... Right down in the gut I felt good" (194). Despite the fact that the economic viability of the Port Kembla Steelworks depended entirely on the availability of migrant labour, the acceptance of such labour is extremely circumscribed. Reggio soon discovers that, unlike the British, Dutch, and German migrants, the qualifications of Italian skilled workers were not recognized, a state of affairs that led to paradoxical situations in which the foreman sought "advice from the [Italian] fitter's labourer because he knew more than the tradesman himself" (Tedeschi, *53B* 182), while "the humblest, the dirtiest, the most impersonal jobs ... were especially reserved ... for the Italians" (183) – in line with the universal capitalist practice of assigning the lowest jobs to the lowest workers.[25] Paradoxically, however, "the big Diesel locos which pulled the trains on the railway network inside the Steelworks, showed in big letters the [Italian] name ANSALDO" (183).

However, these constraints notwithstanding, Reggio's initial perception of Australia is positive and enthusiastic, though critical and not necessarily accepting in all its aspects. Australia is seen as a place that offers a fresh beginning, new opportunities, and new experiences, and, in a sense, challenges that need to be resolved. He is engaged in negotiating his way in a natural environment which presents a rugged beauty, despite some hidden dangers (quicksand and poisonous insects), the social environment of the Berkley migrant camp, where tolerance and acceptance is only skin deep ("We can make backwards somersaults, offer them the moon wrapped in ribbons but on the first occasion that dormant sense of distrust and contempt towards us will spark alive immediately" [186]), and a work environment that relegates him to the bottom of the hierarchy. Despite these difficulties, Reggio's first year in Australia has changed him from the passive, limp, withered human being who had set foot on the boat in Genova to an assertive, self-confident, and critical individual, whose perceptions of the world have been set in focus and whose horizons have been widened (190), thus forming a basis for further exploration and contact with the new country and, potentially, for identifying with it. In this process, he has shed the relationships formed during the voyage to Australia and in the Berkley migrant camp (except for Sandro, with whom he shares his new lodgings in a Warrawong Italian boarding house), freeing him to form new relationships, both at work and socially. His initiation into the industrial environment of the steelworks has played an important part in this transformation.

Alberto, on the other hand, has, over the years, formed his own world, which is Italian-Canadian at home (solidly based on the family) and socially — throughout the novel the only social activities are a visit from his *compare* (old pal) and a dinner organized by the local Italian community in honour of his son Bill, who has become a famous ice-hockey player. At the steel plant, he has formed contacts with migrant workmates (his best friend there is the Ukrainian Yukich), while his only contact with "real" Canadians is with the young worker he disciplines and who contributes to his accident and with the officials who visit him at home after the accident.

Alberto's sense of identification with Canada is also qualified. While appreciating the material benefits of life in the new country and how they have been instrumental in allowing him to provide for his family, he is also aware that this has been achieved at the cost of a less rich and varied life and of daily toil, both through his work at the steel plant (economically viable because of the migrant workforce), as well as the time and effort required to repair and refurbish his home. For Alberto, Canadian values are questionable, in some cases incomprehensible, and present the potential "loss" of his children. He considers ice hockey deviant, and cannot understand Bill's passion for the sport or why he leaves school to play the game professionally.[26] Aldo's religious crisis, which dashes the high expectations he had for his son (in the hometown cultural tradition, it was considered highly desirable to have a priest in the family), is, in Alberto's view, triggered by Aldo's relationship with the Canadian Evylyn, while Lorianna's less-than-ideal marriage to Lorenzo is welcomed because he is Italian (not Canadian), although Lorenzo's initial position in refusing to accept any of the ways of the new country (including the language) is instrumental in provoking Lorianna's desperate marital plight.

Both Paci's and Tedeschi's novels relate their respective protagonists' rapport with the industrial and socio-cultural environments of the new country in a context where the two protagonists, Alberto and Reggio, are emblematic representations of the migrant workforce that ensured the economic viability of the steel industry in Canada and Australia. Although the protagonist of each novel is represented at different stages of his migration and workplace experiences, they can be seen as providing a sort of continuity, in that Reggio, the newly arrived migrant worker, is engaged in the somewhat optimistic process of coming to terms with and initially adjusting to his new situation, while Alberto represents a less-optimistic long-term dynamic process of adjustment, re-definition and creation of an Italian-Canadian space.

The narratives by Paci and Tedeschi thus constitute a valuable contribution to the substantial corpus of fictional and non-fictional accounts that represent a view of the physical and socio-cultural environment encountered by working-class Italians who have migrated to Canada and Australia and have experienced the dislocation caused by geographical, climatic, and social situations so different from the ones they had left behind in Italy. Together with other Italian–Australian/Canadian narratives, they give voice to a largely silenced migrant working-class experience and help show how the individuals who produced them came to terms with their new environment, negotiating, each in his own way, the liminal divide that is an integral part of the process. This is, in fact, also the case of the two novels discussed in this chapter, which describe how Alberto creates his niche in Italian-Canadian space over the twenty years of his migration experience and how Reggio copes with the initial impact of living and working in Australia by engaging to some extent in cultural negotiation.

In parallel with their engagement with the migration experience, both novels also highlight working-class themes that range from pride in (manual) work and cultural memory, despite dealing with problems ranging from marginality to the risks of working in heavy industry. Aside from the brief image of the steel plant that "swallows" workers alive, there is, surprisingly, nothing about workplace risks and dangers to be found in Tedeschi's novel, although in conversations about the Port Kembla steelworks, the author has remarked on unsafe work practices. By contrast,

Alberto's pride in his work at the Marionville plant is to a large extent overshadowed by his increasing weariness and, in particular, by the accident that marks a premature end to his working career.

In line with the corpus of Italian-Australian and Italian-Canadian narrative writing, Paci's and Tedeschi's novels can be considered as providing an interesting example of Bhabha's general observation regarding the potential provided by Australia's pluricultural society (an observation that can be extended to all such societies) to present views from the periphery: "the nations of Europe and Asia meet in Australia: the margins of the nation displace the centre; the peoples of the periphery return to write the history and fiction of the metropolis."[27] It can be claimed that the regional and localized differences articulated in the two novels contest dominant notions of history and nation, thus contributing to the interrogation of the national as emergent from both local communities and global diasporas.

## NOTES

1 Pivato, *Echo*, passim.
2 Zandy, *Hands*, 84.
3 Coles and Zandy, *American Working-Class Literature*, xx.
4 Paci, "Tasks of the Canadian Novelist," 39, 40.
5 Bhabha, *Introduction*, 4.
6 Bhabha, *DissemiNation*, 313.
7 Bromley, *Narratives*, 4.
8 Bottomley, *From Another Place*, 90.
9 Said, *Culture and Imperialism*, xiii. See also Joseph Pivato's discussion of Said in the context of Italian-Canadian writing: "Representation of Ethnicity."
10 Deleuze and Guattari, *A Thousand Plateaus*, 380.
11 Rogaly, "Disrupting Migration Stories," 528, 541.
12 It can also be noted that, in the Italian-Australian context, personal accounts, memoirs, and autobiographies by first-generation writers constitute a long-standing tradition going back to the mid-nineteenth century (Rando, "Il racconto dell'esperienza migratoria" 317–18). Their publication has continued up to the present time, in accounts such as Salvatore di Bella's bilingual memoir *Lo strano Diario di Sam / The Strange Diary of Sam* (2014). This type of life writing seems equally popular in the Italian-Canadian context (e.g., Giuseppe Ricci's *L'orfano di padre: le memorie di Giuseppe Ricci*, 1980).

13 This is also the case in Italian-Canadian narrative – e.g., Maria Ardizzi's *Il sapore agro della mia terra* (1984), Bianca Zagolin's *Une femme à la fenêtre* (1988) – Joseph Pivato, personal communication, October 2004.
14 Papalia, "Icon of Resistance," 197, 206. Papalia has also observed that another and perhaps more significant mechanism is religious celebrations. See Papalia, "Migrating Madonnas."
15 Gibson, *Seven Versions*, 170–1.
16 Typewritten autobiographical notes by Pietro Tedeschi (ca. 1988), 4; English translation by the author.
17 Ibid.
18 Pivato, *Echo*, 211.
19 Pivato, "Interview," 231.
20 Paci, *The Italians*, 121.
21 Tedeschi, "The Steelworks," 182.
22 Paci, *The Italians*, 26, 122.
23 A theme analyzed in Zandy, 40.
24 Ibid., 43–4, 89.
25 Ibid., 144.
26 Sport as a new country identifier expressed through ice hockey is an important theme in a number of Paci's novels. It is virtually non-existent in Italian-Australian narrative, despite the considerable value placed on sport in Australia. The only short story that presents sport as a central theme is Archimede Fusillo's *Memories of Sunday Cricket in the Street* (1987), while in Andreoni's *Cenere* (1982), the second-generation protagonist becomes captain of the First XI cricket team at school as part of an all-out, but ultimately unsuccessful, attempt to become completely Australian.
27 Bhabha, "Introduction," 6.

## BIBLIOGRAPHY

Andreoni, Giovanni. "Cenere." In *L'australitaliano come linguaggio letterario. Un racconto documento*. Quaderni del Veltro 19. Rome: Il Veltro Editrice (1982): 4–81.
Bhabha, Homi. "DissemiNation: Time, Narrative and the Margins of the Modern Nation." In *Nation and Narration*, edited by Homi Bhabha, 291–322. London: Routledge, 1990.
– "Introduction: Narrating the Nation." In *Nation and Narration*, edited by Homi Bhabha, 1–7. London: Routledge, 1990.
Bottomley, Gillian. *From Another Place: Migration and the Politics of Culture*. Cambridge: Cambridge University Press, 1992.

Bromley, Roger. *Narratives for a New Belonging: Diasporic Cultural Fictions*. Edinburgh: Edinburgh University Press, 2000.
Coles, Nicholas, and Janet Zandy. *American Working-Class Literature: An Anthology*. New York: Oxford: Oxford University Press, 2007.
D'Aprano, Charles. *Tears, Laughter, and the Revolution*. Brunswick West, Victoria: Insegna Publishers, 1998.
Deleuze, Gilles, and Felix Guattari. *A Thousand Plateaus: Capitalism and Schizophrenia*. Minneapolis: University of Minnesota Press, 1987.
Gibson, Ross. *Seven Versions of an Australian Badland*. St Lucia, Queensland: University of Queensland Press, 2002.
Gunew, Sneja. "A Conversation between Sneja Gunew and Yiu-Nam Leung. May 2003." 30 July 2015. http://faculty.arts.ubc.ca/second generationunew/LEUNG.HTM.
– "Denaturalising Cultural Nationalisms: Multicultural Readings of 'Australia.'" In *Nation and Narration*, edited by Homi Bhabha, 99–120. London: Routledge, 1990.
– *Haunted Nations: The Colonial Dimensions of Multiculturalisms*. London: Routledge, 2004.
Hutcheon, Linda, and Marion Richmond, eds. *Other Solitudes: Canadian Multicultural Fictions*. Toronto: Oxford University Press, 1990.
Paci, Frank. *The Italians*. Ottawa: Oberon Press, 1978.
– "Tasks of the Canadian Novelist Writing on Immigrant Themes." In *Contrasts: Comparative Essays on Italian-Canadian Writing*, edited by Joseph Pivato, 35–60. Montreal: Guernica Editions, 1985.
Papalia, Gerardo. "Icon of Resistance: *Vecchiu carrubbu* – The Old Carob Tree." In *Bernard Hickey, a Roving Cultural Ambassador: Essays in his Memory*, edited by Maria Renata Dolce and Antonella Riem Natale, 197–208. Udine: Editrice Universitaria Udinese, 2009.
– "Migrating Madonnas: The Madonna della Montagna di Polsi in Calabria and in Australia." *Fulgor* 3, no. 3 (November 2008): 57–71. http://ehlt.flinders.edu.au/deptlang/fulgor/volume3i3/papers/Papaliav3i3082.pdf (accessed 25 July 2015).
Pivato, Joseph, ed. *Contrasts: Comparative Essays on Italian-Canadian Writing*. Montreal: Guernica Editions, 1985.
– *Echo: Essays on Other Literatures*. Toronto: Guernica Editions, 1994.
– "Interview with F.G. Paci." In *Other Solitudes: Canadian Multicultural Fictions*, edited by Linda Hutcheon and Marion Richmond, 225–32. Toronto: Oxford University Press, 1990.
– "Representation of Ethnicity as Problem: Essence or Construction." *Journal of Canadian Studies* 31, no. 3 (1996). engl.athabascau.ca/faculty/jpivato/ethnicity.php (accessed 23 July 2015).

Rando, Gaetano. "Il racconto dell'esperienza migratoria." In *Italo-australiani: La popolazione di origine italiana in Australia*, edited by Castles Stephen, Caroline Alcorso, Gaetano Rando, and Ellie Vasta, 317–36. Turin: Edizioni della Fondazione Giovanni Agnelli, 1992.
– "*Italo-Australiani* and After: Recent Expressions of Italian Australian Ethnicity and the Migration Experience." *Altreitalie* 20–1 (January–December 2000): 64–85.
Rogaly, Ben. "Disrupting Migration Stories: Reading Life Histories." *Society and Space* 33 (2015): 528–44.
Said, Edward. *Culture and Imperialism*. London: Chatto and Windus, 1993.
Tedeschi, Pietro. *Senza Camicia*. Milan: Editrice Nuovi Autori, 1983.
– "The Steelworks (from 53B, a novel in progress)." In *Italians in Australia: The Literary Experience*, edited by Michael Arrighi, 181–94. Wollongong, New South Wales: The University (Department of Modern Languages), 1991.
– *53B*. Wollongong, NSW: The Author, 1993.
Zandy, Janet. *Hands: Physical Labor, Class, and Cultural Work*. New Jersey: Rutgers University Press, 2004.

# Gunn, Edwards, and di Michele: Nomadic Spaces

*Anna Pia De Luca*

## INTRODUCTION

People in constant movement have become a characteristic of modern social life, as they hop trains or planes for new destinations and new experiences. In the light of new migrant literary studies, concepts of transculturality, which place emphasis on the dialectical interaction of diverse cultural influences, contribute to a new understanding of the complex processes involved in the formation of individual identities. As underlined by Wolfgang Welsch, transculturality also implies "a culture and society whose pragmatic feats exist not only in delimitation, but in the ability to link and undergo transition."[1] Much critical investigation, however, is still needed to understand how traditional concepts of culture are reconceptualized from a transcultural perspective to underline how transnational networking can become a decisive factor in redefining identity-formation and cultural adaptation.[2] What emerges is that, within this framework of mobility, transformation, and cultural interaction, cultural identities can never be fixed, but are rather flexible and open to redefinition and reconstruction.[3]

The mapping of a Canadian identity, in constant flux as a result of Canada's kaleidoscope of multicultural, multiracial, and multilingual enclaves, has generated a polyphonic literature, in which the so-called "nomadic" writers can give voice not only to personal perspectives of expatriation and relocation, but above all to new and original artistic forms, which underline their cross-cultural experiences. The main frame of reference found in these Canadian texts is the recurrent shift between cultures, and as their juxtaposition frequently intimates, many characters find themselves on the threshold of diverse borders, whether real or imaginary, foregrounding the multiplicity and ambiguity of identity. In fact, as argued by Arianna Dagnino, it is undeniable "that the kind of imposed or deliberately provoked uprootedness experienced by those on the move simultaneously across physical and cultural ... borders has radical effects on one's sense of identity and belonging."[4] In this chapter I will explore Genni Gunn's major works in the context of these nomadic trajectories. I will also make some comparisons to specific works by Mary di Michele and Caterina Edwards, with reference to language choices and ethnic identities.

In the light of women's travelogues, dream journeys, and quests for identity, Genni Gunn is one of these Canadian writers whose fictional and poetic works navigate the complexity of her multiple identities. Initially a professional musician and singer travelling across Canada and the United States to perform with various rock bands, in the 1980s she settled down to become a writer, poet, and translator. Her publications include two short-story collections – *On the Road* (1991) and *Hungers* (2002) – two poetry collections – *Mating in Captivity* (1994) and *Faceless* (2007) – three novels – *Thrice upon a Time* (1990), *Tracing Iris* (2001), and *Solitaria* (2010) – and a travelogue memoir – *Tracks: Journeys in Time and Place* (2013). She has also translated from the Italian two collections of poems by Dacia Maraini and written the libretto for her opera, *Alternate Visions* (2007). Her translations were awarded the John Glassco Translation Prize and the Premio Internazionale Diego Valeri, while her second novel was made into a feature film with the title *The Riverbank*. The eclectic nature of her numerous publications and awards pays homage to her dynamic creative abilities.

Gunn was born in Trieste, which after the Second World War, between 1947 and 1954, had been proclaimed by the United Nations as the Free Territory of Trieste, a neutral border zone in Central Europe between Italy and Yugoslavia, administered by an Allied military government. Her father, a Friulan from Udine, engaged during the war with British Intelligence, collaborated with the British command support units in protecting the Free Territory of Trieste (Zone A) before it was disbanded and handed over to Italy. The native language of Friuli is Friulan, recognized as a minority language in Italy. Gunn's birth in a multilingual and multicultural hybrid space at the northeastern edge of Italy and at the threshold of other emerging national spaces is significant, because it emphasizes a precarious world of displacements and relocations, which condition one's way of defining self in relation to a specific social and cultural identity.

In many of her poetic and prose works, in fact, travelling and mobility become the core of the symbolic structure around which her narratives are built. Her women characters are often uprooted migrant subjects in constant motion, crossing the length and breadth of cities, towns, and countries in search of new landscapes and emotional terrains. As underlined by Gunn during a conference in Udine in 2007, when one travels, there is always something new to discover about oneself and about others. And this escape into the familiarity of alienation – one that characterizes many of her female protagonists – reflects her own personal restlessness and need to experiment with different environments.[5]

In the past, Gunn had refused to be labelled as Italian-Canadian, with its confining and limiting spaces, but rather preferred to assume a crypto-ethnic identity,[6] as testified to by both the choice of concealing her original name, Gemma Donati, and her particularly creative and experimental use of the English language. As underlined by Deborah Saidero, in Gunn's poetic works, the question of ethnic identity is never the focal point of her attention, just as the transcultural dimension of her writings is never limited to reclaiming her original Italian cultural heritage.[7] Her interior spaces related to family and culture, based on memory, are juxtaposed with exterior Canadian spaces, where spatial/temporal chronotopes not only take on new meanings but in particular underline the author's desire to give voice to her vision of liminality. We must also note that very few Italian words appear in her publications.

## ITINERANT WOMEN IN SEARCH OF IDENTITY

In *Mating in Captivity*, Gunn's first collection of poetry, the author reconstructs only fragmented moments of the Donati family's immigration to Canada. The collection, composed of five cycles of lyrical dream poems resembling a five-act play, foregrounds Gunn's ambivalent sense of isolation and displacement as she shifts from natural to artificial environments, in particular when confronted with a socio-cultural ambience that compels her to live in cage-like spaces that create voids of silence and deconstruct any definition of self-identity. Filled with images relating to forms of silence, fields of geology, meteorology, and astronomy, the poems strive, through these forms of metaphorical trans-codification, to transcribe the difficulty of interpersonal relationships felt by the poet in diverse spatial/temporal periods of her life. Language, which is seen as the medium through which meaning is produced and expressed, here becomes the mode through which meaning is lost. But for Gunn, language can be recovered by way of dreams, as they bridge the gap between our awareness and our unconscious mind, thus enabling an interpretation that is inherently dialogical, plural, and syncretic.

In particular, in the first cycle, under the heading "Natural Habitats," the narrating female voice travels through memory and dream sequences that surrealistically superimpose sensations and moments in time, in a reflective desire to understand and come to terms with the distances she has created between herself and others, and specifically between herself and her family. The first poem, "Variations of Silence" points to moments of stifling household inarticulateness, symbolically represented through a paradigmatic layering of the sounds of silence. As in Bach's *Goldberg Variations*, where the main melody is superimposed on two or more melodies with perfect structural balance, Gunn recreates sounds not heard or understood in her relationships with family or lovers: "words flutter" (8), "silent accusation" (9), "the loss of words," "aphonia, the loss of voice," "unable to utter sound" (10), "a thick silence" (11), "white noise" (13), "soundless," "tell no one" (14). The voices that come and go become imprisoned, impenetrable and silent as the earth. In displacements of time and space, the narrator is unable to cross personal borders as she metaphorically blurs roles: daughter, wife, lover, gardener, geologist, gold digger. But as the narrator recalls these moments, epiphanic revelations take place, images condense, sensations are displaced, and meanings shift.

As a child, the narrating voice recalls writing letters "dictated by an aunt in a foreign tongue" (8) to an absent and bewildered father overseas, who lived in an indefinite place without borders called "America" (59). Yet it is the surprised reaction of the poet, years later, when she receives these letters from her mother, along with a childhood doll, that trans-codifies a process of diachronic re-imagining and re-thinking of the essence of her feelings. "It's not the letters, or the meaning, or the act of writing you recall," she writes, "but the moment, years later, when you discover he has kept them all." As she removes the elastic band around the envelopes of the letters, the thin, light paper cascades into her hands like "blue wings." The doll, on the other hand, "with her hard straw body and splintered porcelain crown," where eyes "shut each time her head inclines," contains secrets which the child tries to discover by smashing the doll's head: "to uncover the mystery behind the eyes" (8). In dreams, the doll as symbol often refers to a return to infancy or a desire for protection. The head, on the other hand, could signify wisdom, understanding, a perception of the world, or an image of self. Here and throughout the other poems of the cycle, the doll is symbolically envisioned as the narrator herself: a woman split and fractured both in mind and heart, at times unable to see or to feel, and who, like the doll, for years had kept her eyes shut. "It's what you carry with you whenever you move from one decisive space to another" (8), she writes, but what she carries with her is the nightmarish realization that, since "history is cyclical, and fate inevitable," her unearthing of the past, like any gold digger, will only reveal "Fools' gold" (9). In the end, the three fundamental images of the poem, the doll's metal arm, her straw body, and the light wings of the letters, condense as the narrator realizes that it is the surprise of these treasures that she feels again and again in lovers' beds, as she responds to "their metal arms" with flapping wings "to ignite straw hearts" (8). The poems in the collection foreground Gunn's growing awareness of the difficult processes of reconsidering and recuperating one's past in order to reconstruct an identity, because, ultimately, she realizes that her frustrated search for words to express affection and love are nothing but "a construction/destruction of words" (14).

Gunn's metaphoric representation of her sense of alienation and displacement is reminiscent of Caterina Edwards's Canadian short stories, and in particular her 1999 essay titled "Where the Heart Is" (31). In the essay, Edwards presents a self-analysis of her own dual cultural identity, of her being "at home and not at home" (29) during her many trips to Venice, and in particular of her realization that, though she speaks Italian, in Italy she is "an outsider ... a foreigner" (29). She writes: "Home is a feeling, a haven, a cage, a heaven, a trap, a direction, an end, and the generator of more metaphors than Venice. If I claim that I am both not at home and at home in Venice, it is longing that keeps the contradictory states from cancelling each other out" (31). In her definition of Venice as the geographic space of home, it is interesting to notice the binary oppositions regarding her conflicting feelings – haven/cage, heaven/trap, direction/end – which, as for Gunn, create the tension and metaphor for her writing.

Gunn's early short stories, collected in *On the Road*, present a fascinating, partially autobiographic world that is ironic and tense, and where the language and life of the characters – musicians or singers on the move – intersect with the syncopated rhythms of rock music. While the stories deal with the newly gained freedom of Gunn's generation, filled with expectation and desire for women who had the courage to escape social restrictions and enclosure, in the collection *Hungers*, on the other hand, female characters trapped in difficult interpersonal situations yearn for love and human contact. Yet, because of lack of compassion or understanding, they find that every effort at reconciliation is ineffective. The title of the book serves as a leitmotif within each story as it explores the secret self under a public guise to discover the unfathomable depths of the human personality. Again partially autobiographical, many of the stories have a mysterious and cryptic tone, with sudden changes of environment and shifts in time. These, along with associative links to memories that surface in the minds of the characters, leave the reader with the feeling that human experience can never be fully understood, and human actions can only be perceived as fragmentary, and often illusory. Nonetheless, Gunn's narrative skills and poetic ability in shaping language make the stories rich with nuances, ironically emphasizing the deceptions that surround people.

In the stories set in foreign countries, Canadian protagonists are rushing about in search of something that is always beyond their grasp. In "Public Relations," for example, Magda, because she chooses to be a pop singer and on the road with a group of musicians, is disowned and disinherited by a father she unexpectedly meets up with in Mexico. Defeated and resentful, she "hops buses, escapes into their familiarity. Day trips to Playa de Santiago, Manzanillo, El Colomo Cuyutlan, Pascuales. Night rides over a narrow ribbon of black through mountains and valleys. She finds herself in Guadalajara, Colima. The air thick with diesel fumes, moisture and dust. She could be anywhere" (55).

Some of the stories, such as "Fugue" and "Rondeau," play with the structures of musical compositions to develop and give voice, either singularly or polyphonically, to shifts in the themes of complicity, cunning, and subterfuge. Other stories highlight the bitter disappointments of characters, like Paula, an abandoned wife in "The French Woman," who looks forward to a trip to Italy in order to recreate and rediscover the thrill of love. The protagonists, in search of themselves, are forced to face painful failures and faults, making them aware of the invisible, deceptive threshold between pain and pleasure or truth and fiction.

In the last story, "Hungers," which gives the title to the collection, Gunn explores the mysteries of the intense love that unites two sisters, despite the rift and animosity between them. The story is divided into five parts, which develop chronologically from childhood to the present, when the already middle-aged sisters are travelling through the deserts and canyons of Utah. The landscape is corroded, fragmented, and unstable, evocative of the psychological fractures that have deteriorated their relationship: "a word, a phrase repeated, a small gesture" (229) can become violent forces in the stability of any bond of kinship. The narrating voice is that of Clair, who recounts episodes of manic suicidal disorder in the life of her older sister, Marcia, and how Clair had been duped and manipulated into making reckless and audacious choices in the belief that these would alleviate Marcia's potential distress. During the journey, the two sisters finally confront their past, with a growing consciousness of their faults and of their mutual complicity with regard to actions or choices they have made, an awareness that is juxtaposed with the image of the Aztec child who willingly climbs the stairs of the temple, mindful of the sacrifice that awaits him as the priests tear out his still-beating heart. Here the analogy underlines how familial relationships, like the canyons eroded by water, salt, and wind, shift and change but always reappear as before: "nothing is what it seems; the earth [is] a shape-shifter" (227).

Gunn's cryptic, autobiographical references to her sister Ileana, in "Hungers," could be viewed as a precursor to one of the most interesting segments of her travelogue, *Tracks: Journeys in Time and Place,* titled "Discoveries," which covers her numerous trips to Myanmar between 2006 and 2010 to visit Ileana and her husband, Peter, residents and teachers in this former British colony, now ruled by an oppressive military junta. Together they take trips to remote areas and temples in Myanmar, liminal spaces forbidden to most travellers, but which trigger both historical and personal memories in the two sisters. Even the old Burmese colonial homes, surrounded by luxuriant vegetation, bring back recollections of their father's home in Friuli where Genni and Ileana spent childhood summers playing in the garden, now in retrospect seen as Eden "idealized in memory" (103). Ileana becomes Gunn's mentor as together they re-evaluate their past, their cultural identity, and their sense of home since their father's undercover anti-fascist activities had rendered them homeless: "My father was cloaked in political mystery and intrigue. I knew nothing about his whereabouts or doings, but I understood that I could not ask" (100). The girls had lived separate lives in Italy before immigration, Genni in southern Rutigliano with an unmarried aunt and Ileana in northern Pozzecco with paternal grandparents, while their parents moved back and forth across oceans or criss-crossed Italy by train. "Those tracks were lifelines: they carried us to and from each other, bore newspapers and gifts, absorbed the longing of our letters" (99). Thus, the trips to Myanmar permitted both Genni and Ileana to escape peer pressures and family misunderstandings and come to terms with their split pasts.

The dilemma of an identity based on misleading appearances is given prominence in her collection of poems, *Faceless,* in which she explores the theme of the mask and its multiple possibilities for inventing and re-inventing the self. The traumatic experience of a woman who undergoes a face transplant, after her dog had mangled her face in its attempts to awaken her from a suicidal sleep, becomes the *mise en scène* for subsequent poems where the poet explores the paradox of external camouflage, which, like the chameleon, shifts or changes according to the situation or environment. Like the grotesque statues on display at the *Body Works* exhibit of Los Angeles, where cadavers "stalk the galleries / their skinless arms / bat softballs / row canoes" (33), the faceless woman is unable to recognize herself: "without your face / you could be no one" (32). As argued by Deborah Saidero, the parable of the woman without a face, which Gunn presents in these poems, seems particularly relevant to the traumatic experience of the migrant woman who, because of her geographic, cultural, and linguistic dislocation/relocation, finds herself donning a series of diverse masks to protect herself from derision and prejudice.[8]

Undoubtedly the most enigmatic figure in Gunn's works is that of her father, Leo. In the last cycle of poems, entitled "Departures," which concludes *Mating in Captivity*, the figure of a charismatic father is again reintroduced, as the author turns her attention to an errant soldier that had fought the Second World War from offices in Britain, while his young family awaited his return to Italy. In the title poem of the series, "Departures," the father, seen as one of the Magi, first returns on the day of the Epiphany, where the echo of his shoes on the cobblestones, "Morse code," are encoded telegraphic sounds to fill the void of expectation created by his absence. He appears in full uniform, with pockets full of gifts to ease his conscience, but the poet feels his impatience to move on, "to map new soils; and his eyes blue with other skies" (58). Ironically these are feelings that she will later learn to understand in herself, as predicted by her mother: "It's a matter of genes ... Your father has given you his errant eyes" (16). The religious image of the Epiphany is significant, as it is the one in which the Magi appeared when Christ first made himself apparent to humankind, therefore the trope of the Epiphany in Gunn's poems is about revelation, understanding, and recognition. In the end, the father becomes the central force in "Departures," granting expectation and renewal, but also betrayal and disillusion, ironically defined however by the poet as "safe and familiar" (62), since continuity with the father can only be seen as finite and transient.

Often in works that narrate migratory experiences, the processes of re-appropriating a submersed identity occur following a long-postponed return trip to one's original homeland. In this light, the last poem in the series, "The Return," becomes the catalyst through which Gunn can reconsider her own itinerant wayfaring. After 1976, she returns to Friuli, a land now devastated by an earthquake, wearing shoes manufactured in Canada, designed to protect her from the schism and the modernity of industrial globalization: "Your father's home lies in the midst of a fault, split open by an earthquake ... the air is charged with dust, fear, melancholy, superstition, an industrial disease seeping into the pores" (69). Although Gunn had returned to set foot in the land of her past and be reconciled with generations of ancestors buried under marble gravestones, her real spirit still remained anchored to her vivid experiences of Canada, just as those of her father, whose "feet balanced on two hemispheres" (59), had been tied to his dreams of Italy.

A similar image of feet in balance between two worlds is anticipated by Mary di Michele in the poem "Enigmatico," from her collection *Bread and Chocolate*. Here the eye of the poet is focused on the theme of the double and on the unfathomable fate that not only brought her to Toronto with her parents, but in particular, as she looks back and envisions her mother, on the fact that the mother is enigmatically transfigured into the poet herself: "with one bare foot in a village in Abruzzo, / the other laced into English shoes in Toronto, / she strides the Atlantic legs stretched / like a Colossus" (5).

This woman with her legs spread, like the Colossus of Rhodes straddling the Atlantic, intensifies the concept of a split identity, but at the same time it allows di Michele to identify with a land from which she has not entirely separated. In reality, her two worlds are juxtaposed, as shown by the two opposite pictures of a girl described at the end of the poem. One is dressed in a gypsy costume for the carnival season in Italy, and the other in academic robes trimmed with rabbit fur in Canada. Although the narrator is now a mature woman who has found her voice to describe the past, the impressions we have of di Michele are only visual and in passing: faded photos of a quiet and motionless girl in different poses. She seems powerless and submissive, as required in a patriarchal society, but in this way di Michele invites the reader to look at her while she manipulates the power of speech, highlighting the distinction between one who sees and what is seen and one who speaks and what is expressed. Unlike Gunn, Mary di Michele freely uses Italian words in her poetry.

The return trip to Italy in Italian-Canadian literature has had a diverse significance for many writers over the years. For many migrant writers, the theme of the journey becomes a metaphor for the discovery of the self, as the writers provide a retrospective view about their sense of identity and displacement.[9] Many of the works written by Italian-born authors in the 1970s and 1980s reflected the despair that affected immigrants in discovering the inconsistencies between their expectations and the reality of an Italy in constant change. An example is found in the Italian-language novel *Made in Italy*, by Mary Ardizzi, in which the protagonist, Nora Moratti, returns to Italy to bury her husband, Vanni, a man who in Canada had sacrificed everything, including his loved ones, as a result of his nostalgic desire to return to his native hometown as a wealthy man. Ironically, he returns, but dies suddenly in the underdeveloped village of his youth. On the other hand, as pointed out by Joseph Pivato, Nora, in spite of "her feelings of exile in Canada and of alienation from modern society,"[10] realizes that a return is impossible, because what she remembers of Italy can only exist in the past and in her memories: "I recognize this place but it doesn't recognize me ... My places have remained unchanged only in my imagination and I can possess them only with the imagination."[11]

In the 1970s and 1980s, however, the return trip for the children of immigrants allowed many writers to reconnect to their past and rediscover the families of their ancestors and the places of their Italian heritage. In the works of women of the generation after Ardizzi, the return trip, as in Catherina Edwards's *The Lion's Mouth*, highlights the inner conflict between two cultures and worlds that seem antithetical: Italy, the land of ancestors, and Canada, the spaces of youth and education. Through Canadian eyes, Edwards, in her journey of reverse migration, underlines the tension resulting from a dual identity and language, while her metaphoric trip to Venice brings to the foreground her need to give voice to that sense of diversity or inadequacy that the experience of immigration had created in her. In her metafiction, Edwards narrates her double journey: the first physically, during her summer trips to Italy, in which she describes the gradual evolution and change in her way of seeing and feeling her country of origin, and the second imaginatively, through the creative process of writing. In this second journey she describes her various attempts at writing her novel, while at the same time exploring the world of words, of language, and the ambiguous boundary separating the real from the illusory or fact from fiction: "Why have I spent my winter telling your story? I needed to exorcise my dream of Venice. I needed to rid myself of the ache of longing that I have carried for so long."[12] It is, however, through writing that she is able to recognize herself as whole and bring to light a wider knowledge of the two worlds, both linguistic and cultural, that coexist within her. Edward's life has been a continual crossing of borders and geographic displacements, from Wellingborough in England to Edmonton in Canada, from Venice in Italy to her mother's native city, Lussino, now part of Croatia. Consequently, her personal sense of cultural and national identity is in constant transition and flux. Thus, to create herself through her many writings and give shape and meaning to her memories, she deconstructs her imaginative visions of past and future geographical spaces, especially her ethnic spaces in Canada, in order to acknowledge not only her cultural diversity but above all her strong sense of being Canadian.

Similarly, the fundamental themes of Gunn's short stories and poems, with autobiographical references to the ambiguities of communication, a sense of alienation as a result of ties and obligations derived from her family's errant nature, and a need to define the various masks she creates to overcome her preoccupation between being and appearing, are reiterated in her first two novels, *Thrice upon a Time* and *Tracing Iris*. In particular, as she is travelling through British Columbia and Washington State, Gunn's journeys can be considered further displacements and metaphorical returns to places of birth in search for personal identity. Presented through the genre of mystery fiction, involving a mysterious death or a crime to be solved, her two novels delve into the troubled past of the protagonists, whose lives have been conditioned, because, at a very young age, they had been abandoned by their mother. These novels ambiguously underline Gunn's personal malaise in her search for a familial and cultural heritage, and yet interestingly foreground a quest that is psychologically and culturally resolved in her travelogue, *Tracks*.

In *Thrice upon a Time*, Gunn's search for the identity of a mother, whose baby girl was left adrift in a canoe near Prince Rupert, is narrated in a framed story by detective Paul Evans, responsible for looking into their identity. Newspaper clippings, diary entries, letters, poetry, recorded tapes, and a battered manuscript, part of the sparse evidence available, lead Evans into a web of historical relationships stemming from the Caribou Gold Rush days of Barkerville in the mid-nineteenth century to present-day Porcher Island. The women protagonists of the core story appear to be re-creating an ancient Indian legend, that of Esileh, an infant girl abandoned at the mouth of a river. And it is through this myth that Gunn recounts the matrilineal saga of the split lives of three generations of women, originating with Catherine Steward, who, in the first generation, was forced by a domineering husband to abandon her illegitimate daughter, Sarah, the fruit of a relationship with a Native Indian. In the novel, the myth of Esileh is re-enacted by Elise Slayte, Catherine's great-granddaughter, who, after the death of her parents in a road accident, is given a wooden box full of notes and diaries that inform her of her own abandonment and adoption. She travels back to the island of Porcher, where Sarah, Catherine's illegitimate child of mixed ancestry, began her own family, and where Elise, like her mythological namesake, falls in love with Sarah's grandson, David. They give birth to Gitrhawn, the abandoned baby girl who began the story, thus completing the cycle of *"we are women with an hereditary gene which makes us unable to mother"* (24). In the end, all the reader can perceive is that the fragmented facts narrated are only constructs. Yet, since "one cannot exist in the present without knowledge of the past" (14), Elise recreates and then rewrites her own myth and that of her women ancestors in a manuscript, later discovered by Evans, the investigating police detective. In this way it is through the power of the written word that Elise, in the last generation, deconstructs then reconstructs identity to give visibility to personal female history.

Even in her second novel, *Tracing Iris*, Gunn narrates a horizontal and vertical voyage into the past of the protagonist, Kate Mason, an anthropologist specializing in endangered cultures, in search of Iris, the mother who had abandoned her when she was just a child. Kate travels back to her father's house, looking for clues that could help her discover the enigma behind the mother's disappearance and bring to light artifacts of a vanished civilization, the hidden mysteries. The funeral of her stepmother, Elaine, who Kate later discovers was her mother's older sister, becomes the opportunity to return to the places where Kate had lived as a child, before her forced removal following her father's second marriage. In her will, Elaine had left Kate some property located in Kitimat, a small northern town in British Columbia where Elaine and Iris were born, and an envelope with pictures, notes, recollections, and letters addressed to Kate regarding Iris's childhood. Through Kate, Gunn also travels back to Kitimat, where she herself had resided after her immigration to Canada with her sister, Ileana, to join their parents, who had emigrated from Italy a few years earlier. Autobiographical memories give shape to and fuse with Kate's narrative regarding the two sisters and their particular relationship with their father, to the point that the reader is uncertain about which childhood father is being remembered, Genni's or Iris's: "your memory of him shaped and reshaped until even you don't recognize him anymore? The ghosts linger" (70).

Working with the patience of an anthropologist, Kate methodically begins to piece together all the fragments of her mother's life, starting with the photographs, letters, and other items rediscovered in a panelled cabin behind the Mason home. Fragmentary information from witnesses and friends, unspoken sentences, newspaper clippings, and Kate's own childhood letters to an absent Iris are reviewed through a process of spatial and temporal reorganization. As she picks up the pieces, trying to decipher the colours, designs, and shape of objects, memories of her mother surface and overlap in time and space, giving the reader the impression that Kate manages to revive the past in the present. This permits her to become aware of how her surroundings, her family, lovers, and friends take on new meanings as they are unveiled through the transformations of memory.

In reconstructing these memories, and pressing her father, Joe, for answers, Kate discovers that Iris had abandoned a son born from a liaison with a lover who, unable to convince Iris to leave her family, murders her with one of Joe's guns. Her father, a well-known policeman, had tried to protect both Kate and himself from this tragic incident, especially since he had shot Iris's lover. Kate, now destitute, frustrated, and full of rage, is unable to do anything but take note of an inevitable truth. Her new gained knowledge of a so-much-desired and sought-out mother, now lost forever, was ironically highlighted in the early stages of the novel with a lexical play in the semantic field of motherhood – "mother goddess, mother figure, motherfucker, mother love, mother earth, mother tongue ... motherless" (59) – that creates a subtle linguistic grid between the real world and the need to understand and redefine with words Kate's ambivalent feelings about the loss of Iris. In reality, her mother had not abandoned her, but the events narrated disclose how truth can be arbitrarily created. All that remains is only acceptance of a past filled with disillusionment, abandonment, violence, and misunderstanding. "There's no turning back, not really, the past an expanding universe," thinks Kate; "There's only moving ahead, reinventing herself" (246).

Moving ahead and reinventing self, in fact, is what Gunn tries to do in the novel *Solitaria*, where she moves beyond the wilderness of Kitimat and the shores of western Canada to return to Italy to rediscover her matriarchal roots in Puglia. Gunn's re-appropriation takes place slowly but fluidly, as she crosses diverse cultural borders towards a vision of the world that is not limited to multicultural acceptance but rather embraces transcultural interaction. In *Solitaria*, the descriptions, motivations, and consequences of the return trip have been transformed and enriched with new and interesting nuances, which also involve the fluid adaptation of literary forms and genres that freely cross borders to create new spaces for self-expression. Gunn has often pointed out that a journey also implies a return: "If you are away for long enough, the familiar place seems slightly altered, discordant, like a melody played in the wrong key. With each return, there is a new memory, until the landscape is littered with it, superimposed on the place and the people."[13] Gunn is inevitably attracted to these transformations of memory, seen as dangerous because constantly changeable, since what remains of the past can no longer be found in the present. Here, in the imaginary journey through Puglia, in search of places, myths, superstitions, and beliefs of her mother's ancestors, Gunn turns the journey into many stories within other stories, which in a transcultural aesthetic fluidly adapt to different but interchangeable literary genres: mystery novel, historical fiction, family saga, diary, autobiography, but also intertextual postmodern fiction and reality show. The story unfolds through the character of David, an Italian-Canadian university professor from Vancouver and Gunn's alter ego. He returns to Puglia with his mother, Clarissa, a famous international opera singer, to discover the truth about the mysterious death of his uncle Vito.

The body of Vito Santoro had been unexpectedly discovered by construction workers while they were demolishing the ruins of a deserted mansion in Fregene in 2002, but the brothers and relatives only learn of his death through a popular Italian television program *Chi l'ha visto?* The program, which recreates the scene of the murder, focuses on the garden of the mansion, with close-ups on the excavation site where the body was buried. Since Vito's sister Piera, for the past fifty years, had always proclaimed that Vito had abandoned his wife, Theresa, and his son to flee to Argentina, the Santoro family members are bewildered and upset. As a consequence, they gather in Italy from different parts of the world in a search for answers, but their arrival causes nothing but renewed age-old family conflicts and resentments. They all have their own grudges and discordant stories to tell, but, like many narrators, they are unreliable, because they can only reveal fragments of truth that reflect their own personal prejudices regarding events of the past.

In the many flashbacks that make up the novel, the past surfaces primarily from the point of view of Piera, the matriarch and self-named *solitaria*, who, locked in her room, refuses to speak to anyone, except to David, her beloved nephew. Through David, who also serves as mediator for the various stories, the reader learns of the difficult childhood of the Santoro family, of their life during the fascist period, when they survived on rationed bread and wild dandelion weeds, and of the immense debts faced by Vito, a charming but ambiguously deceitful older brother. With the hope of rescuing the family from further financial losses, Piera, at a very young age, sacrificed herself to marry Sandro Valente, a wealthy and noble older magistrate. Now a widow, Piera bemoans the fact that the family has failed to respect and understand her commitment to assist her siblings, even if this meant using questionable methods. In addition, her husband's impotence had rendered her life miserable and lonely. Unaware of her hardships, however, the family maintains that Piera has been too critical, arrogant, and despotic. Even the villagers make the sign of the cross when passing her house, indicative of the dread that she transmits.

As the various stories evolve, the reader becomes aware of Piera's self-delusion and the consequences of her actions on others. For example, after Sandro's death, Teresa had spent her life "serving that ungrateful witch" (137), while Clarissa secretly feels that "Piera was a monster" who "tortured that poor wonderful man," and, had Clarissa been allowed to marry Sandro herself, they would "all have had different lives" (134). In a similar manner, all the siblings find fault and personal offence in the way they were treated by their sister. Nonetheless, it is through the various voices that overlap the conflicting and often-manipulative tales of Piera that Genni Gunn explores the unreliability of memory, creating a novel of malaise, in which truth is always a bit out of reach. Amidst these passionate Italian intrigues, David tries to filter the information obtained from all the protagonists, for he is perhaps the only one able to decipher the messages and to understand the situations. The stories of his aunt Piera, assisted by an album full of pasted photos, documents, pieces of material, letters, and other jotted notes, allow him not only to shed light on the death of Vito, but also to unearth the silences that concerned his own birth, his unmarried mother, and their migration to Canada. Slowly, the past comes to light, as the reader begins to suspect the truth about the ambiguous relationship between Piera and Vito, their drama of incest, and the violent reaction of their father, who eventually murders and buries Vito to save their family honour. In particular, the denouement foregrounds the joyless relationship between Piera and her husband, Sandro, who, rather than accept the birth of an illegitimate child, forces David's biological mother, Piera, to abandon her baby and send him to Canada with Clarissa.

In the complex plot of *Solitaria*, the theme of incest remains a thorny element; nonetheless, it becomes one of the threads that determine the outcome of the novel. By examining the role of women and how they interact within the dynamics of this southern-Italian family, with its secrets and misunderstandings, Gunn explores in depth, as underlined by Val B. Russell in her review of the novel, "the burdens and expectations placed on girls from a very young age to sacrifice oneself for the family unit." In establishing a parallel between the various stories of women, Gunn shows how many women are still abused because of patriarchal power, yet these stories also serve to illustrate how experiences and memories, even of the same events, are very different from each other. From this perspective, the example of Piera is significant, because from the position of victim she ultimately becomes a symbol of transformation and of the regenerative capacity of women.

Moreover, by juxtaposing historical realism during the fascist years in Italy with fictive biography of the Santoro family during the postwar years, Gunn demonstrates a creative ability that crosses literary and cultural borders to enhance and give voice to her multifaceted Italian heritage. Even the inclusion in her account of Italian superstitions like the *malocchio*, next to the reclaiming of Italian legends like that of the Roman *Bocca della Verità*, seen as "fascinating" by the reviewer Elizabeth Bricknell, can be envisioned as a way to go beyond the simplistic identification of Italian beliefs as silly superstitions. Rather than undermine the cultural aspects of these rural Italian beliefs, she attempts to understand their deeper meanings. Thus, through the adoption of cross-cultural perspectives in *Solitaria*, Gunn has gone beyond cultural boundaries, allowing her to recognize a plurality of voices that speak to each other without prevarication.

Like Gunn, Mary di Michele also returns to Italy, but this time to Friuli, in a transcultural search for self and personal identity. She had originally seen her 1972 return trip to her mother's village in Italy as a *rite de passage*, whereby she could come to terms with her Italian heritage. Yet, in retrospect, the spiritual, psychological, and cultural consequences of di Michele's many returns are evident in her later works, in particular in *Flower of Youth*, where a trip to Casarsa della Delizia, Pier Paolo Pasolini's hometown, is transformed into rewriting and metamorphosis. While the political and cultural background of the fascist period remains as backdrop, as in *Solitaria*, di Michele travels through the problematic past of Pasolini as a youth, trying to understand his surroundings, his life, his interior turmoil, and how these must have conditioned his writing. At the same time, she mirrors herself in his pursuit of creativity, passion, understanding, and perhaps even forgiveness. Framed by a short prologue and epilogue, which describe di Michele's personal pilgrimage in search of the places where Pasolini began *La meglio gioventù*, his poetical autobiography written in the Friulan language, the poems which make up the largest section of what di Michele calls a "novel in verse," entitled *Impure Acts*, are "based on the experiences, feelings, Pasolini describes in the memoir" (*The Flower of Youth* 84). Written in the first person as if they were a transcription of his memories, these poems focus on his homosexual longings and encounters, often in conflict with his religious beliefs. Eventually these relationships led to a scandal that forced him to leave the village of Vilute, where the poems are set, but in *Flower of Youth,* autobiographical references to homosexual and religious anxiety in Pasolini's memoirs are skilfully translated and transformed by di Michele's poetic sensitivity. And it is through these rewritten verses that di Michele's trip to Casarsa not only becomes an additional return home from Canada, but also the symbolic return of Pasolini to a Friuli that had forced him into exile. Perhaps what unites the two poets is their artistic temperament. She feels a strong empathy with Pasolini's sense of alienation, frustration, and guilt, but also with his determination to become an established writer and film director after his resettlement in Rome.

Further evidence of di Michele's empathy can be found in the poem "The Return," in which Pasolini recalls his return to Casarsa after having completed his studies in Bologna at the beginning of the war:

> I woke up to that crisp and candid air I knew
> so well, to the smells of fire, of polenta,
> of the iron pot, my grandmother stirring it.
>      All around I heard breathing:
>
> horses, humans, the whooshing wheels of bicycles.
> Bells were calling us to vespers, voices
> rose in prayer, in gossip, the incredible
>      cadence of that tongue,
>
> the open vowels, the sibilants, fricative,
> strangely familiar inflections, flowering,
> deflowering my ear. (27)

The impression is that di Michele is transferring her own memories of an Abruzzi home onto the nostalgic memories of food cooked over the hearth by Pasolini's Friulan grandmother. Like the poet, di Michele also hears voices with "strangely familiar inflections," which could have been either in Friuli or Abruzzi, announcing future "joys" and "triumphs" for the two poets, but also "enormous losses and extraordinary consolations" (28). Pasolini fills the volume with his strong presence as he becomes support and inspiration for di Michele. She, on the other hand, has translated and transformed his Friulan memoirs into English, but only after having filtered them through her own mother tongue, Abruzzese. In this way, di Michele, moving beyond any restrictive ethnic borders and through a process of transculturality, is able to internalize Pasolini's spaces, his thoughts and his voice.

The latest book by Genni Gunn, *Tracks: Journeys in Time and Place*, also moves beyond spatial, cultural, and linguistic borders. It is not only a travelogue, but also an inner journey into the realm of memory linked to a rootless migrant family in constant motion. In her introduction, she writes: "Sometimes I travel to enter a state of alienation – an anonymity that reflects my restlessness, my need for diverse landscapes, new experiences, not as flights to and from anything, nor as quests, but as journeys into the unexpected, through which even the ordinary becomes extraordinary" (8). Memories of her numerous voyages to diverse geographical and social spaces across Canada, Cambodia, Mexico, Hawaii, Myanmar, and Italy are juxtaposed with unexpected childhood memories of her family and sister, Ileana, as Gunn travels in a search "for that elusive imagined *home*, like trying to catch a mirage on a hot desert highway, the illusion shimmering and enticing" (7).

Subdivided into four chronological segments entitled *Escap(ad)es, Explorations, Discoveries*, and *Excavations*, which symbolically exemplify Gunn's restless compulsion to travel through diverse terrains, the essays in each section, enriched with photos and visual images, not only explore the magic and allure of foreign places, but also inquire into the mystery of family ties and concepts of origin and destination. From Sunday outings across northern forests near Kitimat, where her father had been relocated after the war, to excruciating non-stop, on-the-road band tours throughout Canada, Gunn, in the first segment, digs into a past that offers the reader an autobiographical and visual background to many of her earlier published works. Furthermore, the errant natures and artistic fervour for painting and music of both her parents come to the foreground, qualities that Gunn herself has inherited and skilfully used in her works. Her fascination with the destructive/creative forces of nature, for example billows, caves, volcanoes, and ruins, described in the second segment of the book, provokes a sense of awe, but also becomes symbolic of a creative energy generated by her escapes into the unknown, "a constant attraction/distraction" (9), through which everything is relived and renewed.

In the poetic and narrative works of Gunn, the protagonists have always moved in a frustrating and painful search for family and identity. Incredibly, in her travelogue, the two sisters have been able to rediscover one another, not in Italy or even in Canada, but through affection and reconciliation in a foreign country: "My imagined utopia is almost palpable, just out of reach, a receding horizon, spurring me on, inviting belief in magic, in the spiritual world" (113). In *Tracks*, the question of how identity is shaped by movement and displacement is symbolically depicted in a series of mixed-media paintings done by Ileana Springer in Myanmar. Two specific examples of the series, titled *Displacement, Identity* and *Spaces of Desire*, are on the cover pages of Gunn's books *Faceless* and *Solitaria*. Ileana states that, in these various works, she was "examining identity and the loss of it when we move country to country," because even if "the immigrant moves towards the fantasy of a better life – the space of desire – the loss of identity causes new problems" (110). Both these paintings contain references to music, railway tracks, and utopian gardens to be reached either with an outstretched arm or through a far-seeing imagination. Even the painting *Origins*, reproduced in black and white in the book, creatively depicts three women who represent the past, the present, and the beginnings of a new future, symbolically surrounded by trees whose roots delve deep into the earth and spread beyond imagination.

## CONCLUSIONS

In the end, it is the capacity of Genni Gunn, Caterina Edwards, and Mary di Michele to understand, rewrite, and relocate themselves through diverse artistic forms and geographic dislocations as they track their spaces of desire. Gunn's roots, like those of the trees in her utopian gardens, extend beyond immobility and conformism. Edwards, in her non-fiction narrative, *Finding Rosa*, moves beyond her concern with a split identity to also embrace her Welsh and Croatian spaces, while di Michele rewrites herself through the musical and poetic inspirations of Enrico Caruso and Pier Paolo Pasolini. According to Arianna Dagnino, what distinguishes contemporary transcultural authors from those writing a "literature of mobility" is specifically their flexible, "neonomadic attitude when facing issues linked to displacement, rootlessness, nationality, cultural allegiance and identity." In their most recent works, Gunn, Edwards, and di Michele fluidly move across borders and cultures as they reinvent identity – thus demonstrating all the characteristics of the trancultural writers analyzed by Dagnino – writers who intentionally aim "at being culturally and/or geographically dislocated, or 'dispatriated,' in order to gain a new perspective: on the world, on different cultures, on humanity, and, ultimately, on themselves."[14] Genni Gunn, in fact, whose genes are similar to those of her nomadic family, and Caterina Edwards and Mary di Michele have ultimately and freely crossed geographic, social, linguistic, and cultural borders in their search for personal identity, not specifically as Canadian or Italian-Canadian but as professional writers and women of global modernity.

## NOTES

1 Welsch, "Transculturality," 200.
2 A central contribution to the field of transculturalism and migration in Canada is the work done by Klaus-Dieter Ertler and Martin Löschnigg at the Centre for Canadian Studies in Graz. They edited *Canada in the Sign of Migration and Trans-Culturalism: From Multi- to Trans-Culturalism*.
3 De Luca, "Transcultural Encounters," 19.
4 Dagnino, *Transcultural Writers and Novels*, 115.
5 De Luca and Saidero, "Esperienze di scrittura migrante," 40–1.
6 The term is taken from Linda Hutcheon's essay "A Crypto-Ethnic Confession," in *The Anthology of Italian-Canadian Writing*, edited by Joseph Pivato. Hutcheon underlines how her maiden name, Bortolotti, had been secretly hidden in the folds of her married name.
7 Saidero, "Le maschere dell'io," 90.
8 Ibid., 88.
9 Pivato, "The Return Journey," 169–76.
10 Ibid., 171.
11 Ardizzi, *Made in Italy*, 125. The translation from the Italian is by Joseph Pivato.
12 Edwards, *The Lion's Mouth*, 179.
13 De Luca and Saidero, "Esperienze di scrittura migrante," 41.
14 Dagnini, "Transcultural Writers," 9.

## BIBLIOGRAPHY

Ardizzi, Maria. *Made in Italy*. Toronto: Toma Publishing Inc., 1982.

Bricknell, Elizabeth. "Review of *Solitaria* by Genni Gunn." *The Winnipeg Review* (2 Feb. 2011). http://www.winnipegreview.com/wp/2011/02/solitaria-by-genni-gunn (accessed 12 September 2014).

Dagnino, Arianna. *Transcultural Writers and Novels in the Age of Global Mobility*. West Lafayette, IN: Purdue University Press, 2015.

– "Transcultural Writers and Transcultural Literature in the Age of Global Modernity." *Transnational Literature* 4, no. 2 (May 2012): 1–14.

De Luca, Anna Pia. "Transcultural Encounters in Re-Inscribing Identity: European Memories and Ethnic Writing in Canada." In *Europe – Space for Transcultural Existence?* edited by Martin Tamcke, Janny de Jong, Lars Klein, and Margriet van der Waal, 195–206. Göttingen: Universitätsverlag Göttingen, 2013.

De Luca, Anna Pia, and Deborah Saidero. "Esperienze di scrittura migrante a confronto: le testimonianze di tre scrittrici canadesi di origine friulana." *Oltreoceano* 2 (2008): 33–47.

di Michele, Mary. *Bread and Chocolate*. Ottawa: Oberon Press, 1980.
– *The Flower of Youth*. Toronto: ECW Press, 2011.
Edwards, Caterina. *Finding Rosa: A Mother with Alzheimer's, a Daughter in Search of the Past*. Vancouver: Douglas & McIntyre Publishing, 2008.
– *The Lion's Mouth*. Edmonton: NeWest Publishers Ltd, 1982.
– "Where the Heart Is." In *Palinsesti Culturali: Gli apporti delle immigrazioni alla letteratura del Canada*, edited by Anna Pia De Luca, J.P. Dufiet, and A. Ferraro, 27–35. Udine: Forum, 1999.
Ertler, Klaus-Dieter, and Martin Löschnigg, eds. *Canada in the Sign of Migration and Trans-Culturalism: From Multi- to Trans-Culturalism*. Frankfurt am Main: Peter Lang, 2004.
Gunn, Genni. *Alternative Visions* (opera libretto). Montreal: Chants Libres, 2007.
– *Faceless*. Winnipeg, MB: Signature Editions, 2007.
– *Hungers*. Vancouver: Raincoast Books, 2002.
– *Mating in Captivity*. Kingston, ON: Quarry Press, 1993.
– *On the Road*. Ottawa: Oberon Press, 1991.
– *Solitaria*. Winnipeg, MB: Signature Editions, 2010.
– *Tracing Iris*. Vancouver: Raincoast Books, 2001.
– *Tracks: Journeys in Time and Place*. Winnipeg, MB: Signature Editions, 2013.
Hutcheon, Linda. "A Crypto-Ethnic Confession." In *The Anthology of Italian-Canadian Writing*, edited by Joseph Pivato, 314–23. Toronto: Guernica Editions, 1998.
Maraini, Dacia. *Devour Me Too* (poems). Translated by Genni Gunn. Toronto: Guernica, 1987.
– *Travelling in the Gait of a Fox* (poems). Translated by Genni Gunn. Kingston: Quarry, 1992.
Pivato, Joseph. "The Return Journey in Italian-Canadian Literature." *Canadian Literature* 106 (Fall 1985): 169–76.
Russell, Val B. "*Solitaria* by Genni Gunn." http://www.hercircleezine.com/2011/09/01/solitaria-by-genni-gunn (accessed 10 September 2012).
Saidero, Deborah. "Le maschere dell'io: identità transculturale nella poesia italo-canadese." *Oltreoceano* 3 (2009): 87–93.
Welsch, Wolfgang. "Transculturality: The Puzzling Form of Cultures Today." In *Spaces of Culture: City, Nation, World*, edited by Mike Featherstone and Scott Lash, 194–213. London: Sage, 1999.

# Peasant Boots, Dancing Boots: Assimilation and Hyphenation in Vera Lysenko's *Yellow Boots* and Hiromi Goto's *Chorus of Mushrooms*

*Jolene Armstrong*

In this chapter I will first examine the problem of assimilation in Vera Lysenko's Ukrainian-Canadian novel *Yellow Boots* and then follow this reading with a comparative analysis of Hiromi Goto's Japanese-Canadian novel *Chorus of Mushrooms*. This comparative study explores the conflicts with changing ethnic identity, memory, and old-world customs, the condition of women in immigrant communities, and the role of women in navigating hybrid ethnic minority cultures and mainstream Canadian society. I hope to demonstrate that the methodologies of Comparative Literature are well suited to exploring the languages of ethnic minority texts within the context of world literature in English.

When Vera Lysenko published *Yellow Boots* in 1954, it followed one of the first English-language histories of Ukrainians in Canada, her *Men in Sheepskin Coats: A Study in Assimilation*, published in 1947. Lysenko's third book, *Westerly Wild*, appeared in 1956. Vera Lysenko was a first-generation Ukrainian-Canadian, born to Ukrainian immigrant parents in Winnipeg, Manitoba, in 1910. She is one of the first Ukrainian-Canadian women to have attended and graduated with a bachelor of arts from the University of Manitoba in 1929, after which she worked as a teacher, nurse, journalist, social historian, playwright, poet, and translator. She wrote under the names Vera Lysenko (changing her name from Lesik to Lysenko in order to make her name sound more Ukrainian) and Luba Novak. Her novel *Yellow Boots*, while generally assumed to be at least semi-autobiographical, portrays a family that is radically different from Lysenko's own family. Given Lysenko's interest in both Ukrainian culture and social history, the novel reads like a cultural history of the Ukrainian immigrants in Manitoba during the first and second wave of immigration from Ukraine. The novel is rich in ethnographic detail and cultural scenarios. It also traces the process of the assimilation of immigrants, as they try to negotiate the fine balance between retaining the culture of their homeland while becoming full citizens of their new country.

Lysenko was an early feminist and worked throughout her career to promote the status of women, and, as Lisa Grekul points out in her book *Leaving Shadows: Literature in English by Canada's Ukrainians*, Lysenko "anticipated the emergence of multiculturalism and feminism, years before either movement became firmly entrenched in public discourse on identity in Canada" (34). Unfortunately, Lysenko's pioneering efforts to raise the status of women and minority ethnicities would be overshadowed by concerns about a perceived communist sympathy in her writing, in particular in her social history, *Men in Sheepskin Clothing*. Strangely, it was the lack of an overt statement denouncing communism – Soviet control of Ukraine specifically – rather than any actual statements in favour of it that landed Lysenko on a blacklist of communist sympathizers in the years following 1946 and the defection of Igor Gouzenko, as well as the McCarthy communist witch hunts occurring south of the border. Further, a McMaster University professor by the name of Watson Kirkconnell felt that, because Lysenko did not outline communist affiliations of many Ukrainian-Canadian cultural organizations, she must naturally be a sympathizer. Lysenko's response indicated that she felt that Ukrainians in Canada were more concerned with their lives in Canada than with the politics of a distant motherland (Campbell). Nevertheless, the accusation clung to Lysneko's literary career at a vulnerable time, and her work was subsequently relegated to the dusty corners of Canadian ethnic literature. The almost-forgotten novel *Yellow Boots* was rescued from oblivion in 1992, when it was republished by Edmonton's NeWest Press and the Canadian Institute of Ukrainian Studies, long after Vera Lysenko's death in 1975.

The novel uses the device of a neglected daughter of a large, rural Bukovynian[1] family to illustrate the way of life of early Ukrainian immigrants in the 1920s and 1930s. Lilli, who is actually named Oksana, but whose name is all but forgotten by her parents, who view their small, sickly child as more of an inconvenience than a family member, embodies the challenges and opportunities that are at times culturally specific to the Ukrainian immigrants, and at other times symptomatic of the gender inequalities of the time period, as well as the difficult economics of the time, and finally the isolation of early farm life on the Canadian Prairies. When the novel opens, the unnamed protagonist is gravely ill and being sent home by her aunt and uncle. At the age of six, she had been lent out for five years by her parents to her aunt and uncle as free labour. As she travels by jigger, piloted by a section hand by the name of O'Donovan, readers also meet the new schoolteacher, Ian MacTavish, who is also being delivered by this rather unconventional method of travel to the town of Prairie Dawn in Manitoba. It is the spring of 1929. No one expects the girl to live, but the scene allows a certain contextualization – from an outsider's point of view – of the Ukrainian farmers of the area. The two men assess the condition of the girl and comment upon her size (small for her age, likely older than she appears) and the fact that "it's hard to tell about some of these immigrants' children. They don't always keep a record of births" (5). Additionally, her hands are observed as calloused, rough, "more like a labourer's than a girl's" (5); O'Donovan adds, "riding up and down this line, on these homesteads I've seen young girls doing tasks grown men would do among us" (5). The outsider's assessment of the Ukrainian immigrants is surprisingly unflattering in a novel written by an author who hoped to show the Ukrainian settlers in a better light. However, perhaps that is exactly what Lysenko had hoped to achieve: O'Donovan and MacTavish, as Anglo-Scots-Irish representatives of dominant Canadian ethnicity, are outsiders, and their outsider status is revealed in their comparison between what "they" (the Ukrainians) do versus what "we" (the Canadians) would do. What has yet to be revealed are the harsh conditions that Ukrainian immigrants – indeed many immigrants – faced in terms of the disparate economic reality of financially viable farming during this era. Rather than condemning the Ukrainians of Prairie Dawn as a harsh and uncaring people, readers are to understand the conditions of the immigrants, who, despite being observed in the 1920s in the novel, are working as the pioneers did thirty years earlier. As Ian MacTavish writes in his diary: "Today I have learned something of the cost of settling our country. These sheepskins who settled here with little assistance from our government had little to sustain them in their pioneering life except their conviction: 'Free land and strong hands open the door to the future for our people'" (61).

As the novel continues, readers learn, somewhat unbelievably, that during the five years that their daughter has been sent away to work, her parents have forgotten her name, and refer to her as "Gypsy." Again, the light in which the immigrants are portrayed is anything but flattering, as the young girl remains nameless until she is given a name on the first day of school by Ian MacTavish. Nevertheless, the family's dis-ease around their daughter is fraught with ancient beliefs rooted in old-world superstition. Readers eventually learn that "Gypsy" (or Lilli, or Oksana) is described early in the novel as having "been attended by misfortune" (16) since birth, resulting in the family, at times, referring to her as "Luckless" (16). As the novel progresses, more information is gleaned about the unfortunate circumstances of Lilli's birth. Born the third daughter, when Anton Landash, her father, had so desperately wanted a boy to further his aspirations as a landowner, Lilli is given the nickname "Gypsy" for a band of gypsies that happened to have passed through town on the day she was born. Further, she was a small baby, a feature that only inspired further disappointment in her father: "Not much of anything... A gypsy brat" (18).

Finally, it is revealed that Lilli's birth is also coloured with superstition in that she "had been born at the twilight hour, and was clothed in a caul, for which reason Grandmother Yefrosynia had predicted that the child would have second sight" (65). So, while her birth as a female was already inauspicious for a farmer who already had plenty of daughters and was in need of more sons to provide labour for the farm, she also brought with her the folk beliefs and superstition assigned to those born with a caul. While generally such individuals are regarded as good luck, and although she does not exactly display the ability of second sight, the unusual power and ability of this small girl appear to be too much for the Landash family to cope with: "It was true that Lilli possessed many curious powers" (65).

When the girl miraculously recovers from her illness, she proves to be a good worker on her father's farm, and a large section of the book is dedicated to detailing her coming of age, as the town and family move through the seasons of the year and of life. The scenes detail spring festivals, the duties of harvest and the preservation of food, marriage, death, and finally the near-miss of an arranged marriage for Lilli that her father brokers with a man with a terrible reputation as a brute. Lilli escapes the impending ordeal with the help of Ian MacTavish, and the remainder of the novel takes place in Winnipeg.

Once Lilli arrives in Winnipeg, she does what many unskilled and uneducated women and men do: she works in a factory. She also joins an ethnic choir, as she has always enjoyed singing and possesses a natural talent for singing; she even has a chance at becoming a concert singer, a career she rejects in favour of singing folk songs and working as a dressmaker. Eventually, she marries the Austrian choirmaster, Matthew Reiner.

Toward the end of the novel, Lilli returns to Prairie Dawn while she is on tour with the folk choir, and she is shocked at the transformation of the town and its people in such a short time. Worried at first by her family's potential reaction at seeing her again, she is soon welcomed by her mother and father. To Lilli's surprise and disappointment, it seems that the Ukrainian immigrants of Prairie Dawn, including her own family, have completely embraced "Canadian" styles of dress and furniture, even dispensing with cumbersome customs and traditions in favour of a more generically Canadian way of life: clothing ordered from a mail-order catalogue; a modern stove in place of the old clay and wood ovens. As her mother entrusts her with the care of the yellow boots, it becomes clear that it will be up to Lilli (now remembered as having been named Oksana at birth, but preferring the name Lilli) to preserve the traditions in song and dance and story as relics of a bygone time. However, despite the reader's trust in Lilli to be a faithful preserver and curator of these traditions, it is also clear that their place in day-to-day actions and beliefs has now been relegated to that of museum status. They are relics, and can only be revived in an artificial manner, through performance and ritual. They are no longer the lived experience of a people.

Much like her first book, *Men in Sheepskin Clothing: A Study in Assimilation*, this novel, too, is a study in that process – the pains and sorrows, and sometimes the joy, of a people forced by the circumstance of history and immigration to take up a new life, and eventually a new language and culture, and finally a new identity. Lysenko's novel resists the temptation to make the old ways too nostalgic; after all, women in particular were subject to rather rough treatment, as is keenly depicted in Lilli's early years. Further, the immigrants are often depicted as outsiders; the only way in which the outsiders can become insiders is to assimilate. Some of the transformations are considered good and are indicative of modernization in general; other transformations draw attention to cultural loss and homogenization, and, by the end of the novel, the reader should be questioning whether or not multiculturalism is a truly attainable ideal, or merely a utopian ideology, a failed social experiment. As Lilli wonders early in life, "am I a gypsy, Granny?" (29), she draws attention to the essential homelessness of the immigrant, who must shed one identity for another and somehow make a new place home while maintaining enough of her former identity as not to be lost – and therefore forever homeless. In the process, traditional songs, foods, dancing, and articles of clothing become the signifiers of culture, the anchors to which an immigrant might secure herself, as she navigates the new and unfamiliar world she finds herself in. The yellow boots in the novel function in that manner.

About two-thirds of the way through *Yellow Boots*, Lysenko makes the distinction between "Peasant Boots and Dancing Boots" in the title of one of the chapters (171). Perhaps knowingly, Lysenko is demonstrating to the reader the way in which various cultural objects function as both practical objects and aesthetic artifacts, not only in the novel but in the immigrant experience of adapting to life in a new cultural environment. As artifact, the yellow boots referred to in the title function as a link between past and present, between one generation and the next, between Ukraine and Canada. The yellow boots are both a practical object and an expression of traditional belief, whose original meaning remains intact while in possession of Lilli's mother and when worn by Lilli's sister Fialka to get married; however, the status of the boots as practical object, and their ability to ensure the continuation of specific cultural beliefs and practices, is broken when the boots are given to Lilli, even though their survival as cultural objects is likely more secure in her care. The practical and symbolic meaning and function of the boots is complicated by the transplantation of both boots and people from Ukraine to the Canadian prairies.

Archaeologist Andrew Jones explores the interconnection amongst "history, memory and identity," and asserts in his book *Memory and Material Culture* that "things help societies remember" (5). He bases much of his argument on the theory that "artefacts are the only class of historic event that occurred in the past but survive into the present" (4), providing an authentic link to the past, and as such can be "re-experienced" (4). Memory is the result of the interacting fields of mind, body, and world, and memory based on experience and knowledge is gained through "embodied engagement with the world and is dependent upon contingent interactions amongst brain, body and world" (10). Memory then is "a process of pattern re-creation" (11); Jones asserts an essential relationship between the brain and body in the creation of memories, and, by extension, identity. According to this view, "memory is effectively sedimented in the very movement of the body" (11). Further, "bodily memory constitutes the ground for individuals to perceive themselves as discrete and continuous entities," providing a sense of constancy and orientation in the world around us. There is also a relationship between body memory and cultural practices. Our habitual body movements also "incorporate the correct usage of extrabodily instruments and objects" (12). Jones proposes that "objects cannot be treated purely as symbolic media; rather the materiality of objects is best seen as impinging on people sensually and physically at a fundamental level ... physical traces of past events ... aids to remembrance" (19).

Also useful to this examination of the boots in the novel is the notion of the memory trace, first proposed by Freud as the notion of objects as "physical traces of memory" (Jones 20), an idea that was expanded upon by Walter Benjamin and later by Jacques Derrida, for whom "the trace evokes the absences of full and present meaning" (20). For the purposes of my argument here, objects shall be considered physical traces of past action, whereby they physically embody memory. The use of the word memory in relation to objects such as the yellow boots enables me to describe the relationship between the object and the people who created and used the object: as Jones says, "objects provide the ground for the humans to experience memory" (22). What Jones is developing is a strategy for interpreting objects whose context of production and use may be to greater or lesser extent missing; in other words, his strategy is specifically useful in archaeology, or when, in the case of the novel, there is both a physical and temporal gap large enough to cause a lapse in memory, for an object to fall out of use, for the owner to forget the object. In the case of reading the material culture of a novel such as Lysenko's *Yellow Boots*, the context of the production, people's remembering, and use of the object in question is made explicit through the narrative. However, his argument for how these objects can be "read" is still pertinent in the way in which Jones's line of thought enables a deeper understanding of the object's transformation through time and space as the boots immigrate with the people from Ukraine and transfer from one generation to another. Both cultural context and the passage of time function to transform the boots' meaning and function throughout the course of the novel. It is in this aspect of Jones's theory that objects do not simply stimulate a retrieval of information about the past, but rather enable people to recall the past through a "process of sensory experience, by inferring the presence of past events" (24), that they function in their ability to evoke remembrance" (25). The act of remembering is dialogic in its core, and as an act of remembrance, the objects' presence as a memory device for both the mother and Lilli in the novel already suggests that they are no longer practical objects, but sensual, nostalgic artifacts that link present and past, Canada and Ukraine.

The first time the boots are mentioned in the novel, Lilli and her mother, Zenobia, are taking a lunch break after spending a morning working in the garden under the hot sun. At the best of times, the relationship between Lilli and her mother is strained and awkward, owing to the inauspicious circumstances of her birth, the father's disappointment that Lilli had not been born a boy, and the fact that Zenobia is better able to recognize Lilli's usefulness around the homestead than she is able to recognize her as a child first, as Lilli is uncannily good at gardening, baking, and cooking. It is out of this reluctant respect for the child's obvious talent and usefulness on the homestead that Zenobia is willing to divulge the story of the yellow boots to Lilli, when Lilli asks, "Mother, how did you come to marry father?" (69).

Zenobia responds to Lilli's question by stating, "[y]our father married me because I had a new pair of yellow boots"; Zenobia describes the boots, handcrafted by her father, as "made of the finest leather, soft as a stocking, tall as my knee, yellow as gold" (69–70). Zenobia recalls that she walked twenty miles to a dance in a neighbouring village, and "those yellow boots of mine attracted many eyes ... bounding and leaping, whirling, they sang out as I stamped and glided about the room, and seemed to say, 'Look at my new boots! Look at my boots!' Who could resist such boots? And then – Zenobia sucked in her breath at the memory of it – then my boots caught the eye of Anton Landash, a handsome young man of the district ... He came to me, seized my wrist and whirled me off – my yellow shoes dancing all the while ... It was the beginning of our courtship, for we were married six weeks later. Yes Lilli when I put on those yellow boots, I never dreamed how far they would take me" (70).

For Zenobia, the yellow boots are not simply practical objects to protect the feet; they are recognized as works of art, for, as she tells Lilli, her father was an artist – people came from miles around to have him make boots. As works of art, Zenobia cherishes them as both aesthetic and nostalgic objects; she feels that "as long as she had the yellow boots, she would not lose contact with the girl she had once been" (70). For Zenobia, the boots function primarily as memory traces, as a way in which to access not only her past, but also past spaces, for they not only belong to her life as a young girl, but also to her life in Ukraine, in the Carpathian Mountains. She holds on to the boots, as the narrator points out, "relegated now to the obscurity of an immigrant's trunk" (70), in order to maintain a link to her past, in order to maintain her memory of her life and identity. In contrast, for Lilli, the boots become an imaginative site, a "magic talisman in a fairy tale ... symbolical of peasant craftsmanship" (70). To Lilli, they symbolize something she cannot access, "all those old things – which she felt belonged to her somehow" (70). But these things that she believes belong to her "somehow," do not really belong to her. These are her mother's memories, her mother's experiences. Lilli, who was born in Canada, can only appreciate them via her mother's own nostalgia, as much as she might long to appropriate them for her own use, for her own memories, and for her own identity. In reality, all Lilli can do with these "old things" is act out what she believes were their original purposes and try to give them new life in a new context. And act them out she does, as a singer/performer in a travelling show.

Later in the novel, when Lilli is becoming a young woman, she prepares for the midsummer's eve celebrations. She casts a love spell by floating a wreath of flowers in the creek in the direction of the family farm of her sweetheart, Vanni, and, placing a lump of sugar in the stream, speaks charms in order to make him fall in love with her. In the morning she packs a picnic and the yellow boots and goes out to meet Vanni. At one point during their meeting, Lilli takes out the yellow boots and puts them on, much to Vanni's admiration. It is hard not to see this action as an attempt on Lilli's part to re-enact her mother's own courtship with Lilli's father. Lilli tells Vanni the story of the boots in the old country, and Vanni suggests that they dance in them now. Lilli even sings a song about the yellow boots, how charming they are, how they sing and take their wearer far. The entire scene with Lilli's contrived desire to re-enact the love scene of her mother and father's meeting is an act, because that is all that Lilli can do in her contemporary context. In this new country, in which traditions and culture are being remade by the moment, the presence of the yellow boots points to the nostalgia for the old country that has been passed on to the children who have never even been to the old country. But as artifacts, they allow Lilli to reimagine their meaning and purpose; they allow her to access through her body's ability to dance, sing, and therefore remember ancestral values and memories. Nevertheless, their status changes from artistic, but practical, object to symbolic artifact when Lilli tries to integrate the boots into contemporary times. Rather than becoming the love token she wishes them to be for herself, as they were for her mother, they become an anachronistic costume piece that reminds the people who see them of the old days, reinforcing the idea that they belong to times past and places far away.

For example, the boots are also featured at the wedding of Lilli's sister Failka, as part of her wedding attire. While much of the ceremony is sombre, signifying the loss of Fialka as daughter to her family and the sadness of the trials she will face as a wife, after the formal part of the wedding is over, the true function of what the yellow boots symbolize takes over as the village celebrates the happy union. Throughout the novel, the village schoolteacher, Ian MacTavish, functions as a sort of participant/observer/anthropologist. He takes a keen interest in the culture and language of the Bukovinian people of the village, and Fialka's wedding becomes a rare opportunity for him to witness the old customs that are fast disappearing as the Bukovinian immigrants modernize – Canadianize. Throughout the wedding chapter, MacTavish makes several observations about the behaviour and dress of the people, including remarks about the yellow boots worn by the bride. For him, they symbolized "a vanishing world." In his estimation, "it was possibly the last time these boots would dance in their proper surroundings; they were like actors playing their last role" (136). The boots stand in contrast to the other signs of modernization observable around him – the sound of the threshing machines, for example, or the factory-made dresses that many of the women wear. Even MacTavish laments that "for these embroideries ... they will substitute the machine made variety; for handmade costume, the dress from the mail-order house; for the peasant poetry of their ceremonies, the cut and dried responses of a civil ceremony" (136).

MacTavish's observations draw attention to two details that are remarkable here: the fact that the surroundings are changing – in other words, the cultural context in which the boots signify their proper meaning and purpose – and that the boots are like actors – which signifies that, to a certain extent, the boots have already passed into the realm of artifact, relic of days gone by. As Jones pointed out, artifacts help societies remember, and, in this instance, the yellow boots serve as reminder to the members of the community of who they are via who they once were. They are able to do this because who they are has already changed from who they were. In other words, as Derrida pointed out, the boots' presence points to the absence of their full and present meaning.

Absence and loss are notable throughout the novel. Zenobia laments frequently that people are changing and forgetting the old ways. Later in the novel, when Lilli returns home after being absent for several years, Zenobia describes for Lilli how the times have changed: "If I could tell you, how shameful what the girls did with those carpets, embroideries, dress up and laugh! Costumes wear out and new ones not made. Girl will not spend time to embroider when she can order from mail order catalogue, so cheap, so fine! ... No more Killims on wall, all, all take off and instead put on wallpaper, curtains from mail order, range where was old stove, so good to bake bread!" (331). Lilli assures her mother that she still loves the old, which is quite true, since she has dedicated her life to learning, performing, and thereby preserving the folk songs of her people, and those of other immigrants to Canada. In this reunion scene between distanced mother and daughter, Zenobia gives Lilli the yellow boots to take care of, and Zenobia asks her, pleads with her, "[y]ou will save these things for our people?" (332). The boots bring back many memories for Lilli, but it is clear in this instance that the boots have been completely relegated to cultural artifact. Their ability to trigger memory comes from Lilli's own bodily memory of wearing the boots during her wild dance with Vanni, of watching her sister dance with abandon at her wedding, and by imagining her mother's own courtship with Lilli's father. They allow her to access the past, and maintain some continuity to the present, but they can no longer function in the old-world way.

In the final appearance of the yellow boots in the novel, Zenobia's hope that the yellow boots will bring her daughter a good husband comes true, in a way. After Lilli has returned to Winnipeg, she displays the boots for her music teacher and suitor, Matthew Reiner. She describes for Matthew their beauty, highlighting their handmade craftsmanship, explaining their family significance. Then she exchanges her modern pumps for the boots, examines herself in the mirror, and begins to execute a wild and lively dance, flying and whirling about the room, finally collapsing in a chair, breathless but exhilarated. She comments to Matthew, "I suppose every immigrant family has something like these boots – a talisman which they brought from the old country – a pair of boots, a shawl, a carved wooden chest, a samovar, something to get out at family gatherings to symbolize their heritage" (349). While Lilli's greater objective was to seduce Matthew with the beauty of the boots, the way her mother seduced her father so many years before, Lilli inadvertently reveals her own unacknowledged awareness of the artifact status of the boots. While she might desire to hold on to the "old," to preserve it and maintain it, that is all she can do, for the times have changed, for better or for worse, and the embroideries, the carpets, the ovens, and ceremonies have fallen by the wayside in favour of less culturally distinctive, more contemporary, culturally homogenous styles. If people want to access their cultural roots, then they have to rely on performances given by people like Lilli; they have to visit museums or open their musty immigrant trunks and dust off the relics and talismans.

Sociologist Herbert Gans has named the cultural process identified by Lilli as "symbolic ethnicity," a process in which assimilated immigrants develop a nostalgic relationship with old-world objects or traditions which are only manifested on particular occasions, such as celebrations or holiday events. Gans attributed "symbolic ethnicity" to immigrants of white European origins, who can easily assimilate into North American society. He questioned whether it could apply to visible minorities, who cannot so easily assimilate into white society. In my reading of Hiromi

Goto's *Chorus of Mushrooms* (1994) I will consider this problem in terms of the author's use of languages.

In his study of ethnic minority writers, Joseph Pivato has argued that we must recognize that "as immigrants and the children of immigrants these authors were speaking for the first time about their communities ... they have become the authority voices for these immigrant communities" ("Representation of Ethnicity" 153). Pivato continues by explaining that "the use of a new language such as English or French in the new country by the immigrant writer or his/her children presents other problems of translation. Representing the immigrant experience (originally lived in Italian or in Japanese or in Bengali) in English changes the experience. The ethnic minority writer is involved in the process of translation, in the search for the authentic presentation of the experience" (154).

Canadian ethnic writers have approached this in different ways, calling on the dominant language in which they are writing to bend to certain effects, or using language in novel ways to reflect this experience. For instance, Hiromi Goto, in her novel *Chorus of Mushrooms*, uses Japanese words, sentences, and phrases to capture the untranslatable. Even so, the fact that much of the Japanese text in Goto's novel is written phonetically in the Roman alphabet indicates that it has already undergone one transformation. It seems that the cultural transportation of language and cultural practice, whether from Ukraine or Japan, undergoes a type of translation by virtue of its relocation in space and time. While the language and cultural practice point to the original, they cannot be anything but an interpretation because of the translation process in relocation.

Goto's novel highlights how quickly the loss of cultural connection can happen when, in just one generation, there is complete loss of ability to speak or understand Japanese, traditional foods are totally unfamiliar, and the central character must go to extremes to relearn her ethnic culture. Goto emphasizes this loss through language, stories, and food, as Muriel is brought back into Japanese by her grandmother Naoe through the secret sharing of traditional food, as well as Naoe's rebellion against anything not Japanese, even though she reveals to the reader that she is perfectly able to speak and understand English: "*Ohairi kudasai! Dōzo ahairi kudasai.* Talk loudly and e-n-u-n-c-i-a-t-e I might be stupid as well as deaf. How can they think a body can live in this country for twenty years and not learn the language? But let them think this ... I mutter and mutter and no one to listen. I speak my words in Japanese and my daughter will not hear them. The words that come from our ears, our mouths, they collide in the space between us" (4).

The issue of language use, language loss, and the gulf between the generations of immigrants is crystalized in this revealing scene. The image of words colliding in space describes the gulf of experience, the loss that can be experienced by immigrants, as generation by generation, the people assimilate into the dominant culture. While it is true that Naoe's daughter Keiko can understand her, both women refuse to be flexible in their language use. This inflexibility poses the two extremes of alienation for the immigrant. The result is Naoe's eventual wandering off, and Keiko's eventual emotional breakdown, in which the reader realizes that Keiko's connection to the unrelenting steadfastness of her mother to Japanese functions as a sort of identity anchor, which counteracts Keiko's pursuit of the generically Canadian. Naoe's stubborn adherence to her Japanese roots grounds her family in what would otherwise be a lost legacy. The third generation, that of Muriel, will need to make a conscious effort to recover lost cultural and linguistic traditions – which readers understand that Muriel undertakes and achieves – or else they will likely assimilate fully to the dominant Anglo culture. In this scenario, both language and food are used to heal Muriel's mother when she suffers from severe depression. The method is radical, for Keiko/Kaye has renounced her Japanese heritage, including language and food, even going so far as to ensure that her own daughter should not know these things, in favour of assimilation into what she believed was a middle-class, generic Canadian identity. Re-immersion in the cultural flavours and sounds of her youth works to gradually bring her to a place of health and acceptance of her dual identity. This healing is brought about by a daughter, Muriel, who must learn her Japanese heritage from strangers and books now that her grandmother is gone and in order to retrieve her mother from severe disconnection and depression.

Interjecting the minority writer's mother tongue into the text is one method of presenting the linguistic and cultural struggle that ethnic writers portray in their writing. A contrast to Goto's free and rebellious use of untranslated Japanese text is found in a novel such as Lysenko's, in which the language used to write the main narrative is written in "proper" Queen's English. To contrast the narrative voice, which to a certain extent reflects the outsider's perspective, or the dominant Anglo view of the immigrants, Lysenko has her Ukrainian characters speak in broken, accent-inflected English. The unintended consequences of this choice are worth mentioning. In representing a group of people already perceived as outsiders – as othered by virtue of their cultural origins, their language, and their religion – speaking in broken, fragmented English is fraught with the danger of reinforcing stereotypical views of the immigrant as less intelligent, immature, unworldly, and inferior in comparison to the insiders who possess fluency and ease of articulation.

For instance, it isn't long after Lilli begins going to school that she becomes aware of her awkward speech and her inability to communicate all that she is thinking and feeling. She confides in her teacher, Ian MacTavish, who at the beginning of the conversation observes that "she had a thought which struggled like a captive bird for liberation from the dark recesses of her mind" (Lysenko 55). Her reply captures the core of what it means to be assimilated: "Oh, I like to learn to talk like you. My tongue lame like old horse" (56). Lilli assumes that fluency equals full belonging. For her, questions of citizenship and identity are felt only on the subconscious level. But there is also a nascent acknowledgment of citizenship when Lilli observes that, for her brother Petey, "life will be good. He will be a real Canadian" (58), referring to his ability to assume the culture and speech of the dominant group. Moreover, when she is unable to perfectly mimic MacTavish's speech, she laments: "I am so stupid ... All the time, mistakes!" (57). Here it is revealed that fluency translates into perceived intelligence and thoughtfulness. If one is unable to communicate effectively in the language, then one is assumed to be less intelligent; even more disturbing is the observation that the speaker herself begins to believe that. So, while Lysenko chose to portray the accented and imperfect speech of the Ukrainian immigrants, as they struggle, not only with the land, but also with the dominant culture and finding their place within it, she risks diminishing the intelligence of the people that she wishes to elevate in her detailed cultural fiction.

In order to balance this view, to which Lysenko is likely not insensitive, she endows Lilli with a preternatural intelligence that is closely linked to nature and the land. She is frequently described as "wild," "untamable," "like a very young, wild deer, the big eyes, proud, shy" (56). Unfortunately, because of Lilli's desire to learn, to be educated in the modern system, and because of MacTavish's support of her desire, her innate knowledge of nature is replaced with book learning, language cultivation, singing lessons, fashion designing, and other modern notions of knowledge. Indeed, despite her innate abilities to work with the land and nature, Lilli comments to MacTavish, "[s]ometime I dream I am in city, free, happy, can live how I like" (58). For Lilli, the oppression of cultural tradition is somehow conflated with living in the traditional manner. On the one hand, there is comfort in the traditions of the past, but on the other, those same traditions can prove to be oppressive, stifling (as in the case of a child who is denied the opportunity to go to school, and instead has to work). Yet, the double bind that most immigrants face is the way in which to maintain the best of their cultures and blend them with the best of the new culture. How does one adopt one, without completely losing sight of the other? How can one pick and choose one's ethnic origins, which according to these Canadian literatures strike at the heart of identity?

Communicating the barriers posed by language and (un)translatability is one challenge for minority writers; reconciling duelling cultural identities is another. For example, Goto also presents the emotionally difficult struggles with which Japanese-Canadians contend within *Chorus of Mushrooms*. Goto's novel forges new territory for ethnic Canadian literature in general, and Japanese-Canadian literature specifically, in that it extends the discussion of ethnicity beyond the Second World War period and the post–internment camp experience of Japanese Canadians, most importantly and critically examined in Joy Kogawa's novel *Obasan*, and Roy Miki's poetic examination in his body of poetry. We remember that one of the problems in *Obasan* is the silence that Naomi endures, unable to speak about the abuse she suffers.[2] By contrast, in Goto's novel, the war is distant, known only through story, for talkative Muriel – or as she comes to be known, Murasaki – who is born in Canada, does not speak Japanese and is the product of her mother's aspirations to total assimilation and Canadianization. Her experience relates to how immigrants must continue in the second half of the twentieth century to find a harmonic balance between, on the one hand, maintaining, or in Muriel's case relearning, ethnic traditions and, on the other, language fluency and assimilation into mainstream Canadian culture. What Goto's novel articulates in a more sharply critical way is the fact that Canadianization is a somewhat slippery notion. What does it mean to be Canadian, stripped of one's ethnic roots? Is this possible? What does a Canadian look like if you are a visible minority?

In Lysenko's novel, Lilli is able to change quite easily into a new identity. She masters the language sufficiently, and discovers that she is an excellent performer, both as a natural singer and an actor. In her career as a performer, she slides seamlessly into the identities and costumes of any number of ethnic performances. She can do this because she is Caucasian. Goto's Keiko, Muriel, and Naoe face a different challenge that is part and parcel of the paradox of multiculturalism, in that they are not Caucasian. Their task of balancing ethnic identity against an "official" and majority culture is doubly troubled in that, by virtue of a happenstance of birth, they must work harder, assimilate more fully, to be accepted, to belong.

So, while Kaye effectively sheds all detectable elements of Japanese-ness from her lived experience, to the point that she suffers a complete breakdown when her stubbornly Japanese mother disappears, she is constantly fearful, constantly aware, of her own – and even more pointedly, of her daughter's – otherness.

For example, this critical aspect of difference is mentioned early in the novel when Muriel/Murasaki laments that her mother, Keiko, didn't tell tales like her grandmother did, that "the only make-believe she knew was thinking that she was as white as her neighbor" (29). Murasaki's comment reveals her mother's complete denial of her Japanese-ness in order to achieve full assimilation, but also points to the impossibility of achieving that. Naoe describes Keiko as "a child from my body, but not from my mouth. The language she forms on her tongue is there for the wrong reason. You cannot move to a foreign land and call that place home because you parrot the words around you. Find your home inside yourself first, I say. Let your home words grow out from the inside, not the outside in" (48).

Indeed, Keiko's attempt to become fully Canadian misses the mark, in that her assimilation of Canadian-ness is superficial. She buys "pork chops and steaks and macaroni and cheese" (49) in an attempt to erase the tastes and smells of Japanese cooking and therefore the culture. In one of the novel's anecdotes, Murasaki describes her mother's misguided approach, as she recalls the time in her life in which she "came to realize that the shape of my face, my eyes, the colour of my hair affected how people treated me. I never felt different until I saw the look crossing peoples' faces" (175). The crisis of identity comes to a head when Muriel is given the lead role of Alice in the *Alice in Wonderland* operetta at her school. Understandably, Muriel is thrilled that she has been chosen. Things go sideways for Muriel when, at the school meeting, the teacher pulls Kaye aside to address the issue of the colour of Muriel's hair: "Alice is the story about an English girl, you know. An English girl with lovely blonde hair. And strictly for the play, you understand, Muriel will have to have blonde hair or no one will know what part she is playing. You simply cannot have an Alice with black hair" (177). Kaye, eager to comply and prove her Canadian-ness by her willingness to erase all otherness, suggests dying Muriel's hair. Muriel, upon hearing her mother and teacher discuss this approach, is horrified: "Me with blonde hair and living the role of Alice? In Nanton? What could my mom be thinking? I would look ridiculous and stand out like a freak" (177). Accordingly, Muriel changes her mind and rejects the opportunity to play the role. Kaye's uncritical willingness to transform her daughter's physical identity, and acceptance that this transformation is indeed necessary, is contrasted sharply in this scene with that of the mother who storms out of the meeting when it is suggested that her daughter needs to lose weight for the role in the play. The implication is that mothers, rather than sacrificing their children's identities, should protect them. Why couldn't Alice have black hair? In Kaye's defence, her attempt to assimilate her daughter is sincere, if misguided. As Muriel observes, "she made my life easy and easy to assimilate" (68), but it is at the expense of what she calls her "malnourished culture" (99), the cultural impoverishment, the gutting of the family's Japanese identity.

As Muriel's realization of her difference grows, so too does her desire to differentiate into an authentic self, as opposed to the superficial make-believe identity that Kaye tries to construct. As Muriel says, "[i]t was hard growing up in a small prairie town, the only Japanese-Canadians for miles around. Where everybody thought Japan was the place they saw when they watched Shogun on TV" (121). For Kaye, the choice in identity is either/or – there is no blending or hyphenation, as Muriel explains, "she chose the great Canadian melting pot and I had to live with what she ladled" (175). In addition to the fiasco with Muriel's hair colour, her growing self-consciousness about her difference is handed to her by the dominant culture in other ways. She remembers: "You know what I hated most? Valentine's Day. Those press-out Valentine booklets that everyone bought, including me, and I knew what I would always get. At least five of them. Every year. I hated it. The press-out Oriental-type girl in some sort of pseudo kimono with wooden sandals on backwards and her with her hair cut straight across in bangs and a bun and chopsticks in her hair, her eyes all slanty slits. I knew there was something wrong about me getting these cards. What the picture was saying. But the words weren't there to speak out loud yet and all I could do was feel this twisty thing inside me" (62).

Her realization dawns on her slowly and comes from outside as well as inside her own family, that, like the salamander that she and Joe examine in the mushroom barn, "it's very far from home" (106). Yet, for Muriel, this is home, the only home she knows. For her, and inevitably her mother, the trick will be to reconcile the hyphenated identity. While Kaye tries to erase the hyphenation and the "Japanese," Muriel will work to reinsert it alongside her Canadian one. It turns out all along that Naoe knew the necessity of the hyphenation best: "Who is that silly Chinese philosopher? The one who fell asleep gazing at a butterfly and dreamt that he was a butterfly dreaming that he was a philosopher. And when he woke up, he didn't know if he was a philosopher or a butterfly. What nonsense. This need to differentiate. Why, he was both, of course" (44).

In both *Yellow Boots* and *Chorus of Mushrooms*, the first generation born in Canada to immigrant families is faced with being caught between two cultures: the culture of the old country and that of the new. This generation is faced with the dilemma of choosing if and how to balance the two competing forces. Both Muriel/Murasaki and Oksana/Lilli must remake the cultural traditions of their ancestral homelands, which neither character is familiar with first-hand. The challenge for this generation is to find ways in which to make these traditions relevant and meaningful within each generation's context, to make the easing of one tradition into the identity of the other natural, comfortable, and real.

For Lysenko, the inevitability of cultural transformation and loss, for assimilation and homogenization of culture difference, is unavoidable, but not entirely lamentable. In the end, Lilli is depicted as being able to both preserve and remember, through the preservation of folk songs, but also of objects such as the yellow boots, while modernizing and embracing the multicultural – albeit mono-cultural – middle ground of the urban centre. Distinctive cultural practice, ethnic difference, becomes something that is played out in rare ceremony, performance, or in the private sphere of the home. In public, difference becomes erased for something more homogenous. In the end, Lilli is able to appropriate the mannerisms and dress of the urbanite woman, while reserving the wild outbursts of ethnic dance for private moments, or of song during her ethnic performances. While she helps people to remember their old ways, she is also part of the process of forgetting. The more that these old ways are relegated to the realm of artifact and performance, the more distant they become for the people to whom they belong.

## NOTES

1 Located in the northeastern Carpathian Mountains and plains, variously under the purview of the Ottoman Turks, Austro-Hungary, parts of which came under Soviet control, but is now divided between Ukraine and Romania. It is a multi-ethnic region, including German, Polish, Ukrainian, Romanian, and Jewish citizens. Prior to the eighteenth century, the area was referred to as Moldavia. The area was viciously fought over during the Second World War. The Bukovinian people comprised a large number of eastern European immigrants to Canada during what is known as the "first wave" of immigration, between 1891 and 1914.
2 Silence and the silencing of women is a problem encountered by ethnic women writers. When Lysenko was accused of being a communist sympathizer for her *Men in Sheepskin Coats*, it was an attempt to stifle

her criticism of social conditions. Ukrainian-Canadian writer Janice Kulyk Keefer explains her own encounters with the silencing politics of Ukrainian factions in Canada in "The Sacredness of Bridges."

## BIBLIOGRAPHY

Campbell, Sandra. "Lorne Pierce of the Ryerson Press and Vera Lysenko's *Men in Sheepskin Coats* (1947): Resisting the 'Red Scare.'" http://hpcanpub.mcmaster.ca/case-study/lorne-pierce-ryerson-press-and-vera-lysenko-smen-sheepskin-coats-1947-resisting-red-scar?page=1 (accessed 9 August 2015).

Gans, Herbert J. "Symbolic Ethnicity: The Future of Ethnic Groups and Cultures in America." *Ethnic and Racial Studies* 2, no. 1 (1979): 1–20.

Goto, Hiromi. *Chorus of Mushrooms*. Edmonton: NeWest Press, 1994.

Grekul, Lisa. *Leaving Shadows: Literature in English by Canada's Ukrainians*. University of Alberta Press: Edmonton, 2005.

Jones, Andrew. *Memory and Material Culture*. New York: Cambridge University Press, 2007.

Kogawa, Joy. *Obasan*. Toronto: Lester & Orpen Dennys, 1981.

Kulyk Keefer, Janice. "'The Sacredness of Bridges': Writing Immigrant Experience." In *Literary Pluralities*, edited by Christl Verduyn, 97–110. Peterborough: Broadview Press, 1998.

Lysenko, Vera. *Men in Sheepskin Coats: A Study in Assimilation*. Toronto: Ryerson Press, 1947.

– *The Yellow Boots*. Edmonton: NeWest Press, 1992.

Pivato, Joseph. "Representation of Ethnicity as Problem: Essence or Construction." In *Literary Pluralities*, edited by Christl Verduyn, 152–61. Peterborough: Broadview Press, 1998.

SECTION FOUR

# LOOKING BACK AT TRADITIONS

"Many years later, as he faced the firing squad, Colonel Aureliano Buendia was to remember that distant afternoon when his father took him to discover ice."

That is the opening sentence in *One Hundred Years of Solitude* by Gabriel García Márquez, a Colombian novel read in Spanish or English translation in many Comparative Literature courses.

The human mind can behave in strange ways. While we may be trying to live (or die) in the present moment, the mind can take us back to a previous event and reveal an association from our subconscious. Many of the contributions collected here are oriented toward possible future directions in Comparative Literature; nevertheless, several also look back to past practices in our reading habits. The two chapters in this section consider the past and our relationship with tradition.

**BIBLIOGRAPHY**

García Márquez, Gabriel. *One Hundred Years of Solitude*. Translated by Gregory Rabassa. New York: Avon Books, 1970.

# Comparative Literature in Canada: A Case Study

E.D. Blodgett

When Paul Morris, the treasurer of the CCLA/ALCC, graciously invited me to talk to you about Comparative Literature in Canada as I knew it, I hesitated, of course. Did I really wish to venture again into that curious history, and how should I go about it? Would it mean asking once again what comparative literature might be, a question you have no doubt seen frequently raised. English and other languages are, by contrast, profoundly comforting: they know what they are, despite all the internal debates about the curriculum. After all, Proust belongs to French, Dickens to English, and nothing (or everything) belongs to comparative literature. It is a fate that certain scholars have thrived on.

Having once agreed, I proposed a title which was mutually satisfactory. To give the matter some shape, I have chosen a fifty-year period between 1960 and 2010. I chose this period for two reasons: first, because it follows roughly the years of my career, and because it follows the trajectory of the former Department of Comparative Literature at the University of Alberta, the department with which I have been associated. It has a prehistory in two phases, both of which were European. The first student who earned a PhD at the university was a German immigrant named Kuonrat Haderlein (1971), who went on to have a resounding career at the University of Saskatchewan. The other European aspect of our prehistory is, of course, more enduring, inasmuch as it belonged to the tradition in which our discipline took its rise.

As we know, Goethe's notion of *Weltliteratur* was developed in the early years of the nineteenth century, and the idea of comparative literature came into being in the same decades in the lectures of Claude Fauriel (the Sorbonne) and Jean-Jacques Ampère (Collège de France). Why this period and not earlier? one might ask. Because the idea of the monolingual nation possessed a powerful prestige that it acquired during the post-Revolutionary and Romantic periods. Latin as a dominant language standing above national languages did not begin to fade until the seventeenth century. Moreover, the political and other tensions of the emerging nationalisms of the period foreshadow the latent tensions of the century that culminated in the international catastrophes of the two world wars. International solutions were proposed in the United Nations and, on the regional level, by the European Coal and Steel Community (1951), which became the basis for the EU. This was a period that was even more troubled than the post-Revolutionary period, and it is hardly surprising that one of the literary responses manifested itself in the first of the Acts of the Congresses of the ICLA/AILC, *Venezia nelle letturature moderne*.[1]

I mention all this because it is our contemporary point of departure. In the 1950s Europe was the dominant project, politically, financially, and culturally, especially its unity, and it continued to be so in the 1960s when I began its study. As a young graduate student, my larger passions were Greek grammar, Old Provençal poetry, and German mysticism, certainly legitimate, if blithely innocent, areas of exploration for someone at that level. Of course, my horizons quickly expanded, and when I went to inquire about the comprehensive exams, I was told there would be a two-hour oral, all organized around the literatures of Europe and Classical Antiquity. I was handed a book divided into two columns. On the left page were primary works, arranged under six headings: Antiquity, the Middle Ages, the Renaissance, Neo-Classicism, Romanticism, Modernity. On the right-hand page, each period contained a list of the major studies devoted to the primary material. Dismayed, I asked whether there were written exams to fall back on if one did not fare well. The answer was firmly in the negative, but you were given two chances to pass it. A year later, when I was ushered into the exam room, I saw facing me six specialists from other departments. Although my heart sank, I passed. Not long after, I received an offer from the University of Alberta.

You will have noticed that I have spent a fair amount of time discussing historical contexts. As a student, and in my early years at Alberta, in a far-away city of which few know anything, such contexts had not impinged greatly on my imagination. The program gradually expanded until, in 1970, when it became the first department in Canada offering both graduate and undergraduate courses, we had a faculty distribution in the formative years as follows: our chair from Serbia, a member from Belgium, another from Spain, another from Poland, another from Israel, and two from the United States. It should be added that our strongest support in the Arts faculty came from two professors with doctorates from the Sorbonne, one of whom, E.J.H. Greene, had published *T.S. Eliot et la France*, which tacitly placed the approval of French comparatism over the department. Europe was the focus, and perhaps too much so, for in the fall of 1970, during the October crisis, an inspector in the RCMP arrived in the office of our Serbian chair, demanding information on all the aliens in the department. He was coolly sent to see the vice-president. The world, however, had arrived, and I suppose we had already acquired the reputation for political radicalism, a quality particularly noticeable in students of comparative literature, that Leo Strauss and others mention in passing.

Two years later, I began my career as an administrator, by becoming acting chair during the absence of our Serbian chair. As I drove him to the airport, I raised a topic I had already raised several times. Not being sure how much I could rely on German mysticism, I needed advice. The one response I got was: "Don't put anything on paper you would not put in the party newspaper." Sound as this counsel was, it did not help when the advisory committee to the department, consisting of the five department chairs of English and the other languages, put a motion at a faculty meeting that the department be placed in quarantine until the credentials of all staff members had been thoroughly examined for their validity. The motion was withdrawn when the dean advised them that such a motion could be used against them. This, combined with the arrival of the RCMP, made it evident how precarious our presence in the university was, and so it continued for another thirty years, more or less, until we lost department status.

I suppose we might have been more firmly anchored if our founder had been Northrop Frye,[2] which was the good fortune of the University of Toronto. Our fate was, I think, more interesting. It was dispensed by the Serbian member of the department, M.V. Dimić, who was a fine example of the Clerk of Oxenford of whom Chaucer says: "gladly wolde he lerne and gladly teche." Although he did not possess either Frye's rootedness in Canada nor his public éclat nor the international reputation acquired through his book on Blake, his literary theory, and his studies of the Bible, Professor Dimić was more firmly rooted in comparative literature, which resulted, inter alia, in our hosting one of the congresses of the ICLA/AILC. It was a necessary orientation, but it was perhaps too broad, at least in the early years, for the university. When we were organized into a department in 1969, something as emphatically interdisciplinary as our field was in a certain measure a scandal. Most departments in the humanities were concerned with specialization. There were strict rules about the honours programs, and as such they meshed very well with the Faculty of Education, which had difficulty knowing where we fit. That was our first obstacle. Compared to subsequent ones, however, it was manageable, despite a second attempt, not long after the first, to have the department closed down. The other obstacles to our survival were for the most part more subtle and, hence, more difficult to find a way to address.

Two of the most powerful events to move through American universities in the late 1960s and the next decade was French poststructuralism and, concomitantly, feminist theory. Literary theory can almost always be counted on to receive a positive reception. After all, as Frye's *Anatomy of Criticism* does, it appears to give a kind of patina of objectivity to fields that seem to foster nothing more than the reading of novels, while the rest of the academy is striving to add to the useful sum of knowledge with things such as cures, graphs of voting trends, and convenient bombs. Theory appeared a fine way to appeal to legislatures and granting agencies by justifying the happy pouring over of Jane Austen. Sadly, the new theory, especially poststructuralism, openly scoffed at objectivity. In fact, in its contestation of power, essentialism, and patriarchal values, it found very fertile soil in the student protests in Paris in 1968, not to speak of the years of protests against the war in Vietnam, particularly in the United States. Its effect was felt less intensely in Canada. This is perhaps because the political and cultural worlds here were concerned, at least as one is given to believe from the news, primarily with the economy and separatism. Hence, in the 1970s, as theory made its way to Canada, mostly through the filtre of American universities, two events dominated Canadian politics: the War Measures Act and the National Energy Plan. The major impact of the former on the study of literature was to weaken the study of French-Canadian literature in English Canada. Canadian Comparative Literature was the major loser.

The sober reception of literary theory in Canada had a number of facets. The first is that members of my generation for the most part remained satisfied with either the Anglo-American New Criticism or *explication de texte*, and so its fuller effects did not come into view for another decade. Theory, it should be remembered, has two bearings. First, it can be sufficient in itself, making use of literary texts to illustrate its benefits, or, as is more common, the literary text remains central, and theory illuminates it in previously undiscovered ways. One of the early proselytizers of Jacques

Derrida in English departments, for example, one who followed the latter tendency, was Paul de Man, who readily demonstrated that literary texts meant nothing, and therefore hardly lent themselves to the kind of psychological analysis they are so often subjected to. The pleasure of the text is to take the reader to the point where sense, particularly a unifying meaning, is undecidable.

The arrival of French theory opened an invisible breach between our department and English over the very issue of theory in translation, and a number of my colleagues pointed out that the French language as used by Derrida, Barthes, and Foucault, for example, was not quite as clear as the translations suggested. This was not a small point, and it became the beginning of the endless territorial disputes we began to endure. It made it clear that theory belonged to everyone, not so much because it was theory, but because it was available in English. The same is true for reception theory, which originated in the German language. By raising the issue of translation, it prompted a debate that would initiate serious reconsiderations in the following decade of what the academic role of comparative literature might become.

As to the challenge of Cultural Studies, I think it could be asserted that we did not rise to it with sufficient vigour. This may have been a consequence of the Marxist phobia of Professor Dimić. In any event, its value was quickly perceived by members of the Department of French, who began sponsoring seminars on aspects of Cultural Studies as developed by Stuart Hall at the University of Birmingham. We failed to realize, I think, that this was a field of research that resisted departmental specialization, and that its interdisciplinary character could lend it very well to our field, as well as to theirs. Perhaps our caution, without being so extreme as that expressed by Harold Bloom, surmised some years ago that it might be fundamentally destructive of the study of literature as literature, because of the increasing emphasis on questions such as those of hegemony, power, and the role of the reader as agent. Such questions, however, are not only inevitable, but also have sometimes remarkably interesting ways of opening a text to unseen meanings.

Far from Bloom's other argument, that Cultural Studies are just about political correctness on the one hand, and academic opportunism on the other, our view depended on our generally shared view that either Cultural Studies would be a universal perspective on the study of literature or a kind of instrument to be used like literary theory when considered to be most effective in elucidating a text. To choose the latter is, of course, to violate many of the operating principles of Cultural Studies, inasmuch as elucidation is not always, perhaps rarely, the problematizing of texts themselves, which questions what a text is, who controls it, particularly in a classroom, and how it forms kinds of knowledge. To choose the latter, furthermore, was to give the impression that one's field, no matter how avant-garde it may have appeared in the 1960s and 1970s, might be losing its edge.

Nevertheless, Cultural Studies raise yet another problem. For those raised in the European paradigm, it challenges us with crucial questions of power, tradition, and reader practices. What makes, for example, one text more worthy of study than another? What, in fact, is the role of the literary text in cultural formation or, to put it more simply, education? Given the significance of both popular culture and the canon, for want of a better term, how much teaching time should be devoted to either or both? These are questions that, gathered together, amount to asking: What is the teaching of literature for? Given the brief amount of time we have at our disposal in the teaching of a course, how is that time best used? *Ceteris paribus*, these are questions which reach the same level of anguish as Hölderlin's desperate cry: "Wozu Dichter in dürftiger Zeit?" It may be construed that such a sentence that begins in Latin and ends in German, making use of a quotation that assumes you are familiar with it, is a sufficient sign of antipathy with Cultural Studies. Such an assumption is not necessarily valid, inasmuch as Cultural Studies ought to be inclusive. But it also implies something else. Does the classical tradition still have a role to play in contemporary education? If I am to teach world literature, is it to be taught vertically or horizontally? If the latter, what happens to Sophocles? If the former, how do we engage Sophocles with popular literature, or do we rather problematize the text of Sophocles and raise immediately its hegemony in European culture since the Renaissance? It's all very well to argue that it was the political power of Maecenas that gave Virgil the leisure to dictate the *Aeneid*, but in the absence of much popular literature of the time, with the exception of the Greek romances, how *are* we to address its role in Latin literature?

Although these are rhetorical questions, very moving answers to them are proposed in Azar Nafisi's *Reading Lolita in Teheran*, a book that has been unfairly treated as orientalist by some of her fellow Iranians, and that could probably be shown to be a weak response to my questions by a student of Cultural Studies. After all, Nafisi's family was part of Iran's elite, she was given a superior education in Switzerland, England, and the United States, and when she left Iran, she acquired a prestigious position at Johns Hopkins University. She also had, nevertheless, a connection with Marxism and, one might argue, deep feminist sympathies, at the very least. The framework of her book is the teaching of modern English and American in Iranian universities. What her memoir reminds us of is that while a text may belong to a dominant canon, it does not carry any other prestige until it has been suffered. Living with a text and being prepared to suffer torture and death for it confers upon it its canonic value. We might have wanted her to have chosen some texts of popular culture for her students, but she did not. We might wish to believe that her choice was a mark of professorial hegemony that determined the responses of her students, but we would be wrong. In fact, her students took them into their complicated lives and made them their own. It was a process that gave them as readers unusual hegemony, especially for women in a thoroughly misogynistic society.

Anyone who has read Nafisi's book will no doubt recall "the case of the Islamic Republic of Iran versus *The Great Gatsby*" by F. Scott Fitzgerald, the charges laid against it, the brilliant defence, and the triumphant verdict in favour of the novel. The case itself would strike most Western readers as bizarre, but Iran is a special situation, and all of Nafisi's canonized texts become sites initially of ideological firefights over which in the end the imagination triumphs, thus demonstrating that reading only realizes itself as a mental activity when the reader becomes an intensely active agent. As a result, writing and reading become interdependent activities. The defence of *The Great Gatsby* is a radiant response, I believe, to the proposition of Cultural Studies that political oppression and agency are implicitly more readily seen in texts of mass culture. Although the text itself is probably not important, those texts that avail themselves of nuanced analysis of psychological motivation and ethical limitations are the most effective. Hence, Nafisi's book can be read as a significant and moving contribution to Cultural Studies.

That such teaching – within the context of Cultural Studies and without the constraints that Nafisi and her students suffered from – was already being practised in French and English began to pose certain problems for us, problems which have beset us ever since. These were problems, furthermore, that took us to one of the major issues of teaching comparative literature at the undergraduate level. We could not subsist, as all of you know, without the use of translations. I am not going to try to amuse you with the Italian pun, *traduttore traditore*. In many ways it's nonsense: a translator can be wrong, and, of course, no single translation can do justice to a text, but more than one by serious and skilful translators with different objectives do it justice, and this is true even for most poetry. Of course, the original music of a poem cannot be transferred, but it can be suggested. Some rhythms can never really be imitated, such as the rhythms of classical poetry. Most prose, however, responds well to translations, and it never hurts to consult more than one version where possible.

The use of translations, particularly in the Department of English, began to pose problems for us, and it was often difficult to explain to our colleagues that they should, as much as possible, be used in the classroom by those who know the language, so as to enrich the text, even to read it aloud in the original if it is poetry. Our colleagues in English would always make reference to standard versions that had become part of the English canon, particularly of novels and plays. But the use of translation could be abused in surprising ways. One of our colleagues was invited to be part of an MA examining committee on African literature, which involved a translation of a novel in French. She dutifully read all the passages cited, but in French, where she found a sufficient number of errors that the argument of the thesis could be said to be compromised. When our colleague raised this at the exam, the student replied that she had treated the text as if it were in English, and her adviser, an expert in post-colonial literatures, defended her. Such a way of approaching a text is damaging in at least two ways. First, not only is it wrong, but also it leaves the impression that once in English the text *is* English, and its past in another language is quietly erased. Even more damaging, however, is the thoughtless ease in which the English canon is expanded. In those years when translators' names were omitted from the book publication data, the impression that the book was English was only re-enforced.

For us in Comparative Literature, this was the beginning of an intolerable situation, inasmuch as few, if any, of our colleagues in English understood the basis of our criticism. How readily modern drama could now range from Chekhov and Ibsen to anyone else. Nor did it help when Susan Bassnett observed in 1993 in her book *Comparative Literature: A Critical Introduction* that comparative literature had reached the point in its development that it must be considered secondary to translation studies. Fortunately, she saw the error of her ways and recanted in an essay published in 2006, but the damage had been done. Translation Studies, as practised by Belgian and Israeli scholars in the 1980s, is a highly technical mode of intertextual analysis that few of my colleagues in English seemed interested in. Her book, unwittingly or not, opened the door to a general use of translations wherever desired; this could easily prompt a dean to begin to wonder why one might need a Department of Comparative Literature.

The dominant phenomenon of the 1980s and 1990s was the emergence of globalization, a term already invented in the 1960s. Although discussed frequently in the humanities, its primary bearing is on economics, particularly the liberalization of world trade. Despite the eagerness with which departments of English and Comparative Literature embraced it for their own ends, no one should forget its effects on Third World countries, the term McDonaldization rather neatly covering the general business model. Aligned with the business model are the serious effects of homogenization and Westernization on small countries and regions that are drawn to what appear to be the financial advantages of globalization.

Nevertheless, if it is not perceived for what it is, that is, neo-colonialism as practised for the most part by the US, its full negative impact cannot be understood. Departments of English and comparative literature should unhesitatingly take oppositional stances to the damage it is capable of carrying out. That does not mean, however, that it should be ignored, and as Lois Parkinson Zamora remarks:

> the cultural specificity of literary fictions may serve as antidote to current processes of cultural homogenization, and to the perception of homogenization as propagated from critical centers in the U.S. and Europe. For it is surprising how little literary theorists of globalization refer to particular works of literature to ground their generalizations about the leveling of cultures. As intelligent as the discussions often are, they sometimes seem to me to reiterate familiar colonizing trajectories from U.S. and European academic centers to the peripheries: Latin America, Africa, Asia. This, I confess, worries me, for however we choose to structure (or re-structure) our approach to the new spaces of global culture, we will need to continue to direct our attention, and our students' attention, to the specificities of literary texts and their cultural contexts. We will, then, be prepared to measure the dialectics of difference in a world increasingly "globalized." This has always been the aim of the discipline of comparative literature and it continues to be so.[3]

As we know from the most recent report of the ICLA/AILA, *Comparative Literature in an Age of Globalization* (Johns Hopkins Press, 2007), globalization is now on the agenda, as a kind of sequel to the Bernheimer report on multiculturalism (1994). The introduction, prepared by Haun Saussy, makes a number of significant remarks that adjust our understanding of the discipline, and, in fact, lead me neatly toward some of my concluding comments that address the scope of our field, and wonder out loud about the possibility of preparing experts in such a large field that supposes a fair knowledge of the literatures of the world, not to speak of competence in more than the usually accepted three. In other words, globalization poses the question of how we are to continue, an issue that has hovered over Comparative Literature at the University of Alberta for most of its existence. The bibliography on which I was examined when I was just setting forth would now be woefully inadequate, and even the level of language competence, which then amounted to four languages, which were all European, would be clearly insufficient.

Much of Saussy's introductory remarks is devoted to the history of comparative literature, arguing that it is a field constantly in search of itself. While this may be true to a certain extent of English and other literatures, it is evident that they have canons – no matter how subject to change they may be – and that they imply a certain cultural cohesion through their various languages. English can teach the English novel; comparative literature must teach the novels of several literatures, having none – and this is the central point – of its own. Consequently, comparative literature appears to be in a constant identity crisis, fully aware that there may be "no there there." Fortunate indeed is the department or program of comparative literature that does not undergo such crises, but if it did not, it would have little to contribute to the study of literature. Its role seems to be one of regularly creating and managing crisis, as if crisis were the dominant narrative.

By crisis I don't mean something like the subduction of tectonic plates before an earthquake, but rather the sense of a world that is never finished and futures that cannot be predicted. Globalization is simply a contemporary moment of the world, fostering greed in the economic world and something more complex in the world encompassed by literary studies, a pluralistic world, one hopes, of many centres in which the usual hegemonies have a diminished effect. Such a world can no longer follow the model that I was given, in which the European literatures are sufficient. For one thing these are literatures which, if they continue to retain their European cachet, can only foster neo-colonialism. In themselves, however, they are insufficient, and new configurations must be made. It is difficult to imagine how such configurations will unfold, and what kind of critical language will have to be developed or invented that will place disparate cultures on a plane of equality and allow for difference to overcome the desire to establish a *tertium comparationis*. It is equally difficult to imagine how such a transformation will occur without an increase of team research.

To return to the University of Alberta, it was perhaps a blessing that, early in the twenty-first century, the departmental configuration of Comparative Literature was removed, and the surviving unit became part of the division of Interdisciplinary Studies. I fear, however, that such a move was purely administrative, and the challenges of being interdisciplinary were not exactly met. But to think of comparative literature as collaborative, rather than as a group of experts who can offer courses in Romanticism, mediaeval literature, Modernism, etc., is what is now required. The final move that is now about to happen, namely, to transfer the program of comparative literature administratively into the Department of Modern Languages and Cultural Studies, will not rise intellectually to the occasion. Its professors will be subject to the needs of the department for their teaching assignments, and it is unclear how many will wish to take up Cultural Studies along the lines of the Marxism as once practised at the University of Birmingham.

If the driving force of economic globalization is *cupiditas*, it could be said that the driving force of comparative literature is hubris. How many challenges should we rise to, how much should we feel capable of holding within our purview? One of the silly wisecracks that our founding chair used to cast about was: "You name it, we compare it." In our optimistic days, it seemed to fit. Although we all know such optimism is now misplaced, that was part of Professor Dimić's personality, but it had a great deal to do with how the department was shaped. A few remarks are therefore appropriate on who he was and why his name is still associated with one of the university's research institutes. That he was the *rayonnement extérieur* of the department there can be no doubt, and without taking anything from the Centre for Comparative Literature at the University of Toronto, Dimić almost single-handedly put Canada on the international map of research in comparative literature. He was the founding editor of *Canadian Review of Comparative Literature/Revue canadienne de la littérature comparée* (1974–) and among the founding members of the Canadian Association of Comparative Literature/Association canadienne de littérature comparée (1969), which, largely through his efforts, came into existence despite efforts by Canadian colleagues – who argued that the American Association was sufficient – to prevent it. As an immigrant to Canada, Dimić always felt strongly that, when opportunities arose, one should contribute to one's new country. He also brought the world of comparative literature to Edmonton in 1994, when he hosted a conference of the ICLA/AILC, an association that he served as a member of the executive council in a variety of positions. Among the most demanding was his ten-year stint as the coordinating secretary of the editorial committee for the *Comparative History of Literature in European Languages*. Finally, as the director of the Research Institute for Comparative Literature, he organized a number of conferences from 1989 to 1997, among which was a project that was leading toward a comparative history of the Canadian literatures along the lines of polysystem theory.

Of course, his publications were many, and for all these activities he was promoted to the level of distinguished university professor and also made a fellow of the Royal Society of Canada. His energy was enormous, his achievements various, and he might be credited with making comparative literature a viable and internationally recognized field of study in Canada. It was only after his retirement, while he was teaching in Taiwan, that a new dean arrived and peremptorily announced the virtual demise of the department on the Faculty of Arts website. Although the dean did not really follow correct procedures in this, it hardly mattered, and he immediately gave the impression of behaving like any American president. If there is no war going on, find a small Caribbean country and take it over. We were that country. As someone who had worked closely with Dimić since the formation of the department until its end, I would say that he felt more than his usual disgust and anger at the mean-spirited manner with which large institutions are capable of displaying power. Something in him broke, and his post-retirement years in Taiwan, despite what scholarship he kept up with, were markedly despondent years. It's possible to infer, I think, that his immediate, Canadian identity had been removed without the slightest consultation.

But this was not all. The war that destroyed the former Yugoslavia in the early years of the 1990s also took a large psychological toll, as one might expect, in a certain ironical fashion. For, when Dimić came to Canada in the mid-1960s, he was an articulate opponent of nationalism. Not long after the war broke out, however, a fondness for Serbia took hold of him, and he became very active among ethnic Serbs in Canada. This eclipsed the international side of him with which I was more familiar. While everyone knew of his love of Serbian epics, which he could retell with verve and humour, his literary formation in general in Serbia was more significant. It gave him, to an unusual degree, a knowledge of, and openness toward, the literatures of the world, and this clearly left its mark on the formation of Comparative Literature at the University of Alberta. As no one needs reminding, Serbia was historically situated between the Habsburgs and the Ottomans, between Europe and the gateway to the East. It never had, for example, the assurance of a country like France, which could readily produce the first theorists of comparative literature. As far as literary studies were concerned, it was unpretentious, a country that made abundant use of translations and taught literature from an international perspective. It was this global *Weltanschauung* that Dimić brought to our department, which made it, if I may say so, unique among such programs in Canada. For most people such an openness requires a lifetime to acquire. For Dimić it was an innate disposition, as if he were a globalist from the time he went to school.

Thus, his late turn toward nationalism is both easy and difficult to understand, and his disaffection with the university must have had much to do with it. If we put the nationalism to one side, we may discover certain principles that were of value to us and to the field of comparative literature in general. First of all, he was a great believer in diplomacy as opposed to confrontation, the results of which are never predictable. This is because Dimić was also a great believer in coherence and order. Despite all the efforts of scholars of postmodernity to re-order the world, from economics to literary studies, he believed that a possible result might simply be a culture of anarchy. This did not mean he was, therefore, a modernist. He clung to no particular metanarrative, inasmuch as he was more than familiar with the complexity of the human condition. What he understood was the variety of stories we tell ourselves, how they are coloured by the multiplicity of languages and cultures that produce them, and how they form the webs of history we all share in and create. Despite the fact that most of his research and teaching dealt with a variety of romanticisms, it should be said that he seemed to represent the best of the European Enlightenment, deep skeptic as he may have been. In fact, it was just this grain of skepticism that motivated him to continue to extend his horizons. He was, without knowing it, a great believer in the counsel of Hugh of St-Victor's dictum, namely, "Omnia disce, videbus postea nihil esse superfluum." While this may have been possible in the twelfth century, given the state of knowledge in Europe at the time, for us it appears somewhat extravagant. While such a desire may reflect the hubris I have already mentioned, for Dimić it was no more than a desire. He knew his limitations.

Although it may seem I have dwelt on Dimić's character and achievement to an inordinate degree, I have only discussed him because he, the department, and the international presence of comparative literature at the university are so thoroughly intertwined. It may be that the demise of the department and the immanent dispersion of its faculty to Modern Languages and Cultural Studies, without the least notion that it was a part of Interdisciplinary Studies, is symbolic, as if the fragmented world that postmodernity predicts has already taken place. Of course, comparative literature thrives elsewhere in the world, offering differing models of order. Inasmuch as it also thrives on constant self-analysis in its effort to define itself or to prevent definitions of itself, it will continue to mount as many theories as possible and, like Stephen Leacock's famous horseman, ride "madly off in all directions." I am no longer persuaded that such a plan shows much purpose. Because for ineluctable reasons we have collectively chosen, however, to try to learn everything, we have to know how to give up much of our individual ambition. It is now hard to imagine any major undertaking without some sort of teamwork. For example, Dimić proposed to the planning committee of the ICLA in Venice in 2005 the preparation of a dictionary of terms and concepts of poetics, and certainly such a proposal and clear desideratum could not be accomplished otherwise than through teamwork. In fact, most of our activities to date point now in the direction of larger kinds of research that would be beyond the scope of an individual scholar. One such project, developed by the department through the Research Institute for Comparative Literature, was the ambition to write a history of the Canadian literatures through the optics of polysystem theory. The project began in the mid-1980s, continuing with preparatory conferences for a number of years thereafter. Admittedly, the whole project foundered toward the end of these conferences, but Dimić and I were overwhelmed by other matters at the time, and we gradually let it go. Speaking only for myself, I wonder, however, if the actual history would have been written. A near-equivalent was already under way for the literature of Quebec, namely, *La vie littéraire au Québec* (5 vols, 1991–2005), and it is difficult to say how much time this team could have devoted to our project, beyond giving sage advice. Another doubt arose when I was writing my *Five-Part Invention: A History of Literary History in Canada*, as I continually discovered how little English Canadian literary historians were in fact interested in history. But to return to my larger point, it also became very clear to me that my book could serve as a prefatory volume to a number of other volumes that could only be written by a small team working effectively together. The project remains a worthy desideratum in comparative literature, and its time may come. It will not come from the University of Alberta, where no one has carried it on.

It may seem disheartening to conclude on such an unfinished note, a note that is hardly a conclusion, but unfinished is often better than finished. It reminds one of Kenneth Untener's little prayer on Óscar Romero: "Nothing we do is complete, which is another way of / saying that the kingdom always lies beyond us." These words remind us that everything we do has at once an immediate value and, more powerfully, a future resonance. This is why I have concluded with desiderata, inasmuch as one tends to delight more in what might happen, rather in than what has already occurred. Without doubt, the accomplishments in comparative literature across the world have been solid and often groundbreaking. They have brought us to thresholds, however, where more is expected and where whatever we manage to do will best be brought about by working together, enlarging our knowledge of the field from several diverse perspectives.

## NOTES

This article was first published in the *Canadian Review of Comparative Literature* 40, no. 3 (Sept. 2013).

1 Papers given at the congress of 1955, edited by Carlo Pellegrini.
2 Jonathan Hart has compared the two in "CL History: Northrop Frye, Milan Dimić, and Comparative Literature."
3 Zamora, "Comparative Literature," 7.

## BIBLIOGRAPHY

Hart, Jonathan. "CL History: Northrop Frye, Milan Dimić, and Comparative Literature." *Inquire: Journal of Comparative Literature* 2, no. 1. http://inquire.streetmag.org/articles/61.

Pellegrini, Carlo, ed. *Venezia nelle letterature moderne. Atti del Primo Congresso dell'Associazione Internazionale di Letteratura Comparata (Venezia, 25–30 settembre 1955)*. Fondazione Giorgio Cini – Civiltà veneziana – Studi, vol. 8. Firenze: Casa Editrice Leo S. Olschki, 1971.

Zamora, Lois Parkinson. "Comparative Literature in an Age of Globalization." CLC Web 4, no. 3. http://docs.lib.purdue.edu/clcweb/vol4/iss3/1.

# Haunting Tradition Properly: Studies in Ethnic Minority Writing

**Mark A. McCutcheon**

> I want especially to speak of the voices of the dead, which may be considered of especially dubious use by those who question the value of liberal education.
> Constance Rooke, "The Engagement of Self and Other"

> All the old thinking was about loss, and thus resembles all the new thinking.
> Patrick Holland

Since the latter part of the last century, the study of English literature has challenged the traditional ambit and canon handed down from the major British and American universities, by cultivating the interdisciplinary project of Cultural Studies, and by both renovating and moving beyond the literary canon to consider the post-colonial literatures produced by ethnic minority authors. It is perhaps ironic, then, that one of the most active promoters of ethnic minority literature in Canada is an academic and scholar steeped in the traditions of Dante, Chaucer, and Shakespeare. In this chapter I survey the work of Joseph Pivato in the context of post-colonial theories and critically examine his contributions to Comparative Literature, ethnic minority writing, and university governance.

While this chapter could be read as a crypto-Festschrift, I approach it instead as an adaptation *and* a critique of the Festschrift tradition. The Festschrift is a genre of writing highly specific to academia: it is a collection of writings in honour of a scholar, traditionally presented to the scholar on the occasion of her or his retirement. As such, the Festschrift occupies a rather small niche in the already specialized and diversified academic book market, and both market pressures and changes in publishing have, of late, suggested that the Festschrift perhaps now faces retirement itself. Cognizant of the genre's hyper-specialized and occasional audience, many academic publishers categorically do not publish Festschrifts. In self-consciously occupying the Festschrift genre, then, this chapter seeks at the level of form to both preserve and question an important scholarly tradition, just as, at the level of argument, I seek to document the importance – and the querying – of tradition in both Pivato's scholarship and his collegial service.

The Festschrift is to academic culture a bit like what the "lifetime achievement award" is to Hollywood: it is a celebratory object (like a trophy, but a longer read) that is bestowed on a scholar in honour and recognition of her or his significant contribution to research, teaching, service, or a combination of these three, the pillars of university work. A Festschrift represents an important occasion – and it also presents something of an impossible obligation: that which is faced by the contributor, who is tasked with addressing a colleague's formidable body of work, in an impossibly representative way, to do justice to the impact and significance of that body of work. A traditional "Festschrift piece," according to law scholar David Schleicher, consists of three main parts:

1 "Your Work Is Perfect, Don't Change a Thing";
2 "Well, Actually, Come to Think of It, There Is This One Little Thing I Have Questions About"; and
3 "The Only Thing That Could Make Your Work Any Better Is Discussing My Work Just a Bit More."[1]

Accordingly, the recipient, the addressee of the Festschrift, faces a correspondingly impossible obligation – to receive the Festschrift as a double gesture: simultaneously both a tribute to one's own work and a kind of foreclosure of it, an intimation of its conclusion or supersession. As Dustin Hoffman wryly remarked on receiving the Lifetime Achievement Award at the Golden Globes in 1997, "if you ever get one of these you say to yourself, 'are you sure this isn't the Goodbye-and-Good-Luck Award?'" Given the form most Festschrift pieces take, the recipient can be forgiven for receiving this gift as a deconstructive kind of gift: both boon and bane; labour of love and memento mori; a coming to praise *and* to bury. The recipient can be forgiven, even, for hating this kind of gift, even if just a little bit, secretly.

As a peculiarly scholarly genre of occasional writing that encodes such affective opposites – lauding and loathing, recognition and resignation, hailing and haunting – the Festschrift seems eminently amenable to a theorization according to a problematic that has been powerfully brought to bear on the diasporic and post-colonial fields of literary study that Pivato has done so much to build in Canada, a problematic that I would like to adapt here, for the purpose of examining Pivato's own work, and for theorizing the work of the Festschrift as such. The problematic I have in mind is what the Marxist post-colonial scholar Neil Lazarus (whose name alone resonates with what follows) calls "hating tradition properly" (3). I want to propose a variation on this problematic, adapting it to the uncanny genre of the Festschrift, and to the context of diaspora studies like Pivato's, a field that is definitively *uncanny* – in the psychoanalytically fraught, ambivalent sense of the original German term, *Unheimlich*: "un-homelike."

But before elaborating this variation, an explanation of its source theme is in order. In his 1999 book *Nationalism and Cultural Practice in the Postcolonial World*, Lazarus takes from the Frankfurt School scholar Theodor Adorno a notion of "hating tradition properly," which Lazarus reads as a methodological injunction for the publicly engaged scholar to "use one's relative class privilege to combat all privilege" (3) and to "think with modernity against modernity" (6). This modernity Lazarus conceives not only as that of the post-colonially dispensed capitalist world system, but also – critically – as itself a tradition now: that is, *modernity* names a global capitalist order that is "uncritically received as pregiven and unalterable" (6) – as its elite advocates never tire of reminding the multitude whose interests they deliberately misrepresent as their own. For Lazarus, "hating tradition properly" thus comes to mean two things: first, attending to how non-Eurocentric writers and intellectuals both commit to and critique capitalist modernity in the wake of European imperialism; and, second, attending self-reflectively to how the post-colonialist scholar him- or herself both commits to and critiques post-colonial theory – in Lazarus's case, by infusing it with a trenchant Marxism that thus reorients post-colonial theory to a properly global-scale praxis.[2]

Understood in this way, "hating tradition properly" can be seen to operate as a methodological principle in Pivato's own work. His educational background in Comparative Literature, English, French, and Italian studies represents a commitment to academic tradition; and to this tradition, his excavatory, genealogical research on multicultural, ethnic minority[3] literatures, especially Italian-Canadian writing, has posed a long-running critique. Bilingual writer Licia Canton has called Pivato the "father of Italian-Canadian literary criticism."[4] She points out that, in the 1980s, Pivato pursued research on ethnic minority writing when university colleagues warned him that it would compromise his academic career, and when literary-studies journals declined articles on Italian-Canadian authors. Pivato countered the dominance of the traditional English canon and attempts to establish a Canadian literary canon along its lines, as envisioned for instance in the 1978 Taking Stock conference.[5]

The discipline's rejection of Italian-Canadian writers at that time was matched by academics who taught Italian literature and culture in Canada. In his essay "Italianistica versus Italian-Canadian Writing," Pivato exposes the refusal of Italianists to include Italian-Canadian texts in their graduate and undergraduate programs and notes their suspicion toward any challenge to the established Italian literary canon or to their elite notions of literary and cultural value. By the time these academics began to include a few Italian-Canadian writers in their courses, they had already lost a whole generation of students, which he sees as a disservice to the larger Italian community.[6]

The discipline's reception of ethnic minority writing warmed slowly. Pivato's 1985 book, *Contrasts: Comparative Essays on Italian-Canadian Writing*, later became an important stimulus to the development of studies on literary diversity in North America. *Contrasts* belongs to university and public-library catalogues across Canada now, while Pivato's other eleven books are usually reserved to university libraries. In all of Pivato's publications, Comparative Literature structures his approach to literary study and to extending the field beyond European literatures. Less well known, perhaps, is Pivato's role in fostering the publication of studies about minority authors. As academic editor of Guernica Editions' Essential Writers Series, he commissioned books on such writers as M.G. Vassanji, Austin Clarke, Joy Kogawa, Dany Laferrière, Roy Kiyooka, and Dionne Brand, as well as Indigenous writers like Maria Campbell, Drew Hayden Taylor, and Daniel David Moses. By design, the Essential Writers Series focuses on ethnic minority writers and others insufficiently recognized by Canada's literary institutions.

In keeping with his old-worldly character, in his final year at Athabasca University, Pivato published two books: *Sheila Watson: Essays on Her Works* and *From Friuli: Poems in Friulan* by Rina Del Nin Cralli. The first of these challenges established views on Canadian modernist literature, and the second challenges those on Italian literature and Italian minority languages. In his research and publishing initiatives, Pivato has enacted a critical kind of "hating tradition properly."

As Pivato's colleague and fellow sufferer through many a prolonged department meeting or faculty retreat, I can attest, too, that Pivato has definitely elevated "hating tradition properly" to an art form in the carrying out of his university service obligations. Pivato has always maintained a keen and clear vision of the social-justice mission of Athabasca University as Canada's open university: the mission to make university education accessible to those students who would be otherwise obstructed from pursuing studies at a traditional university. Pivato's attention to this mission has informed his sharp, outspoken opposition to transformations of the university that impede this mission: transformations such as multifaceted corporatization and creeping managerialism, which Athabasca, like universities everywhere, now faces under the hegemony of neo-liberal capital. Department and faculty reorganization; increasingly bureaucratic administration; technological changes made for efficiency, not pedagogy: Pivato has vocally and trenchantly opposed changes like these, which compromise or eclipse Athabasca's mission to open educational access. "This," as Len Findlay writes, "is the rocky road from the liberal arts to the neoliberal arts, the path down which we are being urged to proceed by most people in administrative positions outside academic departments and schools and those whose advice they commission and heed."[7]

In these research and service contexts, Pivato's work fits well enough into the problematic of "hating tradition properly" as it is. But I want to adapt this problematic to speak more precisely to his work; I want to add to this problematic the negative capability (and uncanny reverberation) of the prefix *un* – not as a prefix, but rather as an interpolation to change *hating* to *haunting*. This adjustment, the difference of only two letters, transforms *hating*, while still leaving it to signify: to rest in pieces, perhaps. (After all, hating remains integral to so many modes and motives of haunting.) Hence this revised rubric: "haunting tradition properly."

To rewrite this hating as haunting is then to refract Lazarus's postcolonial problematic through the post-structuralist prism of *hauntology*, a term coined by Jacques Derrida that has been widely adopted in critical theory generally and in many specific theoretical schools of thought. "Haunting tradition properly" also seems to me a fitting description of the Festschrift and the kind of work it is called on to do, and I will take up this question of the Festschrift genre in my concluding comments.

In his 1994 book *Specters of Marx*, Derrida coins the term "hauntology" to supplement *ontology*, the philosophical discourse of being, of existence. He introduces the concept thus: "To haunt does not mean to be present, and it is necessary to introduce haunting into the very construction of a concept. Of every concept, beginning with the concepts of being and time. That is what we would be calling here a hauntology. Ontology opposes it only in a movement of exorcism. Ontology is a conjuration."[8] Consistent with Derrida's overall project, the coinage replaces "the priority of being and presence with the figure of the ghost as that which is neither present nor absent, neither dead nor alive" (Davis 373). In Fredric Jameson's gloss, all hauntology "says, if it can be thought to speak, is that the living present is scarcely as self-sufficient as it claims to be" (qtd. in Davis 373).

This revenant coinage has proven resonant and appropriate for a range of subjects and fields, including literary and cultural studies generally, and diasporic, multicultural, and post-colonial literary studies specifically. For literary scholars, "the attraction of hauntology ... arises from the link between a theme (haunting, ghosts, the supernatural) and the processes of literature and textuality in general" (373). In the context of diasporic, multicultural, and post-colonial literatures, this "theme" of haunting becomes legible as more than motif – as an integral meaning-making process in the connected traditions and histories of nation-building, diasporic identification, and cultural globalization more broadly. Diaspora names a social relation or network characterized by hauntology: by legacy and loss, by repression and return, by memory and forgetting. Literature too is structurally and culturally hauntological, in its mediation of dialogues (sometimes impossible dialogues, sometimes chimerical ones) across space and time, in its ability to bring to life and to keep alive, in the present, images and voices of the past.

In Canada specifically, "if we understand the term 'postcolonial' ... less as a descriptive label than as a series of questions that are enabled in the aftermath and continuance of colonialism," as Cynthia Sugars and Gerry Turcotte put it, then "the very persistence of gothic motifs of haunting and monstrosity that invoke the colonial past testifies to the incomplete resolution of these histories" (x). Processes and experiences of haunting in a post-colonial, multicultural, settler-invader nation-state like Canada take many shapes and occupy many contexts: "fears of territorial illegitimacy, anxiety about forgotten or occluded histories, resentment towards flawed or complicit ancestors, assertions of Aboriginal priority, explorations of hybrid cultural forms, and interrogations of national belonging and citizenship" (ix). In short, as Sugars and Turcotte assert, "the Canadian national project is inherently haunted" (xi). And both the minoritized literary production of immigrant communities and the study of this literature by groundbreaking scholars like Pivato attest to this haunting in the simultaneously local and global milieu of Canadian multiculture – the context, that is, "of the 'in-between' nature of identity in Canada" (Sugars and Turcotte xxi).

Pivato has devoted a considerable part of his research career to investigating this "in-between nature of identity in Canada"; he has helped to build a canon of Canadian literature in the shadow of British and US literary canons, but has done so by questioning the Anglo-American assumptions and aesthetics of the nascent Canadian canon, challenging it to include and embrace the work of writers from ethnic minority backgrounds and marginalized cultural traditions. Pivato's work has focused on Italian-Canadian writing, but also encompasses that of black Canadians, like George Elliott Clarke for instance, and other diasporic and minoritized communities. If the theory of hauntology can be thought of as "fundamentally about forces which act at a distance,"[9] and if it "enjoins readers to learn to speak with ghosts – to acknowledge the shrouded and silent – and to move towards a collective sense of redefinition,"[10] then Pivato's work in documenting, theorizing, and critiquing ethnic minority literature in Canada can be thought of as a haunting of the traditions of both canon formation and – if they are not synonymous – literary study.

The very title of Pivato's collection of essays on these "other literatures" – *Echo* – evokes a theme of uncanny repetition and representation, return, and of course classical allusion. In this collection, Pivato reads texts written in English, French, and Italian, and thus he brings comparative methodologies to his literary analysis. Among these essays, questions of tradition and temporality, together with figures of split and doubled identities, conjure spectres of "forgotten or occluded histories" and "hybrid cultural forms." As Pivato writes, "a recurring motif in immigrant Italian writing is the notion that dead ancestors are as real as living relatives" (*Echo* 159). Not only real, but as present in the diasporic community's new homestead (that is, as present as spectral apparitions can ever be) as in the community's old homeland: "For Salvatore, Di Cicco and other writers this country [i.e., Canada] is filled with spirits from the past ... the ghosts of our ancestors are always here, ready to listen. At times these poems seem to be addressed as much to the dead as to the living" (*Echo* 97). Pivato, in turn, addresses diasporic writers like those he names here; and in the process, his scholarship and criticism address, and may be said to haunt, two traditions at once: one, the "linguistic and cultural traditions" (Gunew qtd. in *Echo* 13) of the immigrant writer's homeland and of the literary techniques that characterize work by immigrant writers (e.g., motifs of doubling, figures of alienation, bi- or multilingualism); and the other, the "great tradition" (*Echo* 42), the canon of English literature that was consolidated between Arnoldian education projects under late-Victorian imperialism and the Leavisite elevation of English to university core curriculum between the world wars.[11] As Pivato has reflected, it is important to remember that it was not until the 1970s that Canadian literature – to say nothing still of diasporic and ethnic minority literatures – became legitimate subject matter in Canadian university English programs.[12]

It is against the backdrop of that quite belated legitimization of Canadian literature in Canada that Pivato's de facto inauguration of Italian-Canadian literary studies assumes its groundbreaking (or even, we might venture to say with no little irony, pioneering) significance, and can be understood as both a hating and haunting of tradition, properly: an occupation and reproduction of the tradition that Pivato was thoroughly schooled in, and has full command of; yet at the same time, a critique and interrogation of this tradition. A haunting of "the great tradition" of literature, undertaken in the excavation, recuperation, and redistribution of the "forgotten or occluded histories" that have documented the experiences and subjectivities of displacement and difference, of disorientation and reorientation, in the ongoing socio-historical experiment that is Canada.

Pivato has further developed and expanded this kind of haunting tradition properly in more recent work on black Canadian literature, specifically on the "Africadian" oeuvre of George Elliott Clarke. It should go without saying, and yet can't be emphasized strongly enough, that the black Atlantic – the ocean-traversing African diaspora during and following the Atlantic slave trade – represents a site of hauntological cultural production par excellence, as theorized by Dionne Brand (in *A Map to the Door of No Return*), by Paul Gilroy (in *The Black Atlantic*), and by Clarke himself (in *Odysseys Home* and elsewhere), among others. Pivato recognizes something of this hauntology in his observation that Clarke's incisive critique of Gilroy – "Must All Blackness Be American?" – asks this question as one that "haunts" black Canadian artists (*Africadian* 321). Introducing his work on Clarke, Pivato also identifies himself and Clarke as "fellow minority intellectuals" (2); while this is arguably a problematic gesture, according to the intersectional politics of cultural difference, it is also an important gesture of solidarity across different formations of cultural difference, and more than once has the significance of Pivato's "institution-building" scholarship and research networking been impressed on me by major Canadian scholars of diverse ethnicities and cultural backgrounds.

On the subjects of Canadian literature generally and black diasporic literature specifically, Pivato's research interests overlap with mine, and these shared interests have served us and our university well, in our collaborations to provide graduate-level literary studies for Athabasca

University's MA program. This MA program is emphatically, constitutively interdisciplinary, and so the literary specialization that we have furnished for the program is specifically named the "literary studies" focus area. A committee of several colleagues has worked together to design and launch this focus area, and all deserve great credit; here I want to highlight just one of Pivato's contributions, that of the focus area's name, which, although it appears simple and straightforward, encompasses a proper haunting of university disciplinary tradition. As Pivato pointed out in a program planning meeting in February 2014, "literary studies" is neither "English" nor "comparative literature" – the two more conventional disciplinary formations of literary study – but, rather, an extrapolation of and a departure from both of those extant formations. Literary studies names no national or linguistic canon or tradition, as does English or French; and literary studies both differs from and is indebted to Comparative Literature.

Comparative Literature names a discipline defined "by means of a critical act: the comparison of literatures by the critic."[13] But as Robert Young notes, the name of this field is somewhat illogical, "perfidious": Comparative Literature "suggest[s] that literature, not the critic, is the agent, a literature that carries out a work of comparison."[14] In our MA program, literary studies is indebted to Comparative Literature: in its eschewal of national or linguistic specificity (given that no language like "English" is named here); in its design and deployment by Pivato and a group of colleagues, most of whom are trained in Comparative Literature (and concerned of late to see this discipline's wane at other Canadian universities); and, though it dispenses with the "comparative," in its invocation of plurality – both "literary" and "studies" can here be read as plural, and pluralistic. The resulting disciplinary formation that Pivato helped to innovate – Literary Studies – is thus more capacious, encompassing a range of linguistic and literary traditions, comparative and non-comparative literary forms, and close and contextual reading strategies, as well as a spectrum of theories and methodologies. Students in this area have produced work in diverse forms, such as interactive fiction, magazine articles, and blog posts, as well as more conventional research essays. If "literature" can be tentatively defined as a body of practice of "highly valued writing"[15] – and yet at the same time paradoxically defined as "impossible to define"[16] – then literary studies requires and activates a correspondingly broad disciplinary definition, one we find anticipated, long before the advent of Athabasca's program, in Rowland McMaster's still-timely polemic from 1977, "Why Read?" "The study of literature," writes McMaster, "is a study of what is possible in the effective use of language."[17]

This detour into the nomenclature and function of a subject area offered in Athabasca's MA program is given here as a further illustration of how Pivato's teaching work comprises a kind of haunting tradition properly. It is critical to recognize in this work of disciplinary reformation an institution-building kind of commitment to not only pedagogy and research but also service. The capacious abstraction of Pivato's conception of literary studies, illustrated by the variety of subjects that students have pursued under its auspices and the variety of analytic approaches they have brought to it, is a curricular assertion of academic freedom: freedom from – and resistance to – the ongoing, instrumentalizing transformation of liberal education into *neo*-liberal job training. The capaciousness of literary studies enables and invites an equally capacious research imagination, it invites the student to think big, and to think critically. The abstraction of literary study, similarly, affords the supervisor a kind of authority and responsibility of mentorship, evaluation, and administration that the professoriate in North America enjoys less and less in the neo-liberal milieu of university corporatization, bureaucratic bloat, and the recalibration of learning as training under regimes of learning outcomes, program prioritization, and other such narrow-minded, short-sighted, impoverished metrics and valuations of learning and research.

In this institutional environment of what Bill Readings calls "the university in ruins,"[18] Pivato's insistence on academic freedom, faculty autonomy, and collegial governance of as flat and lean a kind as possible constitutes both a hating and a haunting of tradition properly. Pivato has resolutely and vocally opposed the restructuring of the faculties, the reintroduction of decanal governance, and a succession of technological changes that increasingly seem to be implemented not for pedagogical effectiveness or to otherwise further Athabasca's mission to open access to education, but only for reasons of technical efficiency or cost-effectiveness, which benefit the institution, not the student. Such technological changes include, for instance, the university's push for courses to adopt electronic textbooks, to which such a burden of technological protection measures is too often applied as to render them practically unusable. In opposing such technology implementations that don't serve open education, Pivato exemplifies how "it is evidently possible now to be both ... a desperate radical [and] a hopeless stick in the mud ... at once," in McMaster's memorable phrase.[19]

Although I know Pivato's schooling and career have taken place in Canada, I think that there is something almost old-worldly in the confident assurance with which he wields his polyglot professorial expertise and rank as social and political capital. It is rare to see professorial privilege wielded like this in North America, but it is much more commonly encountered in Europe. Something of the old-world scholarly tradition, then, Pivato can thus also be said to haunt. And yet what is distinctive about how he asserts this privilege is a palpable sense of social responsibility in his dedication to serving students: his warm compassion and understanding of Athabasca's students and their needs; his generosity towards them and a devotion to helping them persevere and succeed in their studies amidst other equally if not more demanding responsibilities of work and family; his desire to both inspire and challenge them.

I recall getting an early taste of Pivato's old-world scholarly style when I first came to Athabasca to be interviewed for the literary studies professorship that I was later offered, and which I have held since. In the presentation I gave as a requisite part of my interview, I talked about my research on adaptations of *Frankenstein* in Canadian popular culture. A question I often get asked about that research is "Why Canada?" and this question did come up at the time of that presentation. I answered then, as I have argued elsewhere,[20] with reference, first, to the peculiar prominence of new media in Canadian culture (part of what Maurice Charland calls a tradition of "technological nationalism")[21] and, second, to the self-consciously factitious, "mosaic" character of Canadian official multiculturalism: "For postcolonial critics, official multiculturalism amounts almost to a Frankenpheme [i.e., a condensed allusion to *Frankenstein*]: an experimental, ideological state apparatus that integrates Canada's culturally differentiated population in a national 'fantasy of unity,' while mystifying the state's neoliberal political economy of mobilizing and managing flows of labour."[22]

As a scholar who entertains a more "positive view of Canadian multiculturalism as actually working when we see different communities acknowledge each other and discuss similar experiences,"[23] Pivato was understandably troubled that my argument risked making diasporic and immigrant communities in Canada "seem like Frankenstein's monster," as he said in response to my answering the question; skepticism and concern were audible in his tone. In that moment I was convinced I had made one of those serious-but-all-too-common missteps that can cost an academic job candidate the opportunity. I had never before, in an academic forum, been so squarely challenged on the implications – and by extension the very value – of my research program. And I had previously presented this work to an academic audience in Germany – where I had seen senior academics challenge other junior colleagues and graduate students with a forthrightness and bluntness that still remains very rare in North American academic culture. It was not until after an offer actually came through from Athabasca that I could reflect otherwise on Pivato's challenge, reconsidering it as a kind of test, as a part of the interview itself: how well can the candidate defend their work against direct, critical interrogation?

And in the contexts of our shared research interests and of my own decidedly more Gothic pursuits, Pivato might be as surprised by my hauntological characterization of his work as he must be unsurprised that this is how I would characterize it. In his long service to the university, at least as much as in his teaching and research, Pivato has very much enacted a proper haunting of tradition. A further instance that cannot go unrecognized is his role as one of the founders of Athabasca's Faculty Association (AUFA), which he helped organize in order to recognize and to protect the university's then-new workforce of doctorate-credentialed professors, whom Athabasca had employed, in its first years, only on limited contracts. Pivato's proper haunting of tradition has consistently involved an insistent pursuit of providing modern, liberal education, and the advocacy of *this* tradition's ideals of mass enlightenment and social justice against the countervailing grain of postmodern, neo-liberal education, which tends instead to narrow both the university's social mission – and its pool of eligible students.

Likewise, Pivato's teaching and research enact a commitment to a conception of education generally as a service in the public interest, and of literary work and literary studies specifically as a project integral to the genuinely representative democracy that is *lived* multiculturalism's ideal, even as it is anathema to *official* multiculturalism and the neo-liberal corporatocracy. Pivato's proper haunting of the related traditions of literary study, canon formation, and liberal education is, then, the kind of haunting that the university today ignores at nothing short of existential peril to itself.

The subject matter of Pivato's expertise – diasporic, ethnic minority, and multicultural literature in Canada – is thus doubly haunting and hauntological, and his academic work in both literary criticism and program development models both the diasporic subject who seeks cultural knowledge of self and the scholarly subject who seeks institutional knowledge of tradition. In these pursuits, both kinds of subject can be seen to haunt (and, admittedly, sometimes to hate) tradition properly, and haunting tradition properly is also a hallmark of the industrious and celebrated scholar who is fortunate, and at the same time cursed, to find her- or himself fêted by a Festschrift. Fortunate: to have tribute paid, by one's colleagues, to the influence and importance of one's work, while one still pursues that work – while one, more fundamentally, still lives to pursue that work. (And here we pause to pour out some parenthetical ink for other colleagues deserving of the Festschrift but departed too soon to receive it.) Fortunate, then, but also cursed: for the invitation of the Festschrift is by the same token an intimation of mortality. At once an expression of gratitude, a celebration of the research imagination, and yet also a form of farewell, a "graveyard of scholarship,"[24] the tradition that is the Festschrift haunts writer and recipient alike.

But properly so.

In itself, the Festschrift is institution-building, institution-strengthening work. The Festschrift documents institutional memory, making the luminary that is its subject a spectral force of authority, a voice of conscience to reckon with for those of us who dwell amidst the ruins of the university, shoring its fragments against the gathering barbarians of capital, those for whom the cultivation of public forgetting and ignorance is a consummation devoutly to be wished, those to whom this voice – the voice *of* tradition *and* against it – remains nemesis.

## NOTES

1. Schleicher, "From Here All-the-Way-Down," 401–2.
2. See the chapter by Ndeye Fatou Ba in this volume, 67–86.
3. In my research and teaching, I use the term "minoritized," rather than "minority." This usage follows Frantz Fanon's theorization of "racialization," instead of "race," as a way to emphasize that categories of identity are not essential but historical, not statuses but processes. In this chapter, however, I use the term "ethnic minority," because this is Pivato's terminology, and because it is consistent with this terminology's use throughout this volume.
4. Canton, "Italian-Canadian Literature," 14.
5. See Steele.
6. Pivato, "Italianistica," 227–44.
7. Findlay, "Rethinking the Humanities," 6.
8. Derrida, *Specters of Marx*, 202.
9. Fisher, "What Is Hauntology," 20.
10. Sugars and Turcotte, *Unsettled Remains*, xiv.
11. Eagleton, *Literary Theory*, 23, 28.

12  Pivato, *Africadian*, 314; see also Monkman.
13  Young, "The Postcolonial Comparative," 683.
14  Ibid., 684.
15  Eagleton, *Literary Theory*, 9.
16  Barnet et al., *A Short Guide*, 65.
17  McMaster, "Why Read?" 58. See Pivato's chapter on languages in this volume, 41–64.
18  Readings, *The University in Ruins*, 19.
19  McMaster, "Why Read?" 58.
20  See McCutcheon, "Frankenstein."
21  Charland, "Technological Nationalism," 196.
22  McCutcheon, "Frankenstein," 739.
23  Pivato, *Africadian*, 2.
24  Taggart, "Gardens or Graveyards," 227.

**BIBLIOGRAPHY**

Barnet, Syvan, Reid Gilbert, and William E. Cain. *A Short Guide to Writing about Literature*. 2nd ed. Toronto: Pearson Longman, 2004.

Brand, Dionne. *A Map to the Door of No Return: Notes to Belonging*. Toronto: Vintage, 2001.

Canton, Licia, and Giulia De Gasperi. "Italian-Canadian Literature: So Much Left to Say." In *Writing Cultural Difference*, edited by Giulia De Gasperi, Maria Cristina Seccia, Licia Canton, and Michael Mirolla, 13–21. Toronto: Guernica Editions, 2015.

Clarke, George Elliott. *Odysseys Home: Mapping African-Canadian Literature*. Toronto: University of Toronto Press, 2002.

Charland, Maurice. "Technological Nationalism." *Canadian Journal of Political and Social Theory* 10, no. 1 (1986): 196–220.

Davis, Colin. "État present: Hauntology, Spectres, and Phantoms." *French Studies* 59, no. 3 (2005): 373–9.

Del Nin Cralli, Rina. *From Friuli: Poems in Friulan with English Translations*. Edited by J. Pivato. Montreal: Longbridge Books, 2015.

Derrida, Jacques. *Specters of Marx: The State of the Debt, the Work of Mourning, and the New International*. Translated by Peggy Kamuf. New York: Routledge, 1994.

Eagleton, Terry. *Literary Theory: An Introduction*. Anniversary ed. Minneapolis: University of Minnesota Press, 2008.

Findlay, Len. "Rethinking the Humanities." *English Studies in Canada* 38, no. 1 (2012): 1–8.

Fisher, Mark. "What Is Hauntology?" *Film Quarterly* 66, no. 1 (2012): 16–24.

Gilroy, Paul. *The Black Atlantic: Modernity and Double Consciousness*. Cambridge: Harvard University Press, 1993.
Hoffman, Dustin. Lifetime Achievement Award acceptance speech, Golden Globe Award Ceremony, Jan. 1997. Reported in http://www.shellworld.net/~emily/dustin/goldglob.txt.
Holland, Patrick. Lecture. Romantic Literature I. University of Guelph, Fall 1993.
Lazarus, Neil. "Introduction: Hating Tradition Properly." In *Nationalism and Cultural Practice in the Postcolonial World*, 1–15. Cambridge: Cambridge University Press, 1999.
McCutcheon, Mark A. "Frankenstein as a Figure of Globalization in Canada's Postcolonial Popular Culture." *Continuum* 25, no. 5 (2011): 731–42.
McMaster, Rowland. "Why Read?" (1977). *English Studies in Canada* 39, no. 2–3 (2013): 43–61.
Monkman, Leslie. "Canadian Literature in English 'among Worlds.'" In *Home-Work: Postcolonialism, Pedagogy, and Canadian Literature*, edited by Cynthia Sugars, 117–33. Ottawa: University of Ottawa Press, 2004.
Nunn, Robert, ed. *Drew Hayden Taylor: Essays on His Works*. Toronto: Guernica, 2008.
Pivato, Joseph, ed. *Africadian Atlantic: Essays on George Elliott Clarke*. Toronto: Guernica, 2012.
– *Contrasts: Comparative Essays on Italian-Canadian Writing*. Montreal: Guernica, 1985.
– *Echo: Essays on Other Literatures*. Toronto: Guernica, 1994.
– "Italianistica versus Italian-Canadian Writing." In *Social Pluralism and Literary History*, edited by Francesco Loriggio, 227–47. Toronto: Guernica, 1996.
– "Representation of Ethnicity as Problem: Essence or Construction." *Journal of Canadian Studies* 31, no. 3 (1996). Rpt. in Athabasca University Web. http://engl.athabascau.ca/faculty/jpivato/ethnicity.php.
– ed. *Sheila Watson: Essays on Her Works*. Toronto: Guernica Editions, 2015.
Readings, Bill. *The University in Ruins*. Cambridge: Harvard University Press, 1996.
Rooke, Constance. "The Engagement of Self and Other: Liberal Education and Its Contributions to the Public Good." In *The Idea of Engagement: Universities in Society*, edited by S. Bjarnason and P. Coldstream, 228–50. London: The Policy Research Unit, The Association of Commonwealth Universities, 2003.
Schleicher, David. "From Here All-the-Way-Down, or How to Write a Festschrift Piece." *Tulsa Law Review* 48, no. 3 (2013): 401–25.

Steele, Charles R., ed. *Taking Stock: The Calgary Conference on the Canadian Novel.* Toronto: ECW Press, 1982.

Sugars, Cynthia, and Gerry Turcotte, eds. *Unsettled Remains: Canadian Literature and the Postcolonial Gothic.* Waterloo: Wilfrid Laurier University Press, 2009.

Taggart, Michael. "Gardens or Graveyards of Scholarship? *Festschriften* in the Literature of the Common Law." *Oxford Journal of Legal Studies* 22, no. 2 (2002): 227–52.

Young, Robert J.C. "The Postcolonial Comparative." *PMLA* 128, no. 3 (2013): 683–9.

# Contributors

**JOLENE ARMSTRONG** is associate professor in Comparative Literature and English in the Centre for Humanities at Athabasca University. Professor Armstrong's scholarly work is in Canadian and American literature, in examining intersections between narrative and mixed-media art, and in studying popular culture in film, theatre, and television. Dr Armstrong has published two books, one on Métis activist and professor Maria Campbell and one on the late British playwright Sarah Kane, with a third on Michael Ondaatje in press, and has written several academic essays and given numerous conference papers.

**NDEYE FATOU BA** received a PhD in Comparative Literature and Culture from Western University (Ontario). She joined Ryerson University as a contract faculty in 2013. She teaches courses for the Department of Languages, Literatures, and Cultures and the Chang School of Continuing Education. Ms Ba is currently the Chang School's academic coordinator for French. Her teaching and research interests include francophone literature, particularly that of Africa and the French Antilles, colonialism and post-colonialism, Francophonie, theories of enunciation, and plurilingualism. She is currently working as a subject matter expert (SME) on a course exploring francophone Caribbean literature.

**E.D. BLODGETT**, FRSC, is distinguished university professor Emeritus at the University of Alberta, and held the Louis Desrochers Chair in Études canadiennes, Campus Saint-Jean (2008–10). His publications include *The Love Songs of the Carmina Burana* (with Roy Arthur Swanson, Garland Publishing, 1987), *The Romance of Flamenca* (Garland Publishing, 1995), *Five-Part Invention: A History of Literary History in Canada* (University of Toronto Press, 2003), and *Les Enfants des Jésuites ou le sacrifice des vierges* (Les Presses de l'Université Laval, 2013). He has also published twenty-seven books of poetry, of which two were awarded the Governor General's Award, the most recent being *Horizons* (Éditions du Blé, 2016).

GEORGE ELLIOTT CLARKE is E.J. Pratt Professor of Canadian Literature at the University of Toronto. His honours include the Portia White Prize for Artistic Achievement (1998), the Governor-General's Award for Poetry (2001), the National Magazine Gold Medal for Poetry (2001), the Dr Martin Luther King Jr Achievement Award (2004), the Pierre Elliott Trudeau Fellowship Prize (2005–08), the Dartmouth Book Award for Fiction (2006), the Poesis Premiul (2006, Romania), the Eric Hoffer Book Award for Poetry (2009), appointment to the Order of Nova Scotia (2006) and to the Order of Canada, and eight honorary doctorates. His landmark volumes of literary criticism are *Odysseys Home: Mapping African-Canadian Literature* (2002) and *Directions Home: Approaches to African-Canadian Literature* (2012).

F. ELIZABETH DAHAB is professor of Comparative Literature in the Department of Comparative World Literature and Classics at California State University, Long Beach. She has published and spoken extensively on the topic of Arab-Canadian literature and has published a monograph entitled *Voices of Exile in Contemporary Canadian Francophone Literature* (Lanham, MD: Lexington Books, 2009; 2011). Her edited anthology, *Voices in the Desert: An Anthology of Arabic-Canadian Women Writers*, appeared in Toronto in 2002. F. Elizabeth Dahab earned her bachelor of arts from McGill University (Montreal) and her master of arts from the University of Alberta. She received her *doctorat de littérature comparée* in Comparative Literature from the Université de Paris – Sorbonne (Paris IV).

GIULIA DE GASPERI received a *laurea* (BA, 2002) in Foreign Languages and Literatures and a *dottorato di ricerca* (PhD program, 2007) from Ca' Foscari University, Venice, Italy. She was the recipient of a Government of Canada Award (2004) and conducted research at the Celtic Studies Department of Saint Francis Xavier University, Antigonish, Nova Scotia, Canada. She was a post-doctoral fellow in Ethnology at the Department of Celtic and Scottish Studies at the University of Edinburgh from 2009 to 2012. She was associate professor in the Departments of Modern Languages and Celtic Studies at Saint Francis Xavier University, Antigonish, Nova Scotia, for the academic year 2012–13.

She currently lives in Prince Edward Island, where she is founder and CEO of Radici Translation and Wordcraft Ltd, a literary agency specializing in translation proposals of Canadian literary works to Italian publishers.

ANNA PIA DE LUCA received degrees from the Universities of Toronto and Trieste. Before retirement, she taught English Language and Literature at the University of Udine. She has published in her main fields of interest: contemporary Canadian and ethnic female literature, Italian-Canadian literature, multiculturalism, and migration and diaspora in Canada. She is co-editor of the volumes *Palinsesti Culturali: gli apporti delle immigrazioni alla letteratura del Canada* (1999), *Italy and Canadian Culture: Nationalisms in the New Millennium* (2001), *Shaping History: L'identità italo-canadese nel Canada anglofono* (2005), *Itinerranze e Transcodificazioni: Scrittori migranti dal Friuli Venezia Giulia al Canada* (2008), and *Transformations of the Canadian Cultural Mosaic* (2012), and editor of *Investigating Canadian Identities* (2010) and *Passion Meets Paintbrush: Albert Chiarandini (Udine 1915 – Toronto 2007)*, 2015. She is founding member and co-director of the journal *Oltreoceano* and of the Centre for Canadian Culture Studies Series. She was director of the Centre for Canadian Culture at the University of Udine from 2009 to 2015.

**SNEJA GUNEW**, BA (Melbourne), MA (Toronto), PhD (Newcastle, NSW), FRSC, has taught in England, Australia, and Canada. She has published widely on multicultural, post-colonial, and feminist critical theory and is professor emerita of English and Women's and Gender Studies at the University of British Columbia, Canada. She was director of the Centre for Research in Women's and Gender Studies (2002–07). Her books include *Framing Marginality: Multicultural Literary Studies* (1994) and *Haunted Nations: The Colonial Dimensions of Multiculturalisms* (Routledge 2004). Based in Canada since 1993, she is currently working on comparative multiculturalisms and diasporic literatures and their intersections with national and global cultural formations. Her new book is entitled: *Post-multicultural Writers as Neo-cosmopolitan Mediators.* http://faculty.arts.ubc.ca/sgunew.

**DOMINIQUE HÉTU** is a postdoctoral fellow (SSHRC, CLC) at the Canadian Literature Centre (University of Alberta), where she explores the interconnections between feminist care ethics, new materialism, critical posthumanism, and Canadian literature by women. She earned her PhD in Littérature Comparée (FRQSC) from the Université de Montréal with a dissertation entitled "Geographies of Care and Posthuman Relationality in North American Fiction by Women." She has published in journals such as *Canadian Literature, Mosaic, TransVerse,* and *Nouvelles vues*.

**LINDA HUTCHEON** is university professor emeritus in English and Comparative Literature at the University of Toronto. She is the author of nine books, including *The Politics of Postmodernism* (1989), *The Canadian Postmodern* (1988), *Irony's Edge: The Theory and Politics of Irony* (1994), *A Theory of Adaptation* (2006), and of four books written with Michael Hutcheon, *Opera: Desire, Disease, Death* (1989), *Bodily Charm: Living Opera* (2000), *Opera: The Art of Dying* (2004), and *Four Last Songs: Aging and Creativity in Verdi, Strauss, Messiaen, and Britten* (2015).

**MARK A. MCCUTCHEON** is associate professor of Literary Studies at Athabasca University, where he teaches and researches literary history, post-colonial studies, and copyright. Recent research articles of his have appeared in *The Explicator*, *English Studies in Canada*, and TOPIA; recent poetry, in *Existere*, EVENT, and *UnLost*. His book on Canadian *Frankenstein* adaptations is forthcoming from Athabasca University Press. Mark's university service has included presidencies of the Athabasca University Faculty Association and the Confederation of Alberta Faculty Associations.

**JOSEPH PIVATO** is professor emeritus of Literary Studies at Athabasca University and was a visiting professor at Australian and Italian universities. His PhD is in Comparative Literature. In 1985, he edited *Contrasts: Comparative Essays on Italian-Canadian Writing*, the first critical analysis of this emerging literature. When he held The Mariano Elia Chair in Italian-Canadian Studies at York University in 1987–88, he offered the first-ever course on Italian-Canadian literature. His publications include: *Africadian Atlantic: Essays on George Elliott Clarke* (2012), *Echo: Essays on Other Literatures* (1994), *The Anthology of Italian-Canadian Writing* (1998), and *Sheila Watson: Essays on Her Works* (2015).

**GAETANO RANDO** is associate professor and honorary senior Fellow in the Faculty of Law, Humanities, and the Arts at the University of Wollongong (Australia) and has published extensively on Italian-Australian studies, recent book-length publications being: *Filicudi Facts Fiction and Fantasy: Pen Portraits of a Magic Italian Island* (2015), co-edited with Diana Santamaria; *Celluloid Immigrant: Italian Australian Filmmaker Giorgio Mangiamele* (The Moving Image / ATOM, St Kilda, 2011), co-written with Gino Moliterno; the translation of, and introduction to, Rosa R. Cappiello's seminal novel *Paese fortunato – Oh Lucky Country* (Sydney University Press, 3rd edition, 2009).

**DEBORAH SAIDERO** is a lecturer in English and Translation at the University of Udine, Italy. She holds a PhD in Literatures and Cultures of the English-speaking World from the University of Bologna. Her main research areas include contemporary Canadian women writers, migrant literatures, with particular focus on Italian and Friulian immigrant writers in Canada, feminist and gender studies, translation studies, and self-translation. She has published essays on Canadian literature, including Italian-Canadian writers like Mary di Michele, Dôre Michelut, Genni Gunn, and Gianna Patriarca, and has edited a collection of essays on Janice Kulyk Keefer (2010) and a volume on feminist translation and translation theory, written by members of the Canadian School (*La traduzione femminista*, Udine, Forum, 2013). She has co-edited collections of essays: *Italy and Canadian Culture: Nationalisms in the New Millennium* (2001); *Transformations of the Canadian Cultural Mosaic* (2012); *Identities in Transition in the English-speaking World* (2011); and *A Word after a Word after a Word Is Power: Saggi per Anna Pia De Luca* (2013), and is also the co-author of the first *Friulan-English Dictionary* (with Gianni Nazzi, Ente Friuli Nel Mondo, 2000). She is a member of the University of Udine's Centre for Canadian Culture and of The International Centre for Migrant Literatures, which publishes *OltreOceano*.

**MARIA CRISTINA SECCIA** is a lecturer in Translation Studies at the University of Hull (UK). She taught in the department of Italian Studies at the University of Glasgow and was a visiting research fellow at the Centre for the Study of Contemporary Women's Writing (Institute of Modern Languages Research, University of London). She holds a PhD in Translation Studies, with a specialization in Italian-Canadian literature, from Bangor University. Her current research project looks at the representation of motherhood in Italian transnational women's writing from a cultural translation perspective. In 2016, Maria Cristina Seccia became the president of the Association of Italian Canadian Writers.

**MONIQUE TSCHOFEN** teaches at Ryerson University, where she works on Canadian literature and cinema, verbal-visual interactions, as well as philosophy and/of art. She is the co-editor, with Jennifer Burwell, of *Image and Territory: Essays on Atom Egoyan* (Wilfrid Laurier University Press), as well as an edited collection of essays on Kristjana Gunnars, and has written about Anne Carson, Betty Goodwin, Caitlin Fisher, Robert Lepage, and the *Jesuit Relations*. She earned a PhD in Comparative Literature from the University of Alberta.

# Index

Aciman, André, 29
ACLA Report, 4, 45, 46, 50
Adams, Parveen, 54
Adichie, Chimamanda Ngozi, 49, 81
African-Canadian, 137
African Francophone, 67–8
African languages, 76, 79
Ager, Denis, 70
Ahmad, Aijaz, 25
Ahmad, Dohra, 28
Akiwenzie-Damm, Kateri, 58
Al-Ghazali, 42
Ali, Anida, 23
Altman, Janet Gurkin, 183
Altoviti, Carlo, 14
American culture wars, 46–7
Anderson, Benedict, 158
Anderson, Kay, 93
Andreoni, Giovanni, 232
*Anne of Green Gables* (Montgomery), 15
Appadurai, Arjun, 190
Appiah, Kwame Anthony, 22, 46
Apter, Emily, 194
Arab-Canadian, 57, 216–24
Arabic, 42
Ardizzi, Maria, 255
Armenia, 175–8
Armstrong, Jeannette, 58
Armstrong, Jolene, 267–85
Arnold, Matthew, 43
Atwood, Margaret, 87–102

Auerbach, Erich, 44, 57
Australia, 229–43
Aziz, Nurjehan, 65

Ba, Amadou Hampathé, 74
Ba, Mariama, 68
Ba, Ndeye Fatou, 12, 67–83
Badami, Anita Rau, 32–3, 203
Bakhtin, Mikhail, 56
Barad, Karen, 89
Barthes, Roland, 55
Bassnett, Susan, 296
Beck, Ulrich, 22
Beckett, Samuel, 11
Benhabib, Seyla, 92
Benjamin, Walter, 273
*Beowulf*, 121
Bernheimer, Charles, 4, 5, 46–8, 297
Bhabha, Homi, 26–7, 81, 158, 230
Blixen, Karen, 11
Blodgett, E.D., 7, 9, 21, 48, 51–2, 289–303
Bloom, Harold, 293
Bobda, Augustin Simo, 75
Boldini, Licia, 65
Boruszko, Graciela, 5
Bougault, Sophie, 113n3
Braidotti, Rosi, 89, 95, 99, 105–12
Brand, Dionne, 33
*Brébeuf and His Brethren* (Pratt, poem), 125–9
Brennan, Tim, 24, 25

Brink, André, 11
Bugul, Ken, 81
Butler, Judith, 23

*Calendar* (film), 65–9
Canadian Comparative Literature Association (CCLA), 7, 8, 299
*Canadian Review of Comparative Literature*, 6, 8, 299
*Canticles* (Clarke), 138–46
Canton, Licia, 306
*Cantos* (Pound), 120–1, 131, 132
Capecia, Mayotte, 81
Capiello, Rosa, 232
Caribbean writers, 67
Carrière, Marie, 65
Casanova, Pascale, 29
Casselot, Marie-Anne, 110
Castro, Adrian, 137
Celtic Studies, 13
Cervantes, 59
Césaire, Aimé Fernand David, 70, 126
Chakrabarty, Depesh, 30
Chamoiseau, Patrick, 72
Chao, Lieu, 65, 200, 211
Charland, Maurice, 314
Cheah, Pheng, 24
Cheng, Anne Anlin, 37n6
Ch'ien, Evelyn Niem-Ming, 28
Chinweizu, Onwuchekwa Jemie, 79, 81
Chouliaraki, Lili, 23
Chow, Rey, 46
Christophersen, Paul, 77
Ciobanu, Calina, 89, 90
Clarke, George Elliott, 57, 117–50, 200, 310
CLCweb, 60
*Cockroach* (Hage, novel), 215–20
Colebrook, Claire, 22

Comparative Canadian Literature, 47, 307
Conley, Tom, 6
Conrad, Joseph, 123, 147nn6–7
*Contrasts: Comparative Essays on Italian-Canadian Writing*, 16, 307
cosmopolitanism, vii, 21–3, 25, 30–6, 226
Crary, Jonathan, 186
critical posthumanism, 87–91
Croce, Benedetto, 41
Croutier, Alev Lytle, 147n8
Cruz, Victor Hernandez, 137
Cultural Studies, 295–6

Dada, Ayorinde, 84
Dagnino, Ariana, 265n5
Dahab, F. Elizabeth, 12, 57, 65, 215–28
D'Alfonso, Antonio, 12, 153–73, 199
Damas, Leon, 70
Damrosch, David, 6
Dante, 42–3, 135
D'Aprano, Charles, 232
Davidson, Joyce, 92
Davis, Colin, 304
De Franceschi, Marisa, 208
De Gama, Vasco, 118
De Gasperi, Giulia, 3–18, 45
de la Cadena, Marisol, 34
De Luca, Anna Pia, 246–65
De Staël, Madame, 42
Del Falco, Amelia, 87, 90, 102, 105
Del Nin Cralli, Rina, 307
Deleuze, Gilles, 27, 215, 231
Derrida, Jacques, 27, 48, 136, 276, 308
Desai, Airan, 32
di Michele, Mary, 56, 246–64
diaspora, 26, 27, 203
digital humanities, 59–60
Dimić, Milan, 7, 45, 291, 293, 300

Diome, Fatou, 81
Djwa, Sandra, 125, 147n9
Dodds, Susan, 96, 98
Dorsinville, Max, 197
Dostoyevsky, Fyodor, 224
Du Bois, W.E.B., 138, 144
Dudek, Louis, 120–4, 127
Dvorek, Marts, 55
dystopian fiction, 87–9

Eagleton, Terry, 27
Eco, Umberto, 28, 55
Edugyan, Esi, 210–12
Edwards, Caterina, 208–10, 246
Egoyan, Atom, 12, 175–95
Eliot, T.S., 125
Elkhadem, Saad, 200, 223
*ellipse* (literary magazine), 9
emotional geography, 90, 91
epic, 117–21
Equiano, Olaudah, 75
Erdrich, Louise, 58
Ertler, Klaus-Dieter, 265n2
ethics of care, 89, 91
ethnic minority, 11, 59, 65, 197, 315, 316n3; literature, 226, 310–1; writing, viii–ix, 7–8, 11, 16, 42, 55–7, 200, 215, 267, 278, 304, 306–7
ethnicity, 26, 155, 159
Etiemble, René, 77
*Evangeline* (Longfellow, poem), 117, 125

*Fabrizio's Passion* (D'Alfonso/Lombardi, novel), 153–66
Fanon, Frantz, 72–3, 80–1, 316n3
Ferrarese, Estelle, 95
Ferry, Jules, 69
Findlay, Len, 308
Fitzgerald, F. Scott, 295

*Flood of Fire* (Ghosh, book), 30
Forsdick, Charles, 69, 81, 83
Foucault, Michel, 48
Francophonie, 68, 71
French School of Comparative Literature, 56
Friedman, Susan Stanford, 92
Frye, Northrop, 7, 117–21, 131–2, 291–2

Gaelic diaspora, 14
Gandhi, Leela, 35
Gans, Herbert, 277
García Márquez, Gabriel, 287
García Zarranz, Libe, 113n3
Geoffroy Saint-Hilaire, Étienne, 216, 227n1
geographies of care, 87, 90, 95
Georges, Karoline, 87, 112
Ghosh, Amitav, 30, 31
Gibson, Ross, 232
Gilroy, Paul, 34, 35, 311
Gladstone, J.R., 73
"Godzilla vs Post-Colonial" (King), 19
Goethe, Johann, 42
Gomez Moriana, Antonio, 7
Goodwin, Kevin, 84n4
Goto, Hiromi, 119, 210, 267, 278–9, 281
Greene, E.J.H., 291
Greene Report (1975), 4
Greenway, Peter, 175–6
Gregory, Derek, 93, 94
Grekul, Lisa, 268
Grosz, Elizabeth, 108
Guattari, Felix, 27
Gunew, Sneja, 21–39, 197, 230
Gunn, Genni, 246–54, 256–61, 263–4
Gunning, Tom, 185, 189

Hage, Rawi, 12, 215–28
Hall, Stuart, 33, 34, 83, 293

Haraway, Donna, 89, 94
Hardy, Thomas, 125
Hargreaves, Alec G., 82
Hart, Jonathan, 10, 303n2
Hassan, Wail S., 6
Hayles, Katherine, 89, 107–8
Heine, Bernard, 78
Held, Virginia, 90
Henriksen, Line, 131, 134
Herbrechter, Stephen, 89
*Hermeneutica.ca*, 60
heteroglossia, 56, 118, 131, 201
Hétu, Dominique, 12, 87–116
Highway, Tomson, 58
Homer, 119, 129, 134
Horace, 53
Hountondji, Paulin, 72
Huston, Nancy, 11, 48
Hutcheon, Linda, 3, 4, 9, 10, 50, 148n18
hypertext, concept, 6, 61; book, 60

Ibekwe, Chinweizu, 78–81
Idowu, Oludare, 72
Ilboudo, Monique, 68
Indigenous writers, 19, 20
Indirect Rule, 75, 76
*Inquire: Journal of Comparative Literature*, 60
Isaacs, Camille, 66
Italian-Canadian, 28, 200, 318

Jameson, Fredric, 25
Jaures, Jean, 70
*John Barleycorn* (London, book), 15
Johnston, Basil, 58
Jones, Andrew, 272–3, 276

Kachru, Braji, 77
Kafka, Franz, 37n4, 215, 220

Kalashnikov, 29
Kamboureli, Smaro, 55, 66, 156
Kane, Cheikh Hamidou, 70
Kant, Immanuel, 22
Keefer, Janice Kulyk, 201, 285n2
Kegel, Katrin, 176
Kellman, Steven, 199, 202, 218
Kermode, Frank, 138
Kincaid, Jamaica, 30, 32, 36
King, Thomas, 19, 58
Kirby, Vicky, 112
Kirkconnell, Watson, 268
Kogawa, Joy, 211, 281–2
Kourouma, Ahmadou, 70
Kramsch, Claire, 73
Kristeva, Julia, 56
Krysinski, Vladimir, 7
Kushner, Eva, 6, 7, 45
Kushner, Scott, 5, 12, 174

La Grandeur, Kevin, 92
Laferrière, Dany, 200, 307
Landow, George, 60
LaRocque, Emma, 19
Larrère, Catherine, 89
Laugier, Sandra, 89, 111
Lazarus, Niel, 306–7, 308
Le Bris, Michel, 83n2
Levin, Harry, 47
Lionnet, Françoise, 50
Lloyd, Genevieve, 97
Lolice, Frederio, 44
Lombardi, Antonello, 164–9
London, Jack, 15
Longfellow, H.W., 117, 126
Lotfi, Mohamed, 225
Lugard, Lord Frederick, 75
Lyotard, Francois, 23, 24
Lysenko, Vera, 267–85

McCutcheon, Mark, 4, 11, 304–19
MacGregor, Sherilyn, 89, 110
MacLennan, Hugh, 13; and Prize for Fiction, 226
McMaster, Rowland, 312
Macri, Francis, 197
*Maddaddam* (Atwood, novel), 113n1
Mahjoub, Jamal, 211
Mannani, Manijeh, 8, 66
Maoist, 32
Maracle, Lee, 19
Maraini, Dacia, 247
Maran, René, 67, 83n1
Mariniello, Silvestra, 7
Massey, Doreen, 91, 95
media, 12, 41, 46, 65, 174–6, 179–81, 183–6, 192, 194, 272, 314; digital, 5, 12, 59; electronic, 5; mass, 193; mediascape, 190–2; non-literary, 174–5; social, 174; studies, 3; technological, 179, 182, 184; visual, 179
memory, 56, 79, 88, 99, 123, 178–9, 182, 210, 248–9, 252, 257–8, 260, 263, 267, 272–4, 277, 285, 309, 316; collective, 79; cultural, 241
*Men in Sheepskin Coats: A Study in Assimilation* (Lysenko, book), 267–8, 284n2
Merand, Patrick, 74
Meyers, Kristi Jane, 111
Michelman, Frederic, 72
Michelut, Dôre, 199, 206–7
Mignolo, Walter, 31
migrant, 36, 135, 157, 163, 170, 177, 205, 206, 224, 231–3, 248, 253; camp, 235–7, 240; experience, 164; family, 235, 263; identity, 168; labour, 239; literary studies, 246; worker/working class/workmate, 134, 229–30, 236, 240–1; writer, 206, 254
migration, 8, 39, 56, 65, 82, 155, 177, 190, 202, 213, 226, 228, 229–33, 241–3, 245, 255, 260, 265
Miki, Roy, 281
Milton, John, 138
minority, 49, 58–9, 65, 118, 135, 156, 197, 209, 222, 227n3, 268, 316n3; group, 11; language, 43, 208, 247; literature/text(s), 56–7, 226, 267, 304, 310–11; writer/writing, viii, ix, 8, 11, 13–14, 16, 42, 55–7, 200, 215, 267, 278–9, 281, 304, 306–7
Mintz, Susannah B., 105
Miron, Gaston, 207
Mistry, Rohinton, 199, 203
mobility, 3, 21, 31, 102, 192, 246, 248, 264
Modernism, 23–5, 299; modernism, 27, 125
Molinier, Pascale, 88–9
Momaday, Scott, 58
monolingualism, 27–8, 47, 51, 202
Montgomery, Lucy Maud, 15
Moody, A. David, 117–18
Mookerjea, Sourayan, 176
Moroni Parken, Anna, 170n30
Morris, Paul, 289
Moser, Walter, 7
Moses, Daniel David, 19, 58, 307
Mouawad, Wajdi, 200, 224–6
Moumouni, Abdou, 70
Moura, Jean-Marc, 82, 84n6
Mouralis, Bernard, 69
Moyes, Lianne, 66
Moyles, Roger, 125, 147n9
multicultural, viii, 25, 49, 137, 216, 246, 258, 284; post-colonial

literature, 306, 309, 315; nation/people/society, 47-8, 210; writer/writing, 34, 197
multiculturalism, 46, 48-9, 216, 224, 268, 271, 281, 297, 314-15
multidisciplinary, 8-10, 15, 88
multilingualism, 3, 202, 310
multiracial, 124, 130, 137, 246
Murdoch, Jon, 91
Murphy, David, 69, 81, 83
Mussolini, Benito, 138, 144, 146

Nafisi, Azar, 294-5
Nancy, Jean-Luc, 22, 34
Nandy, Ashis, 25
nation, 6, 24, 78, 118, 120, 125, 156-9, 162, 164, 204, 210, 242, 263, 290; state, 22, 24, 34, 78, 159, 197, 309
nationalism, 24, 154, 155-7, 162, 168, 290, 300-1, 306, 314
native, 19, 72-5, 77, 127, 137, 208, 217, 220-2, 233, 238, 255; Native, 129, 256; language, 247; writers/writing, 58, 200
Négritude, 69-72
Negro, 80, 123, 130, 139, 148n13, 149n23
Neimanis, Astrida, 94-5, 113n3
Nelson, Tolof, 176
new cosmopolitanism, 21
new world, 96, 178, 231; New World, 123-4, 135, 149n23, 155
Nievo, Ippolito, 14
Nischik, Reingard M., 66
Noddings, Nel, 89
nomadic, ix, 247; belonging, 210-11
non-literary, 5-6; media, 174-5
North America, 4, 8, 19, 44, 46, 51-3, 58, 78, 124, 126-7, 148n13, 178, 208, 215-16, 307, 313-14; North Americanness, 192

Notte, Fabrizio, character, 156
Notte, Guido, character, 160-1
Nova Scotia, 117
Novak, Luba, 267
Nussbaum, Martha, 90

*Obasan* (Kogawa, novel), 211, 281
*Odyssey, The* (Homer, epic poem), 117, 121, 134
Ojibway, 117-18
Old World, 120-1, 155; old world, 118, 178, 231
*Omeros*: poem (Walcott), 129-35; character, 133-5, 149n25
Open Access, 59
Orwell, George, 34, 215
*Oryx and Crake* (Atwood, novel), 113n1

Paci, Frank, 229-30, 234-6, 241-2, 243n26
Padolsky, Enoch, 156
Pamuk, Orhan, 32
Papalia, Gerardo, 232, 243n14
Paperman, Patricia, 88-9
Parker, Gabrielle, 69-70
Pasolini, Pier Paolo, 261-2, 264
Patriarca, Gianna, 207
Pavlenko, Aneta, 206
Pellegrini, Carlo, 303n1
Philip, M. NourbeSe, 135-8, 149n26, 204
Phillips, Caryl, 36-7
Phillips, Judith, 91
Pivato, Joseph, x, 7, 11, 14, 16, 28, 41-63, 148n17, 243n13, 255, 265n6, 265n11, 278, 304, 306-18
Pogge, Thomas, 22
Polish-Canadian, 120, 123
Posnett, Hutcheson Macaulay, 43

post-colonial, viii, 8, 19, 21, 25, 28, 31, 49, 57–9, 67, 74, 81–3, 130, 159, 197, 199, 203, 206, 304, 306, 309; literatures, 81, 304, 309; studies, 3, 19, 26, 28, 49, 67, 81–3
posthuman, viii, 35, 87–101, 103–13
posthumanism, 87, 89–91, 101
Post-modernism, 23, 195; postmodernism, 25, 136
post-nationalism, 23
Pound, Ezra, 121–3, 125, 130–2, 134–8, 146n1, 147n4, 148n18, 149nn26–7
Pratt, E.J., 119–21, 125–9, 131–2, 135, 137–8, 147n4, 148n9, 148n12
Pratt, Marie Louise, 46–7
*Provincialize Europe* (Chakrabarty, book), 30
psychology, 3, 41, 54

race, 71, 93, 118, 125, 127, 130, 205, 316n3
Radway, Janice, 6
Randaccio, Elena Maccaferri, 170n30
Rando, Gaetano, 4, 229–45
Readings, Bill, 313
Reclus, Onésime, 68
Reichenbach, François, 180
Remak, Henry H.H., 44
Research Institute for Comparative Literature, 302
Reynolds, Clarence, 211
Reynolds, Matthew, 65
Ricci, Giuseppe, 242n12
Ricci, Nino, 156
Riffaterre, Michael, 49
*River of Smoke* (Ghosh, book), 30
Robinson, Eden, 58
Rockwell, Geoffrey, 60
Rogaly, Ben, 231
Romero, Óscar, 302

Romney, Jonathan, 175–6
Rooke, Constance, 302
Rorty, Richard, 10
Rose, Marilyn Gaddis, 153
Ross, Stephen David, 99
*Rotten English* (Ahmad, anthology), 28
Roy, Gabrielle, 49, 51, 198
Ruffo, Armand Garnet, 66
Rushdie, Salman, 26
Russell, Val B., 260

Said, Edward, viii, 74, 231, 242n9
Saidero, Deborah, 199–214, 248, 253
Sakr, Rita, 222, 224
Salvatore, Filippo, 200, 207, 310
Sandru, Cristina, 66
Sartre, Jean-Paul, 72, 129–30, 148n14, 215
Sassens, Saskia, 32
Saussure, Ferdinand de, 27
Saussy, Haun, 4, 46, 50–2, 297, 298
Saussy Report, 4
Sayed, Asma, 66
Scambray, Kenneth, 208
Schleicher, David, 305
Schoene, Berthold, 26, 34–5
Schumann, Georg, 147n5
Scott, Walter, 14
Scottish Gaelic, 13–14
*Sea of Poppies* (Ghosh, book), 30
Seccia, Maria Cristina, 4, 12, 15, 153–73
Selasi, Taiye, 35–6
self-identification, 164
self-reflexive, 6, 56, 199
self-translation, 11, 155, 201, 207
Selvon, Sam, 36
Senghor, Léopold Sédar, 70–2, 129
Serrano, Richard, 84n6
Shakespeare, William, 137

Sharma, Ram, 66
Shelley, Percy Bysshe, 125
Sherbrooke School, ix, 7, 9, 51
Sidney, Sir Philip, 53
Siemerling, Winfried, 7, 58, 198
Silko, Leslie Marmon, 58
Simon, Sherry, 7, 51
Sinclair, Stefan, 60
Sirois, Antoine, 7
Slipperjack, Ruby, 58
Smart, Pat, 7
Smith, Mick, 92, 112
Smith, Susan, 93-4
Smith, Zadie, 32
*Song of Hiawatha* (Longfellow, poem), 117
source language, 153
source text, 153-4, 164, 169
*Sous béton* (Georges, novel), 87, 90, 101-3, 105, 107-9, 111
Spencer, Robert, 26
Spengler, Oswald, 124
Spivak, Gayatry Chakravorty, 10, 30, 50, 61
State of the Discipline Report, 5, 174
Steiner, George, 50
Steiner, Tina, 200, 204
Stoicheff, Peter, 147n4
Stratford, Philip, 7
Strauss, Leo, 291
Sugars, Cynthia, 309
Sutherland, Ronald, 7
symbolic ethnicity, 277
Synge, J.M., 27
Syrotinski, Micheal, 72

Tabar, Tania, 216
Tansi, Sony Labou, 70
target language, 153
target text, 153, 163, 165-6, 168

Taseer, Aatish, 32
Tate, Allen, 131
Taylor, Drew Hayden, 307
Tedeschi, Pietro, 229-36, 239, 241-2
Tennen, Dennis, 5
Third World, 25-6, 51, 218, 220, 297
Thomas, Ronald R., 185
Thompson, Veronica, 66
Tötösy de Zepetnek, Steven, 5, 60
*Towards the Last Spike* (Pratt, poem), 125
transcultural, 156, 199, 201-2, 247-8, 258-9, 261, 264; identity, 155, 158, 207, 209; transculturalism, 265n2; transculturality, vii, 202, 246, 262
translation studies, 3, 8, 15, 50-1, 153; Translation Studies, 12, 296
translingual, ix, 207, 210; writer/writing, 199-200, 202, text, 201, 210-11
translingualism, 199-200, 202-3, 206
transmedial, 184
Trivedi, Harish, 83
Tronto, Joan, 89
Trudel, Marcel, 148n13
Tschofen, Monique, 12, 65, 174-96
Turcotte, Gerry, 309
Turner, J.M.W., 136
Tutuola, Amos, 75
Tuzi, Marino, 156
Ty, Eleanor, 66

Ukrainian, ix, 201, 240, 267-9, 271, 279-80, 284n1, 285n2
Ukrainian-Canadian, 267-8
uncanny, 11, 306
Unger, Steven, 50-1
*Unheimlich*, 11, 306
United States of America, 36, 74-5, 118

Untener, Kenneth, 302
"untranslated words," 165, 167–8
Urquhart, Jane, 203

van Herk, Aritha, 201
Vassanji, M.G., 199–200, 202–3, 205–6, 307
Vautier, Marie, 7
Venuti, Lawrence, 153
Verdicchio, Pasquale, 156–7, 162–3
Verduyn, Christl, 66
Vint, Sheryl, 89, 100–1, 113n3
Virilio, Paul, 180
visual arts, 12, 60
Viswanathan, Gauri, 26
von Flotow, Luise, 66

wa Thiong'o, Ngũgi, 11, 49, 71, 73, 78–81
Walcott, Derek, 129–38, 148n16, 149nn25–6
Wali, Obiajunwa, 78–9, 81
Wallace, Jeff, 113n3
Wang, Ban, 6
Warner, Marina, 21
Warren, Austen, 44
*Waverly* (Scott, novel), 14
"ways of seeing," 175, 180–3
*Weird English* (Ch'ien, book), 28; concept, 28, 35
Wellek, René, 19, 44, 61

Welsch, Wolfgang, 202, 246
Welsh, Sarah Lawson, 66
*Weltliteratur*, 42, 44, 289
*Westerly Wild* (Lysenko, book), 267
Western civilization, 135
Whatmore, Sarah, 111
Wheatley, Phillis, 75
Whitman, Walt, 117, 120–1, 125, 147n3, 147n9
Wiens, Jason, 205
Wilson, Janet, 66
Wilson, Rita, 160
Wilson, Sheena, 19, 59
Wolfe, Cary, 89, 113n3
world literature, 29, 34, 42, 202, 267, 294; World Literature, vii, 6, 82

*Year of the Flood, The* (Atwood, novel), 87, 90, 95, 98–100, 110, 113n1
*Yellow Boots* (Lysenko, novel), 267–8, 272–3, 284; yellow boots (objects), 271–7, 284
Young, Robert, 26, 312

Zagolin, Bianca, 243n13
Zamora, Lois Parkinson, 297
Zandy, Janet, 230, 236
Ziolkowski, Jan M., 42
*Zong!* (Philip, poem), 135–7; character, 136
Zumthor, Paul, 7, 45